MW01007857

SMALL CAP STOCKS

Investment and Portfolio Strategies for the Institutional Investor

Robert A. Klein ▲ Jess Lederman

PROBUS PUBLISHING COMPANY
Chicago, Illinois
Cambridge, England

ISBN 1-55738-518-1

Printed in the United States of America

BB

1 2 3 4 5 6 7 8 9 0

Table of Contents

Preface

Nothing in the equity markets has generated more excitement and controversy in recent years than the small cap sector. Some investors, impressed with analyses demonstrating that small cap stocks have generated risk-adjusted returns in excess of 200 basis points higher than large cap stocks, have concluded that small cap stocks represent the "efficient frontier," offering the optimum trade-off between risk and return. Even some of the most conservative investors have begun to build small cap portfolios. But there are many different—often contradictory—theories of how to evaluate and invest in small cap stocks.

Small Cap Stocks is the most comprehensive source of information ever compiled on the mechanics, economics, and trading and portfolio management dynamics of the small cap market. Part One features four chapters that analyze the relative performance of small cap stocks, looking at both historical trends and expected future results. Part Two looks at small cap benchmark indices. The four chapters of Part Three provide an overview of several different techniques for selecting individual stocks. In Part Four we explore strategies for trading and portfolio management. The book concludes with Part Five, which examines opportunities in the international sector.

Many thanks must be given to each of the contributing authors for the time and energy they took from their hectic schedules. We are also grateful to the superb staff at Probus Publishing, without whose help this project could not have been completed.

Robert A. Klein
Jess Lederman

Contributing Authors

Matthew S. Baker
Senior Research Analyst
Sanford C. Bernstein & Co.

Sandip A. Bhagat, CFA
Senior Vice President
Travelers Investment Management Co.

Brian R. Bruce
Vice President and Unit Head
State Street Bank and Trust Company

John S. Brush, Ph.D.
President
Columbine Capital Services, Inc.

Peter Carman
Senior Vice President and
Chief Investment Officer
Sanford C. Bernstein & Co.

Daniel P. Coker
Junior Quantitative Analyst
Prudential Securities, Inc.

Richard A. Crowell
President and Managing Director
PanAgora Asset Management, Inc.

James M. Eysenbach
Director of Quantitative Services
Scudder, Stevens & Clark, Inc.

Kenneth L. Fisher
President and Chief Investment Officer
Fisher Investments, Inc.

Leo Fochtman
Vice President and Quantitative
Analyst—Equity Research
Kidder, Peabody & Co. Incorporated

Philip S. Fortuna
Director of Investment Operations
Scudder, Stevens & Clark, Inc.

William W. Jahnke
Founder
Vestek Systems, Inc.

Ronald N. Kahn, Ph.D.
Director of Research
BARRA

Hans Kaufmann
Head of Swiss Research Department
Bank Julius Baer

Edmund D. Kellogg
Vice President and Portfolio Manager
Keystone Investment Management
Corporation

Michael Keppler
President
Keppler Asset Management, Inc.

Peter G. Leahy
Vice President
State Street Bank and Trust Company

Rosemary Macedo
Vice President, Quantitative Research
Bailard, Biehl & Kaiser

William Martindale
Managing Principal
Martindale Andres & Co.

Claudia E. Mott
First Vice President and Director of
Small Cap Research
Prudential Securities, Inc.

Richard S. Pzena
Director of Investment
Management Research
Sanford C. Bernstein & Co.

E. K. Easton Ragsdale, CFA
Vice President and Chief Quantitative
Analyst—Equity Research
Kidder, Peabody & Co. Incorporated

Gita R. Rao, Ph.D.
Vice President and Quantitative
Analyst—Equity Research
Kidder, Peabody & Co. Incorporated

Marc R. Reinganum
Phillips Professor of Finance and
Director, Financial Markets Institute,
College of Business Administration
University of Iowa

Josh Rosenberg
Senior Consultant,
Equity Model Research
BARRA

Anthony W. Ryan
Manager, Global Investments
PanAgora Asset Management, Inc.

Varilyn K. Schock, CFA
Vice President and Director of
Quantitative Strategies
Denver Investment Advisors, Inc.

Joel Tillinghest
Portfolio Manager
Fidelity Low Priced Stock Fund

Joseph L. Toms
Senior Vice President and
Director of Research
Fisher Investments, Inc.

Heydon Traub
Senior Vice President
State Street Global Advisors

Kevin L. Wenck
Portfolio Manager
G.T. Capital Management

PART ONE: THE RELATIVE PERFORMANCE OF SMALL CAP STOCKS

Chapter 1

Small versus Large Cap Stocks: Quantifying the Fundamental Reasons Behind Relative Market Performance

E. K. Easton Ragsdale, CFA
Vice President and Chief Quantitative Analyst
Equity Research

Gita R. Rao, Ph.D.
Vice President and Quantitative Analyst
Equity Research

Leo Fochtman
Vice President and Quantitative Analyst
Equity Research

Kidder, Peabody & Co. Incorporated

INTRODUCTION

How have small stocks performed relative to large stocks? To answer this question, we measured small-stock performance using the small-stock index from Ibbotson Associates and large-stock performance using the S&P

Figure 1.1—Recent Small Stock Performance Relative to the S&P 500

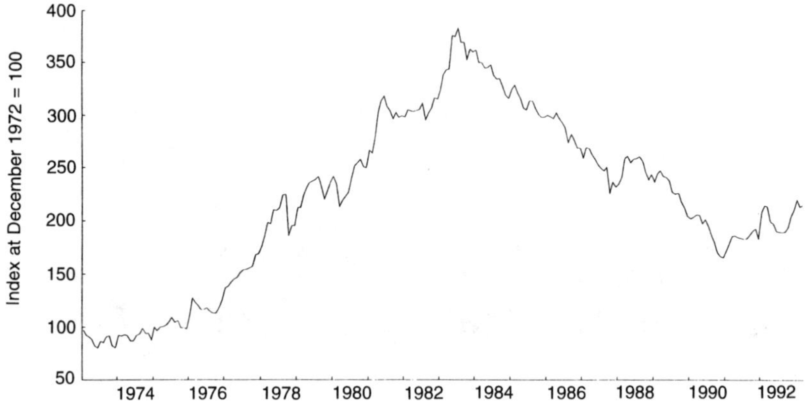

Source: Kidder, Peabody Quantitative Research Group; Ibbotson Associates.

500. Figure 1.1 shows that small stocks outperformed large stocks from June 1973 to July 1983, but then underperformed from July 1983 to December 1990. Since December 1990, small stocks have generally outperformed. As Table 1.1 makes clear, small stocks outperformed in every year from 1974 to 1983 and then underperformed in every year from 1984 through 1990, with the exception of 1988.

It does not take the market seven to ten years to correct significant errors in any stock group's valuation. Rather, prolonged periods of out- or underperformance must be due to fundamentals such as earnings and valuation. The objective of this chapter is to understand both the strong relative market performance of small stocks in the 1974–83 period and their poor relative market performance in the 1984–90 period. Our primary focus is on the earnings fundamentals of small versus large stocks.

In our research, we defined small stocks as the smallest market-capitalization quintile (bottom 20%) of all stocks with data available in the Compustat database. However, to ensure that the smallest quintile contained stocks with at least some relevance to institutional investors, we excluded stocks with market capitalizations below $50 million at the end of 1991. Going back in time, we lowered this market capitalization minimum each year, based on the level of the Ibbotson Associates small-stock index. In order to eliminate survivorship or success bias in our analysis, separate lists of stocks were developed for each year.

What were the results? Over the 1975–81 period of small-stock market outperformance, the aggregate net income of the smallest-capitalization quintile of stocks grew at a compound annual rate of 18.8%, while that of

Table 1.1—Recent Small versus Large Stock Performance; Annual Total Returns (%)

	Small Stocks	S&P 500	Small Stock Relative Performance
1973	−30.9	−14.7	−19.0
1974	−19.9	−26.5	8.9
1975	52.8	37.2	11.4
1976	57.4	23.8	27.1
1977	25.4	−7.2	35.1
1978	23.5	6.6	15.9
1979	43.5	18.4	21.1
1980	39.9	32.4	5.6
1981	13.9	−4.9	19.8
1982	28.0	21.4	5.4
1983	39.7	22.5	14.0
1984	−6.7	6.3	−12.2
1985	24.7	32.2	−5.7
1986	6.9	18.5	−9.8
1987	−9.3	5.2	−13.8
1988	22.9	16.8	5.2
1989	10.2	31.5	−16.2
1990	−21.6	−3.2	−19.0
1991	44.6	30.5	10.8
1992	23.3	7.7	14.6

Compound Average Annual Return (%)

1974–92	18.7	12.9	
1974–83	28.4	10.6	
1984–90	2.6	14.6	
1991–92	33.6	18.6	

Source: Kidder, Peabody Quantitative Research Group; Ibbotson Associates.

the largest-capitalization quintile grew at only 9.1%. However, during the 1982–83 period, small stocks continued to outperform large stocks, despite a deteriorating fundamental performance. We suspect that the 1981–82 recession may have caused investors to miss the secular shift in small-stock fundamentals.

Results were much clearer during the 1984–90 period of small-stock market underperformance. The smallest stocks reported negative aggregate net income for the period, while the largest quintile reported positive aggregate net income and grew 4.3% on a compound annual basis

Thus, earnings fundamentals appeared to play an important role in the 1974–81 period of small-stock market outperformance, offered no explanation for the 1982–83 period of market outperformance, and was clearly important during the period of market underperformance by small stocks.

Taking the analysis one step further, we identified a number of factors that contributed to the shifts in the relative earnings performance of small stocks. The first factor was a shift in relative tax rates, driven by changes in the tax laws and differing rates of capital intensity between small and large stocks. The second factor was a dramatic shift in pension expense, influenced by stock, bond, and real estate returns for pension plans.

Valuation, measured by equity income as a percent of market value, also played a role during both periods. As was the case for earnings fundamentals, however, we found that valuation could not explain the 1982–83 period of small-stock market outperformance.

Small stocks are very attractive for the long term. Factors that should be favorable for small stocks and negative for large stocks include: (1) a slow-growth economic environment favoring smaller, more nimble companies; (2) only minor shifts in relative effective tax rates (turning a negative factor for small stocks to a neutral influence); (3) growing pension expense, which will hurt firms that have older labor forces and more retirees per active employee; and (4) growing post-retirement health care expense, which also will hurt firms with older labor forces and more retirees per active employee.

HISTORICAL PERFORMANCE OF SMALL VERSUS LARGE STOCKS

Over the longer term, small stocks have provided investors with 1.9% greater annual return than the S&P 500 (see Table 1.2). As detailed in Table 1.2, in five of the past eight decades (including the late 1920s and early 1990s), small stocks provided superior returns to those of the S&P 500. With the exception of the 1920s, small stocks tended to underperform by modest amounts, at least when measured over decade-long holding peri-

---

Table 1.2—Total Returns for Various U.S. Asset Classes
Compound Average Annual Returns (%)

	S&P 500	Small Stocks	Long-Term Treasury Bonds	Long-Term Corporate Bonds	Intermediate Term Treasury Notes	Treasury Bills	Inflation (CPI)
1920s[a]	19.2	−4.5	5.0	5.2	4.2	3.7	−1.1
1930s	−0.1	1.4	4.9	6.9	4.6	0.6	−2.0
1940s	9.2	20.7	3.2	2.7	1.8	0.4	5.4
1950s	19.4	16.9	−0.1	1.0	1.3	1.9	2.2
1960s	7.8	15.5	1.4	1.7	3.5	3.9	2.5
1970s	5.9	11.5	5.5	6.2	7.0	6.3	7.4
1980s	17.5	15.8	12.6	13.0	11.9	8.9	5.1
1990s[b]	10.8	11.9	11.0	11.9	10.7	5.6	4.1
1926–92	10.3	12.2	4.8	5.5	5.2	3.7	3.1
1974–83	10.6	28.4	6.0	6.4	8.3	8.6	8.2
1984–90	14.6	2.6	9.7	9.6	7.9	5.1	2.8

Source: Kidder, Peabody Quantitative Research Group; Ibbotson Associates.

(a) 1926–29

(b) 1990–92

---

ods. However, when small stocks outperformed, they tended to do so by large margins.

As noted earlier, the market outperformance of small stocks began in mid-1973 and peaked in mid-1983 (see again Figure 1.1). Looking at annual returns, small stocks returned 28.4% during 1974–83, compared to only 10.6% for the S&P 500 (see again Table 1.1). Small stocks then suffered through seven years of underperformance that began in 1984 and ended in 1990 (1988 being an exception). Over that period, small stocks returned only 2.6% annually, while the S&P 500 returned 14.6%. The 1991–92 period has seen a resurgence by small stocks, which have returned 33.6% annually, versus 18.6% for the S&P 500.

Small stocks experienced pronounced underperformance from mid-1983 through the end of 1990. However, during the preceding ten-year period, the extra return from small stocks was in the double digits. Indeed, over the full cycle from June 1973 to December 1990, small stocks outperformed by 4.2% per year, significantly better than the long-run historical average of 1.9% per year.

Can we explain this pattern of relative market performance by small stocks over the last twenty years? We begin at the beginning, with methodology.

BRINGING SOME METHOD TO THE MADNESS

The methodology used to study small versus large stocks is unusually important. A critical problem centers on defining what is meant by a small stock. At first blush, it might appear that defining a small stock is fairly straightforward. However, we will show that defining size is a fairly complicated problem in its own right. We will also provide evidence that the universe of stocks selected for analysis can dramatically alter the conclusions.

What Is Small and What Is Large?

Investors tend to define size in terms of market capitalization. However, there are any number of alternative measures: sales, assets, and number of employees, to name but a few. For the purposes of our initial analysis, we defined size in terms of both market capitalization and total assets.

Although there is a positive correlation between market capitalization and total assets, a small stock is not necessarily a small firm. It is sometimes the case that a large company falls on hard times; the firm's market capitalization and its share of total market capitalization will usually decline much more than the firm's asset base.

As an example, in late 1983, International Business Machines (IBM) was near its peak as a percentage of the capitalization of the S&P 500. IBM had a market capitalization of $77.1 billion, ranked first in the S&P 500 based on market capitalization, represented 6.28% of capitalization of the S&P 500 Index, and had total assets of $33.4 billion. As of June 1993, IBM's market capitalization has dropped 63% to $28.2 billion, it ranks seventeenth in the S&P 500 based on market capitalization, and it represents only 0.90% of the capitalization of the S&P 500; however, its assets have more than doubled to $85.7 billion. Because of its huge initial market capitalization, IBM remains well entrenched in the top decile of the S&P 500, based on market capitalization; of course, other stocks have not fared as well.

The divergence between ranking on capitalization and ranking on assets may be more modest for large stocks than small stocks. This is because successful companies will be rewarded with a higher market capitalization; successful companies are also likely to grow their asset base. But what are the implications for the smallest quintile? Here, we are more likely to see unsuccessful companies with sharply declining market capitalization but growing or stable assets.

The reader should keep in mind one other point. Sorting on market capitalization introduces a tilt against success among small stocks. Since stock prices reflect market expectations of future earnings, sorting on market capitalization means that large-stock portfolios tend to contain firms expected to do well in the future, while small-stock portfolios tend to fill up with firms expected to do poorly.

We began the analysis with the current S&P 500, sorting stocks into quintiles based both on market capitalization and total assets. Table 1.3 displays the trends in aggregate net income for the current S&P 500 quintiles based on capitalization, while Table 1.4 does the same for the current S&P 500 quintiles based on total assets.

The results based on capitalization quintile were not clear-cut for the 1975–83 period of market outperformance by small stocks. Aggregate net income for the smallest capitalization quintile did not keep pace with that for large stocks. However, the results met our expectations during the 1984–90 period. Poor market performance by small stocks is mirrored in their fundamental, or earnings, underperformance. While net income for the largest capitalization quintile grew 8.0% per year during this period, net income for the smallest quintile rose only 6.7% per year.

What about the current S&P 500 quintiles based on total assets? In the case of the 1975–83 period of market outperformance by small stocks, net income for the smallest asset quintile grew at 8.3% per year compared to 8.4% for the largest asset quintile. During the 1984–90 period of market underperformance by small stocks, the smallest asset quintile actually outperformed on a fundamental basis, with net income growing 7.6% per year compared to 5.4% for the largest asset quintile. In other words, the fundamental, or earnings, results were exactly opposite to the market, or stock return, results.

Even this cursory examination of the data makes it clear that the results based on defining size by capitalization can be very different from the results based on defining size by total assets: Small stocks are not the same as small firms. This should come as no surprise. After all, just as the earnings performance of small stocks is different from that of small firms, it should be the case that the market performance of small stocks is different from that of small firms.

Table 1.3—Aggregate Net Income of Current S&P 500 Stocks
Quintiles by Market Capitalization (Dollars in Billions)

	Quintiles					
	1 Largest	2	3	4	5 Smallest	Aggregate
1992	42.6	9.4	5.1	1.7	−3.98	54.8
1991	71.9	20.9	11.8	4.2	−1.37	107.5
1990	99.7	28.2	15.2	5.9	2.37	151.4
1989	98.4	34.0	20.6	8.4	4.54	166.0
1988	100.3	34.6	22.2	10.6	6.60	174.3
1987	74.7	26.6	14.8	9.0	4.47	129.5
1986	69.3	23.0	10.0	5.6	2.14	110.0
1985	67.3	20.5	10.8	3.2	1.60	103.4
1984	74.0	23.3	12.2	6.7	3.03	119.3
1983	58.3	20.4	9.8	5.7	1.51	95.7
1982	54.3	18.8	8.4	3.3	−0.23	84.6
1981	55.6	21.4	11.5	6.2	4.15	98.9
1980	50.2	20.6	11.6	6.1	3.53	92.0
1979	51.1	17.9	10.1	6.7	4.62	90.4
1978	42.1	14.6	8.5	5.2	3.24	73.6
1977	37.8	12.2	7.3	3.9	2.86	64.0
1976	33.6	10.3	6.7	3.7	3.04	57.4
1975	25.7	8.5	5.7	3.2	2.38	45.3
1974	27.6	8.1	6.2	2.9	2.37	47.2
Compound Average Growth Rate (%)						
1975–90	2.4	0.8	−1.1	−3.0	NA	0.8
1975–83	8.7	10.8	5.2	7.8	−4.9	8.2
1984–90	8.0	4.8	6.5	0.4	6.7	6.8
Average Net Income ($ billion)						
1974–83	43.6	15.3	8.6	4.7	2.74	74.9
1984–90	83.4	27.2	15.1	7.0	3.54	136.3

Source: Kidder, Peabody Quantitative Research Group.
NA Not available/applicable.

**Table 1.4—Aggregate Net Income of Current S&P 500 Stocks
Quintiles by Total Assets (Dollars in Billions)**

| | Quintiles | | | | | |
	1 *Largest*	2	3	4	5 *Smallest*	*Aggregate*
1992	17.4	19.0	10.2	5.6	2.61	54.8
1991	52.9	30.7	13.3	7.3	3.25	107.5
1990	80.5	39.9	18.0	9.1	3.88	151.4
1989	84.0	45.8	22.1	10.5	3.63	166.0
1988	93.0	43.7	23.3	9.6	4.73	174.3
1987	64.7	35.0	18.4	7.7	3.72	129.5
1986	70.2	23.1	9.4	4.4	2.84	110.0
1985	66.0	23.5	9.5	2.3	2.11	103.4
1984	69.0	28.5	12.9	5.4	3.42	119.3
1983	55.6	23.5	10.4	3.9	2.32	95.7
1982	50.4	21.9	6.4	3.9	1.95	84.6
1981	52.6	25.4	11.8	5.8	3.19	98.9
1980	50.1	22.1	12.2	5.0	2.67	92.0
1979	51.3	19.5	11.9	5.1	2.55	90.4
1978	41.9	16.7	9.1	4.0	2.00	73.6
1977	37.4	13.9	7.6	3.6	1.46	64.0
1976	32.8	12.0	7.7	3.3	1.54	57.4
1975	25.1	9.9	6.4	2.7	1.24	45.3
1974	27.0	10.1	6.7	2.4	1.13	47.2
Compound Average Growth Rate (%)						
1975–90	–2.4	3.6	2.4	4.9	4.8	0.8
1975–83	8.4	9.8	5.1	5.7	8.3	8.2
1984–90	5.4	7.9	8.1	12.9	7.6	6.8
Average Net Income ($ billion)						
1974–83	42.4	17.5	9.0	4.0	2.01	74.9
1984–90	75.3	34.2	16.2	7.0	3.48	136.3

Source: Kidder, Peabody Quantitative Research Group.

What Is the Appropriate Stock Universe?

The results based on the current S&P 500 were promising, but this approach suffers from some major weaknesses. In using the current list of S&P 500 stocks for all years, rather than the lists of stocks actually in the S&P 500 for each year, we have based our analysis on portfolios of stocks that could not have been constructed at the time of the analysis. After all, it is impossible to predict in 1974 what stocks will be in the S&P 500 in 1990.

More importantly, we also have introduced survivorship or success bias: Only those stocks that have been successful enough to survive have remained in the S&P 500, while only particularly successful new firms have been selected to replace the often unsuccessful ones that were dropped from the S&P 500 over time.

Research on a wide range of finance problems has made it clear that survivorship or success bias can strongly influence results and conclusions. As a simple example, when studying the returns from a strategy of investing in low-P/E stocks, it is important to consider stocks that no longer trade, since low-P/E stocks that have stopped trading are quite likely to have failed, resulting in stock prices that spiraled down to zero. Neglecting to include stocks that are no longer active may seriously bias upward any estimates of the returns to investing in all low-P/E stocks, not just the ones that happen to survive.

There is an obvious solution to the problem of survivorship or success bias: For each year of the analysis, simply use the list of stocks in the S&P 500 during that year and then sort on market capitalization or total assets. Tables 1.5 and 1.6 repeat the analysis of Tables 1.3 and 1.4, but are based on the historical lists of S&P 500 stocks.

The results using the historical S&P 500 are dramatically at odds with those obtained using the current S&P 500. For example, compare the 1984–90 net income figures for the smallest capitalization quintiles based on the current and historical S&P 500 (see Tables 1.3 and 1.5). In the case of the current S&P 500, net income was never negative, and totaled $24.8 billion for the seven year period. For the historical S&P 500, however, net income was negative in four years and totaled –$2.84 billion. This is a clear-cut example of survivorship or success bias. The current S&P, based on surviving firms as well as especially successful new firms, shows stronger earnings than does the historical S&P, which simply contains stocks in the S&P 500 year by year.

Readers should note that in the case of the largest capitalization quintiles, there is no sign of the survivorship effect; in fact, net income during 1984–90 was virtually identical for the current and the historical S&P 500. Why might this be? Many of the stocks that proved successful should be in

**Table 1.5—Aggregate Net Income of Historical S&P 500 Stocks
Quintiles by Market Capitalization (Dollars in Billions)**

	Quintiles					
	1 *Largest*	*2*	*3*	*4*	*5* *Smallest*	*Aggregate*
1992	41.3	8.7	7.5	0.1	−3.61	54.2
1991	70.6	19.4	10.7	6.9	−3.72	103.9
1990	98.1	29.2	15.3	5.8	−0.82	147.7
1989	101.6	33.2	18.7	6.0	1.49	161.2
1988	103.9	33.8	19.4	11.1	−0.12	168.2
1987	84.1	26.0	8.2	6.0	0.33	124.5
1986	74.9	18.2	10.0	1.5	−2.93	101.6
1985	76.5	17.1	9.5	3.2	−1.66	104.5
1984	75.0	25.1	10.6	3.7	0.87	122.1
1983	69.5	16.4	9.8	5.8	−0.95	101.0
1982	65.7	16.2	7.8	2.2	−1.70	90.2
1981	68.2	20.7	11.6	5.7	1.30	107.5
1980	69.1	17.7	11.4	3.8	0.87	103.0
1979	65.4	16.9	9.6	5.8	1.28	99.1
1978	52.5	13.4	8.3	4.3	1.19	79.8
1977	45.2	11.3	6.9	3.6	0.68	67.7
1976	40.1	10.7	5.5	2.7	0.84	60.0
1975	32.1	8.3	4.0	1.7	0.26	46.4
1974	34.9	8.7	5.2	1.1	1.00	50.8
Compound Average Growth Rate (%)						
1975–92	0.9	0.0	2.1	−12.5	NA	0.4
1975–83	8.0	7.3	7.3	20.7	NA	7.9
1984–90	5.0	8.7	6.6	0.2	NA	5.6
Average Net Income ($ billion)						
1974–83	54.3	14.0	8.0	3.7	0.48	80.5
1984–90	87.7	26.1	13.1	5.3	−0.41	132.8

Source: Kidder, Peabody Quantitative Research Group.
NA Not available/applicable.

Table 1.6—Aggregate Net Income of Historical S&P 500 Stocks
Quintiles by Total Assets (Dollars in Billions)

| | Quintiles | | | | | |
	1 Largest	2	3	4	5 Smallest	Aggregate
1992	16.8	23.1	4.9	6.0	3.47	54.2
1991	47.3	32.5	14.2	6.1	3.73	103.9
1990	78.0	39.0	17.8	8.9	3.88	147.7
1989	83.1	45.5	17.9	9.7	4.88	161.2
1988	90.5	43.7	20.4	9.8	3.81	168.2
1987	64.9	32.9	16.2	7.9	2.49	124.5
1986	66.5	15.9	11.8	5.0	2.44	101.6
1985	70.4	13.6	14.2	3.5	2.77	104.5
1984	72.1	21.8	11.7	6.6	3.02	122.1
1983	64.9	17.1	10.2	5.6	2.55	101.0
1982	61.3	10.5	10.7	5.2	2.49	90.2
1981	62.8	21.9	14.6	5.7	2.52	107.5
1980	61.0	20.1	13.8	5.8	2.25	103.0
1979	60.4	18.6	12.8	5.0	2.19	99.1
1978	49.0	15.1	9.7	4.3	1.59	79.8
1977	42.8	12.2	7.9	3.5	1.31	67.7
1976	39.3	10.6	6.3	2.6	1.06	60.0
1975	30.4	8.4	4.8	1.9	0.99	46.4
1974	34.8	8.3	4.5	2.2	1.09	50.8
Compound Average Growth Rate (%)						
1975–92	–4.0	5.9	0.5	5.7	6.6	0.4
1975–83	7.2	8.4	9.6	11.1	9.9	7.9
1984–90	2.7	12.5	8.3	6.8	6.2	5.6
Average Net Income ($ billion)						
1974–83	50.7	14.3	9.5	4.2	1.80	80.5
1984–90	75.1	30.4	15.7	7.4	3.33	132.8

Source: Kidder, Peabody Quantitative Research Group.

the largest quintile, so the current list of large stocks should look very similar to the historical list of stocks. Evidence to support this argument: 56% of the stocks in the largest capitalization quintile of the year-end 1983 S&P 500 survived to be in the largest capitalization quintile of the current S&P 500, while only 26% of the stocks in the smallest capitalization quintile for the year-end 1983 S&P 500 survived to be in the smallest quintile of the current S&P 500.

At this point, we can conclude that the historical S&P 500 should be preferred to the current S&P 500 and that for our purposes, the capitalization-based analysis is more appropriate than the asset-based analysis. But do the fundamental earnings trends using the capitalization quintiles from the historical S&P 500 match the market returns? Unfortunately, the answer is no; at least, not entirely.

Table 1.5 contains the aggregate net income figures for the historical S&P 500 and each capitalization quintile. Over the 1975–83 period, we can't compute an earnings growth rate for the smallest quintile because of negative net income in 1983. However, even over the 1975–81 period, small-stock net income grew only 30.0%, compared to 95.4% for large stocks.

These results are certainly confusing. After all, if the fundamentals of small stocks are always worse than those of large stocks, why do small stocks offer greater returns? One possible explanation is that the S&P 500 is not an appropriate stock universe for studying small versus large stocks.

The S&P 500 differs from most other indexes in its method of construction. While membership in many indexes is based on market capitalization, membership in the S&P 500 is based on judgment. Given the heavy use of the S&P 500 by passive or index managers, we suspect that Standard and Poor's seeks to minimize the number of name changes in the index. This would result in some poorly performing firms remaining in the index much longer than they would in an index that simply selects new names each year based on market capitalization. This "retention effect" should result in a much larger proportion of poorly performing firms in the bottom capitalization quintile of the S&P 500 than would be found in the smallest capitalization quintile for the full universe of stocks.

What have we learned so far? First, it is not obvious what measure of size should be preferred. Second, the definition of size has a profound effect on the results. Third, the stock universe selected can also have a significant effect on the results. What approach did we choose?

Methodology

We began with all stocks in the Compustat universe, including both active and inactive stocks. However, to ensure that the smallest quintile contained stocks with at least some relevance to institutional investors, we excluded stocks with market capitalizations below \$50 million at the end of 1991. Going back in time, we lowered this market capitalization minimum each year, based on the level of the Ibbotson Associates small-stock index.

Due to data limitations, we were forced to restrict the universe to stocks with fiscal years ending in December. This has the potential to bias the results, since Smith and Pourciau (1988) have shown that stocks with December fiscal year-ends have a number of financial characteristics that are different from those for stocks with other fiscal year-ends. Fortunately, Fama and French (1990), in a study that also looked at small-stock fundamentals, reported that their results were similar whether using all stocks or only those with December fiscal year-ends.

In this study we defined size in terms of market capitalization at the end of each year. All stocks were sorted based on capitalization at the end of the year; thus, we obtained historical lists of stocks. As noted earlier, we then screened out stocks with especially small market value. The number of stocks in the sample ranged from a low of 1315 in 1987 to a high of 1802 in 1974. In the text and tables that follow, we will refer to these annual samples as the "historical stock lists."

The accounting data came from the year following the calculation of market capitalization. This approach introduces a bias toward success, since it requires that the firm continue in business long enough to report results at the end of the following year. However, it appears that any approach that requires the use of fundamental accounting data will have a similar problem. For example, if we used accounting data from the same year as the market capitalization, we would be creating our size portfolios using data not available to us at the beginning of the year. Fortunately, as noted earlier, the fact that we are sorting stocks on the basis of market capitalization introduces a bias toward poor fundamental performance in the smaller capitalization quintiles; this runs counter to the possible bias toward success forced on us by the accounting data.

Finally, for each size quintile, the accounting data were pooled or aggregated as if there were a single firm in the portfolio.

WHAT DRIVES SMALL-STOCK RELATIVE PERFORMANCE?

Identifying and quantifying long cycles of under- and outperformance by small stocks do not answer the question of why these relative performance trends occur. Investors do not get carried away for such long periods of time because of euphoria or animal spirits. After all, the worst of Holland's seventeenth-century Tulipomania apparently lasted only about three years, while England's eighteenth-century South-Sea Bubble lasted less than a year (Mackay, 1852). Rather, these long cycles of under- and outperformance, we believe, are grounded in fundamental factors underlying the valuations of, and demand for, these two stock sectors.

Although we believe that earnings and valuation are important to explaining small-stock relative market performance, alternative explanations have been offered, including market cycles and interest rates.

Just Another Cycle?

Some analysts have suggested that the small-stock effect contains cycles: seven years of outperformance followed by seven years of underperformance, but with the net result being outperformance by small stocks over the long term. Small-stock relative performance back to 1926 (see Figure 1.2) does not show much evidence of cycles.

Figure 1.2—Small-Stock Performance Relative to the S&P 500

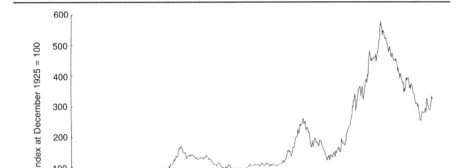

Source: Kidder, Peabody Quantitative Research Group; Ibbotson Associates.

The recent data also do not support the hypothesis of a seven-year cycle (see again Figure 1.1). Small stocks have outperformed in 1991 and 1992, which obviously neither supports nor contradicts the hypothesis. The most recent patch of underperformance lasted from July 1983 to December 1990, or seven and one-half years, which supports the supposed seven-year cycle. However, this period was punctuated by strong outperformance by small stocks during 1988. The last extended period of small-stock outperformance lasted from June 1973 to July 1983, or over ten years. Finally, the previous period of small-stock market underperformance lasted from May 1969 to June 1973, only slightly more than four years. Clearly, there is nothing sacred about the supposed seven-year cycle in small-stocks.

Was It Interest Rates?

One possible explanation for the poor performance of small stocks is the interest rate environment. After all, higher interest rates imply higher discount rates, which are likely to have a more negative effect on small-stock valuations because they are typically riskier and faster growing than large stocks. Fast growth for small stocks means that more of their value lies in future, not current, cash flows and is therefore more sensitive to the rate at which the cash flows are discounted. However, as Figure 1.3 makes clear, the period of outperformance by small stocks from June 1973 to July 1983 encompassed sharply different discount rate environments, with stretches where interest rates were flat, rising, and declining. For example, interest rates rose sharply during 1977–79. Likewise, the period of underperformance by small stocks from July 1983 to December 1990 saw generally declining interest rates; this should have been positive for small stocks.

Figure 1.3—U.S. Interest Rates 1-Year Treasury Bill, 10-Year Treasury Bond

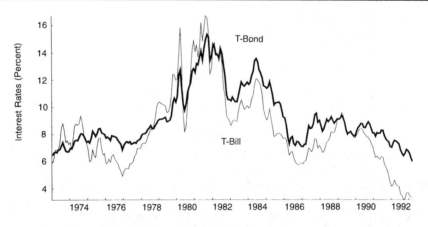

Source: Kidder, Peabody Quantitative Research Group; WEFA.

The Importance of Earnings

A more promising explanation for the period of underperformance is that small stocks failed to generate sufficient earnings growth relative to large stocks. Naturally, this factor is much more difficult to analyze.

The importance of earnings for stock valuation is too obvious to warrant much space in this chapter. However, we would note that in cross-sectional analyses we have conducted in the past, the single most important factor explaining a stock's current price has always been current earnings, typically followed by the projected long-term earnings growth rate. For examples of this type of analysis, interested readers are referred to our December 13, 1989, "Small Stocks" and April 20, 1990, "Growth Stocks" reports.

What Happened to the Earnings of Small versus Large Stocks?

Included in Table 1.7 are the aggregate net income data for each of the five market capitalization quintiles for the historical lists of all stocks (after excluding the very smallest stocks) as well as data for the full stock universe. At the bottom of Table 1.7 are the compound average growth rates for the entire 1975–92 period as well as the two major sub-periods of small-stock market out- and underperformance. Finally, we have included average net income figures for the two major sub-periods of small-stock market out- and underperformance.

The results during the 1975–83 period were not as clear-cut as we had hoped. The earnings growth rate of the smallest quintile of stocks was actually negative, while net income of the largest quintile grew 5.9% annually. To a considerable extent, the results were obscured by the recession of 1981–82, which had a much greater impact on small stocks than on large stocks. Indeed, over the 1975–80 period, small-stock aggregate net income grew 100.0% versus 93.0% for large stocks. Extending the period to include 1981 improved the relative earnings performance of small stocks to 233.3% versus 84.2%. As a point of clarification, readers should note that although the recession began in 1981, it started late in the year and much of the downturn came in 1982.

It may be that the 1981–82 recession caused investors to miss the downturn in the fundamental earnings performance of small stocks. As a result, small-stock relative earnings performance turned negative well before relative market performance.

Fortunately, results during the 1984–90 period were much cleaner. Indeed, the smallest-capitalization quintile reported negative earnings for the period, while the largest quintile reported positive earnings for the period

Table 1.7—Aggregate Net Income of Historical Stock Lists[a]
Quintiles by Market Capitalization (Dollars in Billions)

| | Quintiles | | | | | |
	1 Largest	2	3	4	5 Smallest	Aggregate
1992	47.2	4.3	0.6	1.1	0.66	53.7
1991	76.5	10.4	−2.4	−2.3	−0.17	82.0
1990	118.8	13.7	−0.2	0.4	−0.73	131.9
1989	129.4	13.6	4.7	0.4	0.10	148.1
1988	134.1	16.2	1.8	−0.3	−1.49	150.4
1987	108.8	14.0	1.1	1.8	0.29	126.1
1986	79.9	4.2	1.0	0.3	−0.42	85.1
1985	87.6	6.5	0.9	0.2	−0.31	94.9
1984	104.2	11.8	2.9	0.7	0.21	119.9
1983	88.7	10.0	1.6	0.9	0.01	101.2
1982	84.0	9.1	1.9	0.2	0.12	95.3
1981	97.1	13.0	3.9	1.6	0.70	116.2
1980	101.7	12.0	3.9	1.6	0.42	119.7
1979	96.0	13.9	4.9	1.7	0.53	117.1
1978	74.0	11.5	3.6	1.3	0.60	91.1
1977	65.2	9.0	2.8	0.6	0.39	77.9
1976	59.0	8.3	2.5	0.8	0.34	70.9
1975	47.1	6.3	1.8	0.5	0.25	55.9
1974	52.7	6.2	2.3	0.7	0.21	62.1

Compound Average Growth Rate (%)

1975–92	−0.6	−2.0	−7.4	2.4	6.7	−0.8
1975–83	5.9	5.5	−3.7	2.6	−27.4	5.6
1984–90	4.3	4.6	NA	−9.4	NA	3.9

Average Net Income ($ billion)

1974–83	76.5	9.9	2.9	1.0	0.36	90.7
1984–90	109.0	11.4	1.8	0.5	−0.33	122.3

Source: Kidder, Peabody Quantitative Research Group.

NA Not available/applicable.

(a) Historical stock lists contain all stocks in the Compustat Universe with a December fiscal year-end. Stocks with market capitalization below $50 million in 1991 are excluded, and this floor is raised or lowered going back in time each year, based on the level of Ibbotson Associates' small-stock index.

and grew by 4.3% on a compound annual basis. Given this shift in the rates of relative earnings growth, it is not surprising that small stocks switched from outperforming in the 1974–1983 period to underperforming in the 1984–1990 interval (with the exception of 1988, as we noted earlier).

In some sense, we could end our analysis here: Small stocks clearly outperformed in the 1974–83 period and underperformed in the 1984–90 period, because investors first rewarded them for superior earnings relative to large stocks (at least over the 1974–81 period) and then punished them for sub-par earnings.

These results are certainly helpful in understanding what happened to small-stock relative market performance. However, a more detailed understanding of why small stocks shifted from strong to poor earnings may help us to predict their future performance. Therefore, we will continue the chase.

DISSECTING THE EQUITY GROWTH RATE: A DUPONT ANALYSIS

One method for analyzing the sources of equity growth is a variant of the so-called duPont analysis. The objective of the duPont analysis is to break down the implied equity growth rate into its constituent parts. The full duPont analysis for the aggregate of all stocks with available data is contained in Table 1.22 at the end of this chapter. Readers will recall that the implied equity growth rate is simply the product of the firm's after-tax return on equity (ROE) and its dividend retention rate (or 1 minus its dividend payout ratio).

Equity Growth = After-tax ROE × Dividend Retention

= After-tax ROE × (1 − Dividend Payout Ratio)

In our model, the after-tax ROE is obtained as the product of pre-tax ROA, the interest factor, leverage, and the tax complement:

$$
\begin{aligned}
\text{After-tax ROE} &= \text{Pre-tax ROA} \times \text{Interest Factor} \times \text{Leverage} \\
&\quad \times \text{Tax Complement} \\
&= \frac{\text{Earnings Before Interest \& Taxes}}{\text{Assets}} \\
&\quad \times \frac{\text{Earnings Before Taxes}}{\text{Earnings Before Interest \& Taxes}} \\
&\quad \times \frac{\text{Assets}}{\text{Equity}} \times \text{Tax Complement}
\end{aligned}
$$

$$= \frac{\text{Earnings Before Taxes}}{\text{Equity}} \times \text{Tax Complement}$$

$$= \frac{\text{After--tax Net Income}}{\text{Equity}}$$

Now we will look at the four components of after-tax ROE, starting with pre-tax return on assets (ROA). ROA itself is the product of sales margin and asset turnover:

Pre-tax ROA   = Sales Margin × Asset Turnover

$$= \frac{\text{Earnings Before Interest \& Taxes}}{\text{Sales}} \times \frac{\text{Sales}}{\text{Assets}}$$

$$= \frac{\text{Earnings Before Interest \& Taxes}}{\text{Assets}}$$

The second component of after-tax ROE is the interest factor, a ratio that compares earnings with and without interest:

Interest Factor $= \dfrac{\text{Earnings Before Taxes}}{\text{Earnings Before Interest \& Taxes}}$

The third component of after-tax ROE is leverage, which is captured by comparing assets to equity:

Leverage $= \dfrac{\text{Assets}}{\text{Equity}}$

The fourth and final component of after-tax ROE is the tax complement:

Tax Complement $= 1 - \text{Effective Tax Rate} = 1 - \dfrac{\text{Income Taxes}}{\text{Earnings Before Taxes}}$

Equity Growth Rates for Small and Large Stocks

The full duPont analysis for each market capitalization quintile for the historical lists of stocks as well as the aggregate for the entire list are contained in Tables 1.22 through 1.27 at the end of this chapter. The averages for the largest and smallest market-capitalization quintiles over the key years of 1974–81, 1974–83, and 1984–90 are summarized in Table 1.8.

The duPont analysis illustrates some dramatic differences between large and small stocks. First, the sales margin (earnings before interest and taxes as a percent of sales) during 1974–83 was over two times higher for large stocks than it was for small stocks, 14.2% versus 6.2%. During the 1984–90 period of small-stock market underperformance, margins for small

**Table 1.8—Analysis of the Equity Growth Rate of Historical Stock Lists[a]
Quintiles by Market Capitalization**

		Quintiles	
		1	5
	Period	Largest	Smallest
EBIT/Sales(%)	1974–81	14.54	6.25
	1974–83	14.18	6.23
	1984–90	13.80	5.82
Sales/Assets	1974–81	0.99	1.50
	1974–83	0.98	1.38
	1984–90	0.78	0.80
Pre-tax ROA(%)	1974–81	14.38	9.38
	1974–83	13.90	8.60
	1984–90	10.73	4.44
EBT/EBIT	1974–81	0.82	0.58
	1974–83	0.80	0.51
	1984–90	0.66	0.09
Assets/Equity	1974–81	2.46	2.94
	1974–83	2.49	3.13
	1984–90	3.25	4.58
Tax Complement	1974–81	0.54	0.50
	1974–83	0.55	0.42
	1984–90	0.61	0.92
After-Tax ROE(%)	1974–81	15.57	7.97
	1974–83	15.07	6.46
	1984–90	13.93	−1.55
Retention Rate	1974–81	0.57	0.71
	1974–83	0.55	0.63
	1984–90	0.43	−0.81
Implied Growth Rate	1974–81	8.98	5.69
	1974–83	8.38	4.18
	1984–90	6.12	−6.95

Source: Kidder, Peabody Quantitative Research Group.

(a) Historical stock lists contain all stocks in the Compustat Universe with a December fiscal year-end. Stocks with market capitalization below $50 million in 1991 are excluded, and this floor is raised or lowered going back in time each year, based on the level of Ibbotson Associates' small-stock index.

stocks declined absolutely as well as relative to large stocks. In the case of asset turnover, large stocks were at a disadvantage during all periods. This disadvantage was reduced significantly during the 1984–90 period of small-stock market underperformance.

Multiplying these first two variables gives us the pre-tax ROA. For small stocks, pre-tax ROA was roughly half that for large stocks during 1974–83, before deteriorating both absolutely and relatively. Both margins and turnover contributed to the weaker results for small stocks.

Jumping down to the assets-to-equity ratio, small-capitalization stocks started out more leveraged than large stocks and increased their leverage faster. The ready availability of junk bond financing may be one reason for the greater increase in leverage by small stocks since 1983. In recent years, poor performance may have increased the leverage of small stocks, as shareholders' equity was consumed by losses.

The tax complement (1 minus the tax rate) for small stocks was lower during 1974–83. During the 1984–90 period of small-stock market under-performance, the tax complement for large stocks rose (taxes went down), while the tax complement for small stocks was distorted by losses.

The combination of all the previous ratios in the duPont analysis yields return on equity. Return on equity has historically been significantly higher among large-capitalization stocks. During the 1974–83 period, the spread between large and small stocks was nearly 9%. Over the 1984–90 period, the spread widened considerably, despite a lower return on equity for larger stocks.

In subsequent sections, we will focus on a number of factors that the duPont analysis suggests warrant greater attention.

Sales

On the way to the bottom line, it is always a good idea to start with the top line. As we have already seen, the sales variable plays an important role in the sales margin and asset turnover ratios. The aggregate sales trends for the historical lists of all stocks and each capitalization quintile are presented in Table 1.9.

In isolation, the sales data are not very useful. It is clear that the historical trends in sales for large and small stocks have been almost the reverse of those in market performance and net income. During the 1975–83 period of small-stock market outperformance, sales growth for the large-capitalization stocks, 9.2%, was faster than that for the smallest-capitalization stock, 6.1%. Large stocks actually had slower sales growth during the 1984–90 period of small-stock underperformance, 5.1% versus 6.1%, respec-

Table 1.9—Aggregate Sales of Historical Stock Lists[a]
Quintiles by Market Capitalization (Dollars in Billions)

			Quintiles			
	1 *Largest*	*2*	*3*	*4*	*5* *Smallest*	*Aggregate*
1992	2699.0	500.9	156.7	77.78	50.76	3485.1
1991	2262.2	473.0	147.8	71.66	55.83	3010.4
1990	2421.0	404.3	150.5	72.52	41.23	3089.5
1989	2186.6	364.4	134.6	63.18	36.45	2785.2
1988	2005.0	362.2	120.7	63.69	40.49	2592.0
1987	1883.4	314.0	118.0	65.99	32.02	2413.3
1986	1729.5	278.4	119.1	57.95	32.57	2217.5
1985	1810.2	265.6	118.2	55.60	28.09	2277.7
1984	1819.0	281.9	114.8	69.47	27.66	2312.8
1983	1714.0	282.9	124.8	59.89	27.16	2208.8
1982	1680.8	288.9	142.7	60.46	26.28	2199.0
1981	1668.7	320.3	119.8	57.65	29.76	2196.3
1980	1658.4	293.3	111.3	55.58	25.96	2144.5
1979	1451.6	252.7	97.1	48.44	24.52	1874.4
1978	1205.3	215.8	85.9	40.36	23.36	1570.7
1977	1070.0	201.4	68.9	33.42	19.38	1393.0
1976	935.0	172.7	69.5	31.68	17.16	1226.1
1975	813.1	147.1	63.5	28.74	16.14	1068.5
1974	777.0	144.6	64.9	27.05	16.00	1029.6
Compound Average Growth Rate (%)						
1975–92	7.2	7.1	5.0	6.0	6.6	7.0
1975–83	9.2	7.7	7.5	9.2	6.1	8.9
1984–90	5.1	5.2	2.7	2.8	6.1	4.9
Average Sales ($ billion)						
1974–83	1297.4	232.0	94.8	44.33	22.57	1691.1
1984–90	1979.2	324.4	125.1	64.06	34.07	2526.9

Source: Kidder, Peabody Quantitative Research Group.

(a) Historical stock lists contain all stocks in the Compustat Universe with a December fiscal year-end. Stocks with market capitalization below $50 million in 1991 are excluded, and this floor is raised or lowered going back in time each year, based on the level of Ibbotson Associates' small-stock index.

tively. Clearly, we will have to look elsewhere for insights into what drove small-stock relative market performance.

Leverage

Let's now turn our attention to leverage, measured in the duPont analysis by the ratio of assets to equity. Table 1.10 contains the aggregate leverage figures for the historical lists of all stocks and each capitalization quintile.

The results for the 1975–83 period provided some explanation for small-stock market outperformance. First, on average, small-stock leverage grew slightly faster than large-stock leverage, 3.1% versus 1.3%, respectively. Second, and more importantly, small-stock leverage remained above that for large stocks for every year.

The situation for the 1984–90 period, however, was not as clear. Small-stock leverage actually fell, while large-stock leverage grew 5.6% annually. However, the small-stock figure is clearly sensitive to the unusually low leverage for 1990. In fact, small-stock leverage remained above large-stock leverage for every year but 1990.

As all investors eventually learn, leverage is a double-edged sword. In some situations, leverage increases not at the discretion of management but because steady losses are eroding equity. This may have been what happened to small stocks in the late 1980s and early 1990s. As we discussed earlier, small stocks were, in the aggregate, losing money nearly every year during this period (see again Table 1.7).

Pre-tax Income

At this point, we can examine income before the effect of taxes. The results roughly matched those found for net income (see Table 1.11).

During the 1975–83 period, the annual growth rate in pre-tax income of the smallest quintile of stocks was zero, while pre-tax income of the largest quintile grew 4.8% annually. Once again, the results were obscured by the 1981–82 recession, which affected small stocks more than large stocks. By contrast, over the 1975–80 period, small-stock aggregate net income grew 95.6% versus 74.8% for large stocks. Extending the period to include 1981 improved the relative earnings performance of small stocks to 135.6% versus 57.8% for large stocks.

During the 1984–90 period, the smallest-capitalization quintile reported widely fluctuating pre-tax gains and losses, while the largest quintile re-

**Table 1.10—Aggregate Leverage (%) of Historical Stock Lists[a]
Quintiles by Market Capitalization (Dollars in Billions)**

| | Quintiles | | | | | |
| | 1 | 2 | 3 | 4 | 5 | |
	Largest				*Smallest*	*Aggregate*
1992	4.27	3.52	3.67	4.35	7.47	4.17
1991	3.85	3.78	3.46	6.41	14.34	3.92
1990	3.91	3.74	4.84	7.68	3.51	3.97
1989	3.75	3.72	5.09	4.25	5.68	3.83
1988	3.25	3.82	4.43	5.49	6.21	3.45
1987	3.06	3.71	5.26	4.98	4.14	3.27
1986	3.13	3.39	4.61	3.72	4.02	3.25
1985	2.89	3.76	4.00	3.24	4.22	3.07
1984	2.76	3.79	2.76	3.42	4.25	2.92
1983	2.67	3.48	3.03	2.74	4.01	2.80
1982	2.54	3.66	3.94	2.97	3.80	2.78
1981	2.47	3.72	3.13	3.09	2.98	2.70
1980	2.55	3.16	2.98	2.93	2.87	2.66
1979	2.52	3.08	2.89	3.02	2.88	2.62
1978	2.49	2.68	3.10	2.81	2.99	2.55
1977	2.43	2.83	2.91	2.92	2.85	2.50
1976	2.42	2.85	2.85	2.67	2.99	2.50
1975	2.42	2.78	2.89	2.67	2.91	2.49
1974	2.38	2.78	2.89	2.68	3.05	2.46

Compound Average Growth Rate (%)

	1	2	3	4	5	Aggregate
1975–92	3.3	1.3	1.3	2.7	5.1	3.0
1975–83	1.3	2.5	0.5	0.3	3.1	1.4
1984–90	5.6	1.1	6.9	15.9	−1.9	5.1

Average Leverage (%)

	1	2	3	4	5	Aggregate
1974–83	2.49	3.10	3.06	2.85	3.13	2.61
1984–90	3.25	3.70	4.43	4.68	4.58	3.39

Source: Kidder, Peabody Quantitative Research Group.

(a) Historical stock lists contain all stocks in the Compustat Universe with a December fiscal year-end. Stocks with market capitalization below $50 million in 1991 are excluded, and this floor is raised or lowered going back in time each year, based on the level of Ibbotson Associates' small-stock index.

Table 1.11—Aggregate Pre-Tax Income of Historical Stock Lists[a]
Quintiles by Market Capitalization (Dollars in Billions)

	Quintiles					
	1 *Largest*	*2*	*3*	*4*	*5* *Smallest*	*Aggregate*
1992	183.0	22.3	5.63	2.53	0.97	214.4
1991	141.2	19.9	0.77	−1.23	−0.22	160.4
1990	192.2	23.1	2.37	1.48	−0.51	218.6
1989	199.4	23.4	7.26	1.15	0.64	231.8
1988	200.9	27.3	6.86	0.58	0.38	236.0
1987	178.7	24.2	4.09	2.67	0.74	210.3
1986	136.3	12.1	3.64	1.54	−0.11	153.5
1985	162.5	16.2	3.12	1.41	0.22	183.4
1984	181.2	20.5	7.21	2.04	0.68	211.6
1983	164.5	17.5	4.87	1.79	0.45	189.1
1982	146.9	13.8	4.40	1.13	0.33	166.6
1981	169.6	20.9	7.06	2.72	1.06	201.4
1980	187.9	20.7	7.32	2.80	0.88	219.6
1979	176.2	22.6	8.28	2.76	0.98	210.8
1978	140.7	19.2	6.66	2.36	1.00	169.9
1977	126.5	15.9	4.95	1.90	0.75	150.0
1976	113.1	14.3	4.60	1.70	0.66	134.3
1975	96.7	11.3	3.34	1.09	0.51	113.0
1974	107.5	10.5	4.13	1.41	0.45	124.0
Compound Average Growth Rate (%)						
1975–92	3.0	4.2	1.7	3.3	4.4	3.1
1975–83	4.8	5.8	1.8	2.7	0.0	4.8
1984–90	2.3	4.1	−9.8	−2.7	NA	2.1
Average Pre-tax Income ($ billion)						
1974–83	142.7	19.1	6.23	2.22	0.76	171.1
1984–90	177.3	26.4	6.77	1.99	0.35	212.8

Source: Kidder, Peabody Quantitative Research Group.

NA Not available/applicable.

(a) Historical stock lists contain all stocks in the Compustat Universe with a December fiscal year-end. Stocks with market capitalization below $50 million in 1991 are excluded, and this floor is raised or lowered going back in time each year, based on the level of Ibbotson Associates' small-stock index.

ported consistently positive earnings for the period and grew 2.3% on a compound annual basis.

Taxes

Shifts in effective tax rates can dramatically affect a company's ability to bring earnings to the bottom line. Aggregate tax rates for the historical lists of all stocks and each capitalization quintile are included in Table 1.12.

For the 1974–83 period of small-stock market outperformance, small stocks had an average effective tax rate of 58.3%, compared to 45.3% for large stocks. If we exclude the recession-affected years of 1982 and 1983, tax rates averaged 50.1% for small stocks and 46.1% for large stocks. During 1984–90, tax rates went down for large stocks, averaging only 38.6%. The effective tax rate for small stocks was distorted by recurring losses. The decline in the effective tax rate for large stocks accentuated their relative outperformance.

We suspect that the shift to lower tax rates for large stocks reflected, in part, major changes in the corporate tax law structure. The tax law changes, especially the investment tax credit provisions, tended to help firms with high capital intensity. Since large stocks were helped by the tax law changes, then it should be the case that large stocks were more capital intensive than small stocks. Was that the case?

We examined two measures of capital intensity: Depreciation as a percentage of sales (see Table 1.13) and property, plant, and equipment as a percentage of total assets (see Table 1.14). By both measures, larger stocks were more capital intensive than small stocks throughout the 1974–92 study period. In the case of depreciation as a percentage of sales, large stocks were more capital intensive than small stocks in every year, averaging 5.4% compared to only 3.3% for small stocks. Large stocks also had a greater percentage of assets in the form of property, plant, and equipment in every year, averaging 49.2% versus only 30.5% for small stocks.

Finally, it should be noted that the effective tax rate for the largest stocks bottomed out in 1988, rising in 1989 through 1991. This negative trend for large stocks may have contributed to the most recent period of small-stock market outperformance.

OTHER DETERMINANTS OF EARNINGS GROWTH

There are many other factors that may be important for earnings growth. We will examine two of them: pension expense and exposure to foreign markets.

Table 1.12—Aggregate Tax Rate (%) of Historical Stock Lists[a]
Quintiles by Market Capitalization

	Quintiles					
	1	2	3	4	5	
	Largest				Smallest	Aggregate
1992	36.6	35.7	43.6	39.3	55.3	36.8
1991	38.7	39.7	275.6	−45.4	−63.3	40.8
1990	37.9	39.3	105.4	68.6	−59.2	39.2
1989	35.2	35.2	36.5	63.4	65.4	35.5
1988	35.1	35.8	40.5	167.9	131.0	35.8
1987	38.5	41.4	65.8	41.0	73.8	39.5
1986	39.6	62.7	66.6	74.3	−418.6	42.7
1985	43.0	46.6	64.4	70.6	195.4	44.0
1984	41.0	42.6	47.8	57.8	69.9	41.7
1983	42.1	41.6	55.6	52.3	99.7	42.6
1982	41.9	36.4	55.1	78.7	82.5	42.1
1981	41.3	38.1	44.2	46.0	43.3	41.1
1980	44.2	41.7	42.1	42.5	43.2	43.9
1979	44.0	38.3	39.0	40.6	46.7	43.1
1978	46.1	40.9	43.1	44.0	50.6	45.4
1977	47.2	42.4	43.8	45.2	52.0	46.6
1976	46.7	41.9	44.4	47.2	54.1	46.1
1975	49.7	41.5	44.6	55.1	54.2	48.8
1974	49.8	40.9	43.0	47.5	56.8	48.9

Compound Average Growth Rate (%)

1975–92	−1.7	−0.7	0.1	−1.1	−0.1	−1.6
1975–83	−1.9	0.2	2.9	1.1	6.4	−1.5
1984–90	−1.5	−0.8	9.6	3.9	NA	−1.2

Average Tax Rate (%)

1974–83	45.3	40.4	45.5	49.9	58.3	44.9
1984–90	38.6	43.4	61.0	77.7	8.2	39.8

Source: Kidder, Peabody Quantitative Research Group.

NA Not available/applicable.

(a) Historical stock lists contain all stocks in the Compustat Universe with a December fiscal year-end. Stocks with market capitalization below $50 million in 1991 are excluded, and this floor is raised or lowered going back in time each year, based on the level of Ibbotson Associates' small-stock index.

Table 1.13—Aggregate Capital Intensity (%) of Historical Stock Lists[a]
(Depreciation/Sales) Quintiles by Market Capitalization

	Quintiles					
	1 Largest	2	3	4	5 Smallest	Aggregate
1992	6.15	4.99	5.06	4.47	3.95	5.86
1991	6.46	4.93	6.01	5.01	3.69	6.11
1990	6.00	4.92	4.95	4.24	3.83	5.73
1989	6.12	5.06	4.27	3.87	3.99	5.81
1988	6.21	5.06	4.39	3.71	4.97	5.88
1987	6.20	5.02	4.65	4.30	4.00	5.89
1986	5.99	5.19	4.82	4.48	4.01	5.76
1985	5.52	4.67	4.64	3.78	3.82	5.31
1984	5.00	4.71	4.23	3.47	3.54	4.86
1983	5.47	4.67	4.32	3.56	3.50	5.23
1982	5.16	4.44	3.92	3.44	3.21	4.91
1981	4.61	3.89	3.79	2.87	2.59	4.39
1980	4.41	3.87	3.25	2.44	2.51	4.21
1979	4.43	3.78	2.93	2.47	2.23	4.19
1978	4.77	3.72	2.81	2.66	2.34	4.43
1977	4.72	3.42	2.91	2.96	2.44	4.37
1976	4.80	3.61	2.96	2.70	2.67	4.45
1975	5.08	3.82	3.08	2.99	2.78	4.70
1974	4.85	3.47	2.70	2.79	2.54	4.43

Compound Average Growth Rate (%)

1975–92	1.3	2.0	3.6	2.6	2.5	1.6
1975–83	1.4	3.4	5.4	2.7	3.6	1.9
1984–90	1.3	0.8	2.0	2.5	1.3	1.3

Average Capital Intensity (%)

1974–92	5.37	4.38	3.98	3.48	3.30	5.08
1974–83	4.83	3.87	3.27	2.89	2.68	4.53
1984–90	5.86	4.95	4.57	3.98	4.02	5.61

Source: Kidder, Peabody Quantitative Research Group.

(a) Historical stock lists contain all stocks in the Compustat Universe with a December fiscal year-end. Stocks with market capitalization below $50 million in 1991 are excluded, and this floor is raised or lowered going back in time each year, based on the level of Ibbotson Associates' small-stock index.

Table 1.14—Aggregate Capital Intensity (%) of Historical Stock Lists[a]
(Property, Plant & Equipment/Total Assets) Quintiles by Market Capitalization

| | Quintiles | | | | | |
| | 1 | 2 | 3 | 4 | 5 | |
	Largest				Smallest	Aggregate
1992	31.7	42.8	34.2	25.3	29.6	32.8
1991	38.3	42.0	39.9	25.1	22.4	38.2
1990	36.8	43.4	34.5	22.7	26.4	36.9
1989	38.0	46.0	30.1	24.8	18.0	37.9
1988	41.3	41.2	33.5	18.1	20.6	39.8
1987	47.2	41.5	29.3	27.3	28.6	44.5
1986	46.1	44.7	32.7	34.2	36.8	44.7
1985	48.9	38.3	37.9	40.1	26.5	46.2
1984	48.8	39.8	51.6	41.6	28.8	46.9
1983	54.0	43.1	48.4	44.7	33.4	51.5
1982	58.3	42.5	38.4	47.3	30.6	53.7
1981	58.1	44.0	48.4	35.8	36.8	54.1
1980	54.9	49.7	44.4	36.3	35.8	53.0
1979	54.7	46.2	40.8	35.1	32.0	52.2
1978	55.2	48.8	34.8	35.5	33.7	52.8
1977	55.8	46.5	34.9	36.1	35.1	53.0
1976	55.5	47.2	35.6	35.5	33.2	52.8
1975	55.6	50.7	35.2	35.8	36.6	53.3
1974	55.0	48.1	37.8	35.4	33.3	52.6

Compound Average Growth Rate (%)

1975–92	−3.0	−0.6	−0.6	−1.8	−0.7	−2.6
1975–83	−0.2	−1.2	2.8	2.6	0.0	−0.2
1984–90	−5.3	0.1	−4.7	−9.3	−3.3	−4.6

Average Capital Intensity (%)

1974–92	49.2	44.6	38.0	33.5	30.5	47.2
1974–83	55.7	46.7	39.9	37.7	34.1	52.9
1984–90	43.9	42.1	35.6	29.8	26.5	42.4

Source: Kidder, Peabody Quantitative Research Group.

(a) Historical stock lists contain all stocks in the Compustat Universe with a December fiscal year-end. Stocks with market capitalization below $50 million in 1991 are excluded, and this floor is raised or lowered going back in time each year, based on the level of Ibbotson Associates' small-stock index.

Pension Expense

Long before focusing our attention on the issue of small versus large stocks, we had studied the impact on S&P 500 reported earnings of fluctuations in pension expense. Kidder Peabody's reports, "Pension Expense, a Hidden Source of Past Profit Growth Is Fading" dated April 7, 1990, and "Pension Expense, a Hidden Source of Past Profit Growth Is Now Hurting" dated August 6, 1990, provide an in-depth analysis of the impact of the decline of pension expense on the profits of the S&P 500. Given the dramatic shifts we observed in pension expense for the entire S&P 500, it was natural to examine whether the decline in pension expense varied as a function of market capitalization. Indeed, in the second pension expense report, we showed that for the (then) current S&P 500, large stocks had received a much greater benefit from declining pension expense than had small stocks.

Included in Table 1.15 are the aggregate pension expense trends for the historical lists of all stocks and each capitalization quintile. For all stocks, aggregate pension expense peaked in 1980, declined to a trough in 1988, and recently climbed back.

The data in Table 1.15 make it clear that the large stocks have been more dramatically affected by shifts in pension expense. It is also clear that the impact of pension expense for small versus large stocks closely matched the relative market performance of these two groups. Shifts in pension expense clearly played an important role in the relative performance of small stocks.

During the 1975–83 period of small-stock market outperformance, pension expense grew annually at only 4.5% for small stocks, but 8.8% for large stocks. During the early portion of the period, from 1975 to 1980, sharply rising pension expense clearly hurt large stocks. Pension expense for the largest stocks increased 130.7% while it grew 120.0% for the smallest stocks.

During the period of small-stock market underperformance, small stocks saw pension expense grow only 0.8% annually, while large stocks experienced an 12.4% annual decline. During the early part of the 1984–90 period, from 1984 to 1988, large stocks received major benefits from declining pension expense. Over this time frame, large-stock pension expense fell 64.4%; small-stock pension expense declined only 12.5%.

Why did pension expense decline so dramatically between 1980 and 1988? One likely factor would be the impressive returns pension funds were able to earn from stocks, bonds, and real estate during 1981–88. In the case of stocks, the S&P 500 compound average annual total return for 1981–88 was 14.2%, compared to the long-term figure of 10.3%. In the case of intermediate Treasury notes, the compound average annual total return

Table 1.15—Aggregate Pension Expense of Historical Stock Lists[a]
Quintiles by Market Capitalization (Dollars in Billions)

| | Quintiles | | | | | |
	1 Largest	2	3	4	5 Smallest	Aggregate
1992	15.0	1.55	0.91	0.31	0.26	18.0
1991	11.4	2.56	0.67	0.43	0.35	15.4
1990	8.6	1.83	0.80	0.38	0.16	11.7
1989	9.2	1.41	0.63	0.27	0.13	11.6
1988	7.7	1.53	0.62	0.31	0.14	10.3
1987	8.5	1.43	0.68	0.27	0.11	11.0
1986	9.3	1.60	0.74	0.25	0.15	12.0
1985	15.9	2.22	0.92	0.39	0.13	19.6
1984	18.4	2.41	0.93	0.50	0.14	22.4
1983	21.6	3.01	1.21	0.50	0.16	26.5
1982	22.4	3.71	1.77	0.51	0.21	28.5
1981	21.8	4.01	1.40	0.54	0.22	28.0
1980	23.3	3.99	1.21	0.47	0.22	29.2
1979	22.2	3.31	1.01	0.39	0.21	27.1
1978	19.2	2.77	0.88	0.35	0.20	23.4
1977	16.6	2.45	0.74	0.28	0.16	20.3
1976	14.3	2.22	0.72	0.27	0.11	17.7
1975	12.2	1.90	0.61	0.21	0.11	15.0
1974	10.1	1.53	0.64	0.19	0.10	12.5
Compound Average Growth Rate (%)						
1975–92	2.2	0.1	1.9	2.7	5.1	2.0
1975–83	8.8	7.8	7.3	11.1	4.5	8.6
1984–90	−12.4	−6.8	−5.8	−3.9	0.8	−11.0
Average Pension Expense ($ billion)						
1974–83	18.4	2.89	1.02	0.37	0.17	22.8
1984–90	11.1	1.77	0.76	0.34	0.14	14.1

Source: Kidder, Peabody Quantitative Research Group.

(a) Historical stock lists contain all stocks in the Compustat Universe with a December year-end. Stocks with market capitalization below $50 million in 1991 are excluded, and floor is raised or lowered going back in time each year, based on the level of Ibbotson Associates' small-stock index.

during 1981–88 was 12.8%, versus 5.2% for the long-run. The real estate market also provided excellent returns to pension funds. The appreciation in these markets pushed many pension portfolios to overfunded positions and contributed to a sharp reduction in the pension expense for many corporations.

Another factor contributing to the shifts in pension expense may have been labor force reductions by many of the major industrial companies. Table 1.16 contains the aggregate employment trends for the historical lists of all stocks and each capitalization quintile. For all stocks, aggregate employment grew 1.5% per year over the full 1975–92 period. However, from the peak in pension expense (1980) to the trough (1988), aggregate employment grew only 0.6% annually.

Employment trends also matched the pattern of relative market performance of small and large stocks. During the 1975–83 period of small-stock market outperformance, employment grew 1.2% for small stocks and 1.3% for large stocks. However, during the 1984–90 period of small-stock underperformance, employment grew much faster for the small stocks: 8.1% versus 2.3%.

Foreign Exposure

A number of analysts have suggested that differences in exposure to foreign markets may represent one explanation for shifts in relative earnings performance between small and large stocks. Unfortunately, data on foreign exposure are rather limited; most firms have been providing such data only since the early 1980s and many small firms still do not provide these data. Therefore, we will restrict our examination of foreign exposure for the current S&P 500 stocks.

Table 1.17 shows the trends in three measures of foreign exposure: Foreign sales as a percent of total sales; foreign sales and exports as a percent of total sales; and foreign operating earnings as a percent of total operating earnings. Clearly, by any measure, S&P 500 foreign exposure has grown significantly. Readers should note that the Compustat database only retains foreign exposure data back through 1986; the figures for earlier years were constructed using the list of S&P 500 stocks for August 1991 and therefore are not strictly comparable with the figures for later years.

In Table 1.18 we have detailed the percentage of total revenues that foreign sales and exports represent for the current S&P 500 and each quintile of capitalization from 1983 to 1991. The largest stock group derived the greatest percentage (32.8% in 1992) of total sales from foreign and export sales. Foreign exposure declines steadily with capitalization, leaving the

**Table 1.16—Aggregate Number of Employees: Historical Stock Lists[a]
Quintiles by Market Capitalization (Thousands)**

			Quintiles			
	1 *Largest*	*2*	*3*	*4*	*5* *Smallest*	*Aggregate*
1992	11.8	3.6	1.54	0.80	0.41	18.1
1991	11.3	3.8	1.61	0.62	0.46	17.8
1990	12.2	3.2	1.39	0.61	0.37	17.8
1989	12.0	3.0	1.58	0.52	0.36	17.5
1988	11.7	2.8	1.42	0.50	0.41	16.9
1987	12.0	2.8	1.16	0.67	0.34	16.9
1986	11.8	2.5	1.00	0.75	0.25	16.3
1985	11.5	2.0	1.35	0.61	0.22	15.8
1984	11.6	2.2	1.29	0.48	0.34	16.0
1983	10.5	2.3	1.30	0.47	0.21	14.8
1982	10.9	2.5	1.46	0.51	0.18	15.6
1981	10.9	2.8	1.48	0.51	0.29	15.9
1980	11.0	2.7	1.46	0.54	0.31	16.1
1979	11.3	2.9	1.46	0.51	0.32	16.4
1978	10.3	2.7	1.38	0.45	0.32	15.2
1977	10.3	2.3	1.13	0.60	0.25	14.6
1976	9.4	2.3	1.16	0.59	0.20	13.7
1975	9.0	2.3	1.17	0.57	0.22	13.2
1974	9.4	2.4	1.15	0.68	0.19	13.7
Compound Average Growth Rate (%)						
1975–92	1.3	2.3	1.6	0.9	4.4	1.5
1975–83	1.3	−0.3	1.4	−3.9	1.2	0.8
1984–90	2.3	4.8	0.9	3.7	8.1	2.7
Average Number of Employees (thousands)						
1974–83	10.3	2.5	1.32	0.54	0.25	14.9
1984–90	11.8	2.7	1.31	0.59	0.33	16.7

Source: Kidder, Peabody Quantitative Research Group.

(a) Historical stock lists contain all stocks in the Compustat Universe with a December fiscal year-end. Stocks with market capitalization below $50 million in 1991 are excluded, and this floor is raised or lowered going back in time each year, based on the level of Ibbotson Associates' small-stock index.

Table 1.17—Trends in Foreign Exposure for the Current S&P 500

	Foreign Sales as a % of Total Sales	Foreign Sales and Exports as a % of Total Sales	Foreign Earnings as a % of Total Earnings
1992	25.0	27.0	37.7
1991	24.5	26.5	43.7
1990	24.5	26.3	42.0
1989	22.4	24.2	40.1
1988	21.7	23.4	38.6
1987	21.3	22.8	37.8
1986	19.9	21.4	36.8
1985	20.3	22.1	33.6
1984	21.0	22.8	31.5

Source: Kidder, Peabody Quantitative Research Group.

smallest quintile deriving only 14.3% of total sales from exports and foreign-based operations. Since foreign exposure increased the most for the smallest-capitalization group, this may explain why their relative sales growth in the last five years accelerated to match that of the largest-capitalization group.

Table 1.18—Foreign Sales as a % of Total Sales for the S&P 500

	Quintiles					
	1 Largest	2	3	4	5 Smallest	Aggregate
1992	32.8	22.0	18.9	18.0	14.3	27.0
1991	32.8	20.8	18.4	17.3	15.3	26.5
1990	32.9	19.8	17.5	17.1	14.9	26.3
1989	30.5	18.9	15.9	15.4	13.7	24.2
1988	30.0	17.6	15.2	14.4	12.5	23.4
1987	29.7	16.7	13.5	13.1	12.3	22.8
1986	27.9	15.5	12.9	12.4	10.7	21.4

Source: Kidder, Peabody Quantitative Research Group.

The truth of the matter is that we don't have sufficient data to make a strong judgment about the importance of foreign exposure. Given the relative lack of data on foreign exposure, it is fortunate that there is some strong evidence that foreign exposure is not likely to be an important explanation for the market underperformance of small stocks. Figure 1.4 makes it clear that the period of July 1983 to December 1990 included sharply different exchange rate environments, where the U.S. dollar was first rising strongly, then declining sharply, and finally drifting slowly lower with brief periods of strengthening. These shifts in the value of the U.S. dollar don't seem to be mirrored either in the relative earnings or market performances of small stocks.

Figure 1.4—Exchange Rates Trade-Weighted Dollar, Deutsche Mark/Dollar, Yen/Dollar

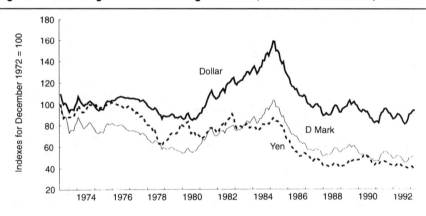

Source: Kidder, Peabody Quantitative Research Group; WEFA

Don't Forget to Accentuate the Positive

There is one more point that should be made. Although small stocks underperformed on a fundamental basis during 1984–90, there were several trends favoring small-stock earnings. At the top line, small stocks exhibited better growth in total sales than large stocks, as well as faster growth in foreign sales and exports. Small stocks' leverage also increased more (of course, this is a double-edged sword). Nevertheless, investors clearly focused on the bottom line, punishing small stocks for weaker earnings growth.

VALUATION

Up to this point, we have relied exclusively on earnings fundamentals when trying to explain the relative market performance of small stocks. Clearly, however, valuation should be considered. The key question is: What does a dollar of earnings cost the investor in the marketplace?

Table 1.19 provides aggregate data on one measure of valuation, equity income (income before extraordinary items, minus any preferred dividends, plus deferred taxes) as a percentage of market value. This valuation measure was suggested by Fama and French (1990). During the 1974–78 period of small-stock market outperformance, investors could consistently buy a greater level of earnings for each dollar invested by purchasing small stocks rather than large stocks. During the 1979–82 period, earnings and valuation fundamentals did not match market performance for small stocks. However, during the 1984–90 period of small-stock market underperformance, small stocks were consistently more expensive than large stocks.

Similar results were obtained when we sorted stocks within each capitalization quintile on the basis of equity income as a percentage of market value and examined the median values (see Table 1.20).

Finally, we also should point out that in the case of median equity income as a percentage of market value, beginning in 1991, small stock relative valuations improved significantly. As we have noted before, this was the most recent period of market outperformance by small stocks.

LOOKING TO THE FUTURE: THE FUNDAMENTALS

As we look to the future, there are a number of factors that should lead to changes in the relative earnings performance of small versus large stocks. Our forecasts are partly predicated on our expectations of a slow-growth economic environment in the United States over the longer term and somewhat faster growth in Japan, Europe, and portions of the third world (especially South America and eastern Asia).

We believe the key factors influencing the relative fundamentals of small versus large stocks will be taxes, pension expense, and post-retirement health care expense. Many of these factors have shifted from being negative for small stocks to being positive or at least neutral. We will also discuss foreign exposure.

In addition, we have some evidence that valuations have shifted back in favor of small stocks. Readers should recall the data on median equity income as a percent of market value displayed in Table 1.20.

Table 1.19—Aggregate Ratio of Equity Income to Market Value (%) of Historical Stock Lists[a] Quintiles by Market Capitalization

| | Quintiles | | | | | |
	1 Largest	2	3	4	5 Smallest	Aggregate
1992	3.85	3.88	2.30	2.57	0.54	3.89
1991	3.96	3.76	-2.56	-7.18	-5.45	3.50
1990	5.75	4.91	-1.02	0.72	-5.57	5.25
1989	8.65	6.13	6.08	0.52	0.21	8.04
1988	9.39	8.98	6.45	-3.13	-3.11	8.96
1987	8.81	7.62	1.63	5.07	0.89	8.25
1986	8.51	2.39	2.14	1.84	-4.83	7.21
1985	11.47	6.79	2.03	2.59	-2.16	10.22
1984	12.23	8.73	7.38	4.06	1.93	11.29
1983	13.50	8.92	4.87	4.98	0.48	12.26
1982	13.90	8.69	5.28	2.52	1.70	12.55
1981	14.15	13.12	10.58	10.61	10.33	13.80
1980	17.80	14.46	13.71	14.25	10.52	17.13
1979	19.05	19.96	22.78	19.54	15.17	19.27
1978	15.38	17.56	18.33	16.90	16.32	15.73
1977	12.40	15.02	15.44	15.79	14.66	12.78
1976	13.67	18.77	19.85	18.50	16.17	14.31
1975	14.68	21.47	21.17	13.62	19.34	15.35
1974	10.88	14.20	19.66	15.46	11.07	11.36

Compound Average Growth Rate (%)

1975–92	-5.6	-7.0	-11.2	-9.5	-15.4	-5.8
1975–83	2.4	-5.0	-14.4	-11.8	-29.5	0.8
1984–90	-11.5	-8.2	NA	-24.2	NA	-11.4

Average Ratio of Equity Income to Market Value (%)

1974–83	14.54	15.22	15.17	13.22	11.58	14.45
1984–90	9.26	6.51	3.53	1.67	-1.80	8.46

Source: Kidder, Peabody Quantitative Research Group.

NA Not available/applicable.

(a) Historical stock lists contain all stocks in the Compustat Universe with a December fiscal year-end. Stocks with market capitalization below $50 million in 1991 are excluded, and this floor is raised or lowered going back in time each year, based on the level of Ibbotson Associates' small-stock index.

Table 1.20—Median Ratio of Equity Income to Market Value (%) of Historical Stock Lists[a] Quintiles by Capitalization

	Quintiles					
	1 Largest	2	3	4	5 Smallest	Aggregate
1992	5.70	5.67	5.23	5.05	4.79	5.43
1991	5.92	6.15	6.12	5.59	4.52	5.80
1990	6.42	6.42	5.57	4.93	3.16	5.71
1989	8.95	7.79	7.67	6.90	4.25	7.46
1988	9.41	9.39	8.70	7.68	4.80	8.21
1987	8.95	8.19	6.53	6.43	4.95	7.30
1986	8.85	7.60	7.00	6.36	4.12	7.20
1985	11.37	9.44	8.53	8.70	6.38	9.28
1984	11.82	8.92	9.19	8.55	6.83	9.13
1983	12.10	10.45	10.47	10.29	8.85	10.54
1982	13.32	10.76	9.81	9.37	8.31	10.52
1981	13.23	12.99	12.66	12.54	11.87	12.67
1980	16.75	15.68	14.68	14.77	11.73	14.98
1979	18.66	18.90	18.70	18.63	16.60	18.52
1978	15.50	16.71	17.38	18.00	20.06	17.25
1977	13.11	14.64	15.64	17.36	19.51	15.47
1976	14.83	18.82	19.73	21.20	23.55	19.00
1975	16.39	21.63	23.36	22.31	29.63	21.31
1974	12.18	14.21	17.11	16.19	16.87	14.88

Compound Average Growth Rate (%)

	1 Largest	2	3	4	5 Smallest	Aggregate
1975–92	−4.1	−5.0	−6.4	−6.3	−6.8	−5.4
1975–83	−0.1	−3.4	−5.3	−4.9	−6.9	−3.8
1984–92	−8.6	−6.7	−8.6	−10.0	−13.7	−8.4

Average Ratio of Median Equity Income to Market Value (%)

	1 Largest	2	3	4	5 Smallest	Aggregate
1974–83	14.61	15.48	15.95	16.07	16.70	15.51
1984–92	9.40	8.25	7.60	7.08	4.93	7.76

Source: Kidder, Peabody Quantitative Research Group.

(a) Historical stock lists contain all stocks in the Compustat Universe with a December fiscal year-end. Stocks with market capitalization below $50 million in 1991 are excluded, and this floor is raised or lowered going back in time each year, based on the level of Ibbotson Associates' small-stock index.

Taxes

We see little to change the effective tax rates of either sector on a relative basis; however, it is likely that everyone will pay higher taxes. Politicians are once again talking about some variant of an investment tax credit. However, at this time it appears that any tax credit will be rather circumscribed. Thus, shifts in relative tax rates are not likely to influence the performance of small versus large stocks. In this case, a factor that had been negative for small stocks should shift to having no significant influence.

Pension Expense

For a number of reasons, we had previously concluded that pension expense would no longer be a major contributor to corporate pre-tax profit growth, as it was for the years 1982 to 1988. The results for 1989–91 have certainly supported these conclusions. Where declining pension expense previously favored large-stock earnings, rising pension expense should penalize large stocks for the next few years. Stock, bond, and real estate returns in the 1990s are not likely to match the high levels seen in 1982–88.

Post-retirement Health Care Benefits

Data on the impact of FAS 106 (post-retirement health care benefits) are just now becoming available. FAS 106 is increasingly important to investors as it becomes clearer that its impact will vary considerably, even among firms within the same industry. We believe that post-retirement health care benefits will have the same differential effect as pension expense. Just as rising pension expense has had a negative influence on the earnings of companies, especially larger ones since 1988, post-retirement health care benefits should play a similar role in the 1990s. This should be an especially important problem for larger companies with their large numbers of unionized employees and retirees per active employee.

Foreign Exposure

As we noted earlier, the important point to remember is that there is little evidence that foreign exposure played a role in the relative fundamental performance of small and large stocks. Nevertheless, differences in foreign exposure may play a role in the future. Large stocks have the larger exposure to foreign markets. The increasing awareness of the international nature of competition should push small stocks to grow their foreign sales and exports more rapidly. Over time, the difference in foreign exposure should decline, making this factor less important to relative fundamental performance.

Employment

For the largest stocks, massive restructurings by many large firms caused employment to decline in 1991 (see Table 1.16); employment was up in 1992, but remained below its peak. Going forward, large stock employment should either grow more slowly or even decline. For the smallest stocks, employment grew in 1991, but declined in 1992. It is likely that employment will grow more rapidly for the smallest stocks. The key question, and one we can't really answer here, is, Which group of stocks will be able to achieve greater labor productivity?

THE OUTLOOK FOR SMALL- VERSUS LARGE-STOCK PERFORMANCE

Based on the above analysis of the fundamentals of large and small stocks, we feel that in the 1990s, small stocks will outperform large stocks by margins that exceed their long-run average of 1.9% per year. The caveats to this forecast generally favor even better returns from small stocks.

First, as discussed earlier, in decades when small stocks outperformed the overall market, it was by a wide margin. This would suggest that our prediction that small stocks will simply beat the long-run average is conservative.

Second, many analysts believe a shift of portfolios toward increased weightings for small stocks could give a further boost to the relative market performance of these stocks. During the 1980s there was a strong movement by pension fund sponsors toward passive investments in the S&P 500 index. This led, in part, to the so-called "S&P 500 index effect": Stocks in the S&P 500 index provided greater returns, on average, than stocks outside the index. In the 1990s, there are two discernible trends that may reverse these results. First, passive investment in S&P 500 index funds seems to have peaked. Second, the emergence of popular small and mid-cap indexes (the Russell 2000, Wilshire 5000, and S&P Midcap indexes, for example) make it easier for pension fund sponsors to invest passively outside the S&P 500. The result of these trends may be to create a small capitalization index effect, boosting the returns from small stocks.

In Table 1.21, we have reported current institutional holdings by market capitalization quintile for three different stock universes: (1) the most recent of our historical list of all stocks (at the end of 1991); (2) stocks in the current S&P 500; and (3) stocks remaining in our most recent historical list of all stocks after excluding the S&P 500. Readers should note that in the top section of Table 1.21, each universe of stocks has been sorted into its own set of quintiles. This means that a different set of market-capitalization quintile cut-off values have been applied to each universe.

Looking at the data in the top section of Table 1.21 for our most recent historical stock list, it is clear that there is a strong tendency for institutional ownership to decline with market capitalization. Average institutional ownership for the largest stocks is 50.3%; it is lowest for the smallest stocks at 27.6%. These figures suggest that there is potential for institutional ownership of small stocks to rise, supporting their relative market performance. Of course, investors will continue to face liquidity constraints among the smallest stocks.

Given the large amounts of money that have gone into S&P 500 index funds over the last decade, it should not be surprising that the range of institutional ownership varies less among the S&P 500 market capitalization quintiles. Average institutional ownership ranges from a high of 62.8% to a low of 55.0%. What is interesting is that institutional ownership of S&P 500 stocks is greatest in the middle of the market capitalization distribution and lowest among the largest and smallest stocks.

In the bottom section of Table 1.21, we have used the market-capitalization quintile cut-off values for our historical stock list to assign stocks in the other two universes to a market capitalization sector. This second analysis has two purposes: (1) to provide an analysis of institutional holding based on a consistent set of capitalization sectors, and (2) to identify where the S&P 500 stocks are located within the market-capitalization distribution.

In the case of the S&P 500 stocks, most of them (294) are collected in the largest market capitalization sector. There is a considerable decline in institutional holdings in the three smallest sectors. The range, from a high of 61.2% to a low of 36.0%, is much greater than that seen in the top section of Table 1.21.

For the stocks remaining in our historical stock list after excluding the S&P 500, the results are quite dramatic. We again see that the largest and smallest stocks tend to have lower institutional ownership than the so-called "mid-cap" stocks. The largest stocks not in the S&P 500 are significantly under-represented in institutional portfolios. Perhaps the recent rush into mid-cap stocks has been overdone.

Table 1.21—Institutional Holdings (%)

A. Market-Capitalization Quintiles Based on Each Stock Universe

Quintiles	Most Recent Historical Stock List [a]			Current S&P 500			Historical Stock List Excluding S&P 500		
	Average	Median	Obs.	Average	Median	Obs.	Average	Median	Obs.
1	50.3	55.0	292	55.0	56.5	100	41.0	36.0	226
2	50.6	53.0	292	60.1	60.5	100	43.8	44.5	226
3	42.8	43.0	292	62.8	66.0	99	37.9	35.0	226
4	36.7	35.5	292	62.5	64.0	99	33.5	34.0	226
5	27.6	25.0	292	55.3	57.5	100	26.3	24.5	226

B. Market-Capitalization Quintiles Based Only on the Most Recent Historical Stock List

Quintiles	Most Recent Historical Stock List [a]			Current S&P 500			Historical Stock List Excluding S&P 500		
	Average	Median	Obs.	Average	Median	Obs.	Average	Median	Obs.
1	50.3	55.0	292	59.3	61.0	294	28.4	25.0	84
2	50.6	53.0	292	61.2	62.0	147	45.7	43.0	198
3	42.8	43.0	292	55.4	54.0	36	41.8	41.0	272
4	36.7	35.5	292	45.6	47.0	11	36.5	35.0	287
5	27.6	25.0	292	36.0	35.5	4	27.4	25.0	289

Source: Kidder, Peabody Quantitative Research Group.

(a) Historical stock lists contain all stocks in the Compustat Universe with a December fiscal year-end. Stocks with market capitalization below $50 million in 1991 are excluded, and this floor is raised or lowered going back in time each year, based on the level of Ibbotson Associates' small-stock index.

SUMMARY AND CONCLUSIONS

What have we found? Lessons learned can be grouped into three areas: Methodology, specific results about factors that drive small-stock performance, and unresolved issues.

Methodology

By now, it should be obvious that methodology is very important when studying small stocks. We have seen that the definition of size has a profound effect on the results. In addition, the stock universe selected can also have a significant effect on the results. Investors should be very careful about generalizing results based on a particular size definition and stock universe to other definitions or samples.

Factors Driving Small-Stock Market Performance

We have identified a number of factors that clearly contributed to small-stock relative market performance. A central factor was earnings growth, whether measured by pre-tax income or net income. Earnings growth was influenced by a number of factors: taxes, capital intensity, and pension expense. Finally, shifts in relative valuation were also important.

Unresolved Issues

There are a number of issues left unresolved and tasks left unfinished. Most importantly, we have been unable to identify any fundamental earnings or valuation factors to explain the continued market outperformance of small stocks during 1982–83. We can only speculate. First, it is possible that in the midst of the 1981–82 recession and its aftermath, investors were unable to recognize the secular shift to fundamental underperformance by small stocks. Second, interest rates may have played a role. Interest rates peaked in late 1981 and declined significantly during 1982.

Third, during the 1974–81 period, small stocks did not exhibit the strong earnings outperformance suggested by their market outperformance. However, as we have seen, valuations remained reasonably attractive for small stocks. This valuation differential should have contributed to small-stock market outperformance even in the face of earnings growth that was roughly on par with that for large stocks.

Expanding upon this point, perhaps we expected too much from this analysis. As we noted earlier, sorting on market capitalization introduces a bias against success among small stocks. Since stock prices reflect market expectations of future earnings, sorting on market capitalization means that large-stock portfolios tend to contain firms expected to do well in the future, while small-stock portfolios tend to fill up with firms expected to do poorly. Thus, it shouldn't come as a surprise that small stocks tend to exhibit poor relative earnings performance in the year after they were ranked low based on market capitalization. Perhaps the most we should expect to see in periods of strong small-stock performance is that small-stock portfolios show implied growth rates that remain below those of large-stock portfolios, but by a smaller margin.

Table 1.22—Analysis of Implied Growth Rate of Historical Stock Lists[a] Aggregate

	Ebit/ Sales (%) ×	Sales/ Assets =	Pre-Tax ROA % ×	Ebt/ Ebit ×	Assets/ Equity ×	Tax Complement =	After Tax ROE % ×	Retention Rate =	Implied Growth Rate (%)
1991	10.710	0.660	7.071	0.496	3.917	0.592	8.128	0.039	0.320
1990	12.861	0.689	8.866	0.549	3.967	0.608	11.752	0.339	3.988
1989	14.296	0.684	9.784	0.580	3.824	0.645	14.004	0.448	6.268
1988	14.061	0.742	10.434	0.646	3.444	0.642	14.892	0.450	6.707
1987	12.928	0.764	9.876	0.672	3.268	0.605	13.110	0.428	5.610
1986	11.342	0.768	8.707	0.610	3.248	0.573	9.882	0.250	2.466
1985	12.066	0.848	10.234	0.667	3.069	0.560	11.719	0.421	4.937
1984	13.057	0.885	11.552	0.701	2.919	0.584	13.787	0.526	7.248
1983	12.359	0.886	10.944	0.693	2.802	0.574	12.202	0.451	5.499
1982	11.586	0.932	10.799	0.654	2.778	0.579	11.364	0.409	4.649
1981	12.681	1.038	13.159	0.723	2.704	0.589	15.135	0.554	8.389
1980	13.186	1.068	14.080	0.776	2.666	0.561	16.343	0.591	9.652
1979	13.876	1.052	14.594	0.810	2.626	0.568	17.655	0.621	10.972
1978	13.391	1.001	13.405	0.808	2.552	0.546	15.091	0.581	8.766
1977	13.235	0.995	13.162	0.814	2.509	0.534	14.348	0.565	8.107
1976	13.492	0.962	12.981	0.812	2.504	0.539	14.227	0.591	8.411
1975	13.312	0.919	12.238	0.794	2.498	0.512	12.429	0.556	6.916
1974	14.709	0.975	14.341	0.818	2.465	0.512	14.801	0.612	9.055
Averages									
1974–91	12.953	0.882	11.457	0.701	2.987	0.573	13.382	0.468	6.553
1974–79	13.669	0.984	13.454	0.810	2.526	0.535	14.759	0.588	8.705
1980–89	12.756	0.861	10.957	0.672	3.072	0.591	13.244	0.453	6.142
1990–91	11.785	0.675	7.969	0.523	3.942	0.600	9.940	0.189	2.154

Source: Kidder, Peabody Quantitative Research Group.

(a) Historical stock lists contain all stocks in the Compustat Universe with a December fiscal year-end. Stocks with market capitalization below $50 million in 1991 are excluded, and this floor is raised or lowered going back in time each year, based on the level of Ibbotson Associates' small-stock index.

Table 1.23—Analysis of Implied Growth Rate of Historical Stock Lists [a] Largest Quintile by Capitalization

	Ebit/Sales (%)	×	Sales/Assets	=	Pre-Tax ROA %	×	Ebt/Ebit	×	Assets/Equity	×	Tax Complement	=	After Tax ROE %	×	Retention Rate	=	Implied Growth Rate (%)
1991	11.863		0.643		7.624		0.517		3.861		0.611		9.285		0.103		0.957
1990	13.811		0.694		9.582		0.574		3.861		0.620		13.174		0.377		4.969
1989	15.021		0.698		10.482		0.606		3.632		0.647		14.911		0.467		6.959
1988	14.701		0.774		11.385		0.668		3.223		0.648		15.884		0.455		7.222
1987	13.338		0.796		10.616		0.702		3.058		0.615		14.021		0.460		6.450
1986	12.036		0.817		9.829		0.650		3.007		0.605		11.616		0.334		3.881
1985	12.245		0.941		11.520		0.731		2.747		0.570		13.190		0.456		6.009
1984	13.712		0.922		12.638		0.730		2.758		0.590		15.011		0.547		8.214
1983	13.345		0.903		12.051		0.722		2.670		0.580		13.475		0.474		6.386
1982	12.320		0.973		11.991		0.719		2.546		0.579		12.711		0.448		5.695
1981	13.257		1.095		14.519		0.776		2.478		0.584		16.312		0.569		9.274
1980	14.153		1.084		15.345		0.803		2.555		0.556		17.490		0.598		10.456
1979	14.749		1.051		15.503		0.829		2.524		0.559		18.131		0.610		11.055
1978	14.189		0.980		13.910		0.819		2.482		0.538		15.220		0.559		8.505
1977	14.293		0.972		13.891		0.826		2.430		0.527		14.688		0.547		8.029
1976	14.681		0.936		13.736		0.824		2.423		0.532		14.606		0.571		8.344
1975	14.810		0.883		13.079		0.812		2.428		0.502		12.939		0.541		6.994
1974	16.652		0.932		15.513		0.838		2.379		0.500		15.484		0.599		9.282
Averages																	
1974–91	13.843		0.894		12.401		0.730		2.837		0.576		14.341		0.484		7.149
1974–79	14.896		0.959		14.272		0.825		2.445		0.526		15.178		0.571		8.701
1980–89	13.413		0.900		12.038		0.711		2.867		0.597		14.462		0.481		7.054
1990–91	12.837		0.668		8.603		0.545		3.861		0.615		11.230		0.240		2.963

Source: Kidder, Peabody Quantitative Research Group.

(a) Historical stock lists contain all stocks in the Compustat Universe with a December fiscal year-end. Stocks with market capitalization below $50 million in 1991 are excluded, and this floor is raised or lowered going back in time each year, based on the level of Ibbotson Associates' small-stock index.

Table 1.24—Analysis of Implied Growth Rate of Stocks[a] Larger Quintile by Capitalization

	Ebit/ Sales (%) ×	Sales/ Assets =	Pre-Tax ROA %	×	Ebt/ Ebit	×	Assets/ Equity	×	Tax Complement =	After Tax ROE %	×	Retention Rate	=	Implied Growth Rate (%)
1991	8.856	0.727	6.434		0.524		3.762		0.615	7.793		0.203		1.579
1990	12.001	0.664	7.968		0.513		4.007		0.617	10.113		0.362		3.659
1989	13.296	0.668	8.881		0.513		4.166		0.662	12.560		0.426		5.352
1988	14.193	0.672	9.544		0.636		3.763		0.651	14.863		0.505		7.508
1987	13.867	0.654	9.066		0.613		3.668		0.596	12.145		0.296		3.597
1986	10.375	0.573	5.945		0.476		4.050		0.418	4.792		-0.651		-3.120
1985	14.698	0.550	8.078		0.446		4.403		0.542	8.592		0.311		2.675
1984	12.443	0.696	8.660		0.589		3.607		0.576	10.589		0.426		4.506
1983	11.143	0.756	8.421		0.615		3.322		0.579	9.964		0.394		3.924
1982	11.130	0.760	8.456		0.432		3.566		0.645	8.401		0.250		2.103
1981	12.184	0.833	10.144		0.547		3.558		0.640	12.628		0.490		6.182
1980	11.015	0.917	10.097		0.678		3.099		0.593	12.579		0.519		6.528
1979	11.933	0.959	11.439		0.750		3.048		0.616	16.108		0.636		10.239
1978	12.073	0.992	11.983		0.780		2.754		0.589	15.145		0.644		9.749
1977	10.914	1.005	10.966		0.770		2.794		0.576	13.600		0.620		8.432
1976	10.978	0.968	10.632		0.768		2.851		0.584	13.606		0.660		8.979
1975	10.197	0.978	9.971		0.739		2.739		0.584	11.773		0.625		7.352
1974	10.299	1.033	10.642		0.740		2.778		0.590	12.892		0.644		8.305
Averages														
1974–91	11.755	0.800	9.296		0.618		3.441		0.593	11.563		0.409		5.419
1974–79	11.066	0.989	10.939		0.758		2.827		0.590	13.854		0.638		8.843
1980–89	12.434	0.708	8.729		0.554		3.720		0.590	10.711		0.297		3.925
1990–91	10.428	0.695	7.201		0.518		3.885		0.616	8.953		0.282		2.619

Source: Kidder, Peabody Quantitative Research Group.

(a) Historical stock lists contain all stocks in the Compustat Universe with a December fiscal year-end. Stocks with market capitalization below $50 million in 1991 are excluded, and this floor is raised or lowered going back in time each year, based on the level of Ibbotson Associates' small-stock index.

Table 1.25—Analysis of Implied Growth Rate of Stocks[a] Middle Quintile by Capitalization

	Ebit/ Sales (%) ×	Sales/ Assets =	Pre-Tax ROA %	Ebit/ Ebit ×	Assets/ Equity ×	Tax Complement =	After Tax ROE % ×	Retention Rate =	Implied Growth Rate (%)
1991	6.456	0.780	5.034	0.299	3.485	0.147	0.773	-129.638	-100.202
1990	7.228	0.727	5.253	0.337	4.490	0.283	2.250	-4.079	-9.176
1989	11.737	0.597	7.005	0.526	5.123	0.610	11.511	0.292	3.363
1988	10.450	0.692	7.227	0.508	4.605	0.580	9.807	0.388	3.802
1987	9.227	0.707	6.527	0.453	4.568	0.396	5.341	-0.184	-0.982
1986	8.716	0.715	6.233	0.420	4.258	0.401	4.469	-0.347	-1.550
1985	7.996	0.694	5.547	0.409	4.076	0.408	3.770	-0.554	-2.089
1984	10.528	0.888	9.347	0.641	2.997	0.540	9.696	0.416	4.030
1983	7.452	0.921	6.866	0.495	3.146	0.453	4.836	-0.041	-0.197
1982	8.209	0.885	7.267	0.403	3.785	0.466	5.175	-0.068	-0.354
1981	10.162	0.978	9.942	0.560	3.129	0.548	9.541	0.451	4.304
1980	9.747	1.161	11.321	0.664	2.893	0.582	12.655	0.608	7.700
1979	11.625	1.119	13.012	0.737	2.906	0.609	16.986	0.730	12.404
1978	10.718	1.053	11.288	0.758	2.992	0.575	14.738	0.717	10.563
1977	9.236	1.111	10.259	0.765	2.888	0.561	12.727	0.702	8.941
1976	9.118	1.136	10.354	0.766	2.815	0.554	12.354	0.737	9.111
1975	8.007	1.074	8.600	0.687	2.878	0.556	9.459	0.665	6.293
1974	9.154	1.160	10.622	0.709	2.859	0.567	12.210	0.739	9.027
Averages									
1974–91	9.209	0.911	8.428	0.563	3.549	0.491	8.794	-7.137	-1.945
1974–79	9.643	1.109	10.689	0.737	2.890	0.570	13.079	0.715	9.390
1980–89	9.422	0.824	7.728	0.508	3.858	0.498	7.680	0.096	1.803
1990–91	6.842	0.753	5.143	0.318	3.988	0.215	1.511	-66.858	-54.689

Source: Kidder, Peabody Quantitative Research Group.

(a) Historical stock lists contain all stocks in the Compustat Universe with a December fiscal year-end. Stocks with market capitalization below $50 million in 1991 are excluded, and this floor is raised or lowered going back in time each year, based on the level of Ibbotson Associates' small-stock index.

Table 1.26—Analysis of Implied Growth Rate of Stocks[a]Smaller Quintile by Capitalization

	Ebit/ Sales (%) ×	Sales/ Assets =	Pre-Tax ROA % ×	Ebit/ Ebit ×	Assets/ Equity ×	Tax Complement =	After Tax ROE % ×	Retention Rate =	Implied Growth Rate (%)e
1991	3.826	0.586	2.241	-0.385	4.824	1.620	-6.738	1.468	-9.895
1990	8.572	0.570	4.886	0.274	7.030	0.347	3.263	-1.079	-3.521
1989	9.022	0.671	6.058	0.311	4.434	0.502	4.203	-0.166	-0.698
1988	7.568	0.561	4.242	0.198	5.270	-0.041	-0.181	3.640	-0.658
1987	8.304	0.679	5.640	0.476	5.258	0.580	8.189	0.486	3.984
1986	6.747	0.795	5.362	0.379	3.824	0.233	1.807	-2.121	-3.833
1985	6.084	1.136	6.910	0.446	3.204	0.346	3.411	-0.317	-1.083
1984	6.720	1.220	8.199	0.486	3.269	0.449	5.851	0.257	1.502
1983	6.315	1.206	7.613	0.519	2.812	0.477	5.303	0.191	1.013
1982	5.735	1.169	6.702	0.386	2.938	0.300	2.281	-1.282	-2.925
1981	8.664	1.193	10.338	0.568	3.045	0.546	9.752	0.545	5.316
1980	8.572	1.246	10.683	0.589	3.197	0.578	11.642	0.653	7.601
1979	8.574	1.406	12.055	0.687	2.875	0.602	14.342	0.750	10.753
1978	7.870	1.449	11.403	0.709	2.714	0.559	12.269	0.715	8.773
1977	7.859	1.264	9.933	0.716	2.878	0.552	11.303	0.722	8.163
1976	7.480	1.282	9.590	0.721	2.672	0.525	9.708	0.714	6.928
1975	6.555	1.236	8.101	0.623	2.647	0.480	6.412	0.606	3.885
1974	7.365	1.399	10.304	0.677	2.659	0.530	9.826	0.717	7.048
Averages									
1974-91	7.324	1.059	7.792	0.466	3.642	0.510	6.258	0.361	2.353
1974-79	7.617	1.339	10.231	0.689	2.741	0.542	10.643	0.704	7.592
1980-89	7.373	0.988	7.175	0.436	3.725	0.397	5.226	0.189	1.022
1990-91	6.199	0.578	3.563	-0.056	5.927	0.983	-1.738	0.195	-6.708

Source: Kidder, Peabody Quantitative Research Group.

(a) Historical stock lists contain all stocks in the Compustat Universe with a December fiscal year-end. Stocks with market capitalization below $50 million in 1991 are excluded, and this floor is raised or lowered going back in time each year, based on the level of Ibbotson Associates' small-stock index.

Table 1.27—Analysis of Implied Growth Rate of Stocks[a] Smallest Quintile by Capitalization

	Ebit/ Sales (%) ×	Sales/ Assets =	Pre-Tax ROA %	Ebt/ Ebit ×	Assets/ Equity ×	Tax Complement =	After Tax ROE % ×	Retention Rate =	Implied Growth Rate (%)
1991	4.559	0.655	2.984	-0.187	25.948	1.315	-19.063	1.432	-27.289
1990	2.722	0.913	2.487	-0.474	3.541	1.575	-6.581	1.396	-9.185
1989	7.842	0.632	4.960	0.232	5.289	0.369	2.239	-4.113	-9.209
1988	6.304	0.629	3.962	0.148	5.920	-0.327	-1.140	1.779	-2.028
1987	6.700	0.789	5.289	0.342	3.934	0.275	1.957	-2.881	-5.639
1986	4.234	1.004	4.250	0.035	3.904	-9.211	-5.309	1.385	-7.354
1985	5.644	0.859	4.850	0.199	4.069	-0.451	-1.766	2.029	-3.583
1984	7.272	0.788	5.730	0.341	4.321	0.309	2.611	-0.656	-1.712
1983	6.508	0.849	5.524	0.265	3.858	0.044	0.247	8.692	2.150
1982	5.533	1.002	5.546	0.241	3.796	0.207	1.051	-3.001	-3.154
1981	7.440	1.373	10.215	0.504	2.963	0.566	8.632	0.599	5.168
1980	6.577	1.461	9.609	0.542	2.882	0.562	8.438	0.603	5.084
1979	6.799	1.567	10.655	0.588	2.947	0.539	9.953	0.741	7.373
1978	6.723	1.522	10.235	0.648	3.136	0.500	10.391	0.771	8.009
1977	6.272	1.488	9.330	0.637	2.875	0.486	8.308	0.745	6.189
1976	6.093	1.419	8.648	0.638	2.953	0.468	7.622	0.781	5.952
1975	5.506	1.397	7.694	0.539	2.908	0.424	5.117	0.739	3.780
1974	5.373	1.552	8.338	0.539	3.003	0.436	5.888	0.709	4.172
Averages									
1974–91	6.006	1.106	6.684	0.321	4.903	-0.106	2.144	0.653	-1.182
1974–79	6.128	1.491	9.150	0.598	2.970	0.475	7.880	0.747	5.912
1980–89	6.405	0.939	5.994	0.285	4.094	-0.766	1.696	0.444	-2.028
1990–91	3.641	0.784	2.735	-0.331	14.744	1.445	-12.822	1.414	-18.237

Source: Kidder, Peabody Quantitative Research Group.

(a) Historical stock lists contain all stocks in the Compustat Universe with a December fiscal year-end. Stocks with market capitalization below $50 million in 1991 are excluded, and this floor is raised or lowered going back in time each year, based on the level of Ibbotson Associates' small-stock index.

REFERENCES

Fama, Eugene F., and Kenneth R. French, "Small-Firm Fundamentals," working paper, University of Chicago, April 1990.

Mackay, Charles, *Extraordinary Popular Delusions and the Madness of Crowds*, New York: Farrar, Straus and Giroux, 1932 (originally published 1852), pp. 46–97.

Smith, David B., and Susan Pourciau, "A Comparison of the Financial Characteristics of December and Non-December Year-End Companies," *Journal of Accounting and Economics*, 10 (1988), pp. 335–344.

Chapter 2

Sizing Up the Small Stock Effect

Philip S. Fortuna
Director of Investment Operations

James M. Eysenbach
Director of Quantitative Services

Scudder, Stevens & Clark, Inc.

INTRODUCTION

Simple ideas exert a powerful sway over our minds. Supported by a moderate amount of evidence, they can quickly become dogma, resisting further exploration. Small cap investing is such an idea.

The justification for small stock investing is intuitively appealing. It is generally acknowledged that security prices are driven by earnings and especially by the growth of earnings. Conceptually, it is much easier for small companies to sustain a high growth rate than it is for the boring behemoths. Therefore, the argument goes, small company stocks as a group should offer superior opportunities for return.

Although few investors are directly aware of it, the plausibility of this argument has been strengthened by academics such as Rolf Banz[1] and Roger Ibbotson. For example, oft-quoted data from Ibbotson Associates suggests that over the period from 1926 to 1992, small stocks have experi-

enced an annualized return of 12.2% versus 10.3% for U.S. large stocks.[2]
Statistics like these have led to the creation of a $30 billion market for
small-stock mutual funds.

The sophisticated investor is likely aware of additional studies that
demonstrate that small firms experience positive risk-adjusted returns.[3]
While recent work suggests that these abnormal returns stem from a failure to measure risk properly, few have doubted the basic proposition that
small firms *appear* to offer abnormal returns.

The case for small cap investing appears compelling from both an absolute and a risk-adjusted return perspective. Yet on closer examination,
much of the work on which the case for small cap investing rests is beset
by methodological and/or practical concerns:

- *A question of size.* The basic academic studies define small stocks as
  some variant of those stocks that make up the fifth (smallest) market cap quintile of the NYSE. For example, the Ibbotson Small
  Company index contains the 2,681 companies that make up the
  smallest 20% of the NYSE as measured by market cap as well as
  stocks on the AMEX and OTC markets within the same capitalization bounds.[4]

  On the surface, this definition is reasonable. No one would deny
  that these are small companies. However, they may be too small
  for practical mutual fund investing. Stocks in the Ibbotson Small
  Company index range from less than $1 million in market value to
  $198 million in market value. A great number of these companies
  fall into the so-called "micro" cap range (less than $50 million in
  market value). Because micro cap stocks are often difficult to trade
  in large amounts, they tend to be avoided by small cap mutual
  funds. In fact, as of early 1993, only one of 110 small cap mutual
  funds had a median market cap of less than $50 million. The typi-
  cal small cap fund has a median market cap of $440 million.[5]

  Note the interesting conundrum. Small cap investing is justified by
  studies that show that the smallest firms offer superior returns. Yet
  the products that have been developed to provide the general public with access to these returns do not *in practice* invest heavily in
  these stocks.

- *A question of geography.* Small cap studies generally purport to examine U.S. small cap issues. In practice, studies have used all
  NYSE companies falling within a certain market cap range. However, since foreign securities are traded on U.S. exchanges in the
  form of ADRs,[6] many studies may have inadvertently confounded

a foreign stock effect with the small cap effect. Since foreign stocks often have quite different returns from the U.S. market, the inclusion of these stocks can bias the results.

- *Then you saw it, now you don't.* Many studies on subsets of the small cap marketplace have been plagued by survivorship bias. It has generally been difficult to access a historically complete database of fundamental firm data. Most sources of such data will drop a company from the database if it ceases trading. Thus, takeovers and bankruptcies cause companies to disappear from the historical record over time. While third parties usually put these delisted companies into a research file, it is fairly difficult to access more than ten years of such data on a quarterly basis. A survivorship-bias is likely to misstate the magnitude and possibly the direction of the effect being studied.

- *Now you see it, then you didn't.* Some researchers have used fundamental data with insufficient lags. These studies have assumed that financial data was historically available on the last day of the quarter or the year. In practice, it can take up to six months for financial data to be made public.[7] Thus, researchers who have studied growth rates or P/E ratios have often implicitly assumed perfect forecasting ability. It is not clear whether the excess returns found in such studies are the result of true inefficiencies, or the result of implicitly investing on the basis of nonpublic information. This so-called "look-ahead" bias can be quite severe.

These four concerns suggest that the time is ripe for a re-examination of the small cap effect.

METHODOLOGY

The scope of previous studies of the small cap effect suggest that we should try to include as many years as possible, while including as much fundamental information as feasible. The tradeoffs between these twin objectives led us to utilize the following data:

1. Standard & Poor's Compustat Services Industrial and Research information over the 16-year period from June 30, 1976, to June 30, 1992. We further reduced the universe by focusing on only those U.S.-incorporated companies with market capitalizations greater than or equal to $50 million.

2. Institutional Brokers Estimate Service (I/B/E/S) database over the period from June 1976 to June 1992. This information consists of

historical earnings estimates from security brokers. Unfortunately, a sporadic survivorship bias exists in the version of the I/B/E/S database available from a widely used third-party data service. To date we have been unable to obtain data free of survivorship bias in a format consistent with Compustat data.

Utilizing the above data sources allows one to deal directly with the concerns noted earlier:

Relevant size. We deliberately did not include micro cap stocks in this study. By including only those stocks with a capitalization greater than $50 million, we were able to focus on the portion of the equity market that investment practice has defined as the small cap marketplace. We chose to keep the $50 million cut-off in all time periods, rather than use a smaller cut-off in the 1970s. After discussing the matter with professional institutional investors, we concluded that at some *absolute* point, a stock's market value is too low to permit its widespread use in funds or institutional accounts. Some small cap funds do occasionally purchase stocks with market caps less than $50 million. However, given the small quantities a manager can generally purchase, micro cap stocks tend to have a negligible impact on overall portfolio returns. Parenthetically, the $50 million lower bound almost exactly corresponds with that of the Wilshire Small Cap Index.[8]

Domestic U.S. stocks. We used supplementary data in the Compustat database to exclude companies incorporated outside the U.S. This should effectively eliminate any foreign stock effects.

Survivorship bias. We took great care to obtain Compustat data on all companies that ever existed in the Standard & Poor's database. To the extent that Standard & Poor's has successfully captured data on companies with market valuations greater than $50 million, our study should also capture that data. Nevertheless, it is possible that a handful of companies slipped through all the nets.[9] The effect on our conclusions is likely to be negligible. The I/B/E/S data does have a survivorship bias, thus any conclusions we reach using that data should be viewed as tentative.

Look-ahead bias. Virtually all companies report financial results within six months after the end of the fiscal year. Since most companies have a December fiscal year, six months is the typical lag used in our study, based on the June 30 starting date for our analyses. For companies with other than December fiscal years, the lag was never less than five months. I/B/E/S data were not lagged because consensus estimate information was available at month-end.

In all of the analyses reported below, deciles and quintiles are arranged such that the lowest values are in category 1. Thus, the smallest companies are in decile or quintile 1, while the largest are in decile 10 or quintile 5. Earnings yield is used in place of P/E so that companies with negative earnings are grouped with low EPS yield (high P/E) companies. Likewise, we used common equity/market cap rather than market cap/common equity or price/book. We calculated monthly total returns and defined excess return as the security's return minus the equally weighted universe return. Therefore, our returns are *not* risk-adjusted. The intent of this study is to look at returns as the general investor would view them. Later work will examine risk-adjusted returns.

In all cases we equally weighted returns. This assumption is likely to be more controversial amongst academics that amongst investors. In practice, managers' holdings tend to be closer to equal weighting than to market-cap weighting.

On balance, we have taken care to minimize the sources of bias or error in our analyses. Nevertheless, we acknowledge that some problems remain. Of particular worry to us is the often poor quality of the underlying data. For example, after our initial work, we discovered one company (Crystal Oil) had a reported market cap of over $1 trillion in 1981! This error was caused by an unaccounted-for split. After re-analyzing the data, we were relieved to discover generally negligible changes in the results. Certainly, none of the conclusions changed. However, we retain the sneaking fear that there are less obvious Crystal Oils out there and that our results are somewhat contaminated by them. (More detail on methodological issues is presented in the Appendix to this chapter.)

THE SIZE OF THE SIZE EFFECT

Although most of the attention has been directed toward companies with small market values, a few practitioners have claimed that the small cap effect is actually a small company effect. Alternative measures of size that have been proposed include assets, sales, and common shareholders' equity.

The argument in favor of these alternative definitions is a simple one. Many "hot" small companies can experience a faster growth in market value than in sales, assets, etc. However, since earnings growth potential is postulated to be a function of the asset, equity, or sales base, not market value, a focus on capitalization could cause an investor to overlook companies that are in reality still small and capable of rapid growth.

The Case for Small Cap Investing

We first re-examined the case for small capitalization investing. The first step was to split up all of the stocks in our universe into ten size deciles as of June 30 of each year. We then calculated the average excess return to each decile over the following year. Finally, we aggregated the results for each decile over all years to determine the average excess return to the decile.[10] All of the returns presented in the tables that follow begin and end on June 30 of the years indicated.

One conclusion emerged immediately: The vast majority of stocks in our study would be classified as small by most institutional investors. Institutional money managers and third-party evaluators suggest that the top of the small cap range falls somewhere between $500 million and $1 billion. With the growing popularity of mid-cap indexes, a top range of $500 million seems increasingly reasonable. As Table 2.1 shows, most stocks fall below the $500 million market cap level.

Table 2.1—Average Market Cap of Firm in Decile (in $ millions)*

Market Cap Decile	Average 1976–91	Average 1976	Average 1991
1	$56.82	$54.98	$58.30
2	72.86	67.39	79.30
3	94.59	83.73	105.95
4	126.76	108.46	151.59
5	174.58	147.71	212.91
6	249.56	205.91	316.69
7	378.62	301.73	518.72
8	626.43	484.10	903.10
9	1181.59	804.44	1872.71
10	5147.42	3590.44	9089.76
Total	811.32	586.55	1331.85

* Averages were used to provide a general sense of the size of the typical company in each decile. For many applications, it would be more appropriate to take the log of market cap. However, the distortions caused by the skewness of the market cap distribution become apparent only in decile 10.

In 1976, over 75% of the universe fell into the small-stock category. Even though there was significant market appreciation between 1976 and 1991, over 60% of the universe would still be classified as small in 1991. In fact, given the doubling of the number of companies in each decile over this time period, there are actually many more small companies available for investment today (1500+) than in 1976 (1,000+).

Our initial analysis focused on the excess returns to capitalization. The results displayed in Table 2.2 are ambiguous. If there is a small cap effect, it was not very pronounced over the entire period from 1976 to 1992.

The picture changes dramatically if one looks at sub-periods. We broke down the 1976 to 1992 period into three periods of six, five, and five years, respectively. These periods roughly coincide with three distinct market environments.[11] As Table 2.2 illustrates, the classic small cap effect was visible only in the late '70s. The '80s, by contrast, were a terrible time for small cap investing.[12] On balance, at the decile level, there does not appear to have been much of a small cap effect over the last 16 years.

Table 2.2—Annual Excess Return versus Universe for Market Cap Deciles (%) 1976–1992

Market Cap Decile	Excess Return 1976–1992	Excess Return 1976–1982	Excess Return 1982–1987	Excess Return 1987–1992
1	0.79	5.70	-0.32	-3.98
2	-1.17	3.27	-2.16	-5.52
3	1.20	6.01	-1.18	-2.18
4	1.19	3.58	0.74	-1.24
5	0.51	1.41	1.21	-1.28
6	0.76	-0.36	1.21	1.67
7	-0.50	-2.52	-0.36	1.78
8	0.33	-2.29	0.71	3.10
9	-0.80	-5.27	0.06	3.71
10	-2.30	-9.49	0.11	3.94
Total	0.00	0.00	0.00	0.00

Sometimes aggregating data makes patterns emerge more clearly. The market cap analysis was re-sliced using quintiles rather than deciles. Each quintile now contains 20% of the universe. Table 2.3 displays the results.

Table 2.3—Annual Excess Return versus Universe for Market Cap Quintiles (%) 1976–1992

Market Cap Quintile	Excess Return 1976–1992	Excess Return 1976–1982	Excess Return 1982–1987	Excess Return 1987–1992
1	–0.19	4.48	–1.24	–4.75
2	1.19	4.79	–0.22	–1.71
3	0.64	0.53	1.21	0.19
4	–0.08	–2.40	0.17	2.44
5	–1.55	–7.38	0.08	3.82
Total	0.00	0.00	0.00	0.00

If anything, the case for a small cap effect is weakened by aggregating into quintiles. However, another set of effects becomes clearer. The stocks in the middle (currently between $180 and $400 million in market cap) have outperformed in each sub-period. Thus, it appears that by avoiding the smallest capitalization issues, small cap managers have been fishing in productive waters.

The Case for Alternative Definitions of Size

As noted above, the small cap "effect" might be nothing more than a proxy for another type of small-firm effect. For example, some investors have postulated that companies with small *sales* have excess returns. If this were the true underlying effect, then even if capitalization *by itself* had no relation to return, there would still appear to be a small cap effect, since most small cap stocks have small sales.

There are a number of companies with large capitalizations but small sales. Therefore, if the excess return to small sales hypothesis were true, we would expect to see two things. First, the small sales effect in isolation would be stronger than the small cap effect in isolation. Second, in the interaction between sales and capitalization, sales would appear to be the more important factor in determining excess return.

We examined three alternative definitions of size:[13]

1. Total Assets
2. Common Shareholders' Equity
3. Annual Sales

Since these three measures are alternatives to market cap, we have
compared the excess returns for all three side by side with market cap. For
analytic ease, we report the total period and sub-period results separately.
Also for ease of presentation, we have displayed quintile rather than decile
returns. The conclusions *do not* change if deciles are used.

Table 2.4 presents the excess returns for the full period from July 1976
to June 1992. A quick look at the table reveals that these alternative measures of size have similar returns. Once again, there does not appear to be a
small firm effect. In fact, there appear to be stronger *negative* returns to
very small size. On average, the lowest quintile of assets underperformed
the universe by 188 basis points per year, while the smallest quintile of
sales underperformed by 335 basis points per year.

Although the magnitude of the effect is fairly small, there did appear
to be some type of medium size effect. The second and third quintiles of
all four size measures outperformed over this sixteen-year period.

Table 2.4—Annual Excess Return versus Universe for Size Quintiles (%)
Full Period 1976–1992

Quintiles	Market Cap	Assets	Common Equity	Sales
1	−0.19	−1.88	−2.23	−3.35
2	1.19	0.35	0.51	0.55
3	0.64	1.02	1.91	1.43
4	−0.08	−0.81	0.53	1.78
5	−1.55	1.42	−0.57	−0.30
NA (return)	NA	0.10	−2.04	−2.73
NA (number)*	0.0	16.6	18.4	15.6

* NA (number) signifies the average number of companies missing data per year.

Perhaps the small-firm effect is masked by some type of interaction
effect. For example, the companies with medium to large market caps but
small sales might outperform. We directly examined this concept by measuring the average returns to each combination of market cap and sales
quintiles. The results are displayed in Table 2.5.

Table 2.5—Annual Excess Return versus Universe for Size Quintiles (%)
Sales and Capitalization* Full Period 1976–1992

Market Cap Quintile	1	2	Sales Quintile 3	Quintile 4	5	All Quintiles
1	−3.93	3.86	3.09	1.02	—	−0.19
2	−2.65	0.86	5.75	3.36	—	1.19
3	−3.25	−1.58	1.63	3.54	2.00	0.64
4	−0.09	−3.01	−2.82	2.30	0.79	−0.08
5	—	—	−4.53	−2.25	−1.07	−1.55
All Quintiles	−3.35	0.55	1.43	1.78	−0.30	0.00

* Cells with fewer than 10 observations on average are not reported. They are marked with "—".

Contrary to the theory outlined above, companies with small sales (quintiles 1–3) and larger capitalizations (quintiles 3–5) appear to underperform. If anything, cap effects seem to dominate sales effects for these stocks. Extremely similar effects were found for asset size and common equity, but are not reported here.

Table 2.5 does not quite close out the case for alternative measures of size. After all, size may have a strong effect in each sub-period, but the effect may somehow be hidden in the aggregate numbers. To investigate this possibility, we looked at excess returns for the four size measures in each of three different time periods. The results are tabulated in Tables 2.6 to 2.8.

Although the pattern of the quintile returns is basically similar across measures, this table has a few interesting features. First, the market cap effect was by far the strongest over the late '70s. There were over 1200 basis points separating the best and worst performing market cap quintiles, while there was only a 600 basis point difference between the best and worst asset quintiles.

Second, all size measures show sizable *negative* excess returns to large size. In all cases, the largest companies underperformed by an average of at least 250+ basis points per year during this period. Finally, sufficient data were available for each of the alternative measures for them to be of practical use as a screening tool.

Given the strength of the small cap effect, the late '70s should provide a good test of the hypothesis that small companies (defined by sales) can thrive even if they have moderate to large market caps. Table 2.6A displays the excess returns associated with sales and market cap categories over the 1976 to 1982 period.

Table 2.6—Annual Excess Return versus Universe for Size Quintiles (%)
First Period 1976–1982

Quintiles	Market Cap	Assets	Common Equity	Sales
1	4.48	0.98	2.59	3.18
2	4.79	2.64	2.27	2.50
3	0.53	2.19	2.38	1.24
4	-2.40	-3.36	-1.81	-1.86
5	-7.38	-2.59	-5.55	-5.16
NA (return)	NA	2.33	2.06	-1.34
NA (number)*	0.0	9.7	10.3	11.2

* NA (number) signifies the average number of companies missing data per year.

Table 2.6A—Annual Excess Return versus Universe for Size Quintiles (%)
Sales and Capitalization* First Period 1976–1982

Market Cap Quintile	1	Sales Quintile 2	Quintile 3	4	5	All Quintiles
1	4.71	4.19	5.27	0.65	—	4.48
2	3.07	4.44	8.16	0.81	—	4.79
3	-0.27	0.04	1.47	0.20	-0.11	0.53
4	-0.06	-1.85	-4.28	-1.18	-2.14	-2.40
5	—	—	-12.26	-7.21	-7.28	-7.38
All Quintiles	3.18	2.50	1.24	-1.86	-5.16	0.00

* Cells with fewer than 10 observations on average are not reported. They are marked with "—".

Once again, the market cap effect seems to dominate the sales effect. Smaller sales (quintiles 1–3) and larger capitalization (quintiles 3–5) were associated with *negative* excess returns even though low sales by itself was associated with positive returns. Similar results were observed for assets and common equity.

Table 2.7 examines returns to the four size measures over the period from July 1982 to June 1987. While market cap displays a slight increase in return as size increases, the other measures of size show much stronger relationships between size and return. In particular during the mid '80s, sales had a very strong relationship to excess return. Unfortunately for small company investors, it was in the wrong direction.

**Table 2.7—Annual Excess Return versus Universe for Size Quintiles (%)
Second Period 1982–1987**

Quintiles	Market Cap	Assets	Common Equity	Sales
1	−1.24	−3.33	−3.57	−9.33
2	−0.22	−1.70	−0.96	−0.23
3	1.21	0.84	2.27	2.54
4	0.17	0.08	1.25	4.50
5	0.08	4.52	1.43	2.97
NA (return)	NA	−5.13	−6.58	−8.01
NA (number)*	0.0	27.6	28.4	25.2

* NA (number) signifies the average number of companies missing data per year.

Given the weakness of the market cap to return relationship and the strength of the sales relationship, one might expect sales to dominate market cap when the two are examined together. As Table 2.7A illustrates, this is generally the case. Unfortunately, moderate sales (quintile 3) combined with larger market caps (quintiles 4 and 5) generated negative returns even though each quintile alone generated positive returns. Given the relative weakness of the market cap, assets, and common equity to excess return relationships observed during this period, it is not surprising that our analysis of interaction effects for these other measures did not turn up any consistent patterns.

**Table 2.7A—Annual Excess Return versus Universe for Size Quintiles (%)
Sales and Capitalization* Second Period 1982–1987**

Market Cap Quintile	1	Sales 2	Quintile 3	4	5	All Quintiles
1	−10.78	7.00	5.94	12.36	—	−1.24
2	−8.43	−0.90	7.93	9.11	—	−0.22
3	−8.05	−3.28	1.81	9.62	1.45	1.21
4	−2.72	−7.19	−3.85	3.12	5.92	0.17
5	—	—	−1.19	−3.70	1.60	0.08
All Quintiles	−9.33	−0.23	2.54	4.50	2.97	0.00

* Cells with fewer than 10 observations on average are not reported. They are marked with "—".

Finally, there is the exciting and somewhat puzzling July 1987 to June 1992 period. Table 2.8 shows that avoiding small cap stocks may have been the key to investment success during this period. All four measures showed strong relationships between size and excess returns. In general, the larger the company, the better the return, and by a sizable amount.

Table 2.8—Annual Excess Return versus Universe for Size Quintiles (%)
Third Period 1987–1992

Quintiles	Market Cap	Assets	Common Equity	Sales
1	–4.75	–3.88	–6.69	–5.20
2	–1.71	–0.36	–0.15	–1.00
3	0.19	–0.22	0.97	0.55
4	2.44	1.34	2.63	3.43
5	3.82	3.13	3.40	2.26
NA (return)	NA	2.65	–2.42	0.87
NA (number)*	0.0	13.8	18.0	11.2

* NA (number) signifies the average number of companies missing data per year.

Once again, an examination of the interaction between sales and market cap reveals that larger cap and smaller sales is not an attractive combination. Table 2.8A gives the details. For most market cap ranges, smaller sales levels translated to lower returns. Low levels of assets and common equity also tended to have a depressing effect on returns within the mid to large cap range.

Table 2.8A—Annual Excess Return versus Universe for Size Quintiles (%)
Sales and Capitalization* Third Period 1987–1992

Market Cap Quintile	1	Sales 2	Quintile 3	4	5	All Quintiles
1	–7.46	0.32	–2.37	–9.89	—	–4.75
2	–3.74	–1.67	0.67	0.68	—	–1.71
3	–2.04	–1.83	1.65	1.49	5.08	0.19
4	2.50	–0.22	–0.05	5.66	–0.84	2.44
5	—	—	1.42	5.17	3.71	3.82
All Quintiles	–5.20	–1.00	0.55	3.43	2.26	0.00

* Cells with fewer than 10 observations on average are not reported. They are marked with "—".

Summarizing the Size Effect

It is time to take stock. The above tables present a vast amount of information, some of it ambiguous. We believe that taken together, these analyses suggest the following conclusions:

1. While smaller stocks outperform the largest stocks over the full period, there is not a consistent small cap stock effect. Sometimes the market favors smaller stocks; in other periods it favors larger issues.[14]

2. The four measures of size (market cap, assets, common equity, and sales) tend to have the same general relationship to excess return at the same point in time. Sales tended to have even more extreme performance swings from sub-period to sub-period than market cap.

3. Quintile 3 of all four size measures tended to have positive excess returns in each sub-period suggesting a medium size effect. The analysis in this section cannot provide any explanation for this (small) effect if indeed it exists.

4. The proposition that the market rewards companies with small sales (or assets or equity) rather than those with small caps is not supported by this evidence. If anything, the market appears to penalize stocks with small to moderate sales and moderate to large market capitalizations.

NEGLECTING THE SIZE EFFECT

A sizable group of academics and practitioners believe that those small stock effects that do exist are primarily manifestations of another effect—the neglect effect. In brief, this theory holds that if market participants know a great deal of information about a company, that company is likely to be relatively efficiently priced and to have risk-adjusted excess returns close to zero. Furthermore, if these stocks are deemed to be "investment quality" by large institutional investors, the price of these stocks may include a "blue chip" premium and thus may even offer below-average excess returns.

On the other hand, if little information is known about a company, then the risk associated with evaluating the company's potential is relatively high. This so-called estimation risk causes investors to demand a higher than normal return.[15]

Practitioners have interpreted this theory to mean that if a company is widely followed by brokerage houses, then there is likely to be a great deal of information available to investors about that stock. Conversely, if few or no analysts cover the stock, then the odds for higher than normal returns are enhanced.

Studies conducted in the early to mid 1980s demonstrated the existence of the neglect effect. Since most large companies are widely followed by analysts and most small companies are not well followed, the small cap effect was postulated to be little more than the neglect effect in disguise. Professor Avner Arbel presented evidence to suggest that the neglect effect dominated the small cap effect. In other words, large companies with low analyst coverage had superior performance and smaller companies with high coverage had inferior performance.

Most of the basic studies on this topic examined the period from 1970 to 1982, a period during which small cap stocks had superior performance. Given the evidence outlined in the last section, we might expect to find that the neglect effect disappeared in the '80s.

Table 2.9 presents evidence on the neglect effect during the period from 1976 to 1992 as well as three sub-periods. The number of analysts covering each company was provided by I/B/E/S.

Table 2.9 is exceedingly bizarre. Look closely at the excess returns for 1982 to 1987. All companies with coverage experienced positive excess returns! The culprit is the large number of companies missing estimates. Unfortunately, we cannot assume that all of these companies were truly neglected. As noted earlier, there is a problem with a survivorship bias in the estimate data. While we have reason to believe that most of the NAs did not have any analyst coverage, some NAs were widely followed. Therefore, the following conclusions should be considered tentative:

1. Stocks without any analyst coverage *may* tend to underperform. Note that in the late '70s the NAs (which are mostly companies with no coverage) had the highest excess return. Over time, the excess returns of these companies has dropped to the point where they were the worst performers in the universe during the '80s. While survivorship bias is ultimately likely to explain some of the negative excess returns to the NAs in the '80s, that bias has been shrinking over time. Thus, it is quite likely that companies with no coverage were "earning" significant negative excess returns.

2. Overall, there did not appear to be a neglected-firm effect. If anything, over the entire period there was a moderately-followed-firm effect. Firms with from three to ten analysts tended to have positive excess returns in a variety of market environments.

Table 2.9—Annual Excess Return versus Universe for Analyst Neglect Categories (%) 1976–1992

Number of Analysts*	Excess Return 1976–1992	Excess Return 1976–1982	Excess Return 1982–1987	Excess Return 1987–1992
1–2	0.05	2.05	1.44	–3.75
3–5	0.24	0.18	0.46	0.10
6–10	0.52	–1.75	1.43	2.35
11–20	–2.33	–9.35	0.68	3.07
21+	–3.12	–11.13	0.48	2.89
NA**	–1.41	2.59	–2.28	–5.36
Total	0.00	0.00	0.00	0.00

*   The assumption of equally weighting each time period can cause a problem when using absolute rather than relative category sizes. Simply put, very few companies had 21+ analysts following them in 1976 while there were quite a few such companies in 1991. If one is interested in the returns one might have earned by investing in a portfolio of all companies with 21+ analysts and rebalancing that portfolio yearly, then our methodology would be appropriate. However, if one were interested in the excess returns associated with the *typical* overfollowed company, then another methodology would be needed.

Specifically, one would then weight each year's excess return observation by the fraction of all overfollowed companies that occurred in that year. This would have the effect of giving more weight to later years in the case of the overfollowed companies. Fortunately, these two weighting approaches give roughly the same result for most coverage ranges:

Weighted Average Excess Return to Analyst Coverage (%) 1976–1992

Number of Analysts	Equal Weighted Excess Return	Observation Weighted Excess Return
1–2	0.05	–0.04
3–5	0.24	0.22
6–10	0.52	0.98
11–20	–2.33	–1.50
21+	–3.12	0.83
NA	–1.41	–0.08

The one noticeable exception is for overfollowed stocks. These stocks are large underperformers on an equally weighted basis, but become outperformers on an observation weighted basis. Neither conclusion is incorrect. The appropriate weighting to use depends on one's purpose. Fortunately, sub-period returns are more likely to be similar than full-period returns.

**   NAs also pose a problem. In 1977, 46% of the universe was missing estimates for one reason or another (including having no coverage). By 1991, only 12.5% of the universe was missing estimates. The huge number of missing estimates explains why all estimate categories had positive excess returns in the middle testing period.

3. Except for the period examined by initial studies of the neglect effect, heavy analyst coverage has *not* led to negative excess returns. Note, however, that the strength of the neglect effect in the first period has a significant impact on the full-period averages for categories 11– 20 and 21+. This highlights the importance of examining sub-periods. An examination of the full period might lead one to conclude that heavy analyst coverage does lead to negative excess returns, when, in fact, this effect was limited to the first six years of the sixteen years studied.

4. None of the neglect effects are consistent over time.

Size + Neglect = ???

Although the large number of not available (NA) data points makes it extremely dangerous to reach firm conclusions about the interaction of size and neglect, a preliminary analysis of these interactions could shed light on some of the puzzles found earlier. Table 2.10 displays the interactions between market cap and neglect for the entire period from July 1976 to June 1992.

To the extent that the NA category primarily consists of companies without analyst coverage, it would appear that true neglect leads to significantly below average returns across the entire range of market capitalizations. In each market cap quintile, the NA coverage category underperformed the quintile as a whole.

**Table 2.10—Annual Excess Return versus Universe for Size and Neglect Categories*
(%) Full Period 1976–1992**

Market Cap Quintile	# of Estimates						Total
	1–2	3–5	6–10	11–20	21+	NA	
1	0.51	−0.44	−2.85	—	—	−2.04	−0.19
2	0.52	−1.17	2.53	0.80	—	0.27	1.19
3	0.85	1.46	−0.70	−0.60	—	−1.70	0.64
4	−4.35	0.55	1.10	−1.66	−0.51	−0.69	−0.08
5	—	0.44	−0.87	−2.51	−3.07	−3.47	−1.55
Total	0.05	0.24	0.52	−2.33	−3.12	−1.41	0.00

* Cells with fewer than 10 observations on average are not reported. They are marked with "—". Because these missing values are included in the totals, it is possible that the column or row totals will be slightly larger or smaller than any of the displayed values.

If the size effect were a proxy for a neglect effect, then we would expect to see all of the following: Companies with large capitalizations but small coverage would have positive excess returns, companies with small capitalizations but high coverage would have negative excess returns, and the numbers in each column would tend to have the same sign.

Contrary to expectation, those companies with large market caps and low coverage (1–2 analysts) have negative excess returns (–435 basis points per year). While those companies in the smallest market cap quintile that have moderate coverage have large negative excess returns (–285 basis points), those companies in the second market cap quintile with heavy analyst coverage actually have positive excess returns (80 basis points).

Finally, the column signs do not support the proxy idea. Look at the 3–5 analyst column. Small cap stocks in this group have negative excess returns over the period, while the higher cap stocks have positive excess returns. Neither the neglect effect nor the size effect can explain these results.

As always, it might be possible that the full period results are masking interaction effects that are visible during shorter periods. Table 2.11 shows the data for the three sub-periods.

Table 2.11 presents the information needed to investigate the three effects we would expect to see if size were a proxy for neglect:

- Companies with large capitalizations but small coverage would have positive excess returns. In all three sub-periods, the firms with large capitalizations (quintile 4) and 1–2 analysts had negative excess returns. Most of the larger cap NAs also experienced negative excess returns in each sub-period.

- Companies with small capitalizations but high coverage would have negative excess returns. There were very few companies that were analyst favorites and that also had small capitalizations. The little evidence that exists is mixed. Smaller companies (quintiles 1 and 2) with 6–10 analysts tended to have positive excess returns in each sub-period. Smaller companies with 11–20 analysts had strongly positive returns in one period and negative excess returns in another. On balance, the evidence does not support the claim of negative excess returns for these companies.

- The numbers in each column would tend to have the same sign. While there are a handful of analyst coverage categories that do have the same sign in some sub-periods, most of the non-NA columns have varying signs. Only the 1987 to 1992 sub-period comes close to supporting the hypothesis that neglect dominates the size effect, and in that period the neglect effect was the opposite of

**Table 2.11—Annual Excess Return versus Universe for Size and Neglect Categories*
(%) All Sub-Periods 1976–1992**

Market Cap Quintile	July 1976–June 1982 # of Estimates						
	1–2	*3–5*	*6–10*	*11–20*	*21+*	*NA*	**Total**
1	4.72	1.51	—	—	—	4.21	**4.48**
2	5.11	1.08	0.57	—	—	5.17	**4.79**
3	-2.56	-0.95	-2.05	-0.63	—	1.27	**0.53**
4	-4.80	-2.17	-0.68	-7.13	—	-3.16	**-2.40**
5	—	-5.14	-5.13	-11.36	-11.12	-2.04	**-7.38**
Total	**2.05**	**0.18**	**-1.75**	**-9.35**	**-11.13**	**2.59**	**0.00**

Market Cap Quintile	July 1982–June 1987 # of Estimates						
	1–2	*3–5*	*6–10*	*11–20*	*21+*	*NA*	**Total**
1	0.88	-3.52	-1.47	—	—	-2.27	**-1.24**
2	0.26	-2.73	3.29	9.68	—	-1.25	**-0.22**
3	7.22	5.06	-0.85	-2.88	—	-3.09	**1.21**
4	-6.74	2.18	1.75	0.63	0.75	-3.02	**0.17**
5	—	—	2.81	0.18	-0.10	-2.10	**0.08**
Total	**1.44**	**0.46**	**1.43**	**0.68**	**0.48**	**-2.28**	**0.00**

Market Cap Quintile	July 1987–June 1992 # of Estimates						
	1–2	*3–5*	*6–10*	*11–20*	*21+*	*NA*	**Total**
1	-4.93	0.29	3.69	—	—	-9.30	**-4.75**
2	-4.71	-2.30	4.13	-3.09	—	-4.10	**-1.71**
3	-1.43	0.75	1.06	1.73	—	-3.87	**0.19**
4	-1.41	2.19	2.61	2.61	-5.37	4.61	**2.44**
5	—	-0.89	0.57	5.43	3.63	-6.56	**3.82**
Total	**-3.75**	**0.10**	**2.35**	**3.07**	**2.89**	**-5.36**	**0.00**

*   Cells with fewer than 10 observations on average are not reported. They are marked with "—". Because these missing values are included in the totals, it is possible that the column or row totals will be slightly larger or smaller than any of the displayed values.

what was expected; neglected stocks tended to have worse performance than heavily followed companies.[16]

Given this evidence, we would tentatively add a fifth conclusion to the four given earlier:

5. A neglect effect has not been obscured by interactions between analyst coverage and market capitalization.

THE VALUE OF GROWTH (AND VICE VERSA)

Many small company advocates will be unconvinced by the above evidence. The typical small cap investor is a growth investor, and to date we have only examined small stocks in the aggregate. Perhaps if we teased out the growth stocks we would find a strong small cap effect.

The case for small cap growth is appealing. If stock prices are driven by earnings growth, and if smaller companies are more likely to sustain high growth rates than large companies, then small growth companies should have truly outstanding prospects for persistent excess returns.

Definitions of Growth

Growth stocks tend to be like fine art; it is hard to come up with a definition that satisfies everyone, but an expert knows a good one when she sees it. Some growth managers focus on historic growth rates. Others disdain the historic record and focus on analysts' forecasts of growth. We looked at both types of growth:

1. *Three-year EPS trend.* The regression trend line growth rate utilizing 36 months of trailing year earnings. We also examined five-year EPS trend and obtained similar results.
2. *I/B/E/S long-term growth estimate.* The median long-term growth rate, using estimates provided by brokers. These data were first collected in 1982. The survivorship data problem mentioned in the neglect section applies here as well.

    It should be noted that a significant number of companies were missing the data needed for one or both definitions of growth. Roughly one-fourth of the companies were missing three years of earnings data and roughly one-third were missing estimate data. This is lamentable but unavoidable, since a company must exist for three years before a three-year trend can be calculated and since there will always be companies with no analyst coverage. Therefore, we feel that these growth-rate measures are as comprehensive as can reasonably be expected.

The Performance of Growth Stocks

Since the data for the two measures of growth are available for different periods, we have analyzed them separately. Table 2.12 presents the full period and the sub-period performance breakdowns for three-year EPS trend. Growth quintile 1 stocks have low trend growth, while quintile 5 stocks have high growth. Our hypothesis is that growth quintile 4 and 5 stocks should show large positive excess returns, while growth quintile 1 and 2 stocks should have negative excess returns.

Table 2.12—Annual Excess Return versus Universe for 3-Year EPS Trend Quintiles (%) 1976–1992

EPS Trend Quintiles	Excess Return 1976–1992	Excess Return 1976–1982	Excess Return 1982–1987	Excess Return 1987–1992
1	−0.37	1.17	−0.68	−1.91
2	1.02	0.56	0.48	2.11
3	2.48	−1.10	4.99	4.28
4	2.23	−0.29	4.44	3.06
5	0.32	−1.30	4.12	−1.51
NA (return)	−1.81	1.76	−4.57	−3.33
NA (number)*	557.8	319.8	744.8	656.4

*   NA (number) signifies the average number of companies missing data per year.

Over the full period from 1976 to 1992, there is weak evidence for the growth stock hypothesis. Companies with the lowest growth and with the highest growth have excess returns that are close to zero, while companies with average to somewhat above average historic growth rates perform the best.

The picture becomes even more confusing if we look at the sub-period results. The only growth category that displayed positive excess returns in all periods included companies with somewhat *below* average growth (quintile 2). Even in this case, the excess return was low in two of the three sub-periods.

Very high growth companies (quintile 5) and very low growth companies (quintile 1) experienced negative excess returns in two of three periods. Growth was not rewarded in the late '70s but was well compensated in the mid '80s. The late '80s and early '90s were unusual in that moderate growth rate companies performed well, while those with extremely high *or* low growth rates underperformed.

Finally, those companies without three years of earnings data tended to underperform during this period. In many cases, NA companies represent new corporate entities. These results raise questions about the value of a track record that cannot be answered by our data.

The growth aficionado will point out that we have once again displayed only aggregate growth numbers. Perhaps the performance of small cap growth stocks was especially strong. Table 2.13 looks at this question.

Table 2.13—Annual Excess Return versus Universe for Size and 3-Year EPS Trend Categories (%) Full Period 1976–1992

Market Cap Quintile	3-Year EPS Trend Quintile						
	1	*2*	*3*	*4*	*5*	*NA*	*Total*
1	−0.10	5.14	5.72	1.42	2.74	−3.40	−0.19
2	1.58	1.80	5.70	6.07	3.61	−1.72	1.19
3	−0.23	2.01	1.82	5.03	−0.02	−1.71	0.64
4	−1.93	0.31	2.16	1.32	−1.05	−0.34	−0.08
5	−0.85	−1.35	0.01	−1.62	−3.41	0.64	−1.55
Total	−0.37	1.02	2.48	2.23	0.32	−1.81	0.00

This table has a few interesting features. First, smaller, high growth companies (represented by the shaded cells) experienced significant positive excess returns over the entire period. However, on balance, smaller companies with average three-year trend growth (quintile 3) experienced even higher excess returns.

Second, smaller companies (size quintiles 1 and 2) with growth rate data generally experienced positive returns over the last 16 years. The total for all smaller company returns was pulled down by those firms without three years of earnings data.

Finally, the highest growth companies (quintile 5) had a near linear relationship with capitalization. The higher the market cap, the lower the excess return to growth. In other words, growth seemed to work for smaller companies, but not for larger ones.

Although the above evidence is suggestive, it is not complete until the sub-period results have been examined. Table 2.14 presents the interactions between growth and market cap for each of the three sub-periods.

Table 2.14—Annual Excess Return versus Universe for Size and 3-Year EPS Trend Categories(%) All Sub-Periods 1976–1992

Market Cap Quintile	July 1976–June 1982 3-Year EPS Trend Quintile						
	1	2	3	4	5	NA	Total
1	4.05	3.51	7.41	4.45	6.41	2.39	4.48
2	7.75	2.33	4.93	7.85	2.70	5.38	4.79
3	0.18	2.49	−1.13	3.81	1.06	−2.68	0.53
4	−2.29	−0.67	−1.13	−1.89	−5.70	−1.76	−2.40
5	−4.39	−3.60	−7.69	−10.45	−12.05	5.05	−7.38
Total	1.17	0.56	−1.10	−0.29	−1.30	1.76	0.00

Market Cap Quintile	July 1982–June 1987 3-Year EPS Trend Quintile						
	1	2	3	4	5	NA	Total
1	2.73	7.69	5.82	4.46	4.18	−6.60	−1.24
2	1.79	3.59	6.92	8.22	6.56	−7.17	−0.22
3	−3.61	1.42	6.58	7.21	2.97	−0.73	1.21
4	−4.78	−0.18	3.07	1.88	5.31	−1.34	0.17
5	−1.79	−3.57	3.70	2.24	2.25	−4.14	0.08
Total	−0.68	0.48	4.99	4.44	4.12	−4.57	0.00

Market Cap Quintile	July 1987–June 1992 3-Year EPS Trend Quintile						
	1	2	3	4	5	NA	Total
1	−7.90	4.56	3.58	−5.26	−3.10	−7.16	−4.75
2	−6.04	−0.63	5.40	1.78	1.74	−4.78	−1.71
3	2.66	2.05	0.61	4.33	−4.30	−1.53	0.19
4	1.34	1.97	5.20	4.63	−1.82	2.35	2.44
5	4.32	3.56	5.57	5.11	1.30	0.12	3.82
Total	−1.91	2.11	4.28	3.06	−1.51	−3.33	0.00

During the late '70s, although smaller high growth companies (shaded cells) performed extremely well, smaller low growth (quintile 1) and moderate growth (quintile 3) companies performed just as well. The other outstanding characteristic of the late '70s, as noted earlier, was the overwhelming strength of the small cap effect. In all growth categories, the larger the market cap, the lower the excess return.

The story is much the same during the mid '80s. Smaller high growth companies (shaded cells) had superb excess returns, although once again smaller moderate growth (quintile 3) companies performed equally well. The fascinating phenomenon observed in this period was the tendency for excess return to drop as size increased in each growth quintile. However, in aggregate there was no size effect. The explanation rests with the NA companies. The companies without a three year earnings history experienced a negative size effect that offset the size effect for those companies having growth rates.

The third sub-period is quite different from the first two. Smaller high growth companies (shaded cells) had negative excess returns on balance. However, for the third straight sub-period, smaller moderate growth (quintile 3) companies had superb returns. Smaller low growth companies (quintile 1) were a disaster. In this period, there was a slight negative size effect amongst companies with three-year trend growth rates and a strongly negative size effect for the NAs.

Before drawing conclusions about the extent of a small cap growth stock effect, we should look at the returns associated with a forward looking growth measure. Table 2.15 presents the summary performance statistics for the I/B/E/S Long-Term Growth Estimate. Remember that these estimates are only available starting in 1982.

Table 2.15—Annual Excess Return versus Universe for I/B/E/S LT Growth Quintiles (%) 1982–1992

LT Growth Quintiles	Excess Return 1982–1992	Excess Return 1982–1987	Excess Return 1987–1992
1	2.49	1.25	3.73
2	2.02	2.74	1.29
3	3.73	4.23	3.23
4	−0.09	−0.45	0.27
5	−2.33	−4.01	−0.64
NA (return)	−2.63	−1.11	−4.15
NA (number)*	753.4	795.2	711.6

* NA (number) signifies the average number of companies missing data per year.

Based on the aggregate numbers, there appears to be a negative growth effect using forward-looking estimates. In other words, high forecasted growth rates translated into negative excess returns. Low to moderate forecasted growth seems to perform best, with average growth companies once again the best performers. These effects were observed in both sub-periods. Also of interest is the fact that NAs consistently had negative excess returns. Although some of this effect could be due to the survivorship bias present in our I/B/E/S data, it is likely that companies without estimates truly experienced negative excess returns.[17]

Table 2.16 displays the interaction effects between size and forecasted growth for the 1982 to 1992 period and two sub-periods.

During the '80s as a whole, smaller high forecasted growth companies (shaded cells) significantly underperformed. Once again, smaller cap, moderate growth companies (quintile 3) had superb performance. Smaller low growth companies were acceptable performers on balance. Finally, although larger cap stocks tended to strongly outperform, this effect was generally not visible within a given forecasted growth quintile.

The same basic effect was seen in the first sub-period, 1982 to 1987. In the late '80s, the picture changes to some extent. While smaller high growth companies (shaded cells) are still underperformers, the smaller low growth companies are even worse. However, even though small cap stocks as a whole strongly underperformed, the average forecasted growth companies (quintile 3) once again had very high positive excess returns. In most growth quintiles, a negative size effect was noticeable. Higher cap stocks tended to be associated with higher excess returns.

The Value of Growth

Although the large number of companies with missing growth data and the likely survivorship bias in the I/B/E/S numbers give us pause, we believe the above evidence is firm enough to draw the following conclusions about small cap growth stocks.

1. Contrary to most investment professionals' expectations, historic growth rates appear to have more value than consensus forecast growth rates. This result deserves further analysis. Virtually all experts believe that the market looks to future growth when setting valuations, not past growth. Why then should historic growth rates outperform forecast growth rates?

   We believe one reason is that historic growth rates *on average* do a better job of estimating future growth than do explicit forecasts of future growth. The biases analysts bring to the task of estimating future earnings are well known. People tend to underestimate the chance of negative surprises for those companies with rosy prospects. This leads to a disproportionate number of torpedo stocks

Table 2.16—Annual Excess Return versus Universe for Size and I/B/E/S LT Growth Quintiles(%) All Sub-Periods 1982–1992

July 1982–June 1992

Market Cap Quintile	I/B/E/S LT Growth Quintile						Total
	1	2	3	4	5	NA	
1	0.00	−3.71	5.15	−2.86	−2.88	−4.46	**−3.00**
2	1.04	3.12	3.22	2.09	−3.24	−2.56	**−0.97**
3	4.90	1.47	5.62	0.61	−3.76	−0.99	**0.70**
4	2.38	1.56	2.63	1.26	−2.47	1.37	**1.31**
5	0.92	3.15	2.43	0.69	3.22	−1.92	**1.95**
Total	**2.49**	**2.02**	**3.73**	**−0.09**	**−2.33**	**−2.63**	**0.00**

July 1982–June 1987

Market Cap Quintile	I/B/E/S LT Growth Quintile						Total
	1	2	3	4	5	NA	
1	3.25	−2.63	5.69	−1.53	−2.88	−2.03	**−1.24**
2	4.98	7.04	3.37	4.27	−5.72	−1.51	**−0.22**
3	3.32	−0.04	8.46	1.62	−4.80	1.72	**1.21**
4	−0.86	2.56	2.97	0.50	−3.61	−1.29	**0.17**
5	−2.89	3.24	1.17	−1.95	−0.98	−1.56	**0.08**
Total	**1.25**	**2.74**	**4.23**	**−0.45**	**−4.01**	**−1.11**	**0.00**

July 1987–June 1992

Market Cap Quintile	I/B/E/S LT Growth Quintile						Total
	1	2	3	I4	5	NA	
1	−3.25	−4.79	4.61	−4.19	−2.87	−6.90	**−4.75**
2	−2.91	−0.79	3.07	−0.09	−0.77	3.60	**−1.71**
3	6.49	2.99	2.78	−0.40	−2.72	−3.69	**0.19**
4	5.63	0.56	2.30	2.02	−1.33	4.03	**2.44**
5	4.72	3.06	3.69	3.32	7.43	−2.28	**3.82**
Total	**3.73**	**1.29**	**3.23**	**0.27**	**−0.64**	**−4.15**	**0.00**

among high forecasted growth companies. Also, analysts often have the tendency to fall in love with a stock and overestimate its growth prospects in the first place. Together these tendencies would cause high forecast growth stocks to underperform.

2. Smaller companies with high *historic* growth rates have tended to outperform although not in all market environments. However, smaller companies with average (quintile 3) *historic* growth rates have had even better performance and have sustained this in *all* sub-periods.

3. Small companies with average *forecasted* growth rates have also consistently experienced above average performance.

4. Small companies with high *forecasted* growth rates have underperformed in all sub-periods.

5. Stocks missing growth rate data have tended to underperform rather dramatically.

Overall, the evidence suggests that while high *historic* growth rates were good for smaller stocks, low growth was not bad on balance, and moderate growth was best. Over the 10-year period studied, the highest *forecasted* growth rates were apparently overly optimistic as this category generally produced negative excess returns. It should be noted that while these concensus growth rate estimates do not appear to add value, there may be individual analysts who add significant value. A study of aggregates naturally will not identify superior individual performers.

Definitions of Value

The investment flip side of growth is value. A reasonable number of investors believe that stocks with low price-to-earnings ratios (or similar measures) will outperform over time. Since undervalued stocks tend to have lower growth rates, and high growth companies tend to have higher P/Es, it is commonly believed that growth and value are mutually exclusive philosophies. This need not be true. Value investing is *not* the mirror image of growth investing. Therefore, it makes sense to look at the performance of various measures of value rather than assume that they are the inverse of the growth results.

We examined two measures of value:[13]

1. Common Equity/Market Cap—total common equity divided by market cap.

2. Normalized EPS Yield—trailing three-year average EPS divided by price. We also explored EPS yield based on estimated earnings and found similar results.

Only 18.4 companies per year on average were missing common equity data while 400.1 were missing three years of EPS data. For readers who may be used to thinking in terms of price/book and P/E ratios, note that equity/cap quintile 1 includes stocks with high or negative price-to-book ratios, while quintile 5 includes companies with low price-to-book ratios; similarly, normalized EPS yield quintile 1 consists of high or negative P/E stocks, while quintile 5 consists of low P/E stocks.

The Performance of Value Stocks

Since missing data are not an issue for common equity/market cap, it makes sense to analyze this measure first. Table 2.17 displays excess returns for the period from 1976 to 1992 and each sub-period. If there are excess returns to value, we would expect negative excess returns for quintiles 1 and 2 and positive excess returns for quintiles 4 and 5. In other words, companies with high levels of equity relative to market cap would be considered undervalued and thus over time should have better than average returns.

Table 2.17—Annual Excess Return versus Universe for Common Equity/Market Cap (%) 1976–1992

Equity/Cap Quintiles	Excess Return 1976–1992	Excess Return 1976–1982	Excess Return 1982–1987	Excess Return 1987–1992
1	−3.99	−4.45	−3.52	−3.92
2	−1.37	−1.47	−2.46	−0.16
3	0.29	0.70	−0.65	0.74
4	1.91	1.05	2.05	2.81
5	3.29	4.02	5.00	0.70
NA (return)	−2.04	2.06	−6.58	−2.42
NA (number)*	18.4	10.3	28.4	18.0

* NA (number) signifies the average number of companies missing data per year.

These results are remarkable.[18] quintiles 1 and 2 have negative excess returns over the entire 16-year period *and* over each sub-period. quintiles 4 and 5 have positive excess returns in all periods. Furthermore, the relationship between value and return is virtually linear in each time period.

Having finally found a relationship that appears to consistently add value, we must now examine whether the relationship holds for small cap stocks. Table 2.18 examines the relationship between size and valuation as measured by common equity/market cap.

Table 2.18—Annual Excess Return versus Universe for Size and Common Equity/Market Cap (%) Full Period 1976–1992

Market Cap Quintile	Equity/Cap Quintile					Total
	1	2	3	4	5	
1	−5.67	−1.09	2.68	1.81	2.91	−0.19
2	−2.09	−0.39	1.53	3.75	4.24	1.19
3	−3.53	−0.53	1.18	3.17	2.98	0.64
4	−1.24	−1.12	−0.91	0.93	2.88	−0.08
5	−3.99	−2.92	−2.04	0.23	3.02	−1.55
Total	−3.99	−1.37	0.29	1.91	3.29	0.00

Stocks with attractive valuation and smaller market caps (shaded cells) as a group have significant positive excess returns. Stocks with average valuation also have attractive returns. Note that the excess returns to over-valued (quintiles 1 and 2) smaller stocks tend to be strongly negative. A final point to make is that the value approach appears to work for *all* market cap levels, although it is particularly strong in the smallest cap quintiles.

The final question to be answered about this valuation measure is does it work in different market environments? Table 2.19 sheds light on this question by examining the size and value interactions for three distinct sub-periods.

Although all small cap stock quintiles performed well during the first sub-period (1976 to 1982), smaller cap value stocks (shaded cells) as a group once again experienced the highest positive excess returns in the universe. Despite strong negative performance for large cap stocks in this period, undervalued large cap stocks actually outperformed the universe.

As the middle section of Table 2.19 illustrates, the companies that benefited the most from the stock market boom of the mid '80s were the undervalued smaller stocks (shaded cells). The worst returns were for overvalued smaller stocks (quintiles 1 and 2 of each measure). Thus smaller stocks experienced both the best and the worst returns during this period. Also note that undervalued stocks outperformed once again in all market cap ranges.

Table 2.19—Annual Excess Return versus Universe for Size and Common Equity/Market Cap (%) All Sub-Periods 1976–1992

July 1976–June 1982

| Market Cap Quintile | *Equity/Cap Quintile* | | | | | |
	1	*2*	*3*	*4*	*5*	**Total**
1	4.17	4.87	3.46	3.55	5.90	**4.48**
2	1.36	1.63	5.89	5.71	7.63	**4.79**
3	−4.14	2.13	2.23	0.45	1.36	**0.53**
4	−6.04	−4.42	−0.02	−1.03	0.80	**−2.40**
5	−12.68	−9.14	−6.02	−3.12	1.10	**−7.38**
Total	**−4.45**	**−1.47**	**0.70**	**1.05**	**4.02**	**0.00**

July 1982–June 1987

| Market Cap Quintile | *Equity/Cap Quintile* | | | | | |
	1	*2*	*3*	*E4*	*5*	**Total**
1	−9.94	−5.05	4.00	1.82	5.43	**−1.24**
2	−2.10	−0.72	−3.82	1.77	7.62	**−0.22**
3	−1.58	−3.48	1.85	6.09	3.17	**1.21**
4	0.40	−0.02	−2.15	0.13	4.20	**0.17**
5	−2.07	−2.16	−2.38	1.28	3.50	**0.08**
Total	**−3.52**	**−2.46**	**−0.65**	**2.05**	**5.00**	**0.00**

July 1987–June 1992

| Market Cap Quintile | *Equity/Cap Quintile* | | | | | |
	1	*2*	*3*	*4*	*5*	**Total**
1	−13.20	−4.30	0.41	−0.28	−3.18	**−4.75**
2	−6.23	−2.50	1.65	3.40	−3.20	**−1.71**
3	−4.76	−0.76	−0.77	3.51	4.74	**0.19**
4	2.87	1.76	−0.74	4.08	4.04	**2.44**
5	4.51	3.78	3.07	3.21	4.86	**3.82**
Total	**−3.92**	**−0.16**	**0.74**	**2.81**	**0.70**	**0.00**

All good things come to an end, and in the late '80s undervalued smaller stocks underperformed (shaded cells). However, they substantially *outperformed* overvalued (quintile 1 and 2) smaller stocks. Oddly, smaller cap stocks with average valuation enjoyed above average performance. Although the relationship was not perfect, undervalued stocks tended to outperform across market cap ranges.

Before summarizing the case for value measures, we will briefly visit earnings yield to discover if the effect noted above is a general valuation effect or is specific to equity/cap. If there is a general valuation effect, we would expect high earnings yield (low P/E) stocks to outperform. Table 2.20 displays the full period and sub-period results for this measure.

Table 2.20—Annual Excess Return versus Universe for Normalized EPS/Price (%) 1976–1992

EPS/Price Quintiles	Excess Return 1976–1992	Excess Return 1976–1982	Excess Return 1982–1987	Excess Return 1987–1992
1	–4.77	–4.68	–4.33	–5.33
2	–0.10	–2.11	1.34	0.88
3	1.05	0.05	1.58	1.70
4	2.94	2.48	3.08	3.35
5	4.10	3.15	6.15	3.18
NA (return)	–1.43	2.29	–3.86	–3.47
NA (number)*	400.1	271.0	525.4	429.6

*   NA (number) signifies the average number of companies missing data per year.

There is a linear relationship between earnings yield and excess return in virtually all periods. The lower EPS yield (overvalued) stocks underperformed in each period. High EPS yield stocks outperformed in each period by a sizable amount. Table 2.21 explores the extent to which these relationships held true for small cap stocks over the full period 1976 to 1992.

The results are quite similar to those for common equity/market cap. The undervalued smaller cap stocks (shaded cells) once again had superior performance. However, only the most overvalued smaller cap stocks underperformed the universe. Also note that overvalued stocks underperformed in each cap range and that undervalued stocks outperformed in each market cap range. Although not reported, we also examined the issue of negative common equity and negative earnings companies to see if grouping them into quintile 1 had any distorting effects. In all cases, quin-

Table 2.21—Annual Excess Return versus Universe for Size and Normalized EPS/Price (%) Full Period 1976–1992

Market Cap Quintile	EPS/Price Quintile						Total
	1	2	3	4	5	NA	
1	−4.31	3.56	3.17	9.04	3.22	−3.48	−0.19
2	−2.84	3.30	5.47	4.20	4.97	−1.10	1.19
3	−3.86	−0.16	1.41	2.06	5.05	−0.17	0.64
4	−2.65	0.09	−0.99	1.31	3.44	−1.52	−0.08
5	−3.17	−3.68	−1.61	0.64	2.73	0.26	−1.55
Total	−4.77	−0.10	1.05	2.94	4.10	−1.43	0.00

tile 1 continued to be the worst performing group even when these companies were excluded.[19]

We have chosen not to present the individual period interaction tables, since they display essentially the same patterns as the full period chart and the common equity/market cap tables. The valuation effect thus seems to be a general one.

The Growth of Value

At the very end, we find a surprise. Value seems to work well in general and particularly well for small cap issues. In fact, both value measures proved highly robust, working in virtually all market environments since 1976.

Often, a winning investment approach has limited practical value since there may be only a handful of stocks that meet the necessary criteria. That is not the case here. There are literally hundreds of stocks to be found with low capitalization and attractive valuation.

In some respects, earnings yield is stronger and slightly more consistent than common equity/market cap. Nevertheless, the equity/market cap measure has a major advantage. On average, only 18 out of 2,100 companies were missing the data needed to calculate this measure. Over 400 companies were on average missing the data needed to calculate normalized EPS yield.

One puzzle remains. Small cap growth funds are far more popular than small cap value funds; in fact, the Lipper Mutual Fund Evaluation Service currently only has one category for small-stock funds—Small Cap

Growth Funds. Given the compelling case for value investing and for small cap value investing in particular, why is there this emphasis? However, industry's loss could be the investor's gain. If the number of small value funds grows, the excess returns historically available may disappear. Paradoxically, the value of value may be highest if the growth of value funds is low.

APPENDIX

Research Methodology

I.   Data

We used two data sources to conduct this study on small cap investing:

A.   Standard & Poor's Compustat Services, Inc., Industrial, Industrial Research, PDE and PDE Research files.

B.   I/B/E/S Inc. Domestic Earnings historic database available through FactSet Data Systems.

II.   Horizon

We examined the horizon from June 30, 1976, through June 30, 1992. This horizon was dictated by data availability. The Compustat database provides quarterly data for 10 years and annual data for 20 years. The use of appropriate data lags (to avoid look-ahead bias) and the requirement for subsequent returns up to one year limited the study to a maximum of 18 years. Analyses using I/B/E/S data, only available since 1976, further limited the horizon to the 16-year period beginning June 30, 1976.

III.   Universe

The universe of stocks was defined using the Compustat database. For each year, we selected all U.S. incorporated companies with market capitalization greater than or equal to $50 million as of June 30. In addition to foreign incorporated companies, we excluded all REITs and known duplicates in the Compustat database. We also required that the companies have total returns for at least one full month beginning with July. Membership in the universe ranged from 1,353 companies in 1976 to 2,408 in 1991. The largest universe consisted of 2,727 companies in 1987.

IV.   Categories

All deciles and quintiles are defined such that lowest values are in the first category and the highest values are in the highest category. Thus, the smallest market cap stocks are in decile 1 (quintile 1) and the largest are in decile 10 (quintile 5). Negative values are included in decile 1. Ratios used as style measures are defined such that negative values are appropriately categorized. For example, earnings yield is used instead of P/E so that companies with negative earnings are grouped with low EPS yield companies rather than with low P/E companies.

For the number of I/B/E/S estimates or *analyst coverage*, the following six categories are used:

Category	# of Estimates
1	1–2
2	3–5
3	6–10
4	11–20
5	21+
NA	Not available

V.   Returns

Monthly total returns were calculated from Compustat price and dividend data. It was not feasible within the context of this study to obtain returns for less than one month for companies that stopped trading mid-month. To minimize survivorship bias, however, unavailable monthly returns were replaced with the universe averages. Monthly returns were linked to obtain annual returns. Annual excess returns are defined as the stock's return minus the equally weighted universe return and are *not* risk-adjusted. Excess returns across time are equally weighted.

VI. Data Definitions

Quarterly, when available, and annual accounting data from Compustat were lagged a minimum of five months to account for reporting delays and avoid look-ahead bias. Data definitions:

A.   Sales: net sales

B.   Assets: total assets

C.   Common equity: total common equity

D.   Market capitalization: 6/30/yy price times shares outstanding for the latest reported period on or before 6/30/yy

E.   5-year EPS trend: linear regression slope of 60 monthly trailing year EPS figures normalized by the 60-month average absolute EPS, annualized

F.   3-year EPS trend: linear regression slope of 36 monthly trailing year EPS figures normalized by the 36-month average absolute EPS, annualized

G. Normalized earnings yield: three-year average EPS divided by the June month-end price

H. Common equity/market cap: total common equity divided by market capitalization

I. # of estimates: number of analysts providing current fiscal year EPS estimates in the I/B/E/S domestic database as of June of each year

J. I/B/E/S long-term growth: median long-term growth rate estimate from I/B/E/S

For measures using the Compustat PDE file (items e–g above), we required that the market price also be available on the same dates as the earnings per share data.

ENDNOTES

[1] Rolf W. Banz, "The Relationship Between Return and Market Value of Common Stocks," *Journal of Financial Economics* (1981, Vol. 9), pp. 3–18.

[2] Ibbotson Associates Inc. EnCorr Analyzer, December 1992.

[3] A good summary of recent work is provided in D. Robert Coulson, *The Intelligent Investor's Guide to Profiting From Stock Market Inefficiencies.* Chicago: Probus Publishing Company, 1987.

[4] *The Wall Street Journal*, March 17, 1993. pp. C1, C12.

[5] Morningstar Mutual Funds OnDisc, March 1993.

[6] Seventy-six ADRs on the NYSE out of 1703 companies as of March 30, 1993.

[7] Private communication by authors with COMPUSTAT.

[8] The smallest stock in the Wilshire Small Cap Index has a market cap of $58 million according to *The Wall Street Journal*, March 17, 1993, p. C1.

[9] There are some companies not covered by the Compustat database. Because a number of these are utilities and financial firms, further breakdowns by sector could provide additional insights, but were beyond the scope of this study.

[10] Astute readers will have surmised that the total number of companies in each decile will tend to slowly increase over time. This is indeed the case. Each decile in 1976 contained 135 companies. By 1991, each decile had grown to 241 companies. By equally weighting each year's observation, one is effectively giving each company in 1991 less weight than its 1976 counterpart.

For some purposes this would be a problem, but by focusing on excess returns, we believe that our approach gives a fair idea as to the average returns to investing in a broad set of smaller companies. However, we performed a sensitivity analysis to determine the degree to which our conclusions depended on the weighting scheme used for yearly observations. We did not find substantive differences.

[11] Average annual universe returns for the first period were 14.01%, for the second period 24.37%, and 5.40% for the last period.

[12] Interestingly, the classic articles on the small cap effect were written before the experience of the '80s and were clearly colored by the go-go small cap '70s.

[13] Refer to the Appendix for data sources and lags for these variables.

[14] Ibbotson Associates' analysis beginning in 1926 shows similar effects in the relative returns of small versus large stocks. See *Stocks, Bonds, Bills and Inflation 1993 Yearbook.* Chicago, IL: Ibbotson Associates, Inc., 1993.

[15] See D. Robert Coulson, *The Intelligent Investor's Guide to Profiting From Stock Market Inefficiencies,* op. cit., pp. 118–123, for an excellent discussion of neglected stocks and especially of Professor Avner Arbel's ground-breaking work on this topic.

[16] It is interesting to note that in the July 1976 to June 1982 period, the size effect clearly seemed to dominate the neglect effect. The row values all have the same sign with the exception of size quintile 3. Earlier studies of the neglect effect used data from this period to draw the opposite conclusion. We speculate that removing foreign stocks may play a role in explaining these results. ADRs tend to show up as neglected stocks since there are often few U.S. analysts covering them. They can be heavily followed in their home country. Thus, they only appear to be neglected and can bias the results of a neglect study.

[17] One fairly consistent result in this study was that companies missing estimate data tended to underperform. To the extent that this group primarily consists of companies without any analyst coverage rather than rep-

resenting a survivorship problem, one must ask why truly neglected companies don't earn an estimation risk premium.

One speculative answer is that the scope of equity analysis has changed since the first neglect studies were conducted. There are many more analysts now than there were 15 years ago and each analyst seems to be covering a wider range of companies. It is questionable whether most companies with zero coverage are truly neglected. It is possible that analysts have given most of these companies a quick once-over and have decided that they are not worth covering in depth. There is a cost associated with covering a company completely enough to make informed earnings estimates. If an analyst's investment judgment is that the costs of coverage outweigh the likely investment gains, then the company will not be covered. Therefore, a number of so-called neglected companies may actually have been subjected to some investment research. The negative excess returns may demonstrate that analysts do a superior job of determining which companies should receive coverage. A test of this hypothesis cannot be conducted using our data.

[18] However remarkable the results are, they are hardly unique. In a now classic paper, Professors Fama and French demonstrated that there were not only excess returns to value investing, but excess risk-adjusted returns as well. Please see Eugene F. Fama and Kenneth R. French, "The Cross-Section of Expected Stock Returns," *The Journal of Finance*, June 1992, pp. 427–65.

[19] For example, over the full period the average excess return for Equity/Cap quintile 1 is –3.99% versus –3.81% with negatives excluded. The comparable figures for EPS/Price are –4.77% versus –2.29%.

Chapter 3

Questions of Size: Are Small Stocks Worth a Closer Look?

Edmund D. Kellogg
Vice President and Portfolio Manager
Keystone Investment Management Corporation

WHY SMALL CAP?

Although many causes may carry greater spiritual rewards, over the past sixty-six years of U.S. history, there has been no more rewarding financial investment than small capitalization stocks. The Ibbotson & Sinquefield[1] data cited in numerous studies on this topic show that a dollar invested in "small stocks" on January 1, 1926, would now be worth three times a like investment in larger stocks, and over 80 times the value of a dollar invested in the highest-returning fixed income investment.

WHAT IS SMALL CAP?

Size, like beauty, is in the eye of the beholder. At the start of our research we asked a number of institutional investors if they would define the term "small capitalization stock" for us. What we got in return was a wide range of remarkably self-serving definitions. If the investor worked for a firm managing less than $1 billion, the answer we generally received was that small cap stocks had capitalizations ranging from $50 million to $500 million. Institutional investors responsible for managing several billion were likely to respond that a small cap stock ranged in capitalization from $500 million to $2 billion. These investors clearly formed their response based on their need to minimize what we call the Victor Kiam problem. The name relates to Mr. Kiam's advertisements for his Remington electric razors, as in: "I liked it so much I bought the company." Since absolute answers to this question tended to reflect the trading and legal constraints of the respondent, we decided to conduct our research on a market-relative basis. We hope that this will allow the reader to apply his or her own constraints to the results of our research.

A good starting point to establishing a more general definition for small capitalization is to look at the capitalization of the Ibbotson "Small Stock" series, both because it is cited so frequently in the context of small capitalization investing and because it gives us a first benchmark. The Ibbotson "Small Stock" series is actually composed of two separate series. From 1925 to 1981 the authors used data produced by screening the bottom 20% of the NYSE-listed securities and calculating the returns over five-year periods. In other words, they screened for the smallest 20% of NYSE stocks on December 31, 1925, held and measured that portfolio over the subsequent five-year period, and then repeated the process on December 31, 1930. From 1982 to the present, returns for the Dimensional Fund Advisors Small Capitalization portfolio were used. The principal differences between the 1925 to 1981 series and the more recent series were that the DFA Small Company Fund performance figures included transaction costs, portfolio rebalancing[2] was performed quarterly, and companies from the AMEX and OTC were included if they met the capitalization criteria, i.e., had market capitalizations at or below the bottom 20% NYSE capitalization bound.[3]

From our perspective, the study has two principal strengths. First, the Ibbotson series presents consistently derived return data over a very long span of history. The second major strength of the study is that the results have been vetted by one of the most rigorous audiences available, competing finance professors. If it were possible to effectively refute the Ibbotson & Sinquefield data, it is our assumption that it would have happened already.

The principal drawbacks of the study are that the authors measure only large capitalization (the S&P 500) and *very* small capitalization stocks. As of year-end 1992, the capitalization limit imposed by using only the smallest 20% of the NYSE by market capitalization resulted in a portfolio with a maximum capitalization of $106 million and a median capitalization of $29 million.[4] For most institutional investors this is a very illiquid class of securities indeed. A further drawback of the study is that it is probable that industry and value biases are created when stocks are screened by size in the fashion used to create the Ibbotson "Small Stock" series. We will discuss these issues below.

SIZE, RISK, AND RETURN

In order to investigate the relationships between size, risk, and return in greater detail, we chose the Ford research universe created and maintained by Ford Investor Services of San Diego. The Ford database is composed of 2,000 stocks representing close to 84% of the total market capitalization of the U.S. market.[5] The research method we used was to split the Ford database quarterly into five portfolios (quintiles) by market capitalization, from December 31, 1970, through December 31, 1992, rebalancing portfolios quarterly and measuring subsequent returns quarterly.[6]

As of year-end 1992, the quintiles looked roughly as in Table 3.1. We have included several popular indices as benchmarks for comparison.

Table 3.1—Index as of 12/31/92 ($ Millions)

	Maximum Market Cap $ Millions	Median Market Cap $ Millions	1992 Avg. Monthly Trading Volume $ Millions	Average Institutional Ownership %
Largest quintile	75,905	4,952	365.1	51.3
Second-largest quintile	2,378	1,239	91.4	51.7
Third-largest quintile	786	495	44.3	49.2
Fourth-largest quintile	275	171	13.4	39.4
Smallest quintile	95	51	3.5	30.3
The S&P 500	75,905	3,056	283.2	58.1
The S&P Mid Cap	7,108	846	92.5	53.7
Second-largest quintile	2,378	1,239	91.4	51.7
Ibbotson "Small Stocks"	106	29	NA	NA
Bottom 20% of NYSE	115	54	4	32.3

The use of relative definitions is practical for a number of reasons beyond simplifying the interpretation of our research. One of the debates currently going on in the investment community is how to define mid cap. A market-relative definition of size makes the answer to this question clear. A workable definition of mid cap runs from the lower boundary of the largest market capitalization quintile ($2.4 billion) to the upper bound of the smallest quintile (roughly $100 million).

The challenge for investors is not classification, however; it is performance. Which sectors of the market should perform best over time? There are historical precedents that might help you to narrow the optimal size range for your portfolio. These precedents relate to historic risk/return trade-offs.

HOW LOW SHOULD YOU GO?

One of the central issues to consider, should you decide to invest in smaller capitalization stocks, is just how low to go. The risk return trade-offs as size declines are not linear. (See Figure 3.1.) Over the twenty-two years of our study, the data support Ibbotson & Sinquefield's findings that returns and risk rise as capitalization falls. It is worth noting, however, that as capitalization fell, most of the incremental pickup in returns occurred between the first and third quintile of capitalization. Declining into the fifth quintile by size carried a very high cost in incremental volatility without carrying much additional return. Medium capitalization stocks,

Figure 3.1—Risk and Return by Capitalization Quintile 1971–1992

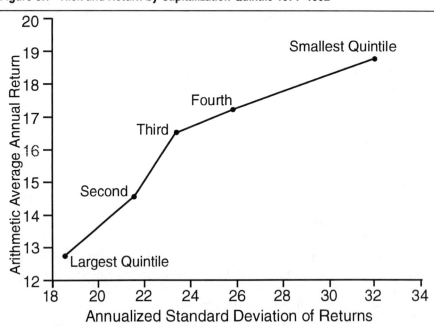

i.e., those ranging from $100 million to $2.4 billion at present, have proven to be a better risk-adjusted investment over time. Lowering the capitalization of a portfolio is best if taken in moderation.

Valuation

One of the great myths of small capitalization investing is that there are large and clearly identifiable valuation swings between small and large capitalization stocks. The seminal chart and root cause of this belief is an advertisement for the T. Rowe Price New Horizons Fund frequently seen in the financial press.[7]

Figure 3.2—T. Rowe Price New Horizons Fund P/E Divided by S&P 500 P/E

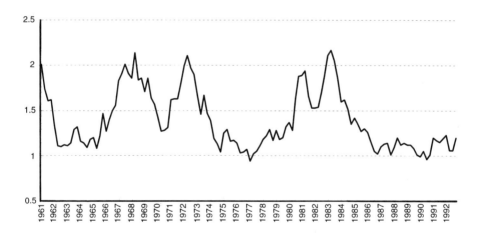

Figure 3.2 shows the P/E of the New Horizons Fund divided by the P/E ratio of the S&P 500. Clearly, the clever investor will buy the New Horizons fund now in hopes of a big gain as P/Es for smaller capitalization stocks double. Perhaps the fund's P/E will double; however, one should understand that this will likely be the result of superior asset management and not anything as simple-minded as the fund's exposure to small capitalization stocks.

Several points on the methodology used to create the T. Rowe Price chart are worth noting. The P/Es used for both the New Horizons fund and the S&P 500 are based on earnings *estimates* for the companies held by both the fund and the companies in the S&P 500. Those estimates are made by T. Rowe Price analysts. Second, the fund is unabashedly a growth fund, which makes the fund's P/E representative of only a portion of the overall market. Finally, it is our guess that the fund's managers actively manage the fund's P/E. The reason for this guess is that our work on the relationship between P/E and capitalization shows nowhere near the dramatic valuation swing implied by the T. Rowe Price chart.

Figure 3.3 shows the average P/Es of our four smaller capitalization-based quintiles divided by the average P/E of our largest quintile shown quarterly over the past twenty-one years. Our methodology for creating the quintiles was the same as described above using quarterly rebalancing of the Ford research universe. The major differences between our approach and that taken by T. Rowe Price were that we used P/Es based on *reported* trailing twelve-month earnings instead of estimated earnings and our research universe was not restricted to growth stocks. Our results show that,

Figure 3.3—Ratio of Smaller-Size Quintile P/E's to Largest Quintile P/E

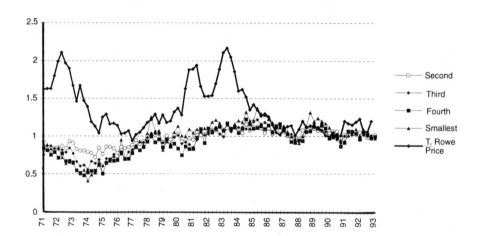

over time, the relationship between P/E and size has been relatively stable between size groupings. Over the time period for which we studied the relationship between P/E and size, the lowest relative P/E came in the smallest size quintile during 1974 at 0.4:1. The highest relative valuation for smaller cap stocks came (again in the smallest quintile) in 1985 at 1.37:1. We include the T. Rowe Price series for reference.

While one can make a convincing case for a strong relative performance by mid cap stocks going forward, we believe that the basis for relative outperformance in the lower capitalization sector will be superior earnings growth and not necessarily a double in relative multiples.

If there is a consistent relationship between size and a valuation measure over time, it is the relationship between size and price to book value as shown in Figure 3.4. On average, smaller stocks have carried lower price to book values than larger stocks over the past two decades. Further, average price to book values fell with each successively smaller size quintile. Our primary explanation for this phenomenon is the industry composition of the quintiles in our study. Over the time period studied, the smaller quintiles tended to have a greater percentage of both utilities and regional

Figure 3.4—Average Price to Book Value by Size Quintile

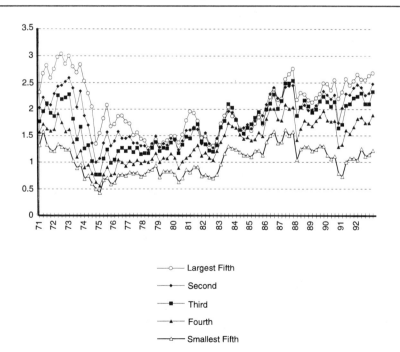

banks than the larger quintiles. Being in regulated industries, these companies have tended to have lower profitability levels and hence lower valuations relative to book value. We mentioned above that there might be
industry and valuation biases associated with the Ibbotson & Sinquefield
"Small Stock" series. Our series, which are derived in a similar manner,
most certainly do exhibit these biases.

Inefficiency

While some will choose to place their small and mid cap investments passively in extended index funds, we would not. One of the most compelling
reasons to invest in smaller capitalization stocks is the greater market inefficiencies to be found there. To draw the comparison between large and
small capitalization stocks in this respect, consider a few selections from
the "Broker's Favorites" list published monthly by I/B/E/S (see Table 3.2).

Table 3.2

	Number of Estimates	High Estimate	Low Estimate	Difference High-Low
Bristol-Myers	44	$4.80	$4.60	$0.20
Merck & Co.	41	6.65	6.30	0.35
Microsoft	40	3.75	3.37	0.38
Pfizer	40	3.35	3.05	0.30
Waste Management	40	2.09	1.80	0.29

Clearly, if you are looking for a place to add value, why would you
want to spend your resources following Bristol Myers when 44 analysts
can discern only a $0.20 difference in earnings per share on a $4.60 base
estimate? Although this is somewhat uncharitable of us to point out, the
"Broker's Favorite" list shown in Table 3.2 was compiled in March of 1992,
showing estimates for fiscal year 1992. As a matter of record, Bristol Myers
actually earned $4.25 in 1992 and the stock spent a good part of the year
on the new low list.

Given the close attention paid to companies in the large capitalization
end of the market, it is quite difficult to add value as a fundamental analyst. Having studied and used numerous quantitative techniques to enhance returns in the large cap sector of the market, we would be the first

to admit that quantitative methods are also losing some of their effectiveness over time. Certainly numerous studies have soured institutional investors on active management in this arena. But just because active investors have had difficulty beating the popular indexes in large cap stocks, this does not mean that they will be unable to add value in the mid and smaller cap sectors, at least for the next few years.

From a commonsense point of view, smaller capitalization stocks are less efficient, at present anyway, because there are fewer people paying attention. Figure 3.5 shows the average number of analysts covering the companies in our capitalization quintiles.[8]

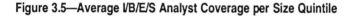

Figure 3.5—Average I/B/E/S Analyst Coverage per Size Quintile

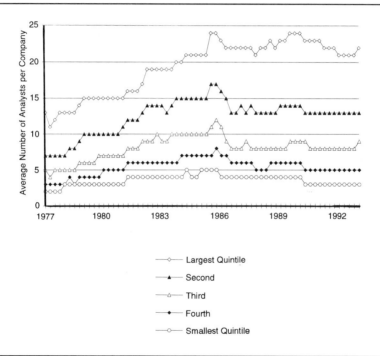

In order to make the further assertion that smaller companies offer better return potential for active managers, however, one has to translate smaller size and lower analyst coverage into market inefficiency. The method we chose for this proof was to split each of our size quintiles into two portfolios according to some well-documented quantitative market inefficiencies.

PRICE TO BOOK VALUE

First we split each of our size quintiles according to their price to book values yielding two 200 stock portfolios in each of our size quintiles. We then subtracted the quarterly return of the "bad" (high price to book value) 200 from the return of the "good" (low price to book value) 200 stock portfolio in each quintile. We rebalanced portfolios quarterly and subtracted a 1% round-trip transaction cost in the largest quintile, escalating the transactions penalty by 0.25% in each successively smaller quintile to attempt to capture the higher transaction costs faced by investors as they reduce their average capitalization. Finally, we created an index of the net value added of picking low price to book value stocks in each quintile. The results are shown in Figure 3.6.

Figure 3.6—Price to Book Performance within Size Quintiles

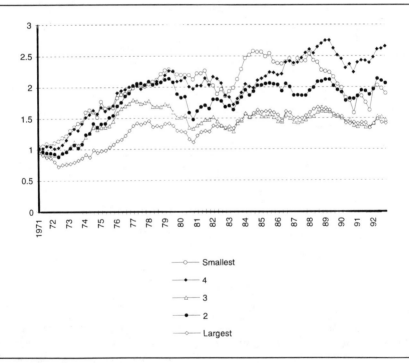

As one can see, low price to book value stocks carried higher returns than high price to book value stocks in all of our size quintiles (all of the index lines rise) over the past two decades. As any value investor will ruefully tell you, however, the relative performance of low price to book value investing peaked in 1989 and has only recently begun to add value again. Of greater interest to us, however, is the pattern of returns by size quintile. While investing in low price to book value stocks produced above-average returns in all capitalization groups, the effectiveness of the strategy tended to be greater in the mid and smaller capitalization quintiles. It is important to note that this performance advantage comes on top of the previously noted tendency of smaller capitalization quintiles to exhibit successively lower price to book values. Further, the incremental performance is also independent of the tendency of smaller stocks to outperform larger stocks over time.

The *relative* performance patterns over time are also interesting to note. The *lowest* capitalization quintile, which was leading the pack during much of the 1971–1985 period, suffered badly between 1985 and 1990. The underlying data make it clear that the economic pressures being felt by larger firms in many industrial areas of the U.S. economy hit hardest in this capitalization range. Small companies with low price to book values had a nasty tendency of going out of business during this time period. If you are a value-based investor, the medium capitalization quintiles have proven to be a far less volatile area for investment.

PRICE MOMENTUM

This relationship between effectiveness (inefficiency) and size is not confined to value-based techniques. We also tested a simple price momentum model,[9] which essentially amounted to ordering stocks by their relative strength over the previous twelve months (see Figure 3.7). Stocks showing high relative strength were considered "good" in our study. This simple price momentum model yielded absolute returns that were superior to our low price book study in all quintiles, with the pattern of smaller size leading to better results remaining essentially the same. The middle quintiles again showed the best performance over time.

In our opinion, if it is possible for the simple strategies that we outlined above to add value, then there is ample opportunity for active management to add value over indexing in the middle and lower ranges of capitalization both through quantitative and fundamental methods.

THE BANDWAGON EFFECT

The final topic we would like to discuss relating to size and return is the most conjectural, but we would maintain, potentially the most powerful.

Figure 3.7—Price Momentum Performance within Size Quintiles

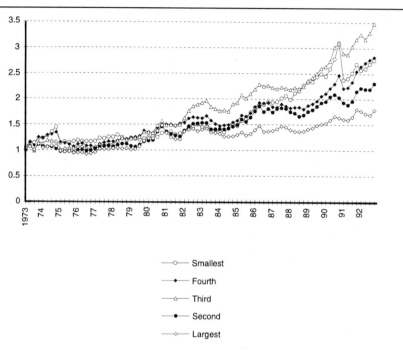

The idea is based on market history, supply and demand conditions in the market today, and finally, human behavior.

First, market history. In order to get a long-term perspective on the performance cycles between small and large stocks, we used the Ibbotson & Sinquefield "Small Stock" and "Large Stock" data series,[10] creating indices for each and dividing the "Small Stock" index by the "Large Stock" index (see Figure 3.8). The resulting series is a relative index line. When the relative index is rising, smaller stocks are winning on a relative basis. When the line is falling, large stocks are winning on a relative basis.

As one would expect, given the long-term outperformance of small stocks, the relative performance index rises over time. Further, there is a very clear and discernible cycle to the relationship. On average, the relative performance cycle between large and small stocks lasts seven years, with an average relative gain in small capitalization stocks of over 200% during up cycles and a relative loss of almost 50% during down cycles. It is our belief that as we write this (early 1993) we are in the second year of a five- to seven-year relative up cycle in smaller capitalization stocks.

Figure 3.8—Timing Is Everything

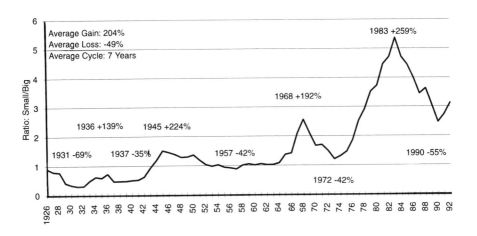

Another reason that we are quite optimistic about the potential for smaller capitalization stocks at this point in time relates to the enormous concentration of capital in the largest quintile of market capitalization at present. In Figure 3.9 we divide the total capitalization of our largest quintile by the total capitalization of all our other quintiles combined over the past two decades. We can see that while there is a perennial concentration of capital in the largest companies in the U.S. market (the average of this relationship is 3.4:1 in favor of large caps) the current relationship is very high by any historic or statistical standard.

The implications for smaller capitalization stocks should even a small percentage of these funds be persuaded to leave the safety of their large cap investments (in IBM, Bristol Myers, etc.) are very inspiring for current buyers of smaller capitalization stocks. In Table 3.3, we show the percent increase in capitalization that would be caused in our mid- and small-sized quintiles given even modest shifts of capital out of the largest quintile.

Figure 3.9—Total Capitalization of Largest Quintile to All Other Quintiles

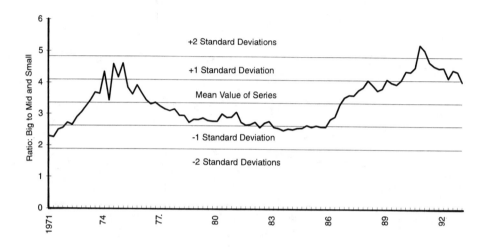

Table 3.3

% Shift out of Largest 400 Stocks	1%	5%	10%	15%
% Average Gain in Second 400	6	32	63	127
% Average Gain in Third 400	17	83	165	248
% Average Gain in Fourth 400	45	226	452	678
% Average Gain in Fifth 400	157	786	1,572	2,357

For example, a 5% capital shift out of the top quintile into the next largest quintile would, all other things remaining equal, produce a 32% increase in the total capitalization of the second largest quintile. Our belief is that over the next four to six years capital *will* flow out of the top quintile and into the smaller quintiles. The flow will first be targeted at the middle capitalization range and then begin to enter the smallest range of capitalization.

The necessary footwork for such a shift is in place. Standard & Poor's along with most of the major consulting firms have created mid and/or small capitalization indices over the past two years. Articles extolling the virtues of smaller capitalization investing are being written. Perhaps belief will come faster this time. Better information flow and the derivatives markets may cause this large cap/small cap cycle to play out faster than previous cycles, but in our view it will play out. If you are considering a downsizing move, the time to consider it is now.

ENDNOTES

[1] Roger G. Ibbotson and Rex A. Sinquefield, "Stocks, Bonds, Bills, and Inflation: Year-by-Year Historical Returns (1926-1974)," *Journal of Business* (January 1976).

[2] In this instance, rebalancing means calculating new market capitalizations for all stocks in the NYSE based on current market prices and shares outstanding, then establishing where the bottom 20% capitalization threshold stood, and buying and selling securities to accurately represent current market conditions.

[3] It is interesting to note that for the period 1926–1981, the Ibbotson small cap series was beating the Ibbotson large cap series (basically the S&P 500) by a ratio of almost 5:1. From 1982 to the present their *large cap series beat their small cap series* by a ratio of 1.4:1. This is not so much an indictment of active management or frequent rebalancing as it is an indication of what happens to a belief too widely shared. When the Ibbotson & Sinquefield series was first published, professional investors and plan sponsors became energetic converts, effectively killing its value as an investment methodology for a good eight years. More on this below.

[4] The year-end 1992 figures come from Ibbotson Associates. It should be noted that these results differ substantially from simply screening for the bottom 20% of NYSE capitalization on the Compustat database. A screen of the bottom 20% of the NYSE yields a maximum market cap of $115 million and a median market cap of $54 million. We suspect that the fund, which held 1,793 stocks at year-end 1992, diversifies its holdings to avoid the Victor Kiam problem described above.

[5] Our estimate for the U.S. equity market is based on totaling the market capitalization of the top 5,000 companies in the Compustat database at year-end 1992. This yields a total U.S. market capitalization of $5.2 trillion, with the smallest company carrying a market capitalization of $6 million.

Companies in the Ford universe had a total capitalization of $4.3 trillion. It should be noted that both of these figures include foreign-based companies listed and traded on U.S. exchanges. The Ford research universe, for example, contains 108 foreign companies, which represent roughly 13% of its capitalization. Many of these are Canadian natural resources companies listed on U.S. exchanges.

[6] For example, there were 2,000 stocks in the Ford research universe on December 31, 1991, which we split into five portfolios of 400 stocks each by market capitalization on that date. The first quintile contained the 400 stocks with the largest market capitalizations, the second quintile contained the 400 stocks with the next highest capitalizations, etc. We measured the performance of each portfolio to March 31, 1992, and then rebalanced the portfolios so that they would reflect the new market capitalizations as of that date.

[7] Source: T. Rowe Price, Baltimore Maryland.

[8] There are currently 1,832 companies with I/B/E/S coverage in the Ford universe. We quintiled this somewhat smaller universe, placing 366 companies in each quintile by size.

[9] John S. Brush, "Six Relative Strength Measures Compared," *The Journal of Portfolio Management* (Fall 1986). The specific model tested is referred to as "Model Q in the referenced article.

[10] Ibid. Roger G. Ibbotson & Rex A. Sinquefield.

Chapter 4

Predicting Size Effect Reversals

Marc R. Reinganum
Phillips Professor of Finance and
Director, Financial Markets Institute,
College of Business Administration
University of Iowa

INTRODUCTION

Predictability of the size effect is a recent phenomenon. My own work on the size effect began nearly fifteen years ago as a graduate student at the University of Chicago. At that time (the late 1970s), the orientation of the academic world was quite different than today. The capital asset pricing model (CAPM) was king. The risk of an individual stock was measured by the stock's beta. The generally accepted view seemed to be that, apart from beta, nothing else could predict a stock's return. This view fit very nicely with the efficient markets hypothesis—a hypothesis that contended all available information was reflected in the price of stock. In the mid- and late 1970s, one could conquer the investment world armed with beta.

This simple view of equities came to an end with the publication of the Ph.D. dissertations of Rolf Banz and myself [for example, see Banz (1981) and Reinganum (1981, 1983)]. These pieces of work established that beta-based benchmarks could be beaten. In particular, Banz and I reported that firm size, as measured by stock market capitalization, is systematically related to stock market performance. On average, small firms outperformed large ones even after adjusting for differences in beta risk. The magnitude of the performance differential was about 20% per year, a number of economic and statistical significance. When initially reported, the size effect was labeled as an anomaly, which suggested that an explanation might come along and squeeze it back into the framework of the capital asset pricing model. Such an explanation has not arisen. Indeed, that which was viewed as anomalous a decade ago is now generally accepted as the mainstream. The creation of the S&P mid-cap index is a testament to the strength and importance of the market capitalization variable analyzed by Banz and me.

In the latter half of the 1980s, the performance of small cap stocks lagged substantially behind that of large cap stocks and indices. For example, from November 1985 through October 1990, the S&P 500 increased in value by 77.46%, whereas the DFA Small Company Fund rose by only 1.15%. Given this abysmal performance, some began to wonder whether the small cap advantage reported in the early 1980s had been fully arbitraged away after wide publicity.

My initial work on the size effect emphasized the long-run nature of the phenomenon. On average, small firms outperformed large ones. This performance differential need not be present in every sub-period. For example, in the period 1969–1974, large cap stocks outperformed small cap stocks. Of course, the reason was not that the large cap stocks did so well, but rather that they lost less than small cap stocks.

Variability over time in the size effect had been highlighted in a paper by Brown, Kleidon, and Marsh (1983). The main finding to be reported here, however, is that variability in the size effect is not entirely random. Rather, over longer horizons, such as five years, the size effect exhibits predictable reversals. That is, a five-year period in which large cap stocks outperform small cap ones is typically followed by a five-year period in which the relative performance is reversed, i.e., small cap stocks outpace large ones.

Predictable reversals in relative performance are inconsistent with the notion of efficient markets espoused in the 1960s and 1970s. Within this framework, stock returns are independently and identically distributed, and past price changes cannot predict future price changes. More recently, the efficient market view of stock return behavior has been challenged by evidence of stock return reversals over longer horizons. De Bondt and Thaler (1985) claim that the stock market tends to overreact; they find that prior performance over a three-year period helps predict the next three years. Previous losers tend to become winners and vice versa. Fama and French (1988) also find predictable long-run stock price behavior. They document negative autocorrelations in long-run stock returns, i.e., the tendency for a period of high returns to be followed by a period of low returns and vice versa. Thus, the empirical evidence suggests cycles in stock returns are a real phenomenon.

The purpose of this research is to investigate whether the relative performance between small and large cap stocks displays cyclical behavior. The question is not whether small stocks or large stocks exhibit cyclical returns. Rather, the issue is whether the differential return between small and large cap stocks reveals cyclical behavior. Stated differently, does the "size effect" follow a pattern of predictable reversals?

THE SIZE EFFECT

The size effect is defined as the difference in returns between a portfolio of small cap stocks and a portfolio of large cap stocks. But how is "small" defined? Academic research often analyzes decile portfolios. The universe of securities is broken into ten portfolios, each with the same number of securities. For example, all New York Stock Exchange (NYSE) common stocks are ranked from the very largest to the very smallest on the basis of their stock market capitalization (price per share times number of shares outstanding). The bottom 10% of this ranking would be assigned to market value portfolio 1; the top 10% of the ranking would be placed in market value portfolio 10. The other stocks would be assigned similarly to the eight intermediate market value portfolios. The portfolio compositions are revised annually.

Figure 4.1 displays the average annual return for these ten market value portfolios assuming dividend reinvestment. For the period from January 1926 through December 1989, the stocks in market value portfolio 1 experienced average annual increases of nearly 24% per year, whereas the portfolio of largest stocks appreciated on average only 11.1% per year. This difference in average annual returns, about 13% per year, is the size effect.

The most dramatic difference in average annual returns is between the two extreme market value portfolios. What size companies are in the smallest (market value portfolio 1) NYSE decile portfolio? At the beginning of 1989, the largest company in this portfolio had a stock market capitalization of just over $48 million (see Table 4.1). The capitalizations of stocks in the next-to-smallest portfolio, market value portfolio 2, never exceeded $100 million. In most academic studies, small stocks are defined as those in the bottom two deciles. However, some institutional investors may consider a small stock to be in the range of $500 million to $1 billion. This corresponds to market value portfolio 7, in the latter half of the 1980s.

Figure 4.1—Average Annual Returns of the Ten NYSE Market Value Portfolios (1926–1989)

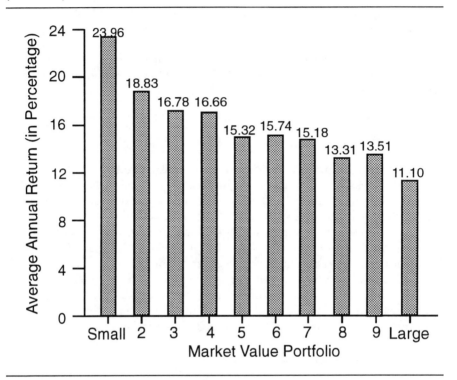

In the next section, potential cycles in the size effect are investigated, using different definitions of a small portfolio. In each case, however, the performance of large firms will be measured in comparison to the performance of market value portfolio 10.

REVERSALS OF THE SIZE EFFECT

On average, smaller cap stocks outperform the largest ones. This performance differential is, however, not constant. Figure 4.2 plots the difference in annual returns between selected small firm portfolios (market value portfolios 1, 3, 5, 7, and 9) and the largest firm portfolio; the other portfolios are omitted from the graph to reduce clutter. Based on market value portfolio 1, the size effect has an annual standard deviation of 34% over the 1926–1989 period. The standard deviation of the size effect declines to just over 6% if small firm performance is measured by market value portfolio 9

Table 4.1—Capitalization Cutoff Values (in $ 000s) for Selected Market Value Portfolios at Start of Year in the Odd Years During 1926–1989

Selected Market Value Portfolio

YEAR	Market Value Portfolio #1		Market Value Portfolio #3		Market Value Portfolio #5		Market Value Portfolio #7		Market Value Portfolio #9	
	MIN	MAX	MIN	MAX	MIN	MAX	MIN	MAX	MIN	MAX
1927	31	2,076	4,225	7,009	10,600	14,750	21,389	36,575	64,201	142,358
1929	150	3,125	6,420	10,093	16,656	23,640	38,500	59,824	109,292	205,215
1931	14	730	1,620	3,340	5,789	8,700	14,388	24,685	47,408	130,349
1933	44	281	656	1,296	1,960	3,020	5,225	10,464	21,656	60,750
1935	44	720	1,581	2,813	4,465	6,827	11,330	21,353	38,025	95,440
1937	135	2,125	4,095	6,599	10,635	15,921	23,000	34,200	60,918	168,663
1939	89	1,111	2,487	4,472	6,950	9,898	14,839	23,625	46,824	122,540
1941	25	920	2,207	3,798	6,016	9,075	12,321	18,624	34,637	91,825
1943	82	906	2,266	3,669	5,398	8,122	11,387	18,600	33,777	84,000
1945	150	3,028	5,329	7,615	10,516	14,700	20,501	28,835	49,344	118,954
1947	969	4,700	7,714	10,500	14,725	20,625	27,135	40,320	66,124	134,692
1949	678	3,424	5,600	8,316	11,520	16,470	23,588	35,350	56,596	127,750
1951	926	5,000	7,968	11,625	16,875	22,935	34,452	49,725	79,670	169,850
1953	292	5,128	8,982	12,992	18,630	27,000	39,990	61,695	102,300	220,986
1955	618	6,651	11,441	17,338	26,426	38,721	56,680	88,596	156,990	296,964
1957	694	7,808	13,637	20,574	31,395	48,081	69,608	110,071	193,162	401,677
1959	650	9,690	17,696	27,196	39,370	57,951	92,750	135,425	253,370	533,265
1961	720	10,255	18,740	28,661	43,865	62,225	96,742	149,786	269,658	579,118
1963	1,350	11,653	20,854	31,428	43,916	64,026	97,902	152,802	296,909	561,015
1965	2,130	16,477	27,031	39,627	56,579	83,132	119,705	195,160	366,816	732,980

Table 4.1 Continued

Selected Market Value Portfolio

YEAR	Market Value Portfolio #1		Market Value Portfolio #3		Market Value Portfolio #5		Market Value Portfolio #7		Market Value Portfolio #9	
	MIN	MAX	MIN	MAX	MIN	MAX	MIN	MAX	MIN	MAX
1967	4,545	19,376	30,443	43,491	64,719	90,182	133,803	209,774	388,613	753,844
1969	5,905	43,922	70,009	94,923	127,820	173,417	246,197	364,289	586,709	1,020,756
1971	1,655	24,860	39,321	59,813	89,697	126,359	178,665	284,718	505,586	847,177
1973	1,750	28,392	42,834	64,749	96,671	138,072	204,402	338,067	554,453	1,014,248
1975	769	8,730	15,535	25,208	36,346	57,623	91,977	152,505	289,513	598,603
1977	1,153	19,894	35,174	54,636	80,910	122,887	198,000	307,453	570,209	997,111
1979	1,932	24,537	39,650	62,415	94,884	142,416	210,005	331,000	556,654	973,780
1981	1,575	31,919	59,181	92,365	150,301	221,350	344,800	534,237	889,948	1,645,734
1983	3,610	43,457	69,819	115,979	174,688	268,278	411,011	635,009	1,024,581	1,803,212
1985	2,840	45,881	83,130	130,492	204,775	316,660	465,347	734,879	1,224,189	2,299,540
1987	1,619	53,177	95,243	145,350	223,579	354,312	596,509	970,305	1,737,365	3,577,391
1989	530	48,231	85,264	134,785	223,094	367,046	594,838	1,049,504	1,899,531	4,123,826

Notes: Decile portfolios are created each year. Market value portfolio #1 is the smallest size portfolio. Market value portfolio #10 (not shown above) is the largest size portfolio. Size is measured as stock market capitalization, i.e., price per share times number of shares outstanding.

Figure 4.2—Annual Size Effect Based on Different Small Cap Portfolios, 1926–1989

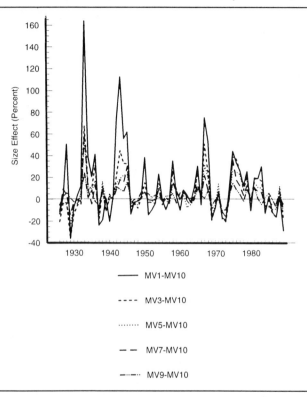

over the same time period. On a year-to-year basis, though, fluctuations in the size effect appear random. What happens to the size effect if one examines an investment window longer than one year? Do patterns appear?

Portfolio returns are compounded over periods ranging from one through seven years to assess potential long-run patterns in the size effect. For example, consider an investment horizon of five years. Is the size effect over the period 1926–1930 related to the size effect of 1931–1935? To answer this question, the correlation of fifty-six pairs of two adjoining five-year periods is computed. This autocorrelation, or the correlation between current returns and past returns, is calculated using different market value decile portfolios as the small firm portfolio. For each small firm portfolio, the autocorrelation is computed for investment horizons ranging from one to seven years.

The autocorrelations of the longer-run size effects are presented in Table 4.2. Over a one-year horizon, the autocorrelations are somewhat positive but not reliably different from zero. For a three-year horizon, the point estimates of the autocorrelations are negative for the size effect using any of the small firm portfolios. This negative autocorrelation means that the size effect tends to reverse itself. The autocorrelations become quite negative and statistically significant at investment horizons of five to six years. Thus, over longer investment horizons, a period during which large firms outperform small ones is typically followed by a period in which the relative performance is reversed.

Table 4.2—Autocorrelations of Size Effect Using Different Investment Horizons and Different Definitions of a "Small" Portfolio, 1926–1989

Investment Horizon (years)	Small Portfolio				
	Market Value Port #1	Market Value Port #3	Market Value Port #5	Market Value Port #7	Market Value Port #9
1	0.277 (0.027)	0.268 (0.033)	0.189 (0.137)	0.083 (0.514)	0.136 (0.285)
2	0.142 (0.272)	0.198 (0.124)	0.154 (0.235)	0.025 (0.842)	−0.027 (0.831)
3	−0.172 (0.191)	−0.141 (0.286)	−0.144 (0.274)	−0.198 (0.131)	−0.233 (0.075)
4	−0.234 (0.079)	−0.284 (0.032)	−0.281 (0.033)	−0.301 (0.022)	−0.341 (0.009)
5	−0.298 (0.026)	−0.398 (0.002)	−0.417 (0.001)	−0.439 (0.001)	−0.387 (0.003)
6	−0.354 (0.009)	−0.455 (0.001)	−0.456 (0.001)	−0.499 (0.001)	−0.331 (0.015)
7	−0.305 (0.029)	−0.485 (0.001)	−0.420 (0.002)	−0.493 (0.001)	−0.291 (0.037)

Notes: The "size effect" is defined as the holding period return of a small firm portfolio minus the holding period return of the largest firm portfolio, market value portfolio #10. P-values are in parentheses. Caution should be exercised in interpreting the p-values since for horizons greater than 1 year observations contain overlapping annual returns. For example, one observation would be the returns from 1926–1930 and 1931–1935; another observation would be the returns from 1927–1931 and 1932–1936.

One way to illustrate the effect of these negative autocorrelations is to count how many times a negative size effect is followed by a positive one (Table 4.3). Again, consider an investment horizon of five years. For mar-

Table 4.3—The Number of Periods with Negative Size Effects Using Different Definitions of a "Small" Portfolio and Different Investment Horizons (1926–1989)

Investment Horizon (years)	Sub-Period	Small Portfolio				
		Market Value Port #1	Market Value Port #3	Market Value Port #5	Market Value Port #7	Market Value Port #9
1	First	25	28	30	26	21
	Second	10	15	16	11	9
2	First	25	26	26	24	20
	Second	11	14	10	9	7
3	First	18	20	23	21	14
	Second	4	7	7	6	5
4	First	14	16	15	16	11
	Second	0	2	0	1	2
5	First	10	17	17	10	9
	Second	0	3	0	1	0
6	First	10	16	12	8	8
	Second	1	3	0	0	0
7	First	9	10	9	6	8
	Second	0	1	0	0	0

Notes: The "size effect" is defined as the holding period return of a small firm portfolio minus the holding period return of the largest firm portfolio, market value portfolio #10. Consider the case the interval length is 5 years. There are 56 rolling (overlapping) 5-year periods in the sample. Using market value portfolio #1, the size effect was reversed 10 times, i.e., the 5-year holding period return of portfolio #10 exceeded the 5-year holding period return of portfolio #1 in 10 cases. For these 10 cases, in the subsequent 5-year period, portfolio #1 outperformed portfolio #10 in each instance; that is, the size effect was reversed 0 times in the second subperiod. Using market value portfolio #3, the size effect was reversed 17 times based on a 5-year interval. For these 17 cases, the size effect remained negative in only 3 of the subsequent 5-year intervals.

ket value portfolio 1, one could find ten five-year periods (potentially overlapping) in which large cap stocks experienced greater total returns than the small cap portfolio. For each of these ten episodes, however, in the following five-year period, the small cap stocks outperformed the largest cap stocks. Using market value portfolio 3 as the small cap portfolio, the size effect was negative in seventeen five-year periods; it turned positive in the next five-year period in fourteen of the seventeen cases. The next-to-largest group of stocks, market value portfolio 9, also exhibits this reversal pattern. This portfolio underperformed market value portfolio 10 in nine five-year periods. In each of these nine instances, during the next five-year period, the stocks in market value portfolio 9 outperformed the largest cap stocks.

The systematic patterns in the long-run size effect are significant not only in the statistical sense of a negative autocorrelation but in the economic sense of actual reversals. For the investment horizon of five years, the details of these reversals are presented in Table 4.4. For example, consider the case when the small firm portfolio performance is measured by market value portfolio 1 (Table 4.4, Panel A). In the 1926–1930 period, this small firm group of stocks lost 11.49% in value, while the largest firms advanced by 32.31%. The size effect for this period was negative, –43.80%. In the next five-year period, 1931–1935, this small cap group gained 357.01%, whereas the largest cap group increased in value by 16.53%. The size effect in this subsequent period was 340.48%. Using market value portfolio 1, the rebound of the size effect averaged 498.44% following periods of negative size effects. The average rebound of the size effect is positive for all small portfolios analyzed in Table 4.4. Even for portfolio 9, the rebound averages 52.81% in periods following negative size effects.

The relationship between the magnitude of the rebound, the capitalization of the portfolio, and the investment horizon is presented in Figure 4.3. In these figures, the average size effect in the rebound is adjusted to take into account the fact that small firms on average outperform large firms. The adjustment is made by subtracting the overall average of the size effect from the average size effect in the rebound periods. For example, consider portfolio 3 in Panel B of Table 4.4. The rebounds averaged 124.25%, but the average size effect over all the possible five-year periods equaled 62.02%. Thus the adjusted rebound is 62.23% (124.25% − 62.02%). These adjusted rebounds are plotted in Figures 4.3A and 4.3B.

The figures reveal that the adjusted rebound effects are nearly zero for one- and two-year investment horizons. The most dramatic changes occur between years three and four. The adjusted rebound effect seems to level off at investment horizons of about five years. Figure 4.3A shows that the adjusted rebound is most pronounced for the very smallest firm portfolio and tapers off rapidly to the next-to-smallest market value portfolio, portfolio 2. However, as Figure 4.3B depicts, the adjusted rebound effects are not zero for market value portfolios 2 through 9 at the longer investment horizons.

As a caveat, one should be aware that reversals over investment horizons of five years do not necessarily imply short-run reversals. For example, consider the following regression equation:

Table 4.4—Negative Size Effects and the Subsequent Returns Using Five-Year Horizons and Selected Market Value Portfolios, 1926–1989

Panel A: Portfolio #1 vs. Portfolio #10

Time Period	Small	Large	Size Effect	Next Period	Small	Large	Size Effect
1926–1930	–11.49	32.31	–43.80	1931–1935	357.01	16.53	340.48
1927–1931	–46.98	–34.74	–12.24	1932–1936	1,225.45	174.61	1,050.84
1928–1932	–58.47	–53.73	–4.74	1933–1937	460.74	101.57	359.17
1935–1939	36.34	61.29	–24.95	1940–1944	410.92	37.61	373.30
1936–1940	–39.94	4.84	–44.78	1941–1945	1,309.30	102.01	1,207.28
1937–1941	–67.41	–27.81	–39.59	1942–1946	1,152.49	116.91	1,035.57
1951–1955	110.38	137.05	–26.66	1956–1960	62.47	54.64	7.82
1952–1956	98.15	115.27	–17.12	1957–1961	113.34	73.06	40.28
1969–1973	–38.18	15.71	–53.89	1974–1978	214.72	13.21	201.50
1970–1974	–31.16	–8.06	–23.09	1975–1979	453.55	85.35	368.19
Average	–4.88	24.21	–29.09		576.00	77.56	498.44

Table 4.4 Continued

Panel B: Portfolio #3 vs. Portfolio #10

Time Period	Small	Large	Size Effect	Next Period	Small	Large	Size Effect
1926–1930	-49.51	32.31	-81.83	1931–1935	71.95	16.53	55.41
1927–1931	-72.45	-34.74	-37.71	1932–1936	454.98	174.61	280.37
1928–1932	-81.05	-53.73	-27.32	1933–1937	198.80	101.57	97.23
1929–1933	-68.65	-48.04	-20.60	1934–1938	82.55	64.50	18.05
1935–1939	42.07	61.29	-19.22	1940–1944	199.26	37.61	161.65
1936–1940	-9.09	4.84	-13.93	1941–1945	420.25	102.01	318.23
1937–1941	-49.42	-27.81	-21.61	1942–1946	411.78	116.91	294.86
1946–1950	43.60	55.31	-11.70	1951–1955	127.10	137.05	-9.95
1947–1951	88.78	91.59	-2.80	1952–1956	114.73	115.27	-0.54
1948–1952	104.67	107.37	-2.70	1953–1957	68.00	70.46	-2.46
1951–1955	127.10	137.05	-9.95	1956–1960	90.31	54.64	35.67
1952–1956	114.73	115.27	-0.54	1957–1961	124.99	73.06	51.92
1953–1957	68.00	70.46	-2.46	1958–1962	134.02	72.90	61.11
1968–1972	13.18	42.75	-29.57	1973–1977	60.79	-5.24	66.03
1969–1973	-41.35	15.71	-57.07	1974–1978	167.85	13.21	154.63
1970–1974	-40.57	-8.06	-32.51	1975–1979	411.55	85.35	326.19
1971–1975	7.72	18.98	-11.26	1976–1980	290.91	87.02	203.89
Average	11.63	34.15	-22.52		201.75	77.50	124.25

Table 4.4 Continued

Panel C: Portfolio #5 vs. Portfolio #10

Time Period	Small	Large	Size Effect	Next Period	Small	Large	Size Effect
1926–1930	-22.03	32.31	-54.35	1931–1935	81.16	16.53	64.62
1927–1931	-57.62	-34.74	-22.87	1932–1936	376.51	174.61	201.90
1928–1932	-69.77	-53.73	-16.04	1933–1937	166.43	101.57	64.86
1929–1933	-52.35	-48.04	-4.30	1934–1938	81.87	64.50	17.37
1935–1939	58.99	61.29	-2.30	1940–1944	123.89	37.61	86.27
1936–1940	0.88	4.84	-3.96	1941–1945	274.91	102.01	172.89
1937–1941	-36.94	-27.81	-9.12	1942–1946	285.16	116.91	168.24
1946–1950	48.80	55.31	-6.51	1951–1955	147.52	137.05	10.46
1947–1951	82.16	91.59	-9.43	1952–1956	129.42	115.27	14.15
1948–1952	101.99	107.37	-5.37	1953–1957	76.15	70.46	5.69
1959–1963	43.41	47.89	-4.47	1964–1968	172.37	56.18	116.19
1960–1964	37.46	53.42	-15.96	1965–1969	85.01	24.20	60.81
1968–1972	29.14	42.75	-13.61	1973–1977	34.93	-5.24	40.17
1969–1973	-30.41	15.71	-46.13	1974–1978	124.79	13.21	111.57
1970–1974	-34.03	-8.06	-25.97	1975–1979	313.77	85.35	228.41
1971–1975	7.61	18.98	-11.36	1976–1980	240.42	87.02	153.39
1972–1976	22.15	25.51	-3.36	1977–1981	150.93	42.60	108.32
Average	7.61	22.62	-15.01		168.54	72.93	95.61

Table 4.4 Continued

Panel D: Portfolio #7 vs. Portfolio #10

Time Period	Small	Large	Size Effect	Next Period	Small	Large	Size Effect
1926–1930	7.11	32.31	-25.19	1931–1935	64.34	16.53	47.81
1927–1931	-42.02	-34.74	-7.28	1932–1936	330.73	174.61	156.12
1928–1932	-62.64	-53.73	-8.91	1933–1937	168.36	101.57	66.79
1935–1939	52.91	61.29	-8.37	1940–1944	97.99	37.61	60.38
1937–1941	-33.86	-27.81	-6.05	1942–1946	251.27	116.91	134.35
1946–1950	52.07	55.31	-3.24	1951–1955	135.59	137.05	-1.45
1951–1955	135.59	137.05	-1.45	1956–1960	83.39	54.64	28.74
1968–1972	27.96	42.75	-14.78	1973–1977	30.06	-5.24	35.30
1969–1973	-20.30	15.71	-36.02	1974–1978	95.81	13.21	82.59
1970–1974	-29.57	-8.06	-21.51	1975–1979	253.23	85.35	167.87
Average	8.72	22.00	-13.28		151.08	73.23	77.85

Table 4.4 Continued

Panel E: Portfolio #9 vs. Portfolio #10

Time Period	Small	Large	Size Effect	Next Period	Small	Large	Size Effect
1926–1930	31.51	32.31	-0.80	1931–1935	41.82	16.53	25.28
1927–1931	-37.54	-34.74	-2.81	1932–1936	258.39	174.61	83.78
1935–1939	50.70	61.29	-10.52	1940–1944	76.37	37.61	38.75
1936–1940	-7.95	4.84	-12.83	1941–1945	191.62	102.01	89.60
1937–1941	-33.72	-27.81	-5.97	1942–1946	205.53	116.91	88.61
1968–1972	31.06	42.75	-11.60	1973–1977	11.26	-5.24	16.50
1969–1973	-11.56	15.71	-27.28	1974–1978	46.39	13.21	33.17
1970–1974	-21.66	-8.06	-13.61	1975–1979	147.57	85.35	62.21
1971–1975	13.61	18.98	-5.31	1976–1980	124.35	87.02	37.32
Average	1.60	11.69	-10.09		122.59	69.78	52.81

Notes: The "size effect" is defined as the holding period return of a small firm portfolio minus the holding period return of the largest firm portfolio, market value portfolio #10.

Figure 4.3—Average Rebounds Following Negative Size Effect

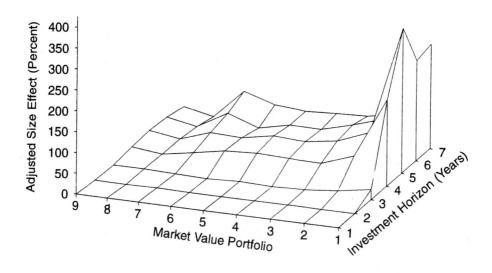

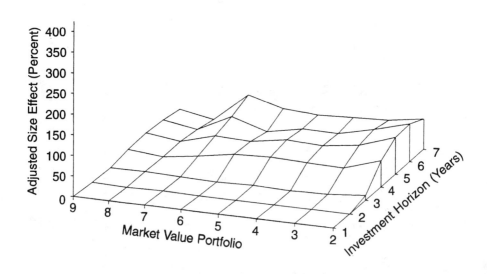

$$(\text{Dif Ret})_y = \beta_0 + \beta_1(\text{Dif Ret})_{y-1} + \beta_2(\text{Dif Ret})_{y-5} + e$$

where:

$(\text{Dif Ret})_y$ = the annual difference in returns between the small and large firm portfolio in year y.

$(\text{Dif Ret})_{y-1}$ = the annual difference in returns between the small and large firm portfolio in year $y-1$, i.e., lagged 1 year.

$(\text{Dif Ret})y-5$ = the annual difference in returns between the small and large firm portfolio in year $y-5$, i.e., lagged 5 years.

In this specification, the impact of recent price changes [$(\text{Dif Ret})_{y-1}$, last year's return differential] and more-distant price changes [$(\text{Dif Ret})_{y-5}$, the return differential five years ago] are allowed to differ. Figure 4.4 plots the regression coefficients, β_1 and β_2. The coefficient β_1 is consistently positive. This means that short-run price movements tend to persist. On the other hand, the coefficient β_2 is consistently negative, which means that the size effect tends to reverse itself at intervals of five years. The point of this caveat is to illustrate that inferences drawn about five-year investment horizons need not apply to year-by-year portfolio decisions.

CONCLUSIONS

The difference in performance between the small cap and the largest cap stocks (i.e., the size effect) can be predicted in part. On average, small cap stocks outperform the largest cap ones, and this is true for almost any definition of a small cap portfolio. This performance advantage, however, is volatile and there are periods during which large cap stocks earn higher returns than the small cap stocks.

The evidence suggests that relative performance of small versus large cap stocks can be predicted at longer-run investment horizons, such as five years. The size effect exhibits a tendency to reverse itself. That is, periods in which the size effect is negative tend to be followed by periods in which the size effect is positive. Stated differently, over longer investment horizons, the size effect is negatively autocorrelated. The strength of these reversals is statistically and economically important. For example, the very smallest firms always outperform the very largest ones following a five-year period in which small-firm returns lagged behind large-firm returns.

Toward the end of the 1980s, many investors began to feel skeptical about the size effect and wondered whether in fact the size effect was dead. This research suggests a very different scenario. The empirical evidence reveals the size effect exhibits a strong tendency to reverse itself in five-year intervals. Given the abysmal performance of small cap stocks in

Figure 4.4—Regression Coefficients Used to Predict Annual Return Differential between Small and Large Cap Portfolios (Based on 30-Year Rolling Windows)

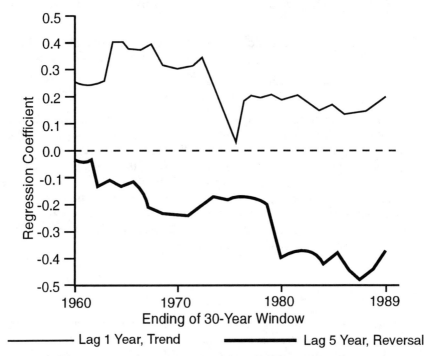

Independent Variables: Difference in Annual Return between Small and
Large Firm Portfolio Lagged 1 Year
Difference in Annual Return between Small and
Large Firm Portfolio Lagged 5 Years

the latter half of the 1980s, history suggests that the first half of the 1990s should be a boom period for small cap stocks. One strongly suspects that small-firm performance will revive in the first half of the 1990 decade. By the mid-1990s, however, this research suggests that the small cap advantage will diminish or perhaps even turn negative.

This chapter documents the statistical regularities associated with predictable reversals in the size effect. Future research will need to establish how the return differentials between small and large cap stocks are related to fundamental economic and firm data. One hopes that such an investigation will yield a deeper understanding of the behavior of small cap stocks.

REFERENCES

Banz, Rolf W., "The Relationship Between Return and Market Value of Common Stock," *Journal of Financial Economics* 9 (1981), 3–18.

Brown, Philip, Allan W. Kleidon, and Terry A. Marsh, "New Evidence on the Nature of Size-Related Anomalies in Stock Prices," *Journal of Financial Economics* 12 (1983), 33–56.

De Bondt, F. M. Werner, and Richard Thaler, "Does the Stock Market Overreact?" *Journal of Finance* 40 (1985), 793–805.

Fama, Eugene F., and Kenneth R. French, "Permanent and Temporary Components of Stock Prices," *Journal of Political Economy* 96 (1988), 246–273.

Reinganum, Marc R., "Misspecification of Capital Asset Pricing: Empirical Anomalies Based on Earnings' Yields and Market Values," *Journal of Financial Economics* 9 (1981), 19–46.

Reinganum, Marc R., "Portfolio Strategies Based on Market Capitalization, *Journal of Portfolio Management* (Winter 1983), 29–36.

PART TWO: SMALL CAP
BENCHMARKS

Chapter 5

Small Cap Benchmarks—Unraveling the Mysteries

Claudia E. Mott
First Vice President and Director of Small Cap Research

Daniel P. Coker
Junior Quantitative Analyst

Prudential Securities, Inc.

INTRODUCTION

Benchmarks, indexes—call them what you will—are the bane of many a money manager's existence. Small cap investors may one day have a standard index like the S&P Composite against which their performance is measured. However, until that day arrives, there are a slew of possibilities and making the right choice is not always easy.

The purpose of this chapter is to provide an in-depth look at the numerous indexes that measure small cap performance. If one of these indexes is going to be used as a performance affecting compensation and even employment—making an informed decision is of utmost importance. Investors need to be aware of the composition nuances and construction idiosyncrasies that affect how these benchmarks perform. Many of the well-accepted so-called "small cap" indexes are far from appropriate when it comes to measuring this segment of the market, as will become obvious in the course of this discussion.

We provide a number of tables that display the results of our analysis. Because they may not be directly referenced in the text, we'd like to provide a brief description at the outset. Note that the S&P Composite is included in all tables for comparative purposes. At the end of the study, we have included an addendum with a brief description of the methodology we used to calculate the fundamental characteristics. Also in the addendum is a focus comparing the measures of central tendency—mean, harmonic mean, median, etc.

- Table 5.1 details many of the characteristics of the indexes. These include the number of companies, rebalancing frequency, weighting methodology, exchange distribution, average size, biggest and smallest holdings, and the percent concentration of the largest 10, 50, and 100 companies in the index.

- Table 5.2 looks at the benchmarks from the fundamental point of view. We have calculated mean, median, and weighted average values for P/E (both with and without negative earnings), price-to-book, price-to-sales, return-on-equity, and debt-to-capital ratios. We have also included the average yield and the number of stocks that are paying dividends.

- Table 5.3 lists the macroeconomic sector breakdown on a percentage-of-companies basis.

- Table 5.4 also breaks the indexes into macroeconomic sectors, but on the basis of the percentage of market capitalization within the index that falls into each group. Differences in index performance are frequently attributable to their sector weightings.

- Table 5.5 divides the companies into size categories, because mean and median market-cap statistics do not provide a thorough understanding of the size distribution of companies within the indexes.

- Table 5.6 also looks at the size distribution of the indexes, but it measures the percentage of the market value in each category rather than the number of companies shown in Table 5.5.

- Table 5.7 shows the average daily volume of the indexes. This table, along with Table 5.8, focuses on liquidity, which may be of special interest to index funds.

- Table 5.8 provides the daily turnover of the indexes. This measure shows the average daily volume as a percent of the shares outstanding.

- In Table 5.9, we look at the annual returns of the indexes from 1980 through 1991. We provide annualized averages for the trailing ten-year period and the standard deviation of the returns.

(Tables appear at the end of this chapter)

WHAT INDEXES ARE AVAILABLE TO MEASURE SMALL CAP PERFORMANCE?

Two of the most popular, and most often referred to, are the Nasdaq Composite and the Value Line Composite, although we will argue later that these may not be the most appropriate. Frank Russell Company provides the Russell 2000 and the Russell 2500. Wilshire Associates offers the Wilshire 4500, the Next 1750, and introduced the Wilshire Small Cap index in 1992. In addition, the University of Chicago Center for Research in Security Prices (popularly known as CRSP), has created the CRSP 6-8, CRSP 6-10, and CRSP 9-10; and Prudential Securities provides the Nasdaq 101+, Nasdaq 201+, and our own Small Cap Universe.

HAVE ANY BEEN EXCLUDED?

To the best of our knowledge, this is the extent of the true indexes with data readily available to the public. By this we mean a list of stocks that is priced daily, monthly, or quarterly and also has returns calculated based on the price changes over the period. Lipper Analytical Services does publish performance on the mutual funds that constitute its Small Company Growth category. The total-return figures represent the average change in the net asset value (with reinvested dividends and capital gains) for the funds in the group.

HOW ARE THE INDEXES DEFINED?

The **Value Line Composite** is based on the stocks in the Value Line Investment Survey.

The **Nasdaq Composite** contains all NASDAQ National Market System issues, including a few warrants, preferreds, and ADRs, as well as all domestic common stocks traded in the regular NASDAQ market. This amounts to just over 4,000 names.

The **Nasdaq 101+** is designed to factor out the impact of the Nasdaq 100 on the Nasdaq Composite. The Nasdaq Composite, like most indexes, is market-cap weighted, which tends to skew performance toward the larger stocks. The Nasdaq 100 comprises the 100 largest industrial stocks traded on the Nasdaq NMS system; while representing only 2% of the names, it is over 35% of the total market value.

The **Nasdaq 201+** starts with the Nasdaq 101+ and removes the 100 largest financial stocks. The result is an almost "pure" small cap Nasdaq benchmark that doesn't have the heavy financial weighting found in the Nasdaq 101+.

The **Russell 2000** represents the bottom two-thirds of the largest 3,000 publicly traded companies domiciled in the United States. Only common stocks are included in the index; in the case of multiple classes of stock, generally only one is allowed. Russell recently dropped its Compustat rule (companies were allowed into the index only if they had two years of data available), which had the effect of significantly raising the financial services weighting.

The **Russell 2500** represents the largest 3,000 publicly traded companies domiciled in the United States, less the largest 500 companies—not less the S&P Composite. The remaining criteria are the same as those for the Russell 2000.

The **Wilshire Next 1750** is derived by taking the top half of the Wilshire 5000 and breaking it into the largest 750 companies and the remaining 1,750. The companies must have fundamental data available through Compustat, but Wilshire uses an expanded universe that enables it to pick up more financial service stocks. Companies must also have two or more years of data available.

The **Wilshire 4500** is a subset of the Wilshire 5000 that contains all U.S. common equities, including ADRs, traded on the three major exchanges. The 4500 excludes the companies in the S&P Composite and is a misnomer because the index contains well over 5,300 companies.

The **Wilshire Small Cap Index** contains 250 companies screened out of the Wilshire Next 1750 for their size, sector, and trading characteristics and is designed to track the performance of small cap stocks. The average market value is higher than the Russell 2000 or the Next 1750, but more in line with typical institutional small cap portfolios.

The **CRSP** indexes are composed of nearly all U.S. common stocks traded on NYSE, AMEX, and NASDAQ NMS within a given market-cap range. The size cutoffs are determined by ranking all NYSE stocks by market cap, forming deciles, and then adding the issues that fit the size ranges from the other exchanges. The CRSP 6-8 represents the sixth through eighth deciles, the 6-10 is the bottom half of the universe, and the 9-10 the bottom 20% of the companies.

The **Prudential Securities Small Cap Universe** is derived by screening the Compustat universe for companies between $40 million and $600 million in market value and with more than two years of fundamental data, with no earnings losses in the most recent two years. In addition, companies must have three or more analysts in the I/B/E/S consensus estimate to be included.

WHICH INDEXES ARE MOST APPROPRIATE FOR MEASURING SMALL CAP PERFORMANCE?

We recommend the Russell 2000, the Wilshire Next 1750 or Wilshire Small Cap, and the CRSP 6-8 as the indexes that would best measure the performance of small cap stocks. Each of these indexes has over 99% of the companies under $750 million in market cap, with similar exchange and sector distributions. Of the three, the Russell 2000 has the lowest mean and median market cap, but all have a narrow range between the mean and median. This tells us the companies are well dispersed in terms of size; there is not an undue concentration in just a few of the larger companies. This is important when returns are market-cap weighted, because a few large names can significantly influence overall returns.

What About the Nasdaq Composite and the Wilshire 4500?

The Nasdaq Composite and the Wilshire 4500, while containing a hefty percentage of very small stocks, also contain enough stocks with market caps over $750 million that their returns are heavily influenced by the larger issues. The largest 100 companies in the Nasdaq Composite represent 42.4% of the index's total capitalization, while that figure is 32.3% for the Wilshire 4500. The weighted average market value for these indexes is $2.3 billion and $2.1 billion, respectively. This is a far cry from what most investors would consider small cap. We feel that these two indexes more appropriately measure performance of the recently dubbed "mid cap" segment of the market.

WHAT MAKES THE VALUE LINE INDEXES INAPPROPRIATE FOR MEASURING SMALL CAP PERFORMANCE?

Over 68% of the stocks in the Value Line Indexes trade on the NYSE, whereas only 26.4% are Nasdaq. This distribution is grossly out of line with all of the other multi-exchange small cap indexes and almost the inverse of the Wilshire 4500. In addition, the universe's exposure to utilities (10.4%) and basic industry (17.9%) is much closer to that of the S&P Composite than to any of the small cap indexes on our list. Because of these differences, the universe contains a lot more large cap companies than it does small cap issues. Even though the geometric and arithmetic indexes are equal-weighted (based on the unweighted average price change of the stocks) such that large caps are treated the same as small caps, the returns end up reflecting the changes in many more large cap stocks. As a measure of the overall direction of the market, these indexes are probably fine.

WHAT ARE THE MAJOR DIFFERENCES BETWEEN THE SMALL CAP SECTOR AND THE LARGE CAPS?

Aside from the obvious average market value differences between the two sectors of the market, there are others that significantly affect index performance. The small cap sector is more heavily concentrated in companies that trade on Nasdaq as opposed to the NYSE. In the Next 1750, 57.4% of the companies are listed on Nasdaq versus 34.1% on the NYSE; for the S&P those numbers are 7.0% and 91.6%, respectively. In addition, the small caps are more heavily weighted toward financial services (22.7% of the Russell 2000), consumer services (14.4%), and technology (12.7%). For the S&P, the heaviest sectors are consumer staples (13.8%), energy (11.5%), and basic industry (11.0). The utility sector is another area where there are many more large companies than small. These sector-weighting differences can significantly impact performance and should be kept in mind when comparing short-term index returns.

WHO WOULD FIND THE NASDAQ 101+ AND THE NASDAQ 201+ USEFUL?

The Nasdaq 101+ and the Nasdaq 201+ provide benchmarks for investors whose sole focus is the small cap over-the-counter market. These indexes are a better measure of the performance of these stocks than the Nasdaq

Composite because the largest stocks are removed from the returns. The 101+ has the largest 100 industrials, representing over 35% of the total market value of the Composite, removed from the returns, and the 201+ has both the 100 largest industrials and the 100 largest financials removed.

WHAT'S THE DIFFERENCE BETWEEN THE VALUE LINE GEOMETRIC INDEX AND THE ARITHMETIC INDEX?

The universes of stocks are the same; it's the index calculation method that differs. A geometric mean tends to be lower than an arithmetic mean and is not so highly influenced by extreme values. The arithmetic average is simply the sum of the percent changes divided by the number of companies in the universe. The geometric mean is the nth root (n being the number of companies in the universe) of the product of the percent changes.

ARE MORE THAN ONE SET OF RETURNS AVAILABLE FOR THE RUSSELL INDEXES?

Yes. The newspapers carry returns that are calculated off the daily indexes provided by a popular pricing service; Frank Russell Company produces its own returns at month-end. The daily index returns are price-only and tend to be close to Frank Russell Company's price-only numbers, but they will vary from the total-return numbers that get published in Russell's quarterly notebooks.

Why Do the Shares Outstanding That Russell Uses Differ from What's in the Stock Guide?

Frank Russell Company's philosophy is that its indexes should represent the investible universe available to buyers and sellers of securities. To this end, the company makes adjustments for cross-ownership both public and, starting this year, private. For example, if Company A owns 10% of Company B's shares, and its president owns another 30%, Russell will use the remaining 60% of the shares outstanding in its index calculation. This affects roughly half of the companies in the Russell 2500, with about 25% of the companies losing 30% or more of their shares to the adjustment process.

AREN'T THE DFA:US 9-10 SMALL STOCK FUND AND THE CRSP 9-10 THE SAME?

If the DFA fund invested in every name that fell in the ninth- and tenth-decile size range, then the two would be the same. However, because of screening constraints, DFA ends up owning about 90% of the stocks. As a result, there will be some differences in the returns that the two indexes produce. DFA will look at the companies that fit the market-cap size range, have been public for at least three years, do not issue multiple classes of stock, and have four market makers. It also excludes REITs, limited partnerships, and investment companies.

ADDENDUM: THE FUNDAMENTAL DATA

All fundamental data were taken from Compustat via Factset as of June 30, 1992. We used latest-12-months earnings per share—excluding extraordinary items and discontinued operations, sales, and net income, as well as most recent quarterly debt, preferred stock, and common equity. When data were not available for the most recent quarter, the most recent yearly data were used. Compustat coverage was limited for the larger indexes due to relatively few small financial stocks available through Compustat—we had a 75% hit ratio for Nasdaq, 90% for Russell and Wilshire, 85% for the CRSP 9-10, and 95% for CRSP 6-8.

Outliers. For some indexes, fundamental data had to be adjusted for outliers. We felt that including a company with a price-to-sales or a P/E ratio of 20,000 times was unrealistic and therefore it was excluded. In most cases if data were above 1000 or below –1000, it was excluded. In no instance was more than 1% of the data excluded as an outlier.

On Average . . .

There is a lively debate as to which type of average—arithmetic, harmonic, median, etc.—is the best measure for a characteristic. Each average highlights different characteristics in a series of data. *Average* and *mean* are terms that can be used interchangeably.

Arithmetic means. An arithmetic mean or simple average is the sum of the fundamental characteristics for each company divided by the number of companies. Negative numbers have the effect of lowering the average. However, for many fundamental characteristics, this is not desirable.

Negative earnings in a P/E ratio would lower the arithmetic P/E, in effect making a more desirable P/E when in fact the negatives are not good.

Medians. The median is the point exactly in the middle of all of the data points. Exactly 50% of the data are above the median and exactly 50% of the data are below. The median may also be misrepresentative. Although the number of data points on either side of the median is the same, the distance of the data points from the median could be different. When the arithmetic mean is different from the median, it shows that the values on one particular side of the median have a greater effect than those on the other side of the median.

Weighted average. The weighted average is derived by summing the product of the fundamental characteristic and the market cap weight. Negative figures have the same effect on a weighted average as they do on the arithmetic average.

Harmonic average. Negative numbers have the effect of actually increasing a harmonic average. It is usually considered a better average for P/E ratios and anything that is a something per something. However, a harmonic average is not easy to calculate, and we have found literature on the subject conflicting and often incomplete. The easiest way to calculate a harmonic average for P/E, for example, is to divide the average price by the average earnings.

One of the drawbacks of the harmonic average is the unusually high P/E that is sometimes derived when negative earnings are included. Occasionally, a large number of companies reporting negative earnings has led indexes to report a harmonic average P/E of over 100 times. The meaningfulness of such a high P/E is uncertain.

Table 5.1—Descriptive Characteristics of Small Cap Benchmarks

	S&P 500	Value Line	Nasdaq Composite	Nasdaq 101+	Nasdaq 201+	Russell 2000	Russell 2500
Number of Companies	500	1,673	4,000	3,894	3,787	2,000	2,500
First Full Year of Return	1920	Geom. 1968 Arith. 1988	1971	1985	1991	1979	1979
Index Rebalancing	As Needed	As Needed	Daily If Needed	Daily If Needed	Daily If Needed	Annually	Annually
Weighting Method	Market Cap	Equal	Market Cap	Market Cap	Market Cap	Market Cap	Market Cap
Returns Calculation	Principal with Income	Principal Only	Principal Only	Principal Only	Principal Only	Principal with Income	Principal with Income
Exchange Distribution Nasdaq NYSE AMEX	7.0% 91.6 1.4	26.4% 68.3 5.3	100.0% — —	100.0% — —	100.0% — —	61.5% 27.5 11.0	55.2% 35.2 9.6
Total Capitalization	$2.8 Tril	$2.6 Tril	$504.8 Bil	$326.5 Bil	$251.8 Bil	$232.4 Bil	$555.3 Bil
Average Size Wtd. Mean Mean Median	$21.2 Bil 5.6 Bil 2.6 Bil	NM $2.6 Bil 686.9 Mil	$2.3 Bil 126.2 Mil 28.5 Mil	$513.8 Mil 83.9 Mil 28.5 Mil	$291.3 Mil 66.5 Mil 25.6 Mil	$194.4 Mil 116.2 Mil 85.3 Mil	$532.0 Mil 222.1 Mil 111.8 Mil
Size Range Largest Smallest	$76.9 Bil 26.0 Mil	$76.8 Bil < 1.0 Mil	$18.9 Bil < 1.0 Mil	$3.4 Bil < 1.0 Mil	$3.3 Bil < 1.0 Mil	$531.3 Mil 3.5 Mil	$1.4 Bil 3.5 Mil
Concentration Largest 10 50 100 Companies	20.6% 34.6 49.1	13.6% 35.4 49.9	15.7% 32.6 42.4	7.7% 19.7 29.1	5.1% 14.8 23.2	2.0% 9.2 17.0	2.4% 10.6 19.3

Note: Data as of June 30, 1992.

Source: Prudential Securities, Inc.

Table 5.1 Continued

Wilshire Next 1750	Wilshire Small Cap	Wilshire 4500	CRSP 6–8	CRSP 9–10	CRSP 6–10	PSI Small Cap	
1,750	250	5,394	1,180	2,619	3,799	1,143	Number of Companies
1978	1980	1975	1982	1982	1982	1987	First Full Year of Return
Annually	Annually	As Needed	Quarterly	Quarterly	Quarterly	Quarterly	Index Rebalancing
Market Cap	Market Cap	Market Cap	Market Cap	Market Cap	Market Cap	Equal & Market Cap	Weighting Method
With Income	Principal with Income	Principal with Income	With Income	With Income	With Income	Principal Only	Returns Calculation
57.4% 34.1 8.7	39.6% 55.2 5.3	70.2% 18.2 11.6	52.5% 37.6 9.8	69.2% 11.2 19.7	62.9% 19.0 18.1	56.3% 34.4 9.3	Exchange Distribution Nasdaq NYSE AMEX
$415.7 Bil	$104.0 Bil	$1.1 Tril	$272.5 Bil	$97.6 Bil	$256.2 Bil	$237.0 Bil	Total Capitalization
$356.0 Mil 237.5 Mil 171.6 Mil	$480.2 Mil 416.1 Mil 404.4 Mil	$2.1 Bil 206.6 Mil 41.1 Mil	$291.2 Mil 231.0 Mil 200.0 Mil	$59.7 Mil 37.3 Mil 29.3 Mil	$230.2 Mil 97.4 Mil 52.7 Mil	$383.7 Mil 210.2 Mil 142.2 Mil	Average Size Wtd. Mean Mean Median
$759.6 Mil 68.9 Mil	$725.8 Mil 81.1 Mil	$18.7 Bil < 1.0 Mil	$704.0 Mil 19.8 Mil	$149.1 Mil < 1.0 Mil	$704.0 Mil < 1.0 Mil	$1.1 Bil 6.9 Mil	Size Range Largest Smallest
1.8% 8.3 15.9	6.9% 31.6 56.1	8.4% 22.1 32.3	2.2% 9.6 17.9	1.4% 6.0 11.3	1.6% 7.1 13.2	3.8% 8.7 15.8	Concentration Largest 10 50 100 Companies

Table 5.2—Fundamental Characteristics of Small Cap Benchmarks

	S&P Composite	Value Line	Nasdaq Composite	Nasdaq 101+	Nasdaq 201+	Russell 2000	Russell 2500	Wilshire Next 1750	Wilshire Small Cap	Wilshire 4500	CRSP 6-8	CRSP 9-10	CRSP 6-10	PSI Small Cap
LTM P/E														
Mean	12.1	13.5	10.2	10.0	9.9	13.8	13.8	13.5	8.7	10.4	14.1	10.8	11.9	17.4
Median	15.5	14.8	10.8	10.5	10.3	13.8	14.2	14.5	14.5	10.8	14.6	8.9	11.5	15.2
Weighted	16.6	16.3	12.7	7.9	5.9	13.4	14.2	12.1	8.2	15.5	13.6	9.8	12.6	18.4
Harmonic	25.8	26.2	113.7	127.3	488.5	35.3	28.8	31.1	20.1	65.2	28.3	N/M	108.5	28.9
-W/O Neg. Earnings														
Mean	28.5	26.9	14.5	29.9	31.3	30.7	29.7	30.6	20.8	30.0	18.1	30.4	30.4	20.6
Median	17.5	16.9	17.5	16.9	17.5	17.0	17.0	17.3	16.3	16.8	17.2	15.8	16.4	17.0
Weighted	22.6	21.3	10.2	12.5	10.5	21.2	22.7	20.7	17.0	21.2	12.4	16.1	20.4	21.4
Harmonic	16.1	17.7	16.1	15.7	16.2	15.6	15.6	16.1	14.6	17.0	16.1	14.1	15.2	15.6
Price to Book														
Mean	2.6	2.2	4.2	4.2	4.3	2.5	2.4	3.7	2.5	3.2	2.8	2.3	2.6	2.0
Median	1.8	1.7	1.7	1.7	1.7	1.4	1.4	1.9	1.7	1.6	1.7	1.1	1.3	1.6
Weighted	3.4	3.1	3.7	2.0	1.8	2.4	2.1	3.5	2.6	2.4	2.6	2.1	2.7	2.6
Price to Sales														
Mean	1.1	1.3	8.5	8.7	8.9	3.7	3.2	4.5	4.8	6.2	3.9	3.6	3.2	1.3
Median	0.8	0.8	0.9	0.9	0.9	0.6	0.7	0.9	0.8	0.8	0.9	0.5	0.6	0.7
Weighted	1.5	1.7	5.2	3.7	3.5	3.4	2.4	3.4	3.7	3.1	3.1	3.8	3.0	1.5
Debt to Capital														
Mean	36.7	34.1	23.0	23.2	23.4	26.9	28.5	27.5	26.7	29.1	27.5	29.4	30.2	25.1
Median	35.3	33.4	11.1	11.4	11.4	19.5	21.5	20.3	20.8	17.7	20.6	17.9	19.2	19.5
Weighted	33.8	31.2	18.6	11.2	9.1	25.3	29.1	26.9	27.0	29.3	25.5	21.9	25.0	24.9
Return on Equity														
Mean	10.5	9.5	-1.1	-1.7	-2.0	5.9	7.6	6.6	12.0	-1.0	8.1	-1.8	1.5	9.3
Median	11.3	10.1	0.0	0.0	0.0	7.5	9.1	9.1	11.0	1.2	9.4	0.3	3.0	10.5
Weighted	16.1	14.0	13.7	5.8	4.0	7.8	11.3	9.3	13.0	12.9	10.4	2.4	8.3	15.1
Yield														
Number of Companies	435	1,167	561	508	445	669	1,018	682	155	1,232	484	407	890	513
Mean	2.7	2.3	0.6	0.5	0.5	1.2	1.4	1.3	1.8	0.8	1.4	1.2	1.0	1.2

Note: Data as of June 30, 1992.

Source: Prudential Securities, Inc.

Table 5.3—Macroeconomic Sector Breakdown—Percentage of Companies

	S&P Composite	Value Line	Nasdaq Composite	Nasdaq 101+	Nasdaq 201+	Russell 2000	Russell 2500	Wilshire Next 1750	Wilshire Small Cap	Wilshire 4500	CRSP 6-8	CRSP 9-10	CRSP 6-10	PSI Small Cap
Basic Industry	18.4%	17.9%	9.5%	9.2%	9.5%	10.6%	11.5%	11.5%	11.2%	12.1%	11.0%	10.2%	10.4%	12.4%
Business Services	4.2	4.4	4.4	4.3	4.4	4.0	4.1	4.3	6.0	4.3	4.5	3.7	4.0	6.2
Capital Spending	6.0	7.0	6.6	6.7	6.9	7.2	6.9	6.2	6.8	7.1	5.5	8.8	7.7	6.4
Conglomerates	1.2	0.1	—	—	—	—	—	—	—	—	—	—	—	0.3
Consumer Cyclical	6.4	5.4	3.6	3.6	3.7	4.0	4.1	4.2	6.0	4.3	4.6	5.4	5.2	5.0
Consumer Services	14.6	15.3	13.9	13.8	14.2	15.4	15.1	15.5	16.0	14.9	16.9	15.0	15.6	16.7
Consumer Staples	6.8	5.2	3.0	2.9	3.0	2.9	3.1	3.3	4.0	3.3	3.5	2.6	2.9	3.0
Energy	8.4	5.6	3.2	3.3	3.4	3.6	3.7	4.0	4.4	4.6	4.5	3.8	4.2	4.9
Financial Services	11.6	14.7	25.2	25.8	23.8	21.3	20.8	18.9	14.0	20.7	18.1	23.5	21.8	10.0
Health Care	5.8	5.4	13.4	13.4	13.7	13.8	12.4	14.0	10.0	11.7	13.0	10.7	11.4	9.1
Technology	10.2	8.6	15.2	14.9	15.3	13.4	12.8	12.8	15.2	13.1	13.4	14.2	13.9	22.8
Utilities	6.4	10.4	2.2	2.1	2.1	4.0	5.5	5.2	6.4	3.9	5.0	2.1	3.0	3.2

Note: Data as of June 30, 1992.
Source: Prudential Securities, Inc.

Table 5.4—Macroeconomic Sector Breakdown—Market-Cap Weighted

	S&P Composite	Value Line	Nasdaq Composite	Nasdaq 101+	Nasdaq 201+	Russell 2000	Russell 2500	Wilshire Next 1750	Wilshire Small Cap	Wilshire 4500	CRSP 6-8	CRSP 9-10	CRSP 6-10	PSI Small Cap
Basic Industry	11.0%	12.7%	8.9%	7.6%	9.8%	11.0%	13.3%	12.9%	10.7%	13.3%	12.0%	10.0%	11.4%	11.4%
Business Services	4.6	2.5	2.9	3.7	4.8	3.7	4.0	5.1	6.6	4.0	5.2	3.8	4.8	6.1
Capital Spending	5.6	4.8	3.8	5.3	6.9	6.7	6.1	6.2	6.6	3.9	5.5	8.5	6.4	5.1
Conglomerates	0.6	0.1	—	—	—	—	—	—	—	0.2	—	—	—	0.4
Consumer Cyclical	3.7	4.2	2.1	2.3	3.0	4.0	3.8	4.8	6.1	2.5	4.6	4.5	4.6	5.7
Consumer Services	10.8	11.0	14.1	11.3	14.5	14.4	12.7	16.1	15.7	12.9	16.2	14.8	15.9	16.6
Consumer Staples	13.8	11.5	3.1	2.4	3.1	2.4	3.3	3.5	4.8	4.1	3.3	2.5	3.1	3.2
Energy	11.5	9.7	0.9	1.4	1.8	4.1	3.9	4.0	3.9	4.7	5.0	3.7	4.7	4.6
Financial Services	9.9	9.5	24.7	36.9	18.5	22.7	21.8	17.7	16.5	21.6	18.5	22.8	19.6	15.7
Health Care	10.5	13.1	12.6	12.6	16.2	12.3	9.4	10.9	8.9	9.5	10.6	13.0	11.2	7.9
Technology	7.6	7.2	21.4	13.8	17.9	12.7	11.4	12.0	12.8	9.9	13.2	13.7	13.3	18.3
Utilities	10.4	13.7	5.5	2.7	3.5	6.0	10.3	6.8	7.4	13.4	5.9	2.7	5.0	5.0

Note: Data as of June 30, 1992.
Source: Prudential Securities, Inc.

Table 5.5—Size Distribution of Small Cap Benchmarks—Percentage of Companies

	S&P Composite	Value Line	Nasdaq Composite	Nasdaq 101+	Nasdaq 201+	Russell 2000	Russell 2500	Wilshire Next 1750	Wilshire Small Cap	Wilshire 4500	CRSP 6-8	CRSP 6-10	CRSP 9-10	P-B Small Cap
Large $3.0B & Over	44.2%	18.9%	0.3%	0.1%	–	–	–	–	–	0.8%	–	–	–	–
Medium–Large $1.5B-$3.0B	24.2	13.4	0.8	0.3	–	–	–	–	–	1.8	–	–	–	–
Medium $750M-$1.5B	17.4	14.9	1.6	0.9	0.3%	–	6.8%	0.1%	–	3.8	–	–	–	1.7%
Medium–Small $250M-$750M	11.4	24.3	7.2	6.5	5.3	10.6%	20.2	35.0	83.2%	11.2	35.2%	11.0%	–	29.0
Small $100M-$250M	1.6	16.6	12.9	13.0	13.1	32.1	26.8	43.7	14.8	14.6	58.6	20.5	3.3%	32.1
Very Small Less Than $100M	1.2	11.9	77.2	79.2	81.3	57.3	46.2	21.2	2.0	67.8	6.2	68.5	96.7	37.2

Note: All data as of June 30, 1992.

Source: Prudential Securities, Inc.

Table 5.6—Size Distribution of Small Cap Benchmarks—Market-Cap Weighted

	S&P Composite	Value Line	Nasdaq Composite	Nasdaq 101+	Nasdaq 201+	Russell 2000	Russell 2500	Wilshire Next 1750	Wilshire Small Cap	Wilshire 4500	CRSP 6-8	CRSP 6-10	CRSP 9-10	PSI Small Cap
Large $3.0B & Over	85.8%	75.1%	17.6%	2.0%	1.3%	–	–	–	–	20.0%	–	–	–	–
Medium–Large $1.5B–$3.0B	9.6	12.0	13.2	7.3	0.7	–	–	–	–	18.0	–	–	–	–
Medium $750M–$1.5B	3.5	6.6	13.4	10.3	4.0	–	30.0%	0.2%	–	18.4	–	–	–	7.2%
Medium–Small $250M–$750M	1.1	4.9	23.4	30.9	30.8	30.6%	39.9	63.4	92.6%	23.4	55.9%	41.1%	–	58.7
Small $100M–$250M	0.0	1.2	15.9	24.1	30.4	42.9	18.9	29.0	7.0	11.2	42.0	33.6	9.8%	24.7
Very Small Less Than $100M	0.0	0.3	16.5	25.4	32.8	26.5	11.2	7.4	0.4	9.2	2.1	25.3	90.2	9.4

Note: All data as of June 30, 1992.
Source: Prudential Securities, Inc.

Table 5.7—Average Daily Volume of Small Cap Indexes

Average Daily Volume in Thousand Shares

Size Category	S&P Composite	Value Line	Nasdaq Composite	Nasdaq 101+	Nasdaq 201+	Russell 2000	Russell 2500	Wilshire Next 1750	Wilshire Small Cap	Wilshire 4500	CRSP 6-10	CRSP 6-8	CRSP 9-10	PSI Small Cap
Very Large	872.0	729.6	2,225.7*	–	–	–	–	–	–	749.3	–	–	–	–
Large	398.3	347.4	993.3	226.9	276.3	–	–	–	–	296.0	–	–	–	–
Medium–Large	253.3	206.8	374.3	187.8	217.0	–	–	–	–	170.6	–	–	–	–
Medium	220.1	170.7	240.5	134.7	236.4	–	174.1	–	–	149.2	110.8	110.8	–	145.3
Small–Medium	144.5	104.5	133.3	119.4	135.1	92.6	111.8	99.6	115.4	95.2	79.3	79.3	–	100.9
Small	135.3	53.2	73.5	72.7	72.6	72.3	72.4	65.0	171.6	63.2	65.8	68.4	23.7	61.4
Very Small	31.4	29.2	23.3	23.1	23.1	39.4	39.6	49.4	119.0	21.9	26.0	68.0	39.1	34.7
Index Average	358.9	179.6	48.8	38.0	36.9	55.5	72.1	73.7	123.9	46.1	39.0	72.0	24.1	64.1

* Only two companies in calculation.

Source: Prudential Securities, Inc.

Table 5.8—Daily Turnover of Small Cap Indexes

Size Category	S&P Composite	Value Line	Nasdaq Composite	Nasdaq 101+	Nasdaq 201+	Russell 2000	Russell 2500	Wilshire Next 1750	Wilshire Small Cap	Wilshire 4500	CRSP 6-10	CRSP 6-8	CRSP 9-10	PSI Small Cap
						Daily Turnover								
Very Large	0.22%	0.18%	0.95%*	–	–	–	–	–	–	0.28%	–	–	–	–
Large	0.29	0.24	0.74	0.41%	0.54%	–	–	–	–	0.22	–	–	–	–
Medium–Large	0.34	0.28	0.56	0.29	0.09	–	–	–	–	0.25	–	–	–	–
Medium	0.40	0.38	0.75	0.49	0.82	–	0.47%	–	–	0.41	0.70%	0.70%	–	0.53%
Small–Medium	0.38	0.39	0.65	0.63	0.72	0.50%	0.52	0.44%	0.47%	0.43	0.45	0.45	–	0.47
Small	0.44	0.35	0.58	0.58	0.58	0.57	0.58	0.47	0.85	0.46	0.52	0.53	0.38%	0.48
Very Small	0.29	0.29	0.38	0.38	0.38	0.66	0.67	0.53	0.72	0.33	0.46	0.77	0.44	0.45
Index Average	0.32	0.32	0.43	0.42	0.43	0.61	0.60	0.47	0.53	0.36	0.47	0.53	0.44	0.46

* Only two companies in calculation.
Source: Prudential Securities, Inc.

Table 5.9—Annual Returns of Small Cap Benchmarks

	S&P Composite	Value Line Arithmetic	Value Line Geometric	Nasdaq Composite	Nasdaq 101+	Nasdaq 201+	Russell 2000	Russell 2500	Wilshire Next 1750	Wilshire Small Cap	Wilshire 4500	CRSP 6-8	CRSP 6-10	CRSP 9-10	PSI Small Cap
1980	32.4%	–	18.3%	33.9%	–	–	38.6%	36.3%	34.0%	–	35.2%	–	–	–	–
1981	-5.2	–	-4.4	-3.2	–	–	2.0	1.8	3.6	4.0%	-1.5	–	–	–	–
1982	21.2	–	15.3	18.7	–	–	25.0	25.9	27.8	29.7	13.6	25.6%	25.2%	24.3%	–
1983	22.5	–	22.3	19.9	–	–	29.1	27.7	29.6	30.3	25.5	28.7	30.4	33.7	–
1984	6.1	–	-8.4	-11.2	–	–	-7.3	-4.6	-1.8	-0.0	-1.7	-0.9	-4.9	-11.5	–
1985	32.0	–	20.7	31.4	20.4%	–	31.1	31.2	33.1	32.9	32.0	32.2	30.1	26.1	–
1986	18.5	–	5.0	7.4	7.5	–	5.7	0.1	11.0	10.0	11.8	8.4	6.7	3.4	–
1987	5.2	–	-10.6	-5.3	-9.4	–	-8.8	-4.7	-5.0	-3.3	-3.5	-6.4	-9.1	-14.1	-13.1%
1988	16.8	6.3%	15.4	15.4	16.0	–	24.9	22.7	22.6	21.4	20.5	23.4	22.4	19.9	23.5
1989	31.5	18.2	11.2	19.3	16.5	–	16.2	19.4	18.6	20.5	24.0	19.1	15.9	8.2	13.1
1990	-3.2	-16.8	-24.3	-17.8	-21.2	–	-19.5	-14.9	-18.5	-15.1	-13.6	-18.1	-20.8	-28.0	-20.9
1991	30.5	38.8	27.2	56.8	52.6	51.8%	46.1	46.7	45.8	51.8	43.5	47.5	48.2	51.6	49.7
1992	7.7	15.1	7.0	15.5	19.2	16.1	18.4	16.2	18.7	14.6	11.9	18.8	21.2	26.0	15.2
Ten-Year Annualized Average	16.1%	–	5.3%	11.3%	–	–	11.8%	12.5%	13.9%	14.8%	13.8%	13.7%	12.2%	9.0%	–
Standard Deviation	11.8	–	15.6	20.6	–	–	19.6	18.4	18.4	18.6	16.7	18.7	19.9	23.3	–

Source: Prudential Securities, Inc.

Chapter 6

Small Cap Indices without Tears

Ronald N. Kahn, Ph.D.
Director of Research
BARRA

INTRODUCTION

Indices play an important role in portfolio management. Beyond measuring economic growth, they can also serve as manager performance benchmarks and can be used to define manager style. But turnover can reduce some indices' suitability as benchmarks. This is particularly true for small capitalization stock indices, which are prone to high turnover. Why do small capitalization stock indices experience high turnover, and is there an approach that will reduce this turnover while preserving the indices' investment character?

INDICES

An index functions as a performance benchmark by representing the achievable return to informationless investing. The index is simply a portfolio of stocks, chosen according to simple, prespecified rules, and designed to capture a particular investment style. The investment manager adds value by using his information to beat the benchmark whose style matches his. Unfortunately, if, by its simple definition, the benchmark is characterized by high turnover, then transaction costs will make the benchmark return unattainable by passive replication. A manager who simply achieves the benchmark return is already adding value in this case.

TURNOVER

Small capitalization stock indices often exhibit high turnover. The problem is simple. Consider an index consisting of the 1,000th to 3,000th largest-capitalization stocks, weighted by capitalization. This simple inclusion and weighting rule should lead to an index appropriate for small capitalization stock investors. Let's just call this the BARRA 2000 for simplicity. This index roughly corresponds to the Frank Russell 2000, ignoring rules governing bank stock holdings, and other specific rules.[1] Its turnover, based on annual rebalancing, was 21.9% per year, on average, over the 1980s. As values fluctuate, the 1,000th largest stock may move up in ranking to 995, and then down to 1,010. So the largest component of the index may regularly move in and out. Imagine the turnover of the S&P500 if that index randomly excluded IBM in 6 out of 12 months!

To be more precise about this problem, we can investigate the turnover of the BARRA 2000 index in more detail. In particular, the total index turnover is a sum of turnover in the holding of each particular constituent. If $h(n,t_1)$ represents the fractional holding in stock n at time t_1, $h^*(n,t_1,t_2)$ represents the fractional holding at time t_2, assuming a buy and hold strategy between t_1 and t_2, and $h(n,t_2)$ represents the fractional holding in the rebalanced index at time t_2, then we can define the index turnover between t_1 and t_2 as:

$$\text{turnover} = \frac{1}{2} \sum_n | h(n, t_2) - h^*(n, t_1, t_2)|$$

We can represent the index turnover as the sum of contributions from each index constituent.

In Figure 6.1, we plot the contribution to turnover from each index constituent, ranked by capitalization. For graphic clarity, we actually gather the constituents into bins of 50 stocks each, ranked by 1988 capitalization. We then plot contribution to annual turnover between 1988 and 1989 for each of these bins. As Figure 6.1 shows, the major contribution to turnover arises from the largest capitalization stocks in the index. The contribution from stocks ranked below 1,000 in 1988 capitalization arises from those stocks whose 1989 capitalization rank ranged between 1,000 and 3,000. Not shown on the graph is a total turnover contribution of 5.5% from stocks not included in BARRA's 1988 ALLUS universe: mainly new 1989 issues. Overall, for this small capitalization stock index, it is the upper

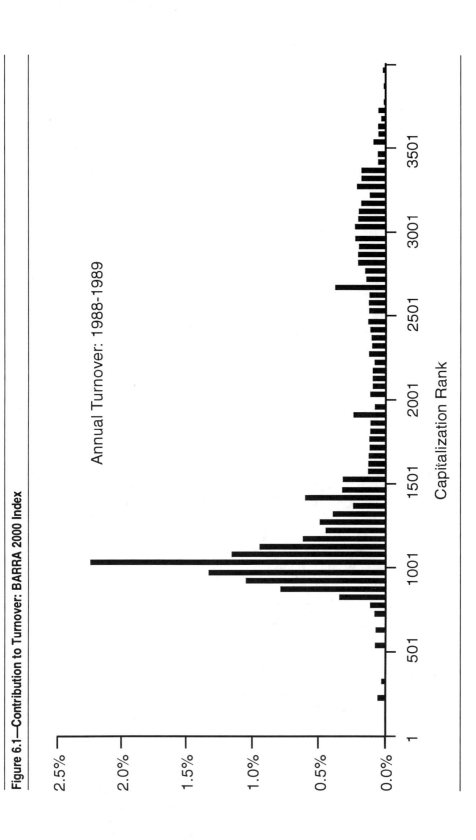

Figure 6.1—Contribution to Turnover: BARRA 2000 Index

Annual Turnover: 1988-1989

Capitalization Rank

capitalization boundary that generates much of the excessively large turn-over.

This is the problem, then. The BARRA 2000 index, as we have defined it, does capture a small cap investment style, but at the price of significant turnover. Can we alter the definition of the index to reduce turnover, while not significantly changing the small cap style of the index?

REDUCING TURNOVER

The above analysis has not only shown the high turnover to the index, it has also pinpointed its origin in the upper capitalization boundary of the index. The largest capitalization stocks in the index face a significant prob-ability of leaving the index before the next rebalancing. Those stocks slightly too large to include in the index face a significant probability of entering the index before the next rebalancing. With this in mind, we can examine various alternative index definitions that try to account for this probability of leaving and entering the index.

The original index definition weighted each stock by its capitalization, so long as the capitalization ranked between 1,000 and 3,000. The new idea is to weight each stock by its capitalization *times the probability that its capi-talization will rank between 1,000 and 3,000 at the time of the next rebalancing.* Assuming annual rebalancing, the 1,000th largest stock would have roughly a 50% probability of ranking between 1,000 and 3,000 in one year's time. The 2,000th largest stock, however, might exhibit close to 100% prob-ability of ranking between 1,000 and 3,000 in one year's time. Also, the 995th largest stock, not in the index at all according to the original mem-bership definition, would exhibit a near 50% probability of ranking be-tween 1,000 and 3,000 in one year's time. So the probability weighting scheme will tend to smooth out the boundaries of the index.

At the same time, simply smoothing the index boundaries according to this probability weighting may change the character of the index. It may now include companies whose capitalizations are traditionally considered large, even though it will underweight such companies relative to their capitalization.

Ultimately, we can treat the specific index weighting as an empirical question. We would like to use this probability weighting approach to smooth the upper capitalization boundary of the index. At the same time we want to keep the original investment character of the index.

SMALL CAP INDICES WITHOUT TEARS

We have empirically investigated indices defined according to the following rules:

1. Include all companies with capitalization rank between 300 and
    3,000.
2. Weight each company by its capitalization times a boundary
    smoothing function:

$$N\left[\frac{\text{rank} - 1047}{\sigma}\right]$$

The function $N[\cdot]$ is the cumulative normal distribution: a probability.
Figure 6.2 plots this index boundary, smoothing function for various
choices of σ. We chose the rank of 1,047 instead of 1,000 based on empirical tests of the observed probability of ranking between 1,000 and 3,000
after one year. We will investigate the behavior of the index for various
choices of σ. We have not attempted to alter the definition of the lower
capitalization boundary of the index, because that boundary definition did
not lead to significant turnover.

So we have investigated the behavior of the index for various choices
of σ. In particular, we have investigated two particular characteristics of
the index. First, what is the index turnover, based on annual rebalancing?
Second, what is the tracking error of the new index, compared to the original index. This tracking error figure should capture the extent to which the
new index preserves the investment character of the original index. Table
6.1 displays our findings.

Table 6.1

Index	Annual Turnover	Tracking Error
BARRA 2000	21.9%	0.00%
s = 300	19.1%	1.53%
s = 367	18.3%	2.11%
s = 400	18.0%	2.37%
s = 500	17.2%	3.06%
s = 600	16.6%	3.26%
BARRA ALLUS	14.8%	11.50%

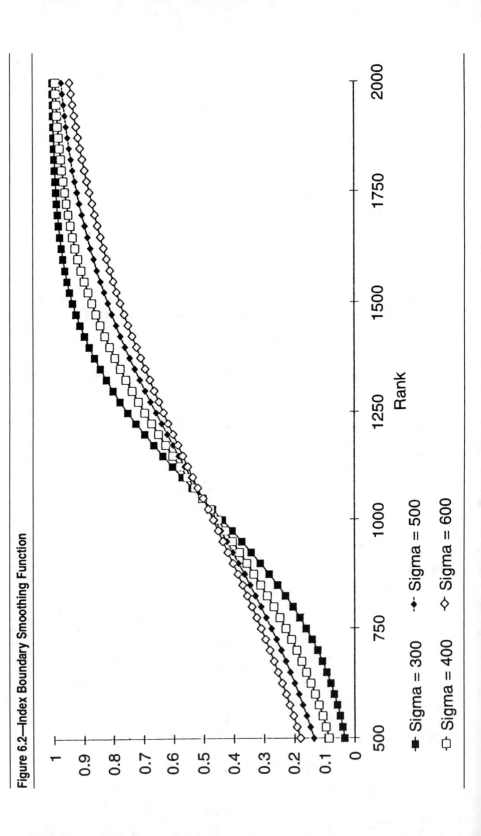

Figure 6.2—Index Boundary Smoothing Function

As the parameter σ increases, further smoothing the upper capitalization boundary of the index, the turnover decreases and tracking error increases. We have also included two other indices in the above table as limiting cases. The BARRA 2000 index has zero tracking error against itself, but 21.9% turnover. It is roughly the $\sigma = 0$ limiting case. The BARRA ALLUS has no upper capitalization boundary, and 14.8% turnover, but a tracking error of 11.5% against the BARRA 2000. It is roughly the $\sigma \Rightarrow \infty$ limiting case.

CONCLUSION

This simple analysis demonstrates one approach to reducing index turnover while retaining the investment character of the index. It is possible to create a lower turnover small cap index: one that tracks the original index, but with reduced turnover. For example, by choosing $\sigma = 367$, we can reduce annual turnover to 18.3%, while tracking the index within 2.11%. This reduction in turnover is significant. It moves the index halfway toward the turnover of the ALLUS index, which effectively represents the maximum reduction in turnover possible with this technical method.[2] Figure 6.3 shows the contribution to annual turnover between 1988 and 1989, from each constituent of this new index, ranked by capitalization and grouped into bins, just as in Figure 6.1. Compared to Figure 6.1, the results in Figure 6.3 show that the contribution to turnover is much more uniformly distributed across capitalization rank.

In general, there is a continuum of trade-offs between turnover and tracking error. More detailed research into this approach, perhaps combined with other approaches to reducing index turnover, may lead to indices that exhibit even lower turnover and track the original index more closely.

ENDNOTES

[1] We focus on this BARRA 2000 index instead of the Frank Russell 2000 index to more simply isolate the effect of the changes we will propose. The general principles discussed here apply to the Frank Russell 2000 as well.

[2] An index like the S&P 500 exhibits much lower turnover than this. However, inclusion in the index is based on more than just capitalization. Additional decision rules help keep member companies in the index, even as their capitalization fluctuates.

Figure 6.3—Contribution to Turnover: Reduced Turnover SMALLCAP Index

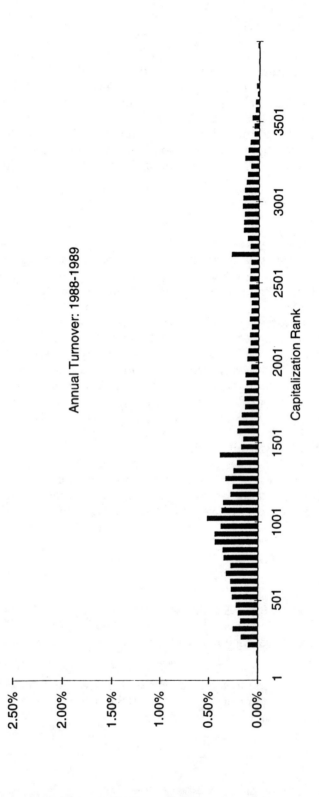

Annual Turnover: 1988-1989

Capitalization Rank

PART THREE: STOCK SELECTION STRATEGIES

Chapter 7

Earnings Surprise Models in Small Cap Investing

Claudia E. Mott
First Vice President and Director of Small Cap Research

Daniel P. Coker
Junior Quantitative Analyst

Prudential Securities Inc.

INTRODUCTION

The introduction of earnings surprise theory dates back to the 1970s, when Henry A. Latané, Charles P. Jones, and Robert D. Rieke coined the term SUE—Standardized Unexpected Earnings.[1]

- Their study found that from 1962 to 1971 companies that reported quarterly earnings above a trendline forecast (positive SUE) exhibited returns greater than the universe average. Conversely, those firms with negative SUEs saw their stocks underperform in subsequent months.

- They also found a strong serial correlation between one quarter's surprise and the subsequent quarter's surprise. Dubbed the "cockroach theory" (like cockroaches, one rarely sees just one surprise), this implied that past quarters' surprises could be used to predict future surprises.

The power of earnings surprise hasn't diminished over the past twenty years, and at Prudential Securities we have found this investment discipline especially useful when applied to the small cap segment of the stock market. This chapter presents performance results from a recent study and offers some thoughts on how to find potential earnings surprises.

Prudential Securities has been running a quarterly earnings surprise model on a small cap universe of stocks since 1988. Although small cap positive surprises tend to be harder to find than negative surprises (see Figure 7.1), the inclusion of this factor has greatly improved the performance of our multifactor model. As a discipline by itself, earnings surprise is also a solid investment tool. Over the 19 quarters of this analysis, positive surprises have consistently outperformed both negative surprises and "no surprises." Negative surprises, on the other hand, have had negative excess returns, with performance deteriorating over time see (Figure 7.2).

Figure 7.1—Small Cap Positive Surprises Are Harder to Find . . .

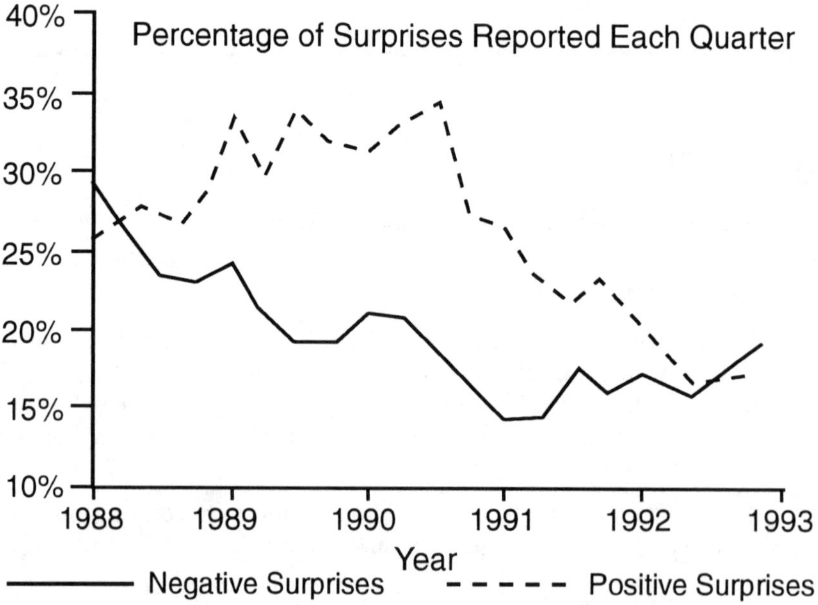

Percentage of Surprises Reported Each Quarter

———— Negative Surprises   - - - - - Positive Surprises

Source: Prudential Securities, Inc.

Figure 7.2—... But Their Outperformance Is Worth It

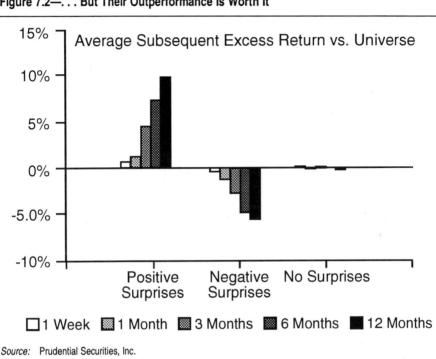

Source: Prudential Securities, Inc.

EARNINGS SURPRISE IS A USEFUL TOOL FOR ALL SMALL CAP INVESTORS

Small cap investors should incorporate an earnings surprise model into any stock selection discipline for several reasons.

- This factor does not play favorites. A technology company is just as likely to announce a positive surprise as a health care company; a financial services company can disappoint just as easily as one in the basic industry sector (see Figure 7.3).

- Stock pickers would be well off avoiding companies that have reported negative surprises, because as performance has shown, more downside comes even after the first week following the report date. Also, the likelihood that another disappointment will be reported in the next quarter is far more probable than the reverse occurring.

Figure 7.3—The Average Percentage of Surprises by Macroeconomic Group

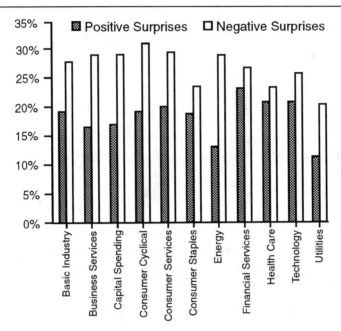

Source: Prudential Securities, Inc.

- Not only can the earnings surprise model be useful in avoiding the purchase of a stock that has disappointed, but actually selling the stocks that have reported negative surprises is likely to enhance portfolio performance.

Obviously, for the bottom-up stock picker, companies on a followed list with reported positive surprises would be more solid purchase candidates.

Many quantitative investors have incorporated an earnings surprise factor in the multifactor valuation models used to drive the stock selection process. No doubt, the experience these investors have had is similar to ours. The earnings surprise factor has had the most consistent performance of any of the nine components of our multifactor model and even the overall composite score itself. Figure 7.4 shows that the rank correlation coefficient between earnings surprise and subsequent 1 month return has been negative in only five months over the past five years. By comparison, the QV Composite, our multifactor valuation model, has had nine months of negative correlations.

Figure 7.4—Earnings Surprise Has Had Better Correlations with Return* . . .

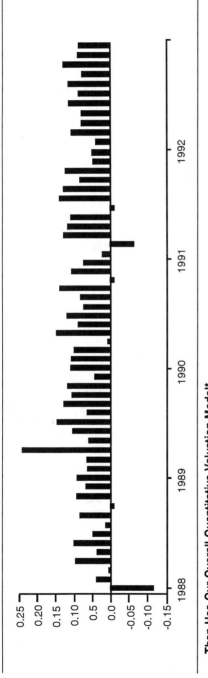

. . . Than Has Our Overall Quantitative Valuation Model*

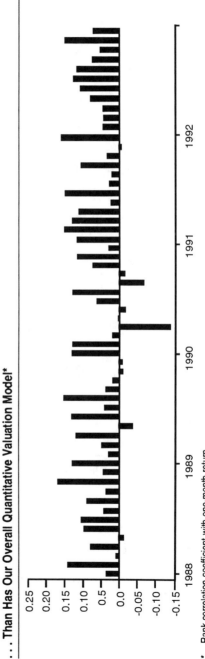

* Rank correlation coefficient with one-month return.

Source: Prudential Securities Inc.

WHAT IS MEANT BY EARNINGS SURPRISE?

The earnings surprise model used at Prudential Securities adheres to the methodology tested by the academics in the 1970s. We calculate a SUE score using the following calculation:

$$SUE = \frac{(Actual\ Quarterly\ Operating\ EPS) - (Consensus\ EPS\ Estimate)}{Standard\ Deviation\ of\ Consensus}$$

The consensus estimate is a blend of the I/B/E/S median forecast and a twenty-quarter seasonally adjusted trendline. These two components are combined based on their variability (inversely). This means that if the standard deviation of I/B/E/S is smaller than the standard error of the trendline, the I/B/E/S forecast will have a heavier weighting in the consensus. Academic studies relied on trendline forecasts, because I/B/E/S forecasts were not available. Although trendline forecasts are often very good predictors of future earnings levels, we feel that the addition of an I/B/E/S forecast may provide more up-to-date market information that a historical trendline cannot incorporate.

A positive surprise is any company that has a SUE score of 1.0 or higher, and a negative surprise has a SUE of –1.0 or lower.

WHAT CONSTITUTES THE DATA SET?

The performance results that will be presented in the remainder of this study are based on a small cap universe that had roughly 640 companies in 1988, growing to 1,100 companies in 1993. In general, these are companies with at least two years of publicly available data and two or more analyst estimates in the consensus estimate. The average market cap for the universe is about $200 million, with few companies exceeding $750 million. The period tested covered 19 quarters from the first quarter of 1988 through the third quarter of 1992. All individual company returns are calculated from the close on the report day through the subsequent ending period, and all averages are arithmetic.

WE ANALYZED EARNINGS SURPRISE FROM MANY ANGLES . . .

We tested the performance of positive, negative, and no surprises by calculating average returns over the subsequent week and month, and 3, 6, and twelve months on an absolute basis and relative to both the overall small cap universe and the Russell 2000. Similar analysis was done at the sector level for the 11 major macroeconomic groups that Prudential Securities divides the world into.

The cockroach theory was tested both for its efficacy and performance by looking at the frequency of companies that repeated their surprise from one quarter to the next and the subsequent stock price performance. In addition, we looked at the frequency of companies that reported surprises in the reverse direction from the previous quarter, another method for testing the cockroach theory. The study also examined the statistical significance of companies reporting three surprises in a row.

Lastly, we tested the performance of surprises by the number of analysts in the I/B/E/S consensus to see whether more information meant fewer surprises or differences in stock price performance.

... AND THE RESULTS WERE IMPRESSIVE

The following were our findings:

- Small cap stocks report fewer positive surprises than negative in any given quarter. An average 19.8% of the companies reported positive surprises over the period, whereas 25.6% of the companies posted earnings disappointments. Over the past five years, the trend has been toward fewer of both types of surprises—i.e., in 1988 closer to 25% positive surprises would be reported in a given quarter, with almost 30% of the universe posting negative surprises.

- Positive surprises consistently beat negative surprises and no surprises on an absolute and relative basis. Positive surprises also outperformed both the universe and the Russell 2000 (the market) in over 90% of the quarters tested after the first week following the report date (we call this the "hit ratio" in Table 7.1). On average, a positive surprise will experience an increase in stock price of 2.1% relative to the Russell 2000 in the first month after reporting earnings; this figure rises to 12.9% over the ensuing twelve months.

- Negative surprises underperform both the universe and the market across all periods with a hit ratio 90% or higher when looking at individual quarterly performance versus the Russell 2000 at all but the twelve-month. Overall, negative surprises fall 0.9% relative to the Russell 2000 in the first month after reporting earnings, with the relative decline falling to 3.5% at twelve months out.

- Companies that report in line with expectations—no surprises—experience flat stock price movement versus the Russell 2000 in the

Table 7.1—Performance of Small Cap Earnings Surprise Model

	Positive Surprises				Negative Surprises				No Surprises			
	Average Return	Excess versus Universe	Excess Versus Russell	Hit Ratio	Average Return	Excess versus Universe	Excess versus Russell	Hit Ratio	Average Return	Excess versus Universe	Excess versus Russell	Hit Ratio
Prudential Small Cap Universe												
1 Week	0.8%	0.6%	0.7%	78.9%	-0.4%	-0.6%	-0.6%	94.7%	0.3%	0.1%	0.1%	57.9%
1 Month	3.1	1.5	2.1	94.7	0.0	-1.5	-0.9	89.5	1.3	-0.2	0.4	42.1
3 Months	7.1	4.4	4.7	94.4	-0.6	-3.1	-3.0	94.4	2.5	0.1	0.3	55.6
6 Months	12.8	7.0	8.1	100.0	0.2	-5.1	-4.3	100.0	5.3	0.0	1.0	47.1
12 Months	24.3	9.7	12.9	100.0	6.5	-6.2	-3.5	86.7	12.7	-0.3	2.7	40.0
Basic Industry												
1 Week	1.2%	1.0%	1.1%	73.7%	-0.2%	-0.4%	-0.5%	63.2%	0.3%	0.1%	0.4%	57.9%
1 Month	3.0	1.4	2.0	78.9	0.1	-1.4	-1.0	78.9	1.1	-0.5	0.4	42.1
3 Months	5.1	2.7	3.2	61.1	0.3	-2.1	-2.0	55.6	2.2	-0.2	1.6	44.4
6 Months	7.8	2.5	4.3	82.4	-1.2	-5.9	-5.3	88.2	3.6	-1.5	2.1	47.1
12 Months	16.4	2.9	5.9	46.7	2.9	-8.7	-6.4	86.7	9.8	-2.6	2.5	33.3
Business Services												
1 Week	1.3%	1.1%	1.1%	68.4%	-0.3%	-0.5%	-0.3%	68.4%	0.4%	0.2%	0.3%	63.2%
1 Month	2.6	1.1	1.2	57.9	-0.4	-1.9	-0.8	78.9	1.7	0.1	0.8	52.6
3 Months	5.9	3.5	3.5	72.2	-2.4	-4.8	-4.1	77.8	1.8	-0.6	-0.4	50.0
6 Months	11.5	6.2	6.3	82.4	-0.2	-4.9	-3.3	70.6	4.6	-0.5	0.4	41.2
12 Months	11.6	2.1	1.5	40.0	8.8	-3.1	0.5	73.3	11.0	-1.3	1.9	46.7
Capital Spending												
1 Week	1.0%	0.8%	0.8%	68.4%	-0.3%	-0.5%	-0.3%	63.2%	0.6%	0.3%	0.6%	52.6%
1 Month	2.6	1.0	1.7	52.6	-0.6	-2.0	-1.3	78.9	1.9	0.3	1.1	57.6
3 Months	8.5	5.1	4.7	66.7	-2.0	-4.3	-4.0	88.9	2.5	0.1	1.9	50.0
6 Months	8.0	1.9	2.2	58.8	-4.0	-8.7	-7.6	94.1	2.5	-2.3	1.4	29.4
12 Months	4.4	-6.9	-4.8	26.7	-1.6	-12.8	-10.5	93.3	10.2	-1.2	4.2	33.3

Table 7.1 Continued

	Positive Surprises				Negative Surprises				No Surprises			
	Average Return	Excess versus Universe	Excess Versus Russell	Hit Ratio	Average Return	Excess versus Universe	Excess versus Russell	Hit Ratio	Average Return	Excess versus Universe	Excess versus Russell	Hit Ratio
Consumer Cyclical												
1 Week	0.6%	0.4%	0.5%	63.2%	-0.3%	-0.7%	-0.3%	63.2%	0.9%	0.7%	0.8%	78.9%
1 Month	1.4	-0.2	0.4	57.9	-0.6	-1.7	-1.3	78.9	1.3	-0.2	0.7	36.8
3 Months	4.4	1.7	2.3	52.6	-2.0	-2.7	-4.0	88.9	1.4	-1.1	-0.5	33.3
6 Months	10.4	4.7	5.9	64.7	-4.0	-3.4	-7.6	94.1	5.0	-0.5	0.9	41.2
12 Months	17.1	2.8	6.2	53.3	-1.6	-5.3	-10.5	93.3	14.3	0.7	3.8	46.7
Consumer Services												
1 Week	1.1%	0.9%	0.9%	73.7%	-0.2%	-0.4%	-0.5%	68.4%	0.6%	0.4%	0.4%	57.9%
1 Month	3.5	1.9	2.8	68.4	0.5	-1.0	-0.6	63.2	1.7	0.1	0.8	52.6
3 Months	7.7	5.0	5.0	83.3	1.0	-1.5	-1.8	66.7	3.2	0.6	0.7	44.4
6 Months	14.1	7.6	8.9	88.2	1.8	-3.9	-3.5	70.6	7.2	1.4	2.3	64.7
12 Months	32.0	15.1	18.5	93.8	8.3	-5.1	-2.9	60.0	15.7	1.4	4.2	73.3
Consumer Staples												
1 Week	0.5%	0.3%	0.7%	63.2%	1.0%	0.8%	0.7%	42.1%	0.2%	-0.0%	0.2%	42.1%
1 Month	0.9	-0.8	0.3	47.4	2.3	0.8	0.7	47.4	1.2	-0.3	0.6	52.6
3 Months	7.0	4.4	4.7	61.1	1.5	-0.7	-1.4	61.1	3.0	0.8	1.2	55.6
6 Months	10.7	5.5	7.4	64.7	3.2	-2.6	-2.3	52.9	7.4	2.7	3.3	58.8
12 Months	26.1	11.3	15.8	80.0	8.2	-4.7	-2.6	60.0	16.9	3.9	7.0	60.0
Energy												
1 Week	-2.2%	-2.4%	-1.8%	33.3%	-0.3%	-0.5%	-0.2%	55.6%	-0.2%	-0.5%	-0.2%	26.3%
1 Month	-0.7	-2.1	-1.0	40.0	0.3	-1.0	-1.2	61.1	1.0	-0.5	0.4	47.4
3 Months	4.3	2.5	4.5	50.0	-0.2	-1.4	-1.8	58.8	2.5	0.7	2.6	50.5
6 Months	2.0	-1.8	1.3	46.2	-5.4	-7.0	-6.9	68.8	2.9	-0.6	3.3	52.9
12 Months	2.6	-13.0	-10.3	45.5	-18.6	-25.7	-24.9	100.0	8.3	-0.9	4.9	46.7

Table 7.1 Continued

	Positive Surprises				Negative Surprises				No Surprises			
	Average Return	Excess versus Universe	Excess Versus Russell	Hit Ratio	Average Return	Excess versus Universe	Excess versus Russell	Hit Ratio	Average Return	Excess versus Universe	Excess versus Russell	Hit Ratio
Financial Services												
1 Week	0.5%	0.3%	0.1%	57.9%	-0.7%	-0.9%	-0.7%	68.4%	0.2%	0.0%	0.2%	52.6%
1 Month	3.3	1.6	1.9	68.4	-0.6	-2.3	-1.5	78.9	1.5	-0.0	0.7	47.4
3 Months	5.3	2.6	3.0	61.1	-4.3	-6.9	-6.7	88.9	3.1	0.6	0.9	55.6
6 Months	13.0	6.6	7.4	70.6	-3.9	-9.3	-8.3	82.4	8.6	2.9	4.1	64.7
12 Months	24.9	8.4	11.3	66.7	-0.3	-13.3	-10.6	80.0	18.8	3.8	7.4	66.7
Health Care												
1 Week	1.6%	1.4%	1.3%	78.9%	-0.3%	-0.5%	-0.5%	63.2%	0.1%	-0.1%	0.0%	47.4%
1 Month	4.4	2.9	3.2	84.2	-0.5	-2.0	-1.8	68.4	2.2	0.6	1.2	57.9
3 Months	12.2	9.4	9.9	94.4	-0.6	-3.1	-3.1	77.8	6.5	3.9	4.0	77.8
6 Months	23.0	16.9	18.2	88.2	2.6	-2.9	-2.8	64.7	11.9	6.1	7.5	76.5
12 Months	52.8	34.5	39.3	93.3	16.2	2.6	2.7	46.7	29.4	14.8	18.8	73.3
Technology												
1 Week	0.7%	0.5%	0.6%	68.4%	-0.7%	-1.1%	-0.7%	68.4%	-0.0%	-0.3%	-0.2%	42.1%
1 Month	3.4	1.8	2.4	73.7	-0.6	-1.7	-1.5	78.9	0.7	-0.9	-0.2	42.1
3 Months	7.0	4.1	4.3	66.7	-4.3	-3.4	-6.7	88.9	1.2	-1.4	-1.2	38.9
6 Months	12.5	6.6	7.5	76.5	-3.9	-5.2	-8.3	82.4	3.1	-2.1	-1.4	35.3
12 Months	20.0	7.0	10.1	66.7	-0.3	-3.5	-10.6	80.0	7.3	-5.0	-2.0	26.7
Utilities												
1 Week	1.8%	1.4%	1.8%	66.7%	-0.1%	-0.3%	-0.4%	55.6%	0.1%	-0.1%	0.0%	47.4%
1 Month	1.4	-0.1	0.2	66.7	-0.5	-1.9	-1.2	66.7	2.3	0.8	1.1	68.4
3 Months	1.6	0.1	-0.4	35.7	1.5	0.1	0.3	52.9	4.8	2.8	3.2	63.2
6 Months	5.7	2.2	0.8	46.2	5.7	2.0	3.4	56.3	7.1	2.5	3.6	47.4
12 Months	10.9	0.4	-3.0	18.2	3.1	-7.2	-3.4	71.4	8.9	-1.8	0.7	26.3

Note: Data are averages based on performance from first quarter 1988 through third quarter 1993.

Source: Prudential Securities Inc.

first three months post-report-date, but they show slight price increases at the six- and twelve-month time frames.

BUYING OR SELLING ON THE REPORT DATE ISN'T CRUCIAL

One of the misperceptions about earnings surprise is that if "I can't buy or sell on the day the company reports, I've lost all the return." We didn't find that to be the case. Overall, positive surprise excess returns versus the universe or the Russell 2000 continue to climb over time while excess return from negative surprises continues to fall, turning up slightly at the twelve-month time period versus the Russell 2000.

EARNINGS SURPRISE WORKS WELL IN MOST SECTORS

Our study showed the earnings surprise model works well in most of the macroeconomic groups that we divide our universe into. All of the following comments refer to excess return versus the universe unless otherwise stated (see Table 7.1).

- In basic industry, negative surprises lose more cumulatively than positive surprises gained.

- Positive surprises in business services show a big upward move in the first week, but those returns diminish as the time period lengthened.

- Capital spending's positive surprise returns are best in the first three months after reporting. The hit ratio for positive surprises is not as good as that for negative surprises. Negative surprises decline steadily relative to the universe.

- In consumer cyclical, returns from positive surprises are best in the first six months after a surprise is reported. On the other hand, the negative surprises underperform the universe consistently.

- The earnings surprise model works quite well in the consumer services area, with a very strong hit ratio for positive surprises and outstanding performance. Positive surprises gain 15.1% relative to the universe over the subsequent twelve-month period. Negative surprises underperformed steadily across all time periods.

- In consumer staples, the negative surprises actually perform better than the positive ones in the short term, but the hit ratio is very low on both sides.

- The earnings surprise model turns in a dismal performance in the energy sector, but it is also hampered by a very small sample size. This group contained few companies until the latter half of 1990. From that point forward, however, both positive and negative surprises were laggards versus the universe.

- Positive surprises in financial services outperformed the universe across all time periods, gaining 8.4% on average over twelve months. The negative surprises turned in the worst performance of any major sector, losing 13.3% over the same time period.

- The performance of the positive surprises in health care was the best of any sector, both in terms of hit ratio and excess return. Positive surprises gained a whopping 34.5% over the twelve-month post-report-date period. The model did not work as well on the negative side, however. Negative surprises in this group get hit hardest in the first three months after the reporting date, but then excess returns become positive.

- In technology, the negative surprises did not turn out to be the worst performers, as might have been expected. The disappointers get hit hard fast, losing 1.1% on a relative basis in the first week after reporting, but performance actually improves from six months to twelve months. Positive surprises show consistently improving excess returns.

- Utilities results were also affected by the relatively few quarters of data, and companies reporting no surprise outperformed the small number of positive and negative surprises reported in this sector.

THE COCKROACH THEORY CAN BE MEASURED BY LOOKING AT SURPRISE REPEATERS . . .

As described earlier, the cockroach theory deals with the repetition of surprises from one quarter to the next. If there was no serial correlation, we would expect to see about 20% (the historical average) of the companies that reported positive surprises in one quarter repeat that surprise in the next. Similarly, about 26% of the negative surprises would repeat.

In reality, 34% of the companies that reported a positive surprise in one quarter repeated the surprise in the next quarter, which is more than two standard deviations above the 20% average and therefore statistically significant (see Table 7.2). On the other side of the equation, almost 41% of companies repeated their negative surprise, also more than two standard deviations above the expected level if no statistical relationship existed.

- From a performance point of view, positive repeaters do not fare much better than first-time surprises in the short term. At three, six, and twelve months, the performance is better by 100 basis points, 320 bp, and 650 bp, respectively.

- Positive surprise repeaters are most frequent in financial services, health care, technology, and consumer services.

- The only macroeconomic groups where the performance of the positive repeaters consistently beat the average surprise were basic industry and health care.

- The two-time surprises in financial services and technology perform better than the first-time surprises, except for the first week post-report-date.

- Capital-spending repeaters actually had negative excess return and underperform the average positive surprise for the sector.

Negative surprise repeaters performed in line with the average first-time disappointer.

- By sector, more than 40% of the companies repeated a negative surprise in business services, consumer cyclical, consumer services, financial services, and technology.

- Consumer services was the only sector where the excess returns for negative repeaters returns were worse than those of first-time negative surprisers.

- In basic industry, business services, consumer cyclical, and technology, the negative surprises actually perform slightly better than first-time surprises, although excess returns are still negative.

. . . AND SURPRISE REVERSALS

Another way of testing the cockroach theory is to calculate the percentage of companies that report an earnings surprise in the reverse direction from one quarter to the next (see Table 7.3). That is, what percentage of positive surprises reverse and turn negative or vice versa. If there were no tendency of surprises to repeat, about the same percentage of companies that report a first-time surprise (20% positive and 26% negative) should reverse direction the next quarter. In fact, only 13.4% of first-time negative surprisers actually report positive surprises (positive reversers), while 15.4% of the positive surprisers reverse and report earnings disappointments (negative reversers).

Table 7.2—Performance of Small Cap Earnings Surprise Repeaters

| | Percent of Repeaters | Positive Surprises That Repeated | | | | |
| | | Average Subsequent Return | | | | |
		1 Week	1 Month	3 Months	6 Months	12 Months
Universe	34.1%	0.5%	3.0%	8.1%	16.0%	30.8%
Basic Industry	32.0	0.6	3.6	7.5	9.0	24.5
Business Services	26.3	0.6	4.0	7.7	18.1	5.7
Capital Spending	24.8	−0.7	−1.0	1.8	−0.9	−14.2
Consumer Cyclical	35.0	0.6	2.2	5.9	8.9	17.6
Consumer Services	36.5	1.1	3.3	9.8	18.4	38.2
Consumer Staples	18.5	0.7	−1.4	0.5	15.3	46.8
Financial Services	39.3	0.3	4.6	8.9	21.6	39.8
Health Care	37.6	1.7	6.8	16.8	29.0	77.9
Technology	36.3	−0.0	2.6	5.8	11.7	19.5

| | Excess Return vs. Universe | | | | |
	1 Week	1 Month	3 Months	6 Months	12 Months
Universe	0.3%	1.5%	5.4%	9.8%	14.9%
Basic Industry	0.4	2.1	4.9	3.5	9.5
Business Services	0.4	2.5	6.0	13.5	−6.6
Capital Spending	−0.9	−2.5	−1.8	−6.9	−24.3
Consumer Cyclical	0.4	0.7	3.3	2.7	3.9
Consumer Services	0.9	1.9	6.8	11.5	20.6
Consumer Staples	0.9	−2.0	−0.8	10.3	20.4
Financial Services	0.1	3.0	6.2	14.0	20.2
Health Care	1.5	5.3	13.9	22.4	53.3
Technology	−0.2	1.0	3.0	5.6	6.7

| | Excess Return vs. Russell 2000 | | | | |
	1 Week	1 Month	3 Months	6 Months	12 Months
Universe	0.3%	2.0%	6.0%	11.7%	19.3%
Basic Industry	0.4	2.6	6.0	6.0	12.3
Business Services	0.4	2.1	5.1	12.6	−1.8
Capital Spending	−0.8	−0.9	0.0	−4.7	−23.4
Consumer Cyclical	0.8	1.0	3.9	3.3	3.9
Consumer Services	1.0	2.6	7.4	13.7	26.1
Consumer Staples	1.3	0.3	1.5	12.7	27.4
Financial Services	0.1	2.8	5.5	14.1	22.2
Health Care	1.5	5.2	13.9	24.8	58.9
Technology	−0.2	1.5	4.1	8.4	12.1

Source: Prudential Securities Inc.

Table 7.2 Continued

	Percent of Repeaters	Negative Surprises That Repeated Average Subsequent Return				
		1 Week	1 Month	3 Months	6 Months	12 Months
Universe	41.0%	−0.4%	0.4%	−0.4%	0.5%	6.5%
Basic Industry	39.1	0.5	0.9	1.2	1.8	4.1
Business Services	45.3	−0.1	−0.0	−1.4	1.2	13.9
Capital Spending	38.6	−0.4	−0.2	−4.3	−5.7	−2.3
Consumer Cyclical	43.4	0.7	0.0	2.3	2.4	7.6
Consumer Services	42.9	−0.4	0.5	0.5	2.2	5.3
Consumer Staples	33.3	0.7	2.9	1.4	−6.4	−3.3
Financial Services	40.2	−0.7	0.5	−4.3	−6.6	−3.2
Heath Care	39.7	−0.4	1.2	0.3	3.7	18.7
Technology	42.9	−0.7	0.1	−0.4	2.0	12.6

	Excess Return vs. Universe				
	1 Week	1 Month	3 Months	6 Months	12 Months
Universe	−0.6%	−1.1%	−2.9%	−5.2%	−6.1%
Basic Industry	0.3	−0.5	−1.1	−3.2	−7.7
Business Services	−0.3	−1.5	−3.9	−4.1	1.4
Capital Spending	−0.6	−1.6	−6.5	−11.0	−12.7
Consumer Cyclical	0.6	−1.1	−0.6	−4.0	−7.3
Consumer Services	−0.6	−0.9	−2.1	−3.7	−7.1
Consumer Staples	0.4	1.2	−1.5	−10.8	−12.8
Financial Services	−0.9	−1.1	−6.9	−12.1	−15.2
Health Care	−0.6	−0.2	−2.3	−1.7	5.3
Technology	−0.9	−1.4	−3.1	−4.5	−1.8

	Excess Return vs. Russell 2000				
	1 Week	1 Month	3 Months	6 Months	12 Months
Universe	−0.6%	−0.8%	−3.3%	−4.7%	−3.6%
Basic Industry	−0.0	−0.8	−1.7	−3.4	−4.8
Business Services	−0.1	−0.2	−3.0	−0.7	7.1
Capital Spending	−0.5	−1.1	−6.4	−9.8	−10.4
Consumer Cyclical	0.4	−0.7	−1.0	−3.0	−3.8
Consumer Services	−0.6	−0.7	−3.0	−3.8	−5.5
Consumer Staples	1.1	0.5	−3.5	−10.3	−12.8
Financial Services	−0.4	−0.3	−7.8	−12.5	−14.5
Health Care	−0.7	−0.0	−2.1	−1.5	8.2
Technology	−0.9	−1.1	−3.0	−3.9	1.1

Table 7.3—Performance of Small Cap Earnings Surprise Reversers

	Percent of Repeaters	Positive Surprises Turned Negative				
		Average Subsequent Return				
		1 Week	*1 Month*	*3 Months*	*6 Months*	*12 Months*
Universe	15.4%	−0.7%	−0.9%	−0.2%	2.7%	12.1%
Basic Industry	17.9	−1.3	−2.3	−1.7	−3.6	4.6
Business Services	20.2	0.2	1.1	−0.9	−2.2	6.1
Capital Spending	18.9	−2.0	−3.3	−5.0	−7.3	−14.9
Consumer Cyclical	15.0	1.6	−0.3	0.8	8.1	25.8
Consumer Services	16.5	−0.5	0.2	5.7	6.7	18.9
Consumer Staples	17.2	1.1	−2.5	3.0	1.0	−12.4
Financial Services	13.9	−0.8	−0.7	−1.3	3.5	−3.4
Health Care	11.1	−0.4	−0.6	2.8	6.3	39.2
Technology	14.5	−1.1	−2.8	−4.4	0.9	16.0

	Excess Return vs. Universe				
	1 Week	*1 Month*	*3 Months*	*6 Months*	*12 Months*
Universe	−0.9%	−2.3%	−2.4%	−2.9%	−1.6%
Basic Industry	−1.5	−3.8	−4.3	−9.2	−8.4
Business Services	0.2	0.1	−2.7	−4.3	−5.3
Capital Spending	−2.4	−5.2	−9.1	−12.6	−21.2
Consumer Cyclical	0.6	−1.3	−1.0	1.0	6.5
Consumer Services	−0.7	−1.1	4.0	0.5	3.3
Consumer Staples	−0.3	−4.0	−4.4	−3.7	−11.9
Financial Services	−1.0	−1.7	−4.5	−4.6	−13.6
Health Care	−0.8	−2.3	−0.8	−0.0	15.5
Technology	−1.4	−4.2	−6.8	−4.8	1.5

	Excess Return vs. Russell 2000				
	1 Week	*1 Month*	*3 Months*	*6 Months*	*12 Months*
Universe	−0.8%	−1.9%	−2.3%	−2.9%	0.3%
Basic Industry	−1.4	−3.0	−3.7	−8.4	−6.6
Business Services	−0.2	0.4	−4.3	−8.3	−5.7
Capital Spending	−1.4	−3.5	−4.3	−8.1	−23.1
Consumer Cyclical	1.2	−0.7	−2.1	1.0	7.7
Consumer Services	−0.8	−1.4	2.2	−1.6	3.8
Consumer Staples	1.1	−2.1	3.5	−1.8	−14.1
Financial Services	−0.7	−1.3	−4.0	−3.8	−9.0
Health Care	−0.7	−2.1	1.1	−0.6	23.1
Technology	−1.8	−4.6	−5.7	−2.4	5.4

Source: Prudential Securities Inc.

Table 7.3 Continued

	Percent of Repeaters	Negative Surprises Turned Positive				
		Average Subsequent Return				
		1 Week	1 Month	3 Months	6 Months	12 Months
Universe	13.4%	1.2%	3.0%	3.2%	7.7%	17.2%
Basic Industry	15.5	1.0	1.4	0.4	0.9	7.2
Business Services	13.8	2.7	5.8	7.9	8.7	4.2
Capital Spending	8.8	−0.2	2.2	2.5	2.5	8.5
Consumer Cyclical	15.2	−0.3	0.5	3.8	7.2	6.3
Consumer Services	11.6	1.1	3.8	2.5	7.2	22.8
Consumer Staples	12.0	1.5	4.8	19.1	15.0	17.2
Financial Services	16.3	0.2	3.7	−0.5	2.8	13.8
Health Care	14.1	2.4	3.5	2.6	5.2	12.9
Technology	16.0	1.4	3.4	4.8	10.2	26.4

	Excess Return vs. Universe				
	1 Week	1 Month	3 Months	6 Months	12 Months
Universe	1.0%	1.6%	0.6%	1.8%	3.6%
Basic Industry	0.8	0.2	−1.6	−3.9	−6.0
Business Services	2.5	4.6	7.0	8.8	−4.5
Capital Spending	−0.3	0.6	0.4	−2.6	−4.5
Consumer Cyclical	−0.4	−0.5	0.5	0.6	−6.9
Consumer Services	0.9	2.3	−0.1	1.1	7.0
Consumer Staples	0.5	0.9	12.0	7.8	−1.4
Financial Services	0.0	2.3	−2.9	−3.9	−1.1
Health Care	2.2	2.3	0.3	0.2	0.3
Technology	1.2	1.8	1.9	3.9	11.9

	Excess Return vs. Russell 2000				
	1 Week	1 Month	3 Months	6 Months	12 Months
Universe	1.1%	2.0%	0.9%	3.4%	8.0%
Basic Industry	1.1	0.6	−0.5	−1.3	0.4
Business Services	2.1	4.4	5.9	8.4	−3.4
Capital Spending	−0.6	0.3	−1.2	−1.6	−0.8
Consumer Cyclical	−0.1	−0.2	1.0	4.3	−2.6
Consumer Services	1.0	3.6	0.2	1.9	11.2
Consumer Staples	1.0	1.7	12.1	10.7	2.9
Financial Services	−0.3	2.6	−1.7	−1.8	1.5
Health Care	2.8	3.2	1.2	2.8	8.5
Technology	1.3	2.3	2.2	5.5	16.9

With relatively few companies in each sector, analyzing returns at that level should be taken with a grain of salt.

- In general, positive reversers have lower excess returns versus the universe than positive repeaters.

- The negative reversers perform most poorly in the early months after reporting, but performance actually improves at twelve months.

"TRIPLE COCKROACHES" ALSO EXIST, BUT IN SMALL NUMBERS

To really stretch the theory, we tested the persistence of small cap surprises for three quarters running.

- On the positive side, 39.0% of companies that had reported two consecutive positive surprises went on to post a third.

- By comparison, 43.7% of double negative surprisers tripled.

And as with the double repeaters, this is more than chance would allow.

Although few and far between, finding companies that report three sequential positive surprises has proven highly profitable. While these issues don't perform much differently than other positive surprises, over the first week or month after reporting, the subsequent three-, six-, and twelve-month excess returns are substantially better than either of the other categories (see Table 7.4). On average, a company reporting three positive surprises gains 7.0%, 13.6%, and 17.4% versus the universe over these periods.

For three-time disappointers, the results aren't as dramatic. These issues do not underperform the universe as badly as their single- and double-surprise counterparts over the longer time periods, while short-term performance is in line with the other categories.

THE NUMBER OF ANALYST ESTIMATES DOES NOT HAVE A HUGE IMPACT ON PERFORMANCE . . .

There is a school of thought that believes stocks with fewer analysts making recommendations are the issues most likely to outperform the market. In the world of earnings surprise, that doesn't seem to hold true.

- Positive surprises based on a consensus estimate with two to four analysts contributing were not the best performing category in the

Table 7.4—Performance of Small Caps Reporting Three Consecutive Surprises

Positive Repeaters	Percent of Repeaters	Average Subsequent Return				
		1 Week	1 Month	3 Months	6 Months	12 Months
Average Return	39.0%	0.6%	3.6%	11.7%	20.3%	35.9%
Excess vs. Universe		0.4	1.8	7.0	13.6	17.4
Excess vs. Russell 2000		0.4	2.3	7.7	15.1	22.5

Negative Repeaters	Percent of Repeaters	Average Subsequent Return				
		1 Week	1 Month	3 Months	6 Months	12 Months
Average Return	43.7%	-0.5%	0.8%	0.3%	0.8%	7.9%
Excess vs. Universe		-0.7	-1.0	-2.6	-4.9	-4.8
Excess vs. Russell 2000		-0.7	-0.6	-3.1	-4.2	-1.4

Source: Prudential Securities Inc.

analysis (see Table 7.5). These issues still produced positive excess returns relative to the universe and the market, but the figures were below those for companies with more analyst estimates.

In addition, the relatively few companies with eleven or more estimates were not the best performers, although this small group of stocks turned in the best one-week performance.

The small cap issues with five to ten estimates turned in the best performance in the long run.

- On the negative side, results are quite different. The stocks with the least number of estimates turned in the worst results, in terms of both excess return and performance, which continued to deteriorate as time progressed.
  The negative surprises with 11 or more analysts declined the most on a relative basis in the first week, but with few stocks in the sample, the performance is quite unstable going forward.

Performance of stocks with 5-7 or 8-10 analysts doesn't really show any marked pattern.

Table 7.5—Performance of Surprises Based on Number of Analysts in Consensus

Positive Surprises

Average Subsequent Return

Number of Estimates	Frequency	1 Week	1 Month	3 Months	6 Months	12 Months
0*	23.5%	0.5%	2.1%	5.4%	8.4%	16.1%
2-4	46.9	0.9	2.7	6.4	11.7	22.4
5-7	20.6	1.0	4.3	8.9	16.1	33.9
8-10	6.6	0.6	3.8	9.3	15.2	31.4
>=11	2.4	1.6	5.0	7.2	12.6	23.5

Excess Return versus Universe

Number of Estimates	1 Week	1 Month	3 Months	6 Months	12 Months
0*	0.3%	0.6%	2.5%	2.1%	2.5%
2-4	0.6	1.2	3.4	5.2	8.1
5-7	0.7	2.7	5.9	9.3	18.2
8-10	0.4	2.2	6.3	8.6	16.0
>=11	1.4	3.4	4.3	6.0	9.1

Excess Return versus Russell 2000

Number of Estimates	1 Week	1 Month	3 Months	6 Months	12 Months
0*	0.3%	1.1%	2.5%	4.3%	4.5%
2-4	0.7	2.0	4.6	7.8	11.5
5-7	0.9	3.1	6.8	12.1	22.6
8-10	0.6	2.7	6.5	11.0	22.1
>=11	1.5	2.8	3.3	6.7	16.6

Negative Surprises

Average Subsequent Return

Number of Estimates	Frequency	1 Week	1 Month	3 Months	6 Months	12 Months
0*	28.5%	-0.3%	-0.2%	-0.4%	-1.0%	4.7%
2-4	44.9	-0.7	-0.5	-1.5	-0.9	3.8
5-7	18.1	0.2	0.7	1.3	2.0	12.3
8-10	5.8	-0.6	0.2	-1.6	4.4	18.0
>=11	2.6	-1.8	-0.1	-2.7	3.5	3.8

Excess Return versus Universe

Number of Estimates	1 Week	1 Month	3 Months	6 Months	12 Months
0*	-0.5%	-1.7%	-3.2%	-6.7%	-7.5%
2-4	-1.0	-2.0	-4.2	-6.6	-8.3
5-7	-0.1	-0.8	-1.5	-3.9	-0.8
8-10	-0.9	-1.4	-4.3	-1.7	4.2
>=11	-2.0	-1.6	5.4	2.5	-8.3

Excess Return versus Russell 2000

Number of Estimates	1 Week	1 Month	3 Months	6 Months	12 Months
0*	-0.5%	-1.1%	-2.7%	-4.8%	-5.9%
2-4	-0.7	-1.1	3.3	4.8	5.1
5-7	-0.2	-0.7	-1.8	-3.0	1.6
8-10	-0.8	-0.6	-3.1	-1.6	4.7
>=11	-1.8	-1.2	-4.8	-3.4	-3.8

* For companies with fewer than two analysts in the I/B/E/S estimate, the SUE score is based entirely on the 20 quarter trendline forecast.

Source: Prudential Securities Inc.

. . . NOR DOES THE LACK OF AN I/B/E/S FORECAST

Analyzing performance by number of analysts also presented the opportunity to see how surprises calculated off the trendline forecast fared. As was discussed previously, academic studies of earnings surprise were based off a trendline calculation of earnings, whereas our consensus forecast combines this trendline with the I/B/E/S consensus. The findings described below confirm our belief that including the trendline forecast has not been detrimental to the performance of the earnings surprise model. (These issues are represented in Table 7.5 as 0 estimates.)

- Positive surprises that are based on trendline forecasts also outperform the universe and the market, albeit to a lesser degree than those positive surprises that included I/B/E/S in the consensus. More importantly, these positive surprises outperformed all negative surprises no matter which category is used for comparison.

- Negative surprises that are calculated using a trendline forecast significantly underperformed the universe and the market across all time periods.

SCREENING CAN TRAP SMALL CAP COCKROACHES

Knowing that the cockroach theory works, we have developed screens that help us trap the likely repeaters. Initial screens combined prior-quarter surprise score with relative stock-price strength, because prices of stocks reporting surprises tend to move in anticipation of the surprise. In 1992, the trend in quarterly earnings estimate was added and greatly improved the results. Since April 1991, the quarterly screens have yielded 134 companies on the potential positive repeater list and 139 on the negative side.

- Of the companies on the potential positive repeater list 57.6% actually repeated, but, more importantly, only 14.1% reversed and reported disappointments.

- Of the potential negative surprises 61.9% repeated, with only 22.6% reversing direction.

SUMMARY

Over the past five years, the small cap earnings surprise model has consistently distinguished between stocks that outperformed the market and those that underperformed. Stocks of companies that reported positive surprises—both overall and in most macroeconomic sectors—were superior performers to those stocks whose earnings fell short of expectations or were in line with consensus. It is our belief that no matter what the investment approach, the use of an earnings surprise model can greatly enhance portfolio returns.

REFERENCES

Bidwell, Clinton M., III, "A Test of Market Efficiency: SUE/PE," *Journal of Portfolio Management*, Summer 1979.

Foster, G., C. Olsen, and T. Shevlin, "Earnings Releases, Anomalies and the Behavior of Security Returns," *The Accounting Review*, October 1984.

Freeman, R., "The Association Between Accounting Earnings and Security Returns for Large and Small Firms," CRSP working paper #192, October 1986.

Jones, Charles P., Richard J. Rendelman, Jr., and Henry A. Latané, "Stock Returns and SUEs During the 1970s," *Journal of Portfolio Management*, Winter 1984.

Rendleman, Richard J., Jr., Charles P. Jones, and Henry A. Latané, "The Determinants of the SUE Effect," (working paper) October 24, 1984.

Rendleman, Richard J., Jr., Charles P. Jones, and Henry A. Latané, "Further Insight into the "SUE" Anomaly: Size and Serial Correlation Effects," (working paper) April 12, 1986.

ENDNOTES

[1] Henry A. Latané, Charles P. Jones, and Robert D. Rieke, "Quarterly Earnings Reports and Subsequent Holding Period Returns," *Journal of Business Research*, April 1974.

Chapter 8

How a Fund Manager Selects Small Caps

Joel Tillinghest
Portfolio Manager
Fidelity Low Priced Stock Fund

INTRODUCTION

The essential job of a portfolio manager is to compare the attractiveness of different investments, and to invest in those that are most appealing. Small cap portfolio managers differ from other portfolio managers mostly in that they consider smaller opportunities, and perhaps make wider comparisons. The population of possible investments expands geometrically as market capitalization declines, and the dispersion of growth rates and valuations broadens. Investment strategies that work with large cap stocks generally work as well with small cap stocks, but the small cap market is less efficient, so less information is required to give the manager an edge. Thus a small cap portfolio manager actually stands a good chance of adding value. This chapter discusses one small cap portfolio manager's stock selection strategy, and provides two examples.

LOW-PRICED FUND OVERVIEW

As manager of Fidelity Low-Priced Stock Fund, my charter is not necessarily to buy small cap stocks, but rather stocks trading at less than $25. (This limit was originally $15.) With a median market cap of just over $100 million, however, the fund has a small cap focus. Assets recently stood at over $2.5 billion. To invest this huge asset base in small companies, the fund holds over 600 names. About half of the companies are traded on NASDAQ, and the rest are listed. About 9% of the fund is invested in shares listed in Toronto, Montreal, London, and other foreign markets.

GOOD BUSINESSES

I manage the funds with the assumption that if I find superior businesses selling at attractive valuations, good results will follow. Thus picking stocks involves two classes of tests: business tests and valuation tests. Business tests are used to identify companies that can predictably sustain above-average returns on investment, particularly incremental investment. Valuation tests are to ensure that I pay less than the fair value for the stock, to be sure its potential isn't fully appreciated by the market. Both tests are vulnerable to competition, which drives returns on most widely analyzed businesses and securities to market levels. One way to avoid losing on both tests is to avoid industries with many recent IPOs. Insiders normally wouldn't be selling if they thought their stock was undervalued. More importantly, the influx of capital generally brings tougher competition within the industry.

A good business is one that predictably earns high rates of return for many years, with growth opportunities that also offer high returns on investment. Good businesses usually have long product life cycles, some element of recurring revenue, but short production cycles and high asset turns. Thus most superior companies earn their profits in cash. Good businesses also have some measure of unused pricing flexibility. This rules out many regulated and competitive industries. Predictability is improved if the business consists of many low-priced items that the buyers see as relatively essential. If demand isn't relatively stable, indicators of business health such as backlog are crucial to investors. Bad businesses, in contrast, are unpredictable, lumpy, faddish, absorb cash, entail long-term commitments for uncertain return, and tend to earn low margins.

Companies that are not capital intensive can exit easily if business conditions deteriorate. The best companies have some barrier to entry that keeps competition from getting difficult. Monopolies and franchise businesses are generally agreed to be superior businesses, but small companies aren't usually monopolies, unless the defined market is tiny. The fact that a small company has entered a business often demonstrates that the industry's barriers to entry are not high. If there are economies of scale, a small business probably isn't the low-cost producer—again, unless it's a tiny market. Some industries such as cable TV, broadcasting, and pharmaceuticals, benefit from major government restrictions on entry, but not profits; again, these tend to be large companies.

Because barriers to entry are low for most small business, the most successful business strategies are generally to differentiate by offering a better product or to focus on niche markets that competitors have ignored or not served properly. Companies that follow an innovative strategy often turn out to be the growth companies in no-growth businesses. These can be terrific stocks if they are valued like their no-growth brethren. One category of underserved market is odd products like ceramic statues (Stanhome) or vitamins (Nature's Sunshine). Another is businesses that seem disagreeable, such as funeral homes, garbage collection, and pawn shops. Yet another includes businesses that modesty forbids discussing—lingerie, tampons.

For companies that lack barriers to entry, nimble management is at a premium. Management skill is one of the most critical factors in the success of an enterprise, but it is also one of the hardest to judge. In meetings with management, I am usually looking to hear a sensible business strategy articulated, with some form of contingency planning. What if demand drops? How is the competition likely to act? Does the company have good financial controls? If something went awry, when would management know? Does the business strategy change frequently, and does it have to change? Does management think like owners?

VALUATION AND EARNINGS SURPRISES

Having determined that a company is at least not a bad business, I try to identify those which are undervalued. This boils down to stocks selling at relatively moderate P/Es or cheap using other conventional valuation methods, including price to net working capital and P/E to growth rate. A dividend discount model is impractical, given that we know pathetically little about earnings, dividend payout, and growth rates over the long time horizons used in the model. Standard brokerage analysis—which basically attempts to guess the next quarter's sales and earnings—isn't always available for all small companies. For those that are covered by Wall Street, estimates revisions and earnings surprises indicate the direction in which the consensus is wrong. Revisions and surprises are generally a short-term tactic, however, and high transaction costs can make it impractical to act on marginal changes. Nonetheless, rising estimates and strong current earnings momentum are usually favored, since they provide a trigger to attract investor attention to an undervalued stock.

Different valuation methods work better with different industries, although most are reasonably covered by relative P/E comparisons. Energy companies, for example, should be considered on a cash-flow and asset-value basis, as well as on earnings. Reported earnings are not always a good proxy for changes in asset value for exploration companies. Similarly, goodwill amortization obscures the profitability of many reverse LBOs. Sometimes a loss-making division needs to be valued separately from the profitable business. To generalize, however, most of my investments are valued on the basis of P/E to three-year estimated growth rate.

SOURCES OF INFORMATION

Investment professionals will find my definition of good businesses and valuation methods quite conventional; their value comes from application to a large number of potential investments rather than their innovativeness. Given the wide range of companies the fund invests in, I find many sources of investment ideas. Regional brokerages such as Wheat First, Robinson Humphrey, and Montgomery are often helpful in pointing out opportunities, and are willing to facilitate meetings with their companies in a variety of ways. Brokerage-sponsored conferences can be good ways to shop for new investments, or meet up with management of existing holdings. Some smaller companies lack research coverage and put on their own road shows, often with the help of PR firms such as Morgen Walke or the Financial Relations Board. Both of these firms publish catalogs describing their clients, making it easy to order information. Business publications (the usual suspects) can be very helpful in spotting opportunities, as can trade publications such as *American Banker, Computerworld, Medical World News,* and *Women's Wear Daily.* An attentive reading of earnings announcements may also suggest avenues of further research, as may screens. I use Factset Data Services to generate screens. Finally, Fidelity has a staff of over 80 equity analysts in the U.S. and abroad who are important sources of ideas and information; however, they're not available to the general public.

EXAMPLE: ANALYSIS OF A FINANCIAL INSTITUTION

The financial services industry provides a good example of my investment approach. The Low-Priced Stock Fund has usually had a sizable weighting in financial stocks, particularly savings and loans. There are hundreds of small banks, thrifts, and insurance companies, and they generally have sold at moderate valuations. Brokerage coverage of financial stocks is very spotty and the differentiation in valuations between attractive and unattractive institutions is also quite uneven. Savings and loans have been especially cheap because of the miserable financial performance of the industry and the associated scandals.

Conversions of mutual S&Ls to stock form have been particularly attractive, due to a quirk in the process. New investors assume title to the institution and get the benefit of their own capital contribution. The old owners of the S&L—the depositors—don't get any direct compensation, but are first in line to buy stock. One example of this was the conversion of NS Bancorp, the holding company for Northwest Savings in Chicago. This company came to my attention through a newspaper item in December 1990, stating that NS Bancorp would convert by selling 10 million shares.

The prospectus described a thrift that was far better positioned than most of its peers. NS Bancorp's assets consisted primarily of 1- to 4-family mortgage loans and mortgage-backed securities. These are among the most conservative asset classes. Consequently, its nonperforming assets were extremely low at 0.30% of assets, and had declined over the previous several years. The average thrift had NPAs of 2.5% of assets at the time. Initially, my primary concern was that NS had purchased many of its loans from other originators, particularly California institutions, and thus lost a measure of quality control. A meeting with management convinced me of their high underwriting standards, however.

Deposit costs and operating costs were also lower than average, reflecting NS Bancorp's position as a plain vanilla thrift serving a moderate income clientele in an urban area. (See Appendix A to this chapter.) Operating expenses were only 1.11% of average assets, versus an industry average of about 2% because $821 million in deposits was held in just six offices. The reliance on purchased loans and a focused range of services offered also kept expenses low.

The net result was that NS Bancorp earned well above average returns on equity—above 14% every year between 1985 and 1989. Returns on assets were also high—above 1.3% during the same period. Because the equity/assets ratios of financial institutions vary widely, I tend to compare ROEs and ROAs by adjusting returns to reflect a "normal" 6% equity/assets ratio. For example, if a bank earns an ROA of 1.00% with equity assets of 8%, and the after-tax return on government bonds is 5%, I adjust down the ROA by (8-6%) × .005 or 0.10%, arriving at an adjusted ROA of 0.90%. Even on an adjusted basis, NS Bancorp had very high returns. NS Bancorp had a 9.9% equity/asset ratio before conversion, but the proceeds from the offering moved this ratio to an extraordinarily strong 15%.

Even though NS Bancorp was more solvent, more efficient, and more profitable than most financial institutions, it was being offered at 43% of book value and four times pro forma earnings. Many other S&Ls were trading at similar valuations, but few had similar characteristics. The stock drifted after being offered at $8, trading as low as $7 3/8.

Management had indicated its intention to use some of its excess capital to repurchase stocks, and, in fact, announced a repurchase program shortly after the IPO. Federal regulations allow converted thrifts to repurchase no more than 5% of stock every six months, and NS Bancorp proceeded to execute new purchase programs each six months. Combined with a steepening yield curve, the stock repurchase plan allowed share earnings to grow from a pro forma rate of under $2.00 in 1990 to $2.46 in 1991 to $3.61 in 1992. Now the stock has almost quadrupled.

EXAMPLE: ANALYSIS OF A TECHNOLOGY COMPANY

Technology is another group that is well represented in the small cap universe. It is a particularly difficult group to invest in, since, in the short run, most technology investors are momentum players, so a value approach doesn't work very well, and long-run prospects are unpredictable here. The correct approach, I think, is based on understanding the length and strength of a company's product cycle.

Sungard Data Systems, one of my fund's holdings, attracted me because its services had longer product cycles and more recurrent income than a typical technology company. These same features kept some momentum investors away, as the quickest acceleration can be seen by companies with short, lumpy product cycles. (My fund will buy these, too, if I think I have the cycle right, and the lumps are breaking right.) In early 1991, Sungard stock was trading around $12, as the company had put out guidance indicating that the year's earnings were likely to be $1.35 to $1.40, marginally better than the $1.35 earned in 1990. (See Appendix B to this chapter.)

With a typical technology stock, it's dangerous to buy when earnings growth is slowing, since this is often a prelude to declining earnings, but Sungard had indicated that it expected to resume mid-teens earnings growth in 1992. Sungard added capacity in its disaster recovery business, and this reduced profit margins in 1991. The average disaster recovery contract runs 4 1/2 years, providing some certainty about baseline revenues, but rising competition from IBM and Comdisco kept revenue growth in the segment to 12%. Sungard's main business, investment support data processing services, accounted for 58% of revenues and 84% of operating profits. Services include securities accounting, trading, and settlement for banks and other financial institutions. Over 80% of revenues in the segment come from maintenance contracts and renewable contracts running one to three years. The renewal rate is high at about 85%. While baseline revenues are quite predictable, growth in the investment support division, other than a fast-growing derivative securities line, had come mostly through acquisition.

Amortization charges were high because of substantial intangibles created by several acquisitions; furthermore, the intangibles were being amortized over short periods. Capitalized software, for example, is amortized over five to seven years. While depreciation expenses of $15.2 million were matched by a like amount of capital spending, amortization of $12.3 million was offset by only $2 million of capitalized software. Thus free cash flow exceeded reported net income by more than 50%.

Despite the high predictability of earnings, a good growth, and large free cash flow, the stock sold at very moderate multiples of earnings, cash flow, free cash flow and revenues. While earnings barely grew in 1991, they grew 17% in 1992, and another year of mid-teens growth is expected in 1993. The stock has more than doubled over two years, yet is still trading at a market multiple.

SELLING STOCKS AND TRANSACTION COSTS

Many investors, including myself, often change their mind about the attractiveness of a stock after holding it for a short period. My fund has averaged about 85% annual turnover. Since valuations for small-company stocks can also be volatile, it's not hard to arbitrage between companies with similar fundamentals but dissimilar valuations, even after transaction costs. These switches are time-consuming, however, so I try to stick to selling when the reasons why I bought are no longer valid. Examples of reasons why I might sell include new competition, declining orders and backlog, and earnings disappointments that seem likely to recur. For every stock that I sell, I need to find a new one, sustaining the never-ending search for new opportunities.

Because transaction costs are high for small cap investors, they can have a major effect on realized returns. Commissions are the smallest and most measurable part of the costs, averaging about 5 cents a share. Institutional commission rates don't vary widely between brokers. Instead, brokers attract business based on research, execution, and relationships. Execution is the major determinant of costs, since bid/asked spreads, market impact, and missed opportunities each generally dwarf commission costs.

Recently, the median bid/asked spread of the stocks in the Low-Priced Stock Fund was quoted at about 6% of their value. It's not clear whether institutions realize tighter spreads than the quoted levels, since unless a market maker has a matching order, the market maker has to supply more liquidity for a large block. To minimize the liquidity cost and market impact, my fund tends to buy small pieces of stock each day for weeks and months on end. Of course, if a stock is clearly mispriced or business is turning rapidly, then transaction costs are less important, and larger orders are appropriate. Larger blocks are also appropriate where recurrent buy or sell orders attract from runners or price-trend followers. Occasionally blocks become available through crossing networks such as POSIT, where buy/asked spreads and market impact are minimized, and the commissions are also low.

The most nebulous cost, but perhaps the largest, is the opportunity cost of transactions that do not get completed. On an average day, only 50-60% of the orders placed by my fund are completed. This compares with a completion rate near 80% for the larger-cap Fidelity Magellan Fund. I adapt to high transaction costs and incomplete orders by tracking a large number of stocks. When these costs become excessive for any one stock, I move on to another opportunity.

SUMMARY

To recap, successful small cap investing is largely a function of hard work and consistent application of traditional analysis. There is a large universe of underfollowed small companies. From these, I try to find the better-positioned companies that are doing something different. The best results occur when the stock is selling at a low valuation because Wall Street has not noticed or appreciated the merits of the company's strategy. Thus, an investor can benefit from both earnings acceleration and an improved valuation of these earnings.

APPENDIX A—NS BANCORE: PROSPECTUS EXCERPTS

SELECTED CONSOLIDATED FINANCIAL AND OTHER DATA OF THE ASSOCIATION

Set forth below are selected consolidated financial and other data of the Association. This financial data is derived in part from, and should be read in conjunction with, the Consolidated Financial Statements of the Association and notes thereto presented elsewhere in this Prospectus.

	At December 31,					At June 30,
	1985	1986	1987	1988	1989	1990
	(In thousands)					
Financial Condition Data:						
Total assets	$697,954	$1,140,073(1)	$1,357,473	$1,249,968	$1,310,863	$1,358,841
Loans receivable, net	510,918	572,751	861,475	783,160	870,759	917,088
Mortgage-backed securi-						
ties, net	98,095	477,442(1)	393,973	347,831	327,373	309,390
Investments	36,470	39,461	39,353	34,088	38,102	38,769
Real estate	9,593	16,108	38,464	54,079	44,551	46,244
Deposits	589,501	619,982	758,960	824,878	843,881	820,910
Bonds payable, FHLB-Chicago advances and other borrowings	34,656	430,416(1)	485,125	288,104	309,370	380,459
Retained earnings, substantially restricted	62,434	78,996	95,999	113,518	131,607	134,524

	Years Ended December 31,					Six Months Ended June 30,	
	1985	1986	1987	1988	1989	1989	1990
	(In thousands)						
Selected Operating Data:							
Interest income	$72,487	$86,397	$118,446	$122,521	$111,998	$55,365	$62,881
Interest expense	44,502	48,995	75,432	82,768	76,604	36,763	43,194
Net interest income	27,985	37,402	43,014	39,753	35,394	18,602	19,687
Provision for loan losses(2) . . .	115	2,248	1,200	1,600	800	—	4,000
Net interest income after provision for loan losses . .	27,870	35,154	41,814	38,153	34,594	18,602	15,687
Other income	4,814	6,605	5,230	4,368	4,523	1,851	1,972
Other expenses	11,060	13,832	14,269	13,919	13,669	6,403	11,848(3)
Income before income taxes	21,624	27,927	32,775	28,602	25,448	14,050	5,811
Income taxes	8,041	11,365	15,772	11,083	7,359	4,063	2,894
Net income	$13,583	$16,562	$ 17,003	$ 17,519	$ 18,089	$ 9,987	$ 2,917

(1) In 1986, the Association issued $300 million of duration-matched collateralized mortgage obligation ("CMO") bonds through its wholly-owned special purpose subsidiary, N.W. Acceptance. The net proceeds from the sale of the CMOs were used to purchase Federal Home Loan Mortgage Corporation ("FHLMC") mortgage-backed securities. See "Business of the Association—Subsidiaries—N.W. Acceptance Corp."

(2) Prior to 1986, the Association recorded reserves only for specifically identified loan losses. In 1986, the Association adopted a policy to establish general loan loss reserves on the mortgage portfolio. During the six months ended June 30, 1990, the Association increased the provision for loan losses based on management's policy of conservatively evaluating the mortgage loan portfolio and its evaluation of the general economy, rather than an increase in loan delinquencies.

(3) Includes a $5.0 million provision for valuation allowance for securities held for sale. See "Business of the Association—Securities Held for Sale."

	At or For the Year Ended December 31,					At or For the Six Months Ended June 30,	
	1985	1986	1987	1988	1989	1989(1)	1990(1)
Selected Financial Ratios and Other Data:							
Return on average assets..................	2.17%	2.09%	1.36%	1.32%	1.47%	1.64%	.44%(3)
Return on average retained earnings	24.41	23.42	18.97	16.37	14.47	16.76	4.28(3)
Average retained earnings to average assets ..	8.90	8.91	7.16	8.09	10.19	9.79	10.18(3)
Retained earnings to total assets at end of period...............................	8.95	6.93	7.07	9.08	10.04	10.37	9.90(3)
Interest rate spread during period(2)........	4.14	4.41	3.24	2.77	2.49	2.73	2.54
Net interest margin(2)(4)	4.67	4.89	3.60	3.16	3.05	3.24	3.07
Other operating expenses to average assets(5) .	1.38	1.37	.93	1.02	1.11	1.05	1.02
Non-performing loans to total loans at end of period...............................	.72	.66	.32	.30	.25	.29	.25
Non-performing loans and real estate owned to total assets at end of period	.63	.79	.30	.29	.20	.23	.18
Allowance for loan losses to gross loans receivable at end of period	.02	.20	.24	.45	.47	.44	.87
Average interest-earning assets to average interest-bearing liabilities	1.07x	1.07x	1.06x	1.06x	1.08x	1.08x	1.08x
Net interest income to other operating expenses(5)	3.25x	3.43x	3.69x	2.94x	2.59x	2.91x	2.87x
Full-service customer facilities	6	6	6	6	6	6	6

(1) Income and expense items have been annualized in calculating ratios for these periods.

(2) Reflects a reduction in the average cost of deposits for interest capitalized to real estate being developed by the Association's subsidiaries. See "Management's Discussion and Analysis of Financial Condition and Results of Operations—Analysis of Net Interest Income—Average Balance Sheet" and "Business of the Association—Subsidiaries."

(3) Includes effect of the Association establishing a $5.0 million valuation allowance for securities held for sale and the $4.0 million increase in the provision for loan losses. See "Business of the Association—Securities Held for Sale" and "—Lending Activities—Allowance for Loan Losses."

(4) Net interest margin represents net interest income divided by average interest-earning assets. Excluding the duration-matched CMOs and related FHLMC mortgage-backed securities which constitute the principal liabilities and assets of the Association's wholly-owned special purpose subsidiary, N.W. Acceptance, the Association's net interest margin would have been 4.52%, 3.85%, 3.77%, 4.05% and 3.68% for the years ended December 31, 1987, 1988 and 1989 and the six months ended June 30, 1989 and 1990, respectively, reflecting the fact that N.W. Acceptance's net interest margin is less than the net interest margin of the Association.

(5) Operating expenses exclude the amortization of goodwill and the provision for valuation allowance for securities held for sale.

| | At or For the Six Months Ended June 30, 1990 | | | |
| | 7,750,000 Shares Sold at the Maximum Price of $10.00 per share | 10,000,000 | | |
		Shares Sold at the Minimum Price of $7.75 per share	Shares Sold at the Midpoint Price of $9.00 per share	Shares Sold at the Maximum Price of $10.00 per share
	(In thousands, except per share data)			
Gross proceeds	$ 77,500	$ 77,500	$ 90,000	$100,000
Less offering expenses and fees	(4,008)	(4,008)	(4,449)	(4,802)
Estimated net proceeds	$ 73,492	$ 73,492	$ 85,551	$ 95,198
Consolidated net income:				
Historical	$ 2,917	$ 2,917	$ 2,917	$ 2,917
Pro forma income on net proceeds	1,859	1,859	2,164	2,409
Pro forma ESOP adjustment(1)	(408)	(408)	(474)	(527)
Pro forma ARP adjustment(1)	(190)	(190)	(221)	(245)
Pro forma net income	$ 4,178	$ 4,178	$ 4,386	$ 4,554
Per share net income:				
Historical	$ .38	$ .29	$ .29	$ .29
Pro forma income on net proceeds	.23	.18	.21	.24
Pro forma ESOP adjustment(1)	(.05)	(.04)	(.04)	(.05)
Pro forma ARP adjustment(1)	(.02)	(.01)	(.02)	(.02)
Pro forma net income per share	$ .54	$ .42	$ .44	$ .46
Stockholders' equity:				
Historical	$134,524	$134,524	$134,524	$134,524
Estimated net proceeds	73,492	73,492	85,551	95,198
Less: Common Stock acquired by ESOP(1)	(6,200)	(6,200)	(7,200)	(8,000)
Common Stock acquired by ARPs(1)	(3,100)	(3,100)	(3,600)	(4,000)
Pro forma stockholders' equity(2)	$198,716	$198,716	$209,275	$217,722
Stockholders' equity per share:				
Historical	$ 17.36	$ 13.45	$ 13.45	$ 13.45
Estimated net proceeds	9.48	7.35	8.56	9.52
Less: Common Stock acquired by ESOP(1)	(.80)	(.62)	(.72)	(.80)
Common Stock acquired by ARPs(1)	(.40)	(.31)	(.36)	(.40)
Pro forma stockholders' equity per share(2)	$ 25.64	$ 19.87	$ 20.93	$ 21.77
Offering price as a percentage of pro forma stockholders' equity per share	39.0%	39.0%	43.0%	45.9%

(1) It is assumed that 8% of the shares of Common Stock in the Conversion will be purchased by the ESOP. The funds used to acquire such shares will be borrowed by the ESOP from an unaffiliated lender. The Association intends to make annual contributions to the ESOP in an amount at least equal to the principal and interest requirement of the debt. The pro forma net income assumes: (i) the Association's total annual contribution is equivalent to the debt service requirement for the year ended December 31, 1989, and the six months ended June 30, 1990, and was made at the end of the respective periods, (ii) the interest rate applicable to the debt was 11.5% for the respective periods; and (iii) the marginal statutory tax rate applicable to the debt was 38.8% for the periods. The amount borrowed is reflected as a liability and as a reduction of stockholders' equity. It is also assumed that the ARPs will purchase an aggregate of 4% of the shares of Common Stock offered in the Conversion for issuance to officers, directors and employees. Funds used by the ARPs to purchase the shares will be contributed to the ARPs by the Association immediately prior to consummation of the Conversion. It is further assumed that approximately 20% and 10% of the amount contributed to the ARPs are amortized expenses in the year ended December 31, 1989, and the six months ended June 30, 1990. See "Management of the Association—Executive Compensation—Employee Stock Ownership Plan and Trust" and "—Association Recognition and Retention Plans and Trusts."

(2) The retained earnings of the Association will be substantially restricted after the Conversion. See "Dividend Policy" and "The Conversion—Liquidation Rights."

APPENDIX B—SUNGARD DATA SYSTEMS: PROSPECTUS EXCERPTS

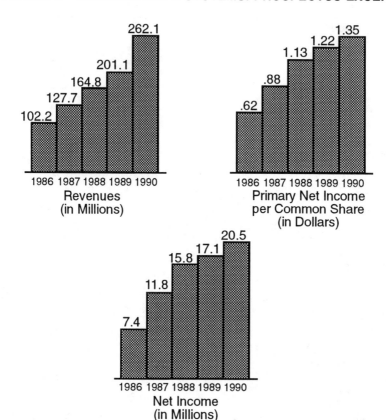

Revenues
(in Millions)

Primary Net Income
per Common Share
(in Dollars)

Net Income
(in Millions)

Selected Financial Information
(in thousands, except per share data)

	1986	1987	1988	1989	1990
Income Statement Data:					
Revenues	$102,156	$127,736	$164,800	$201,093	$262,108
Income from Operations	13,022	18,289	24,273	28,022	40,330
Net Income	7,409	11,764	15,767	17,119	20,480
Dividends on Preferred Stock	345	360	375	32	-
Primary Net Income per Common Share	.62	.88	1.13	1.22	1.35
Balance Sheet Data:					
Total Assets	$68,968	$127,882	$147,737	$193,430	$302,687
Total Notes Payable and Long-Term Debt	2,080	19,151	17,157	37,287	109,232
Redeemable Preferred Stock	3,000	3,000	3,000	-	-
Stockholders' Equity	44,443	81,345	99,482	116,178	140,266

Management's Discussion and Analysis of Results of Operations and Financial Condition
....

Results of Operations:

The following table sets forth, for the periods indicated, certain amounts included in the Consolidated Statements of Income of SunGard Data Systems Inc., the respective percentage that those amounts bear to consolidated revenues (unless otherwise indicated), and the percentage change in those amounts from period to period.

	Year ended December 31, (in millions)			Percent of Revenues (1) Year Ended December 31,			Percent Increase (Decrease) (1)	
	1991	1990	1989	1991	1990	1989	1991 vs. 1990	1990 vs. 1989
Revenues:								
Investment support systems	$ 165.4	$ 151.7	$ 99.2	58 %	58 %	49 %	9 %	53 %
Disaster recovery services	83.5	74.8	64.7	29	28	32	12	16
Computer services and other	34.6	35.6	37.2	13	14	19	(3)	(4)
	$ 283.5	$ 262.1	$ 201.1	100 %	100 %	100 %	8	30
Costs and expenses:								
Cost of sales and direct operating	$ 140.5	$ 127.5	$ 101.0	50 %	49 %	50 %	10 %	26 %
Sales, marketing								
and administration (2)	59.6	56.1	46.1	21	22	23	6	22
Product development	13.4	13.8	10.3	5	5	5	(3)	33
Depreciation	15.2	13.2	8.6	5	5	4	15	54
Amortization	12.3	11.2	7.1	4	4	4	10	59
	$ 241.0	$ 221.8	$ 173.1	85 %	85 %	86 %	9	28
Income from operations (operating margin):								
Investment support systems (3)	$ 36.0	$ 33.7	$ 24.7	22 %	22 %	25 %	7 %	36 %
Disaster recovery services (3)	8.0	7.4	4.9	10	10	8	9	50
Computer services and other (3)	4.4	4.0	1.8	13	11	5	11	122
Corporate administration (2)	(5.9)	(4.8)	(3.4)	(2)	(2)	(2)	27	39
	$ 42.5	$ 40.3	$ 28.0	15	15	14	5	44

(1) All percentages are calculated using actual amounts rounded to the nearest $1,000. (2) Includes merger costs. (3) Percent of revenues is calculated as a percent of investment support systems, disaster recovery services and computer services and other revenues, respectively.

Income from Operations:

INVESTMENT SUPPORT SYSTEMS (ISS):

The primary reason that the ISS operating margins declined slightly in 1991 and 1990 is a change in the mix of ISS revenues. Software license revenues, which typically have higher margins than processing revenues, were a smaller component of total ISS revenues in 1991 and 1990 than in 1989. The primary reasons for this are the February 1990 acquisition of Warrington Financial Systems Inc. (WFS), which significantly increased the remote processing component of ISS revenues, and a $4.5 million, or 19%, decrease in software license revenues in 1991. The Com-

pany expects that the ISS operating margin will improve some-what in 1992 because software license revenues are expected to increase compared to 1991.

DISASTER RECOVERY SERVICES (DRS):

Although the Company expanded its Philadelphia MegaCenter in January 1991, the DRS operating margin in 1991 remained unchanged from 1990. The improvement in the DRS operating margin in 1990 compared to 1989 is attributable primarily to higher capacity utilization in each of the Company's disaster recovery centers. The Company expects

Management's Discussion and Analysis of Results of Operations and Financial Condition
....

that the DRS operating margin will remain relatively constant in 1992 due to competition and ongoing capital requirements.

COMPUTER SERVICES AND OTHER (CS):

CS operating margins have fluctuated in part because of the impact of royalties associated with the Company's sale of its CARS/36 software product to Electronic Data Systems Corporation (EDS) (see Note 9 of Notes to Consolidated Financial Statements). Excluding the impact of these royalties, CS operating margins would have been approximately 8% in 1991, 7% in 1990 and 3% in 1989. The improvement in 1990, and to a lesser degree in 1991, is attributable primarily to cost reductions implemented in response to continued revenue declines in the CARS product line.

Revenues:

Total revenues increased $21.4 million and $61.0 million in 1991 and 1990, respectively. Approximately 49% of the 1991 increase is attributable to a 16% increase in recovery services revenues. The acquisitions of WFS and Phase3 Systems Inc. (Phase3) during 1990 and the inclusion of Money Management Systems, Inc. (MMS) for a full year account for 75% of the increase in 1990 revenues. Recurring revenues — those derived from remote processing services, disaster recovery services, and software maintenance and rentals — increased to approximately $235 million, or 83% of consolidated 1991 revenues, from approximately $213 million, or 81% of consolidated 1990 revenues, and $157 million, or 78% of consolidated 1989 revenues. This percentage increased in 1991 due primarily to the inclusion of WFS for a full year in 1991 and a net decrease in revenues from software license fees and professional services in 1991. This percentage increased in 1990 due primarily to the acquisition of WFS, which had recurring revenues of approximately 91%.

INVESTMENT SUPPORT SYSTEMS:

ISS revenues increased $13.7 million and $52.5 million in 1991 and 1990, respectively. The inclusion of WFS for a full year accounts for 50% of the 1991 increase, and the acquisitions of Phase3, WFS and MMS account for 87% of the 1990 increase.

Revenues from derivative instrument systems increased $2.3 million and $5.2 million, or 8% and 23%, in 1991 and 1990, respectively. Software license revenues decreased $1.7 million, or 12%, during 1991 after increasing $665,000, or 5%, during 1990. The decrease in 1991 software license revenues is due to a lower rate of growth in new foreign markets for the Company's derivative instrument products. Software maintenance revenues increased $3.3 million, or 32%, in 1991 and $3.7 million, or 58%, in 1990, primarily as a result of the respective prior year's license sales. The Company expects software maintenance revenues to continue growing, but at a slower rate due to the 1991 decrease in software license revenues .

During 1991, other investment accounting and portfolio management systems as well as trust and employee benefit systems accounted for $5.6 million of the increase in ISS revenues, which was offset in part by a $1.0 million decrease in revenues from shareholder accounting systems. An increase in professional services revenues is the primary reason for the 1991 net increase of $4.6 million. A $2.7 million decrease in software license revenues in 1991 was offset in part by a $1.6 million increase in software maintenance revenues and a modest increase in data processing revenues. During 1990, trust, employee benefit and shareholder accounting systems accounted for $1.5 million of the increase in ISS revenues. Increases in software maintenance revenues, the number of processing customers and processing volumes of existing customers comprised $4.9 million of this increase, which was offset in part by a $3.4 million decrease in revenues derived from license sales and related professional services.

The Company expects that ISS revenues will increase modestly in 1992, but they may continue to be affected by financial institutions and other investment managers evaluating expenditures at greater length in light of their own financial situations and concerns about general economic conditions. Furthermore, some of the large banks that announced mergers in 1991 are customers of the Company. Some published opinions predict that mergers will continue to occur in the banking industry, but the Company is not yet able to predict whether this apparent trend will continue. The Company believes that announced and future bank mergers will result in some lost revenues, but also will result in some sales of additional services, so that the Company is not yet able to assess the overall net impact on its business.

DISASTER RECOVERY SERVICES:

DRS revenues increased $8.7 million and $10.1 million in 1991 and 1990, respectively, due primarily to net increases in the number of contracts, additional services sold to existing customers and, to a lesser extent, price increases. The 1991 increase is comprised of a $10.5 million, or 16%, increase in recovery services revenues, offset in part by a $1.7 million decrease in software license and professional services revenues. In 1990, software license and professional services revenues remained unchanged from the 1989 level of $7.5 million.

During 1991, the Company experienced a significant increase in DRS revenues from new contracts compared to 1990, offset in part by a significant increase in DRS revenues lost to data center closings and consolidations. Also in 1991, DRS revenues lost as a result of competition from IBM were lower than in 1990, but total DRS revenues lost as a result of competition increased. The Company is unable to determine whether these apparent trends will continue and, if so, for how long.

COMPUTER SERVICES AND OTHER:

CS revenues decreased $1.0 million and $1.6 million in 1991 and 1990, respectively. Revenues from automotive dealer management systems decreased $1.0 million and $2.1 million, or 7% and 13%, in 1991 and 1990, respectively, due primarily to decreases in the number of processing customers, lower processing volumes of existing customers and lower equipment sales. The decreases in automotive dealer management systems revenues in 1991 and 1990 were offset in part by an increase in royalties from EDS (see Note 9 of Notes to Consolidated Financial Statements).

The Company expects that CS revenues will decrease slightly in 1992 as the result of the 1991 sale of a small, unprofitable product line, but the CS operating margin should remain approximately the same. The Company is unable to predict what royalties it will receive from EDS.

Costs and Expenses:

Cost of sales and direct operating expenses increased $13.0 million and $26.5 million in 1991 and 1990, respectively. Approximately 21% of the increase in 1991 and 74% of the increase in 1990 are attributable to acquired businesses. The increase in cost of sales and direct operating expenses as a percent of 1991 revenues is due primarily to the additional costs associated with the Company's expansion of its Philadelphia MegaCenter in January 1991 and to lower software license revenues, which have minimal direct costs. The decline in cost of sales and direct operating expenses as a percent of 1990 revenues is attributable primarily to the relatively lower costs of providing ISS products and services compared to DRS services and, to a lesser extent, to staff and other cost reductions associated with CS products and services.

Sales, marketing and administration expenses increased $3.5 million and $10.0 million in 1991 and 1990, respectively. Approximately 23% of the increase in 1991 and 79% of the increase in 1990 are attributable to acquired businesses. Excluding the effect of merger costs from 1990 and 1989, sales, marketing and administration expenses were 21% of revenues in both 1991 and 1990 compared to 22% of revenues in 1989. The slightly higher percentage in 1989 is attributable primarily to an increase in selling costs associated with an expansion of the DRS sales force and the higher sales volume of derivative instrument systems.

Product development expense decreased $396,000 in 1991 and increased $3.5 million in 1990. Approximately 94% of the increase in 1990 is attributable to acquired businesses. Product development expense for derivative instrument systems increased $1.3 million and $1.6 million in 1991 and 1990, respectively, while spending on other products declined. The decreased expense for other products in 1991 and 1990 is due to lower spending levels, completion of certain projects and the timing of capitalization of development costs. Development costs capitalized aggregated $345,000, $1.0 million and $1.3 million in 1991, 1990 and 1989, respectively.

Depreciation of property and equipment increased $2.0 million and $4.7 million in 1991 and 1990, respectively. Approximately 77% of the increase in 1990 is attributable to acquired businesses. The increase in 1991 and the balance of the 1990 increase are attributable primarily to DRS capital expenditures.

Amortization of intangible assets increased $1.1 million and $4.1 million in 1991 and 1990, respectively. Substantially all of each increase is attributable to acquired businesses.

The increases in interest income in 1991 and 1990 are attributable primarily to higher invested balances and, in 1990, to higher average interest rates.

Interest expense increased $793,000 and $4.8 million in 1991 and 1990, respectively. The increase in 1991 is attributable to a full year of interest on the Company's $86.25 million convertible subordinated debentures (the Debentures), while the increase in 1990 is attributable primarily to the May 1990 offering of the Debentures and to a short-term bank loan.

The Company's effective tax rate was 44% in 1991 and 1990 compared to 39% in 1989. The rate in 1989 reflects the benefit of research and development credits that were not available to the Company in 1991 and 1990. The rates in 1990 and 1989 also reflect the negative tax impact of merger costs associated with the acquisitions of Phase3 and Dyatron Corporation, respectively. Excluding all of these items, the pro forma effective tax rates would have been approximately 44%, 43% and 40% for 1991, 1990 and 1989, respectively. The increases in the 1991 and 1990 pro forma effective tax rates are due primarily to an increase in nondeductible amortization associated with acquired businesses. (See Note 8 of Notes to Consolidated Financial Statements).

The Company believes that its business is not seasonal. Nevertheless, the timing and magnitude of software sales, commitments for equipment and facilities, and product development efforts may cause profitability to fluctuate from one quarter to another.

The Company believes that inflation has not had a material impact on the results of operations to date.

Liquidity and Capital Resources:

Cash flow from operations decreased $7.6 million in 1991 due primarily to an increase in working capital requirements associated with certain development contracts and to unusually high receivable collections in 1990.

1991 financing activities resulted in net expenditures of $22.4 million as the Company made its final payment of $20.0 million to satisfy purchase price obligations related to the 1987 acquisition of Devon Systems International, Inc.

Capital expenditures in 1991 were essentially the same as in 1990. The Company's capital spending for property, equipment and software during 1992 is expected to approximate 1991 spending.

At December 31, 1991, cash and short-term investments aggregated $69.5 million. Of that amount, the Company expects to use $20.5 million in the second quarter of 1992 to complete its recently announced acquisition of Shaw Data Services, Inc. (Shaw). The Company could pay up to an additional $15.0 million in connection with the acquisition of Shaw depending upon the level of Shaw's profits in the three-year period following closing.

At December 31, 1991, the Company's remaining commitments consisted primarily of operating leases for computer equipment and facilities aggregating $90.0 million, of which $30.1 million is due in 1992. The Company believes that its existing cash resources and cash generated from operations will be sufficient to meet its operating, capital spending and debt service requirements.

Report of Independent Accountants

To the Board of Directors and Stockholders
SunGard Data Systems Inc.

We have audited the accompanying consolidated balance sheets of SunGard Data Systems Inc. and subsidiaries as of December 31, 1991 and 1990, and the related consolidated statements of income, stockholders' equity and cash flows for each of the three years in the period ended December 31, 1991. These financial statements are the responsibility of the Company's management. Our responsibility is to express an opinion on these financial statements based on our audits.

We conducted our audits in accordance with generally accepted auditing standards. Those standards require that we plan and perform the audit to obtain reasonable assurance about whether the financial statements are free of a material misstatement. An audit includes examining, on a test basis, evidence supporting the amounts and disclosures in the financial statements. An audit also includes assessing the accounting principles used and significant estimates made by management, as well as evaluating the overall financial statement presentation. We believe that our audits provide a reasonable basis for our opinion.

In our opinion, the consolidated financial statements referred to above present fairly, in all material respects, the consolidated financial position of SunGard Data Systems Inc. and subsidiaries as of December 31, 1991 and 1990, and the consolidated results of their operations and their cash flows for each of the three years in the period ended December 31, 1991, in conformity with generally accepted accounting principles.

COOPERS & LYBRAND

2400 Eleven Penn Center
Philadelphia, Pennsylvania
February 6, 1992

Chapter 9

"Private Market" Small Cap Equity Investing: A Business Management Approach to Systematic Small Company Investing

Kevin L. Wenck
Portfolio Manager
G.T. Capital Management

INTRODUCTION

"Private Market" Small Cap Investing

I define investing as the process of diligently analyzing factual information, applying one's intelligence to envision reasonable future scenarios based on such factual information, and applying conservative valuation principles to value such future prospects. If one accepts this definition as a framework for investing, then a logical and rational process inevitably follows to fulfill such a definition. If investment is based on facts, analysis, and defined valuation principles, a rational foundation for such a process would be based on fundamental economic reality, i.e., what is a fair economic rate of return for an investment having particular financial and operating characteristics?

The reason for my emphasis on concepts such as facts, analysis, valuation, and rationality is my belief that the fiduciary responsibilities of investing are such that it is incumbent on all investment practitioners to find a rational basis for investing, given that most investment activities are done with other people's money. Without such a rational basis, i.e., basing investment decisions on proven valuation principles observed in real economic transactions, then I contend that investment practitioners are actually speculating with their client's funds and, as such, have violated their fiduciary responsibilities.

I am certain that my rambling so far has generated the question about what all this has to do with small cap investing. The connection with small cap investing is that such investing offers an outstanding opportunity to use facts, analysis, and proven valuation principles as a basis for rational investment decision making. Small cap investing is an anomaly in that it both simplifies and complicates the investment process. Small cap investing is more complicated in that, due to relatively less institutional research coverage, most small cap investing must be done through one's own research. Such investing is also more simple than other investing in that small companies are much more easily analyzed than larger companies.

As an example of the above, I would contend that the typical CEO of a Fortune 500 company has barely a clue about the details of the various divisions and operating units of the company. What is achievable in the responsibilities of such a CEO is organization and delegation, not intimate knowledge and close direction of day-to-day activities. The challenge of an investor, however, who desires a rational basis for decision making, is that close knowledge of a business is needed for such rational decision making. If a Fortune 500 CEO cannot closely monitor all the prospects of all of the company's operating units, then I conclude that such knowledge, and the opportunity for rational decision making, is beyond the capabilities of external investors.

I believe that small companies offer greater opportunities for both management knowledge and investor knowledge. In my experience, I have been struck by how closely involved senior management is with the operations of small companies. Four or five executives at the senior level very much control all important activities of most small companies. Such companies are also typically focused on one or two defined market areas, which both simplifies the management task and allows greater opportunity for good investor analysis.

The close and thorough investor analysis possible in small-company investing then offers a much more rational basis for investment decision making—both when buying and when selling. There is a wide diversity of decision-making processes used in the investing world, ranging from looking at charts to employing huge multivariable programs on mainframe computers. My observation about many of these approaches is that they give away many opportunities to move closer to reality in making decisions. For chartists, reality is expressed in price and volume action; for black-box firms, reality is expressed in models using historical statistics; and for many investors, reality becomes the collective opinions of the brokerage community, comprised of various buy, hold, and sell opinions and the ebb and flow of earnings estimates.

I liken such processes to the analogy of the cave given by Plato in the *Republic.* For those who are not familiar, the analogy of the cave is a metaphor for describing the human process of gaining knowledge. At the bottom levels of the process (for those at the bottom of the cave), humans are looking only at shadows but, since they have never seen anything else, the shadows seem to be full reality for those humans. The advancement toward knowledge begins when one questions such apparent reality and works toward finding higher levels of knowledge (advancing up to the sunlight at the mouth of the cave). My observation here is that in thorough small-company investing, one can escape relying on the reality of shadows on which many base their investment decisions. The first level to which one can advance is to realize that there is an opportunity to know the companies themselves very well. The next level of advancement comes when you realize that, based on such company knowledge, you can employ higher levels of real-world experience in valuing such companies when making buy and sell decisions.

Without such close company knowledge, many valuation approaches are like the classic GIGO (garbage in, garbage out) problem in computing. Uncertain or erroneous information goes in to the decision-making process, and so the resultant investment decisions are also likely to be uncertain and erroneous. This is shown even by taking the simple example of using brokerage firm EPS estimates to make valuation judgments in buy and sell decisions. Regardless of whether the brokerage firm estimates are right or wrong, investors are still looking at shadows, since the estimates are not from their own research. Beyond the accuracy of the estimates, however, is the question of an appropriate P/E multiple. Without having done his or her own EPS estimates, an investor would only be guessing at an appropriate P/E multiple for the opportunity of investing in a company with such assumed earnings. There is another side to investing along with opportunity, however, and that is the relative risk of each company. Relative risk would either raise or lower the P/E multiple, depending on the financial and operating characteristics of each business. Without having done one's own research, I would claim that an appropriate decision on risk would be even less likely.

Such problems are simplified when doing one's own research. The EPS estimates are one's own and there will also be greater knowledge about assumptions used to result in such estimates. A complete financial analysis of a company would also include balance-sheet and cash-flow projections, and so such an investor would have higher levels of knowledge about financial risk. A complete research process would also include conversations with company management, and so such an investor would have higher levels of knowledge about business risk. The higher levels of knowledge would then allow more rational and informed decisions about appropriate P/E multiples for each company.

We are now finally to the "Private Market" part of the title of this chapter, and this answers the question of how to justify one's valuation decisions. If you approached the average portfolio manager about a public company that was assumed to have 40% earnings growth in the current year and earn $1.00 a share, the commonplace rule of thumb is that the manager would pay 40 times earnings to include such a company in client portfolios. If you approached the same individual privately, however, about a private company that would earn $50,000 that year, up from $35,000 the previous year, and said that the company could be purchased for $2,000,000, the likely response would be: "Are you nuts? That is only a 2 1/2% earnings yield. I can get more than that in CDs."

My point is that, if this is the case, then why should investment managers go beyond established real-world valuation criteria in making portfolio buy and sell decisions? Small-company investing offers the opportunity to perform private market quality analysis in the research process, but such research would be undermined without also employing private market quality valuation parameters when making investment decisions. A portfolio manager using such real-world parameters as a management discipline is investing. A portfolio manager ignoring such real-world disciplines is speculating.

Business Management Approach for Investing

Investing, as a business, is different from most businesses in that its product—investment returns—is only infrequently evaluated by the marketplace. Most portfolio managers complain about quarterly performance pressures but if the product is being evaluated no more frequently than on a quarterly basis then the manager's pressures are really far less than those of a plant supervisor who needs to run high yields every day or a store manager whose merchandise and customer service must also be of high quality every day.

Such businesses with very frequent evaluation periods have consequently developed sophisticated information and quality control systems to make sure the business stays on track. The manufacturer needs consistent processes to ensure that bad raw materials do not enter the plant, thereby destroying weeks of production, and the store manager needs to ensure that significant merchandising mistakes are not being made so as not to destroy an entire season of merchandising. However unglamorous it may seem, I would contend that the job of a portfolio manager should not be altogether different—especially when dealing with the risks of small cap equities.

One of the earliest things that struck me when entering the investment business was the many different reasons given by portfolio managers for owning different stocks. Some stocks were bought because the companies appeared at a conference, others were bought because of a positive newspaper article, while still more were purchased because a broker thought they were inexpensive. I believe that successful investing is no different from an effective manufacturing process where the means of production are stable and well-defined. As such, a business management approach applied to investing would require a defined and unvarying process for stock selection according to the manager's defined investment style.

Even beyond the many reasons that portfolio managers may have for owning various stocks are the expectations for such stocks. Expectations seem to vary from: "I'm a long-term investor" to "I don't know, I just like the company" to "A broker said the company once sold at 30 times earnings so I am looking for that again." To return again to the manufacturing analogy, if the plant manager did not have established manufacturing processes, standard manufacturing costs from such processes, and standard selling prices based on the economic value of the goods produced, then that manufacturing company, if public, would be a great short.

As in the manufacturing analogy, investing (especially small cap investing), also benefits from the consistent business management approach found in successful goods producing businesses. The manufacturing process is one's thoroughly defined, consistently executed process for manufacturing potential small cap investments. The cost of the product—i.e., the stock—is a given based on the current stock price, and the selling price for the product is the target price derived through the above-discussed "private market" valuation.

If one objects that my analogy is absurd in that there is much more uncertainty of outcomes in investing than in manufacturing, I would very strongly disagree for the following reasons. First, any plant manager knows that while the standard cost of a widget may be $2.33, the likelihood of any individual widget costing exactly $2.33 is rather remote. To manage that problem, appropriate monitoring and control systems are implemented so that, on average, the total lot of widgets will cost $2.33 each. Investors may also manage their manufacturing process in the same way. Although each individual investment will have elements of uncertainty, my experience is that stocks chosen through a consistently applied research and valuation process, with minimum hurdle rates for each individual stock, will produce portfolio (or manufacturing lot) returns converging on that hurdle rate.

In fact, there are more similarities with manufacturing than one might imagine. In manufacturing, a plant manager is looking for yields to various specifications. On the investment side, a portfolio manager is looking for stock appreciation to various hurdle rates. Using an example from the semiconductor industry, there are various clock rates available for microprocessors depending on the quality of the manufacturing process. One silicon wafer containing 300 microprocessor chips may result in 180 16Mhz chips, 90 25Mhz chips, and only 30 33Mhz chips. Similarly, when looking at 300 companies, an investor may find 180 that are likely to go up 10%, 90 that are likely to go up 20%, and only 30 that are likely to go up 30%. And for the investor, if there is any slippage in the tolerances of the manufacturing process, the 10% yield of 30% appreciation stocks could easily decline to 5% or even 2%.

To me, what such an analogy implies is that investors need to define and stabilize their manufacturing process to achieve targeted returns. Commonsense business management would then govern the research and portfolio management process to ensure consistent manufacturing and targeted yields. As any business oriented to such a paradigm would do, this implies understanding what business you are in, setting appropriate goals and operating policies, and implementing information and control systems to monitor progress.

I mentioned very briefly a bit earlier that such an approach is especially useful in small cap investing, and my reason is that small cap investing offers both greater risks and greater opportunities than mainstream equity investing. In mainstream equity investing, investors may be considering a stock that, if it goes up, it may go up 15%, but if it goes down, it may go down 10%. In small cap investing, one is often considering stocks that could go up or down 30%, depending on how correct one's analysis may be. With such a greater possible range of returns, the additional discipline and control of what I call a business management approach is essential.

In addition to mistakes potentially costing an investor much more with small cap stocks, there are additional negative complications from such mistakes. For example, if one had bought Pfizer at $100 and had the misfortune of having the stock decline to $70, the loss would be painful, but at least the company is a widely accepted institutional name that many other investors would find acceptable to be included in a portfolio and the stock also trades in a relatively liquid fashion. On the other hand, if one purchased a small cap stock at $10, which then suffered some operating surprise or opinion change causing a decline to $7, there are usually significant complications for the portfolio manager beyond the absolute loss. Such complications include probably owning 400,000 shares of a stock that may trade only 15,000 shares on a typical day, having over-the-counter market makers discontinue market making activities due to decreased investor interest, having company senior management distracted from operating activities as they are answering all the phone calls about the stock drop, and the portfolio manager having to spend more time monitoring the company. In my experience, the time required to monitor a poorly performing stock is about two to three times that required for monitoring a stock that is meeting expectations. As such, it is far more efficient to design and implement business management practices and faithfully follow them in portfolio management activities than to randomly suffer possible poor performers.

One final comment about what I have called a business management approach to small cap investing. Any realistic business manager understands what is controllable and what is uncontrollable. For a portfolio manager to follow such an approach, the same insight is essential. In looking at investing, many prominent aspects appear uncontrollable, such as overall stock market direction and the short-term trend in individual stock prices. With insight and organization, however, much more is controllable than one may think, and such things substantially mitigate aspects of investing that are uncontrollable. This is the central theme of what I have called a business management approach. In other words, the approach is: Manage what you can manage, be cognizant of but do not waste time with things that you cannot manage. In the rest of this chapter there will be a step-by-step discussion of the process used in such an approach.

PHILOSOPHY (DEFINE THE PROCESS)

Focus on Quality

In real estate, the three rules for success are location, location, and location. In investment management, I believe the three rules for success are selectivity, selectivity, and selectivity. The focus of such selectivity initially is on company quality. A small cap investor, using the Russell 2000 as a possible universe, has 2,000 companies from which to choose. With such a multitude of choices, why even consider companies that are not of extremely high quality? Assuming that acceptable quality is found in only one company out of ten, that still leaves 200 possible investment choices.

I often hear portfolio managers chortling about big gains made in some junky company before the stock ultimately plunged as if such managers were sharp stock pickers. My attitude, however, is why waste your time and complicate the consistent execution of one's business with potentially unstable situations. High-quality companies give investors a great deal of relative stability and control over the investment process. Such companies are less likely to have poor operating execution, bad strategic decisions, distracting management turnover, and financial problems resulting from all the above.

I mentioned above that poor investment decisions require considerably more attention than good investment decisions, and the same is true with operating companies. Poor-quality companies spend time fighting fires; good-quality companies spend substantially less time figuring out how to avoid fires. It is the better quality companies that allow investors more control over their investing activities by allowing more time for positive decisions and less time allocated to determining what to do with disappointing investments.

Focus on Growth

This to me is very simple for the following reasons. Everything else being equal, a company growing earnings 20% a year should have its valuation increase twice as fast as a company growing earnings 10% a year. In the case of disappointments, this comparison is even more significant. If each company's growth rate slips 5%, then the "growth" company, now growing at 15%, is growing *three* times as fast as the other company growing at 5% a year.

Although the above example may seem overly simplistic, I believe there is some underappreciated elegance in the simplicity. The elegance is that, for realistic objectives, I now have one less thing to manage. As stated below in the objectives section, my return goal is 20% annually. As a growth stock investor, to obtain such returns I only need to find fairly valued stocks growing at 20% a year. If such currently fairly valued stocks do grow earnings at 20%, then, in the abstract, they should appreciate 20%. If I were a value investor, my job would be more complicated if I were still looking for 20% returns. As a value investor I would probably be looking at slower growth companies, e.g., growing earnings at 10% a year. In such a case I would now have two tasks instead of one. Task one would be to ensure I was right on my projection of 10% growth. Task two, however, raises the bar because I also must ensure that the company is 10% undervalued instead of just fairly valued to still get the same return.

Such an example suggests that growth stocks do some of the work for you in seeking higher returns because of their intrinsic growth but there are also other examples. One stupid saying I have is that growth stocks are growth stocks because they are growth stocks. In more intelligent prose, growth stocks are growing because they are better companies and their products or services have higher economic value. This not only helps the return side of the equation but also the risk side as well. The higher quality of such companies results typically in fewer disappointments and frustrations, assuming one's research was done properly from the start.

Comprehensively Manage Risk

Investors' primary focus seems to be return, but the other side of return is risk. All investors, in all asset classes, face general risks in their respective markets as well as specific risks from the individual issues in which the investors invest. Small cap stocks are no different and some small cap specific risks are sufficiently serious to demand an aggressive risk management approach.

My risk management approach is: for each identified risk, devise redundant risk management techniques for managing such risks. Some examples follow. Growth stocks use lots of cash, so find those whose financial characteristics allow internal financing and invest only in those with better financial characteristics than competitors. Small cap stocks are difficult to trade, especially in distressed circumstances, so maintain quality in the research process to avoid mistakes and be ready to sell stocks at target prices to avoid distress sales during disadvantageous periods. Small growth company prospects are always changing, so focus not only on the opportunities of such companies but also the risks and, after having finished the original research, employ consistent methods of continual review to constantly monitor company prospects.

The above are a few examples of risk management. More examples will be discussed in specific research and portfolio management sections.

OBJECTIVE (WHAT SHOULD THE PROCESS PRODUCE?)

I have a simple return objective of 20% annually for my small cap portfolios. Although this may seem ambitious compared with long-term overall equity returns of 11% and long-term small cap returns of about 13%, I believe a systematic process makes such an objective reasonable. Such a systematic process must be diligently managed in all steps to ensure proper execution in both research and portfolio management, but a business management orientation makes such diligent management possible.

Achieving defined return objectives involves managing both risk and return. The most salient risk to one's ability to achieve such returns is controlling quality and avoiding mistakes in the research process, as individual small cap mistakes can substantially affect overall portfolio returns. Assuming minimal mistakes in the research process, the next most important factor is maintaining a high return profile for the overall portfolio. This is accomplished by making sure that all stocks purchased are inexpensive relative to return prospects and that stocks are sold when target prices have been reached.

STRATEGY (HOW IS THE PROCESS ACCOMPLISHED?)

Narrow the Universe

The small cap universe, assuming one starts with the Russell 2000 as a reference point, includes at least 2,000 stocks. Individual portfolio managers have different points of view about numbers of portfolio positions but, at an extreme, even if one used 200 stocks, that is only 10% of the total universe. I use only 40 stocks, which is only 2% of the entire universe.

How, then, does one separate the wheat from the chaff? My generic suggestion is to figure out what variables are important for how one defines their investment process. For my specific process, I focus on growth, undervaluation, and unrecognized change. As discussed later within the research process, specific screens for these criteria will be described.

Understand the Opportunities and Risks

For companies identified from one's screens, the next step is to consistently employ a research method that focuses thoroughly on both opportunities and risks. As discussed later, this process should focus on each company as a company while ignoring the company's characteristics as a stock. The objective of such a process is to understand as much as someone outside a company might be able to understand about a company's operations and prospects so as to have superior predictive ability about future company behavior and financial results.

For this process, I stress the word *understand* rather than the word *know*. I make this distinction because of my observation that the investment world is filled with people who know a great deal about individual company details but fail to synthesize such knowledge into an understanding of how all those details will affect the company as a business. Additionally, frequently there seems to be incongruence between the many details that someone may know about a company and the larger factors on which company success or failure depend.

Maintain Portfolios with High Return Prospects

At first glance, this may appear obvious, but I would contend that most managers do not pay any attention to such a concept in actual practice. To suggest that this may be true, I believe that if you ask a manager for the weighted average projected return for his or her portfolio, the most likely answer would be "Huh?"

The reason for this concept is as follows. The objective of investment management is to produce reasonable returns for one's asset class. Portfolios, however, are strange beasts and hard to characterize. The prospects for individual stocks within the portfolio change daily as well as each stock's position within the portfolio. Ironically, stocks that are doing well—precisely those that a manager feels most enthusiastic about—are detracting from the return profile of the portfolio as a whole. The reason is that, assuming a valid target price for each stock, as an individual stock advances toward that target price, the projected return for that stock grows smaller while the position size of the stock grows larger as a percentage of the portfolio. While the manager may very much enjoy the good performance of the stock, the projected future performance of the portfolio has deteriorated. Such subtle portfolio behavior requires monitoring systems allowing the true condition of the portfolio's return profile to be monitored regularly. An absurd example of this problem is shown by a portfolio containing fifty stocks that have all reached their target prices at the same time. In this case the portfolio manager may feel great in that all portfolio stocks have worked perfectly. Investors looking forward to future returns should not feel so good, however, because, at that point, the projected future return of the presently constituted portfolio would be zero.

At this point, all introductory remarks about a business management approach for small cap investing have been concluded. The following will discuss specific functions within the total approach.

STRATEGY EXECUTION

Research and Portfolio Management as Separate Activities

Central to the small cap approach being described is to separate research and portfolio management into two distinct activities. The reason for this separation is to avoid a number of common investment errors when the two activities are blurred together. A common portfolio management mistake caused by a thorough bottom-up research process is that the manager is tempted to automatically buy very good companies discovered in the research process regardless of company valuation. A common research mistake caused by a manager including "inexpensive" stocks in a portfolio is that not enough care is given to finding out why such stocks are apparently inexpensive.

I believe that a small cap process separating the two activities solves such problems. Research serves only to evaluate the quality of individual companies with the aim of ensuring that only the best companies successfully pass through the process. Portfolio management involves using that list of high-quality companies and including them in portfolios only when their valuations are inexpensive. A great deal of discipline is required to follow such a process but, given the opportunity with small companies to do very thorough research, I believe such discipline has many rewards. Some of the more prominent rewards are lower portfolio volatility and more efficient use of overall research/portfolio management resources. Lower portfolio volatility results from a higher quality and more disciplined research process. More efficient use of overall research/portfolio management resources results from the higher quality research allowing one to avoid fire-fighting and emergency calls to portfolio companies when problems arise.

Below is an outline of individual steps within both the research process and the portfolio management process.

A. The Research Process

    1. Initial screening

    2. Opportunity assessment

    3. Comprehensive risk assessment

    4. Continuing review

B. The Portfolio Management Process

    1. Valuation

    2. Investment selection

        a. portfolio composition
        b. trading strategy

    3. Buy discipline

    4. Portfolio monitoring

    5. Sell discipline/Portfolio optimization

Comments on each of these sections follow.

The Research Process

Initial screening. This step narrows the investment universe according to criteria desired by the investor. My approach seeks earnings growth, undervaluation, and unrecognized positive change. For each of the three criteria there is a separate screen. A central theme of all three screens, however, is that they are designed in congruence with my emphasis on being an "early" investor. As such, an additional objective of each screen is to notice interesting situations before other investors.

The earnings growth screen comprises daily monitoring of all small cap companies reporting earnings, with my criteria being minimum year-over-year earnings growth of 15%. Such daily monitoring can often cause notice of promising earnings growth before such growth is noticed by brokers, earnings surprise services, or other investors with less frequent screening techniques.

The undervaluation screen comprises weekly monitoring of small cap companies appearing inexpensive relative to consensus current earnings estimates. Although individual broker research estimates are given little weight in my overall research process, in cases where there are three or four brokers with estimates, I have found that consensus estimates can be quite good as an indication of possible undervaluation. The weekly frequency of this screen is in line with what is usually weekly updating of various earnings estimate services.

The unrecognized change screen uses monthly monitoring of subtle changes in various operating and financial characteristics. I monitor such items as return on equity, return on assets, gross margins, operating margins, turnover ratios, etc. There are two forms of this screen; one compares data from consecutive quarters and the second compares current data to the year-earlier quarter. The premise behind such screens is that before dramatic operating improvement is noticed by many investors, there is often subtle improvement in a few aspects of a company's operations.

All three screens are also sorted by sector and industry to allow some aspect of a top-down view about what is going on in various sectors and industries. Although my specific research process is very much bottom-up in nature, such a top-down view has many synergistic benefits, as all companies being researched are affected by larger macroeconomic trends.

The three screens typically identify about 300 companies a year as being of potential interest. The efficacy of the screens is shown by their ability to eliminate 85% of potential universe companies if one uses the Russell 2000 as an appropriate small cap universe.

Opportunity assessment. The raw material from the initial screens is then subjected to opportunity assessment, which has the object of identifying all favorable aspects about a company. The premise behind opportunity assessment is that companies having more favorable aspects than other companies have both more stability and better growth prospects. There are two defined steps within opportunity assessment. The first is a qualitative assessment of a company's historical record and current condition and the second is a quantitative assessment of the company's possible future financial condition.

The qualitative assessment includes both operational and financial characteristics. Favorable operational characteristics include such things as leading market share, technological dominance, low-cost manufacturing, proprietary products, and products having high economic value. Favorable financial characteristics include such things as high return on equity, superior margins, conservative capital structures, significant sales and earnings growth, and minimal financing needs. I contend that successful companies are superior to other companies in all or most of these characteristics. Although this exercise may appear to be an exercise in stock selection, it is really an exercise in risk management. As the world of economics and investments is highly uncertain and hence, risky, I believe that companies with significant strengths relative to other companies are much less risky as possible stocks for one's portfolio.

The qualitative part of opportunity assessment eliminates about half of the companies originally identified through the initial screens. The remaining companies are then subjected to a quantitative assessment of possible future financial results.

The quantitative assessment uses a financial modeling system that produces comprehensive future financial statements, i.e., balance sheet, income statement, and cash-flow statement from about forty assumptions. Although an exactly precise financial model may not result from this exercise, the model at least demonstrates how a company behaves financially. Very quickly it may be seen whether the company generates cash or uses cash, how volatile earnings per share might be relative to margin changes, and what has to be assumed to result in the consensus EPS estimates found in the weekly undervaluation screen.

Again, while this may appear to be a process of stock selection, it is really a process of risk management. From seeing a company's financial behavior, one may quickly eliminate companies with external financing needs, with potentially volatile margin changes, and whose stated financial models do not make sense within the operating and competitive environment the company is likely to face.

The quantitative part of opportunity assessment eliminates about half again of the then remaining companies that passed through the qualitative part of opportunity assessment. The remaining companies, now numbering about seventy-five each year, then pass through to what is called comprehensive risk assessment.

Comprehensive risk assessment. In simple terms, opportunity assessment was for finding everything good about a company and what is called comprehensive risk assessment is for finding everything bad about a company. This step does not necessarily concentrate on things negative, but its intent is to discover reasons why a potential investment may be too risky to fit into the business management framework that is being outlined.

As small company management can have significant influence over the success or failure of such companies, the primary focus within risk assessment is on company management and on whether those managers have realistic company operating plans. A thorough understanding of the goals, objectives, and behavioral tendencies of company management can substantially mitigate the risks of small-company investing. The opportunity in small-company investing, however, is that senior managers typically are much more available for meetings with the investment community. If such managers do not choose to make themselves available, then that in itself is a company-specific risk to be avoided.

Discussions with company managers proceed from questions generated during opportunity assessment and from industry research. To be most effective, the discussions should generate a number of additional questions for each original question. The objective is to learn more about how the business is run under different operating conditions as well as to gain additional knowledge about the company. With such an objective, an iterative question-and-answer approach allows many deeper levels of understanding about a company, which results in substantially greater understanding of company specific risks.

The most effective approach during this process is to meet separately with three or four senior managers. I start with the chief financial officer to determine the quality of company financial systems and overall financial controls. As our business management approach is to seek companies with relatively low operating volatility, we consequently are looking for a CFO who is an integral member of senior management and who has proper systems in place and the authority to limit business practices having negative financial effects. Without such integration into senior management and such authority, the company is likely to have more volatile operating results than would be desirable under a business management approach.

Assuming the CFO passes muster, I will then talk with the chief executive officer about more general topics, such as company strategy, strengths and weaknesses, and how the business is managed. After talking with the CEO, I will then talk with executives in different functional areas, such as sales, manufacturing, research and development, or operations. These executives will be chosen either to learn more about particular areas of the business to better understand company risks or to become more familiar with an executive in an area in which the company may have had some performance problems.

The overall objective of these discussions is to ensure consistency of company mission across senior executives, an awareness of the company's business environment, that there are realistic profit-oriented business plans, and that the company is forthright with the investment community. This last quality cannot be overemphasized. If you invest in a company, you will need to discuss company operations many times in the future during your holding period. If company executives cannot be forthright about the company in initial discussions, then later conversations about the company are also likely to be unsatisfactory—especially during times of trouble. Although I have given special emphasis to this last item, satisfactory answers must be received in all four areas.

It was mentioned much earlier that the key to investing is selectivity. If one receives any unsatisfactory answers, be selective and do not invest in that company regardless of other positive company qualities. Part of a business management approach is deciding what criteria will govern your activities. If one compromises on one's basic investing criteria, then one has begun to erode the basic business management techniques that could control one's investment process.

It was mentioned within this section that discussions with company management should take an iterative, interactive approach, with the answers to initial questions being followed with additional questions, and so on. I often term this process "hypothesis testing." To provide basic control and business management over one's investment activities, one must have an established hypothesis for each portfolio company to monitor how the company's operations are performing against that hypothesis.

Although only briefly mentioned until now, central to the success of the risk assessment process is thorough financial analysis of each company. Regardless of the intrinsic qualities of each company, above all, one is investing in a business and for that business to be successful, in very simple terms, it must take raw materials and resources at one price and turn such things into products and services for which it charges a higher price. Representing such a process are the company's financial statements.

Although projecting future financial statements is challenging for all companies, small-company investors have an advantage in that the companies typically are far less diversified than larger companies. As such, financial statements are easier to project into the future and such projections are more subject to good analysis.

What governs such forecasting work in my approach is an independent assessment of what is possible for each company. Instead of taking a company executive's comments at face value, first look at the economy and the company's industry in the context of the company's strengths and weaknesses and decide for yourself what is possible for each company. With such a prior hypothesis, one will have a much better framework for subjecting management answers to what I call a reality test. One of the greatest risks to avoid is unrealistic operating assumptions. If company answers about operating plans fail such a reality test, then the analyst has effectively accomplished the risk-assessment process and will avoid a possible investment that would be too risky for a controlled business management approach.

Financial projections also have another use within risk assessment and that is a test of company executives' knowledge about how their business behaves financially. Again, I would emphasize that an investor is investing in a business, and the success or failure of a business is represented in the financial statements. To be successful, I believe that company executives must thoroughly understand how their operating decisions will affect the company financially.

An aid to this part of risk assessment is the integrated financial analysis system used in the research process. With such a system one may interactively question company managers about how their companies behave financially and then immediately test their answers. It is embarrassing how many times I have discovered that a CFO does not know how a 1% margin change will affect earnings per share. Or in other cases, to find executives who are unfamiliar with the cash-flow effects of different operating decisions such as increasing receivables or capital spending for strategic reasons. In such cases, no matter how much an investor may like the *company*, such a company is unlikely to be a dependable *business* which has sufficiently low risk to be acceptable within a business management framework.

An example of an interactive conversation with a CFO follows. One question may concern a reasonable company growth rate for the company over the next two years, and the answer may be "about 20% per year." The next question may be about capital spending plans during those years, and the answer may be "about $10 million a year." The next question may then be about the sales to fixed-asset ratio which, based on the two previous answers, increases this year to 3.3 and the following year to 3.6 from a historical average of about 3.0, and the CFO may reply, "Well, you know, we could actually spend $11 to $12 million this year and $13 to $14 million next year if we do grow at the rate we hope to." The next question may concern receivables and inventories, and the CFO may reply that turns for both may slow a bit, given the strategic objectives of greater sales incentives and a higher in-stock inventory position. The next question may then be about external financing plans, and the CFO may answer, "We expect to be completely self-sufficient for our financing needs." The next question might then be about the $5 million cash deficit this year and the $10 million cash deficit the following year, given the answers to all the previous questions. At this point the CFO may then answer, "Well, a lot of things depend on other things and so it is hard to say what our needs may be at this point."

The deeper levels of questions enabled by the interactive financial modeling system have now allowed the questioner to learn some important things beyond the answers that may be given to basic questions. Concerning capital spending plans, either the CFO does not even know or will not be forthright with investors, which are both risks to be avoided. Concerning financing needs, either the CFO does not know how the company's financial statements behave, or is not an integral part of the company's business planning process, or again will not be forthright with investors, which are additional reasons to avoid investing in the company. An incremental benefit from such a process of interactively questioning company management is that the better companies seem to have more respect for investors who can achieve such a level of knowledge about company operations. Such respect typically results in future conversations with management being much more open and productive.

The above comments complete the description of comprehensive risk assessment. As for how the process works in practice, of the approximately seventy-five companies entering this step each year, only about twenty-five successfully pass through this step. Although that one-in-three ratio may not seem that impressive for such a critical step, the reality is that those twenty-five companies actually were originally from a screened raw material pool of 300 companies, which itself was from a total universe of over 2,000 companies.

Continuing review. The final task of the research process is continuing review of the companies that have originally passed through the initial research process. In a business sense, whereas the first three steps in the research process were defined steps in a manufacturing process that also included its own defined processes and quality controls, continuing review is like the internal audit or separate quality control function.

While the first three research steps manufacture a product through repeated hypothesis testing, continuing review repeats that hypothesis testing at appropriate intervals. The process used in this approach has a structure of daily, weekly, quarterly, and "as needed" tasks to ensure appropriate company progress toward the hypothesis for each company. The importance of a structured and consistently applied continuing review process is that the twenty-five companies passing successfully through initial research each year become part of a continually followed list of 100 to

125 companies. With such a number of companies, a formal organized continuing review process is required to maintain the basic discipline and risk management techniques of the business management approach.

In this process one may begin seeing some of the small cap risk management redundancies built into the investment process. As mentioned earlier, mistakes with small cap stocks can inflict severe damage on a portfolio. Although the original research process is rigorous and contains risk management redundancies in its structured steps, continuing review provides one more safety net and quality control for ensuring the consistency of the investment process.

The Portfolio Management Process

Valuation. Now that the research process has provided a closely followed list of good-quality companies, the next question is, What should one pay for such companies? The abstract answer is that one should pay what can be justified economically. For practical purposes, such an economic valuation would be based on what a prudent, unleveraged purchaser would pay for such a company in a private transaction. As mentioned very early in this chapter, such a valuation approach can be rationally justified as an *investment*, while any price above such a rationally justified price would have to be regarded as *speculation*. This is also the second part of our "private market" approach. The first half is in the research process, where one's analysis aims to be as thorough as it would be in a private market transaction, and the second part is to base valuation decisions on what one would pay in a private market transaction.

The actual process used in my approach is as follows: A by-product of the research process is earnings per share estimates from the financial projections. For each company, I then look at company specific characteristics—such as growth rates, capital structure, financial volatility, industry stability, possible cyclical effects, etc.—to decide on a prudent price/earnings multiple for each company. This multiple is actually from a two-step process. The first step is to decide what an appropriate market multiple should be over the envisioned investment period. For deciding the market multiple, I use a seven-factor macroeconomic model based on historical data, which has had a good record in projecting normalized market multiples. The second step is to decide an appropriate premium or discount to the market multiple for each individual stock. The individual stock premiums or discounts are based on analyzing the company-specific factors listed above as well as noting real-world valuation trends observed in both public market and private market valuations.

As the research process essentially proceeds from a risk management perspective in line with a business management approach, the portfolio management process is also built on such principles. Some of the specific risk management techniques within our valuation process follow. Most importantly is the principle that my approach demands that *the investor* decide on appropriate valuation parameters for each stock instead of relying on common wisdom or brokerage firm opinions about appropriate valuation levels. Such an exercise pays many dividends from the intellectual focus required, resulting in more thorough understanding of one's assumptions about each company.

The next principle is the use of a normalized market multiple instead of the prevailing market multiple. At the time of this writing (in September 1992), based on recession-depressed earnings, the market multiple is in the low twenties. With such a prevailing market multiple, brokers are fond of dredging up some average company selling at "only" twenty times earnings and telling the world what a bargain it is given that it is selling at below the market multiple. If one looks at a long-term record of market multiples and finds that a multiple based on normalized earnings in the current macroeconomic environment should be fifteen, then the abovementioned "average" stock, even giving it a market multiple, is actually 33% overvalued at its current price of twenty times earnings. The same principle also applies in reverse at market bottoms. In such periods, most investors are quite depressed, are convinced that equities will never again be a worthwhile asset class and are happy giving their stocks away at eight to ten times earnings. In such periods, a normalized market multiple from the model described would typically be about twelve times earnings, and so in my infinite pigheadedness, I have been happy buying equities in such depressed periods.

The next risk management principle is to always err on the conservative side when deciding on multiples. This principle is based on a very simple thought, which is, Why talk yourself into buying a stock beyond a price with which you are comfortable? In other words, one should buy stocks only on one's own terms. To do this effectively, one must already be reconciled to knowing that certain stocks eliminated through this discipline will end up doubling in price, but one must remember that we are attempting to consistently manage a business and that the emphasis needs to be on consistent risk management. Another side of choosing conservative multiples is that the maximum individual stock premium assumed is 50% over the market multiple. Statistically, at any given time, less than 5% of one's investment universe will be priced at multiples higher than a 50% premium based on normalized earnings and, from a business management approach, I would hesitate to base consistent portfolio performance on such outliers.

To digress a moment, I would also like to comment on one very common way of valuing growth stocks, which is that the stocks' growth rate gives you an appropriate earnings multiple. If one used a projected secular growth rate over a five-year period one may come up with an acceptable approximation of an appropriate multiple, but in common usage the usual multiple cited is based on the next year's growth rate. My comments in this area are based on my attitude that no matter how attractive a growth story may be, ultimately, trees do not grow to the sky, and growth rates do slow over time. Tables 9.1 and 9.2 illustrate possible returns and risks from using such an approach.

Table 9.1—Projected Return Calculations

Year	1991	1992	1993	1994	1995	1996
Earnings per share	$1.00	$1.40	$1.82	$2.27	$2.72	$3.21
EPS growth rate		40%	30%	25%	20%	18%
Dividends per share		0.00	0.00	0.00	0.00	0.00
Company PE/S&P PE		2.67	2.00	1.67	1.33	1.20
Projected company PE		40	30	25	20	18
Projected price		$56	$55	$57	$54	$58
Cumulative dividends		0.00	0.00	0.00	0.00	0.00
Projected return		40%	17%	12%	8%	8%
Projected yield		0.0%	0.0%	0.0%	0.0%	0.0%
Assumed purchase price	40.00					
S&P multiple	15			Fiscal Year: December		
Months to year-end	12			Current Date: 01/01/92		

Table 9.1 assumes that a company's current-year earnings growth rate is 40% and that the current rate gradually slows over time. As shown in the example, assuming investors at the end of the year will price the company at forty times earnings even though the growth rate will be slowing, the investor has some chance of earning a 40% return for one year. At such multiples, however, projected returns for later years rapidly diminish. Table 9.2 suggests what happens if there is any "slippage" in the current year from the 40% projected growth rate. In this case, growth "slows" to 30%, which is still an outlier when compared to the growth rates of all compa-

Table 9.2—Projected Return Calculations

Year	1991	1992	1993	1994	1995	1996
Earnings per share	$1.00	$1.30	$1.63	$1.96	$2.32	$2.67
EPS growth rate		30%	25%	20%	18%	15%
Dividends per share		0.00	0.00	0.00	0.00	0.00
Company PE/S&P PE		2.00	1.67	1.33	1.20	1.00
Projected company PE		30	25	20	18	15
Projected price		$39	$41	$39	$42	$40
Cumulative Dividends		0.00	0.00	0.00	0.00	0.00
Projected return		–3%	1%	–1%	1%	0%
Projected yield		0.0%	0.0%	0.0%	0.0%	0.0%
Assumed Purchase Price	40.00					
S&P multiple	15			Fiscal Year: December		
Months to year-end	12			Current Date: 01/01/92		

nies. The earnings reported to get to such numbers are not all that different either. Instead of quarterly earnings of, let's say, $0.32, $0.34, $0.36, and $0.38, we are now talking about $0.30, $0.32, $0.33, and $0.35. At an operating company level, such differences are almost noise, but to an investor they are an intolerable disappointment. As such, I would rather be prudent and pay more-conservative multiples in the framework of a business management approach than to speculate that high growth rates can continue and that greater fools will come along to help us exit from such investments.

To digress a bit further, I have one other example of how investors can be hoodwinked into buying stocks with low potential returns. In this case, assume that a company is selling at $20 on January 1, 1992, that the company's fiscal year ends in December, and that consensus estimates are that the company earned $1.12 in FY 1991 and that the company will earn $1.33 and $1.54 in FY 1992 and FY 1993, respectively. In this case, as the story may go, you have to buy the stock, as it is selling at "only" seventeen times 1992 estimates and "only" fifteen times 1993 estimates. Tables 9.3 and 9.4 suggest what one's returns might be, however, when buying such a bargain. Table 9.3 shows returns assuming investors give the stock a P/E multiple equal to the actual earnings growth rate each year. In this case,

Table 9.3—Projected Return Calculations

Year	1991	1992	1993
Earnings per share	$1.12	$1.33	$1.54
EPS growth rate		19%	15%
Dividends per share		0.00	0.00
Company PE/S&P PE		1.20	1.10
Projected company PE	18	18	17
Projected price		$24	$25
Cumulative dividends		0.00	0.00
Projected return		20%	13%
Projected yield		0.0%	0.0%
Assumed purchase price	20.00		
S&P multiple	15	Fiscal Year: December	
Months to year-end	12	Current Date: 01/01/92	

the 1992 return is okay, but the two-year annualized return through 1993 is beginning to be only marginally attractive.

Table 9.4, however, shows what happens if investors use a P/E multiple at the end of each year that is the same as the assumed growth rate for the following year. This is the case currently, given that the stock is now selling at eighteen times the 1991 earnings.

In this example the stock is really a poor purchase, given possible alternative investments.

These examples suggest that stock valuation may deserve more than cursory attention or reliance on "old saw" valuation parameters. As the difference between performance at the bottom of the top quartile and the top of the third quartile is only 3% in many years, one can see how sloppy or thoughtless valuation principles can hurt portfolio performance.

Investment selection. This section is titled "investment selection" because it provides overall principles for selecting portfolios. Specific stock selection guidelines are contained in the buy discipline and sell discipline sections. There are two parts to these overall guidelines. The first part covers overall portfolio composition and typical investment period, and the sec-

Table 9.4—Projected Return Calculations

Year	1991	1992	1993
Earnings per share	$1.12	$1.33	$1.54
EPS growth rate		19%	15%
Dividends per share		0.00	0.00
Company PE/S&P PE		1.00	0.90
Projected company PE	18	15	14
Projected price		$20	$21
Cumulative dividends		0.00	0.00
Projected return		0%	2%
Projected yield		0.0%	0.0%
Assumed purchase price	20.00		
S&P multiple	15	Fiscal Year: December	
Months to year-end	12	Current Date: 01/01/92	

ond part covers trading strategies congruent with our overall business management approach.

Portfolio composition. Portfolio management in a risk-averse, business management approach has a conflict between risk management, which is solved through diversification, and business control, which is solved through limiting the number of portfolio names. What seems to work well within a volatile small cap universe is about thirty-five to forty stocks, which provides sufficient overall diversification across industry groups and also sufficient individual stock diversification in the case of the inevitable disappointments that can occur from time to time with small growth stocks. Individual portfolio positions are roughly equally weighted at time of purchase, although companies with substantially higher return prospects, assuming equal risk, are given higher weights than companies with lower return prospects. Limiting the number of names also roughly corresponds to the number of names with which an individual can maintain a consistent level of expertise. Although, in the approach being described, portfolios of thirty-five to forty stocks are constructed from an "approved" list of 100 to 125 stocks, and all the approved stocks are subject to continuing review, my experience is that an individual's "knowledge advantage" relative to most other investors can be maintained only with about thirty-five to forty stocks at any given time. As such, a business management approach dictates that a "knowledge advantage" be required in all investments. Without such a firm policy, control is lost when one is investing in companies about which one does not have significant expertise, and effectiveness is lost unless one invests only in companies in which one has a significant level of expertise. Both points of view are important but the second is particularly so within a business management framework. If one looks at a portfolio as a set of diversified businesses, why should one invest in any business where one's capabilities doom one's efforts to be at best an also-ran participant in that area? A simple summation again is, Only invest when the investment is on your terms, i.e., when you have an advantage over your competitors in a particular area.

The investment horizon for stocks in my approach is twelve to eighteen months. Beyond that period of time, one's ability to see the future becomes too suspect for a business management approach and to sell before that time is typically an inefficient use of resources, given the amount of work that has gone into each portfolio company. This time period also seems to correspond well with the typical price appreciation pattern of stocks that work best. By design, I am an early buyer, so within the business management framework, there is less competition from other investors while accumulating positions. Many of such "early" stocks seem to do relatively little for three to six months following purchase, as there is a lag before a significant number of other investors begin discovering the stock. Months six through twelve, however, are typically periods of rapid appreciation, at which point an inflection point is reached that is the sell target. Each stock at that point may appreciate another 5% to 15% over the following year, but portfolio optimization forces a swap into higher-return prospect stocks, as the projected portfolio return is more important than incremental individual stock returns.

Some have asked me why I have the patience to wait for the three to six months before the stock starts to appreciate and why I do not instead act like my peers and "buy 'em when they are going up." I resist this idea for three reasons. The first is that if I wait to buy until the stock is "going up" then I will also be competing for stock along with many of my peers. The second is that I am too dumb to know what "going up" means. If someone really could know when stocks were "going up" I promise you that long ago they would have retired with a tidy nest egg. The third reason is based on relative price and return. My small cap approach involves a great many $10 stocks. As a little game, I occasionally ask someone what the difference is between a $10 stock and a $12 stock. The usual answer is: "I dunno, two bucks?" My answer, however, is "20%" which, in the context of a business where the long-term annual rate of return is 11% for all stocks and 13% for small stocks, is a significant excess return. As such, I am happy waiting a year for a stock to go from $10 to $12 instead of waiting, like my more sophisticated peers, to start buying when the stock is "going up."

Trading strategy. There are many different ways to buy and sell stocks but a business management approach dictates that trading is done on one's own terms whenever possible. Part of this has already been suggested above in comments about the advantages of being an early buyer, but the overall approach is to buy when no one is buying and sell when no one is selling. This takes a great deal of organization and discipline to accomplish, but if one is doing one's own original research beforehand and is happy making independent decisions, then the organization part is essentially accomplished.

The discipline part is equally easy. Just decide that such a trading strategy will be your business model and ensure that your traders understand the approach. With small stocks, such an approach does take considerable attention, however, and willingness to act quickly. The organization part is already done, which allows trading decisions to be made rationally based on predetermined projections about a stock's proper valuation. I often say that there are only five days a year when one can advantageously sell a small cap stock, so unless one is organized to respond to such opportunities then such opportunities will be lost. The rule here is very simple—when an active buyer within a day pushes a stock through one's target price, start selling. If one waits until the next day, it is possible either that the buyer may no longer be buying or that the new price levels may bring in other sellers. This is the same as in any commonsense business management approach. In the most basic terms, time to market typically accounts for over half of the incremental profits of any business.

An additional aspect of my trading strategy is, Why pay more when you can pay less, or why sell for less when you can sell for more? The theme behind this idea is patience, patience, and more patience. This part of the trading strategy also has to do with the average stock price and trading spread of the stocks with which I work. Using a $10 stock again as an example, I will occasionally ask what the difference is between a stock at $9.75 and a stock at $10.25. The usual answer is "I dunno, 50 cents?" My answer, however, is "roughly 5%," which is significant in a business where the long-term rate of return is 11%. The importance of this is seen when one notices that the average spread on a $10 over-the-counter stock is 50 cents and if one has the discipline to purchase stock only at the lower end of the spread, and to sell stock only at the higher end of the spread, then one has the opportunity to probably add 2% to 3% to one's returns in the small cap sector.

An understandable question at this point would be, "But just how do you do that?" The answer is patience, patience, patience, plus a little bit of insight. The overall business management approach being described buys only inexpensive stocks. So what are the characteristics of an inexpensive stock? Most prominently it is that "the stock hasn't worked," that the stock "hasn't gone up" and that the stock is "dead money." Doing one's own research, however, provides an advantage in that one has a firm opinion about the economic value of the stock even though an inefficient stock market has failed to recognize that value. Also, for the average portfolio manager, having a stock like that in one's portfolio is an insult to the manager's professional dignity. After all, the portfolio manager specializes in stocks that are "going up," so there must be something wrong with such a stock beyond the control of the portfolio manager.

So what happens when the manager with the business management approach goes into the market? Using the example of the stock bid at $9.75 and offered at $10.25, let's say that the portfolio manager who specializes in stocks that are going up wants to unload 75,000 shares. The initial indication might be that 25,000 will be offered at $10.125 ($10.25 to the buyer) and that the seller will scale up from there. The business management approach buyer might then bid $9.75 for the whole block ($9.625 to the seller). The seller typically will first act insulted and not even respond but an hour later may come back and offer all 75,000 shares at $10.125 because the seller now knows the buyer can at least buy the entire block. The buyer may then raise the bid to $9.875 for the whole block but again the seller will probably not respond. The selling portfolio manager, however, starts thinking more about how frustrating it has been having this terrible stock in the portfolio and that there is a legitimate bid, which will erase this blight on the portfolio. More often than not, at some point later in the day, the seller will agree to the buyer's last bid, thereby allowing the buyer to have just bought the stock at almost a 4% discount from the original offer. Not bad work in a business where, again, the long-term rate of return is only 11% a year.

The same process works similarly when the business management approach manager is selling a stock. In this case the stock is being sold to a manager who specializes in stocks that are going up. As such, the latter manager is typically very proud of the wisdom that caused such a purchase candidate to be selected for the portfolio and is very eager to buy the stock because it is definitely going up from here. This is the opposite of the business management approach whose manager's green-eyeshade emphasis on eighths and quarters dims his enthusiasm for stocks that are going up. The result of such an encounter is that the enthusiastic buyer typically exploits less of the spread than the unenthusiastic seller. If similar bites out of the spread are achieved on both buys and sells, the business approach manager has just made roughly 7% a year before even the effects of stock selection. Again, nice work in a business whose long-term rate of return is only 11% a year.

This concludes my trading-oriented comments within the context of the business management strategy. As suggested, some simple thoughts about the economics and psychology of the business can potentially add significant incremental returns beyond pure stock selection. The next section covers criteria used in deciding what stocks will be purchased for the portfolio.

Buy discipline. At first glance, the question about when to buy a stock seems simple: You buy it when you want to buy it. But what criteria should be used to justify the process? Should one wait for a broker to call and say "hey buddy, buddy, buddy, you gotta own it, own it, own it," like Mars Blackman in *She's Gotta Have It,* saying "hey baby, baby, baby, do you wanna, wanna, wanna," or does one use more rational criteria.

The criteria used in the business management approach being described includes both valuation factors and risk management techniques. The valuation factors are relatively simple and the risk management techniques are more complex.

The simple part of the buy discipline is that unless a stock has a minimum projected annual return of over 20% during our maximum two-year investment horizon then the stock does not get purchased. As Tables 9.5 and 9.6 indicate, the difference between acceptable candidates and unacceptable candidates may appear slight and, in some cases, even absurd, but I emphasize that I am following a consistent business management approach to building high return profile portfolios.

Table 9.5 shows a stock that would be acceptable for purchase based on the valuation part of the buy discipline. The suggested one-year annualized return is 31% and the suggested two-year annualized return is 22%, based on the assumed P/E multiples and the $21.50 purchase price. If the stock was at $23.50, however, as in Table 9.6, the stock would no longer be acceptable for purchase. In this case, although the stock is only two points higher, the suggested one-year annualized return has declined to 20% and the suggested two-year annualized return has declined to 17%. In a systematic investment process, I believe the suggested two-year return difference of 5% is highly significant given that the long-term average rate of return for equities is only 11%. If I had the opportunity to purchase only one stock, then my selection process would likely be different, given the relatively low probability of precisely predicting outcomes with individual stocks. My experience applying this discipline to selecting an entire portfolio has shown, however, that the outlined method, consistently applied to

Table 9.5—Projected Return Calculations

Year	1991	1992	1993	1994	1995	1996
Earnings per share	$1.00	$1.25	$1.52	$1.82	$2.16	$2.52
EPS growth rate		25%	22%	20%	19%	17%
Dividends per share		0.00	0.00	0.00	0.00	0.00
Company PE/S&P PE		1.50	1.40	1.30	1.20	1.10
Projected company PE		23	21	20	18	17
Projected price		$28	$32	$35	$39	$42
Cumulative dividends		0.00	0.00	0.00	0.00	0.00
Projected return		31%	22%	18%	16%	14%
Projected yield		0.0%	0.0%	0.0%	0.0%	0.0%

Assumed purchase price	21.50	
S&P multiple	15	Fiscal Year: December
Months to year-end	12	Current Date: 01/01/92

Table 9.6—Projected Return Calculations

Year	1991	1992	1993	1994	1995	1996
Earnings per share	$1.00	$1.25	$1.52	$1.82	$2.16	$2.52
EPS growth rate		25%	22%	20%	19%	17%
Dividends per share		0.00	0.00	0.00	0.00	0.00
Company PE/S&P PE		1.50	1.40	1.30	1.20	1.10
Projected company PE		23	21	20	18	17
Projected price		$28	$32	$35	$39	$42
Cumulative dividends		0.00	0.00	0.00	0.00	0.00
Projected return		20%	17%	15%	13%	12%
Projected yield		0.0%	0.0%	0.0%	0.0%	0.0%

Assumed purchase price	23.50	
S&P multiple	15	Fiscal Year: December
Months to year-end	12	Current Date: 01/01/92

many possible stocks, results in portfolios with consistently high return profiles.

The more complex part of the buy discipline is what happens to a stock that has an acceptable projected return. At this point the stock is subjected to "an environmental assessment" to find reasons *not* to buy the stock. The environmental assessment includes technical analysis, a survey of brokerage firm opinions on the stock, and some thought about buy-side sentiment concerning the stock. Technical analysis can show suspicious price and volume movements, suggesting that others know more than I know about the stock, which would cause me to avoid the stock if I conclude that this may be so. Regarding broker analyst opinions, although the approach does not use broker recommendations, I have found it unproductive to own stocks about which there are significant negative opinions from the brokerage community. My analysis may be completely right and the broker's analysis may be completely wrong but in such cases, I may not only have to wait a significant period of time before appreciation begins but the stock is often likely to continue declining below my normal purchase point until sentiment at least turns neutral. The most typical broker opinion on stocks that I buy is a neutral rating which, if the stock starts appreciating, will often be followed by a buy opinion. Buy-side opinions about a stock are best obtained through listening to questions asked at conferences and talking to one's peers at such conferences. As with broker opinions, the principle is the same, i.e., neutral opinions are about the best. Neutral opinions make it unlikely that one's stocks will be subject to strong selling interest after purchase and also enable such purchases to be relatively uncompetitive.

Portfolio monitoring. Portfolio monitoring is relatively simple and consists of earlier-described activities within the buy discipline plus a daily review of projected returns for the overall portfolio.

Buy discipline activities that are repeated are the environmental assessment. Although it may seem tedious to focus one's thoughts daily about all portfolio companies, I find such a process to be an effective discipline resulting in very clear thinking about each portfolio position as well as a proactive risk management technique, where necessary changes may be accomplished early and on your terms instead of later and on the market's terms.

Monitoring projected portfolio returns also focuses one's attention for the portfolio optimization methodology described in a following section. The emphasis here is for the overall portfolio to have a high weighted average projected return. If not, low-projected-return stocks should be replaced by high-projected-return stocks. Ironically, as mentioned earlier, it is the stocks that are working best, about which many managers are most enthusiastic, that lower the projected return for the overall portfolio. This results from an appreciating stock having an ever lower projected return while being an ever larger percentage of the portfolio.

Sell discipline/portfolio optimization. The sell discipline is the reverse of the buy discipline, with sell decisions being triggered either by return projections or by a negative environmental assessment. Initial sell targets are reached when the projected returns of individual stocks are lower than money market returns. Some sell decisions may be delayed, however, if sell-side and buy-side sentiment is especially positive. All stocks are sold, however, when projected returns over the next twelve months are negative 10%. If it seems astounding that other investors are buying stocks that one person's fundamental analysis find to be 10% overpriced, my only comment is that many other investors apparently do not mind speculating that even higher prices may be reached. As outlined throughout this chapter, such speculation is inconsistent with a controlled business management approach.

The daily environmental assessment practiced in portfolio monitoring may also generate some sell decisions, although these decisions often remind me of the frustrated decisions made by those portfolio managers who specialize in stocks that are going up. Even so, it would be myopic to ignore negative sentiment or events that could damage asset values even though one's fundamental analysis may be correct over a longer time period.

As mentioned above in portfolio monitoring, portfolio optimization is the process of maintaining consistently high return profiles for the whole portfolio. This is done from both a bottom-up and a top-down perspective. The bottom-up perspective focuses on stocks about which the manager may be relatively indifferent concerning risk or industry group but for which there are substantially different return prospects between the stocks. Stock A may still have a projected return of 10% over the next twelve months which does not trigger a normal sell decision, but Stock B may have a projected return of 30%. In this case it is usually productive to swap from Stock A to Stock B, thereby raising the return profile of the overall portfolio.

The top-down approach to optimization proceeds from the point when the weighted average projected return for the whole portfolio declines below a minimal level. In this case, any number of portfolio stocks with lower projected returns would be replaced by stocks with higher projected returns until the desired projected portfolio return is reached.

RESEARCH/PORTFOLIO MANAGEMENT EXAMPLES

Some brief examples will now be offered to show how my approach has worked with various stocks. Four examples in total will be given, two stocks that were bought that worked well and two stocks that were excluded from portfolios.

Stocks Included in Portfolios

Ramsay-HMO. Ramsay-HMO is a very well-run regional health maintenance organization that dominates the Hispanic health care market in South Florida. I had actually been following the company since its initial public offering in December 1989, but the date of my example is from June 1991. At that time, the stock had declined from a recent high of $16 to around $12 a share, mainly because of an announced secondary equity offering, which was to be split between the company and selling shareholders who had turned the company around some years before. Concern seemed to be high about the selling shareholders but underappreciated in the confusion was that the major selling shareholder was selling mainly to raise money for another business that badly needed capital. There were also concerns about Medicare rates for HMO patients given that 60% of Ramsay-HMO's revenues came from Medicare patients, but a close knowledge of the company would allow an investor to know that the company's costs for its Medicare patients were also quite flexible and could be adjusted depending on Medicare rate decisions. To make a long story short, my earnings estimates for the company were $1.30 for June 1992 and $1.65 for June 1993. The company's growth rate, market position, and financial characteristics warranted a 10% premium to an assumed market multiple of fifteen, resulting in the target prices and projected returns suggested below in Table 9.7.

I decided to take a very significant portion of the secondary offering, which also allowed considerable influence about the pricing of the offering. The end result is that the June 1993 target price was achieved within twelve months and a substantial portion of the stock was sold at or above the target price.

Lattice Semiconductor. Lattice Semiconductor is an example of investor knowledge about a company not catching up with current developments and of a market inefficiency created by a poor company image. Lattice had been regarded as a commodity or near-commodity supplier of programmable logic semiconductor chips. Although this characterization was true for about 30% of the company's product line, the remaining products were

Table 9.7—Projected Return Calculations

Year	1990	1991	1992	1993	1994	1995
Earnings per share	$1.05	$1.08	$1.35	$1.60	$1.90	$2.20
EPS growth rate		3%	25%	19%	19%	16%
Dividends per share		0.00	0.00	0.00	0.00	0.00
Company PE/S&P PE		1.10	1.10	1.10	1.05	1.05
Projected company PE		17	17	17	16	16
Projected price		$18	$22	$26	$30	$35
Cumulative dividends		0.00	0.00	0.00	0.00	0.00
Projected return		N.M.	81%	47%	35%	30%
Projected yield		0.0%	0.0%	0.0%	0.0%	0.0%
Assumed purchase price	12.00					
S&P multiple	15				Fiscal Year: June	
Months to year-end	1				Current Date: 06/15/91	

very high speed (although low logic density) proprietary devices. Completely unappreciated, however, was the company's development efforts in very high speed, high logic density devices. Also affecting the stock was that in the quarter ended December 1990, within about a year of when the company had gone public, the company had "missed" its earnings estimate. In my discussions with various people about the company, there seemed to be no awareness or complete skepticism about the new product line and an almost irrational fixation on the missed earnings estimate. My contact with the company in October 1991 indicated to me that this was a very well-managed company with all the necessary management disciplines for technological and business success. At that point the stock was selling for about $10, which seemed inexpensive based on my earnings estimates of $0.90, $1.20, and $1.50 for the fiscal years ending in March 1992, 1993, and 1994, respectively. Although competitors with similar growth rates were selling at very high P/E ratios, I decided that a conservative multiple to protect myself would be only a 10% premium to a market multiple, which resulted in a projected company multiple of seventeen. Based on my earnings estimates, this implied target prices of $15, $20, and $24 over the following three years, which implied very high projected returns as may be seen from Table 9.8.

Table 9.8—Projected Return Calculations

Year	1991	1992	1993	1994	1995	1996
Earnings per share	$0.92	$0.90	$1.20	$1.50	$1.75	$1.95
EPS growth rate		–2%	33%	25%	17%	11%
Dividends per share		0.00	0.00	0.00	0.00	0.00
Company PE/S&P PE		1.10	1.10	1.05	1.00	1.00
Projected company PE		17	17	16	15	15
Projected price		$15	$20	$24	$26	$29
Cumulative dividends		0.00	0.00	0.00	0.00	0.00
Projected return		N.M.	84%	49%	35%	29%
Projected yield		0.0%	0.0%	0.0%	0.0%	0.0%
Assumed purchase price	10.50					
S&P multiple	15				Fiscal Year: March	
Months to year-end	1				Current Date: 10/05/91	

As with Ramsay-HMO, the projected price targets were also achieved relatively quickly, with the stock selling for over $20 during the third quarter of 1992.

Stocks Excluded from Portfolios

AST Research. AST Research is a pretty well run personal computer manufacturer that has grown very quickly. The computers are very good technically, the marketing has been quite good within a focused market segment (value-added resellers and distributors), using a niche product strategy (notebooks and premium quality machines), and the company has produced high profit levels compared with many competitors. In the summer of 1991, the company was being recommended aggressively by a considerable number of brokers at a time when AST was a large position in a portfolio that I had recently taken over from another manager. Initial research confirmed the company's high quality in a significant number of areas, but I was troubled by the company's financial model, which looked too good to be sustainable in a very competitive industry. The most noticeable aspect of the model was that, at assumed profitability levels, the company generated a considerable amount of cash. At the time, in July 1991, my preliminary earnings estimate for the fiscal year ending in June 1992 was about $2.50 (which was above broker estimates of $2.20 to $2.30) based on the potential opportunities that the company could address. Soon afterwards, the company released final results for the June 1991 fiscal year in which the June quarter results were above broker analyst expectations. The tone on the conference call was jubilant from both management and analysts and most analysts raised their June 1992 estimates to a range of $2.40 to $2.75 after the call. I found a number of things troubling, however, particularly some comments by management (almost as an aside) that because they believed that the company was a low-cost producer they would be willing to match competitor price cuts. After thinking about industry dynamics and gross margin deterioration experienced by PC companies in the past, my new assumptions produced an earnings estimate of $2.20 for June 1992. Although being considerably below consensus estimates was troubling enough, even more troubling was seeing that, even at that level of profitability, the company would add another $10 million to its already large cash hoard of $140 million. In other words, if the company chose to be really aggressive based on its strong balance sheet, company earnings could be considerably below my low estimate. Table 9.9 suggests the poor possible returns based on my earnings estimates.

Table 9.9—Projected Return Calculations

Year	1991	1992	1993
Earnings per share	$2.13	$2.19	$2.13
EPS growth rate		3%	–3%
Dividends per share		0.00	0.00
Company PE/S&P PE		0.70	0.70
Projected company PE		11	11
Projected price		$23	$22
Cumulative dividends		0.00	0.00
Projected return		-25%	–14%
Projected yield		0.0%	0.0%
Assumed purchase price	30.00		
S&P multiple	15		Fiscal Year: June
Months to year-end	11		Current Date: 08/01/91

Based on the poor projected returns, the stock was sold at $30 per share which was helpful given that the stock fell over 50% in the next twelve months.

Employee Benefit Plans. Employee Benefit Plans is a rapidly growing provider of services allowing small and medium-sized companies to self-insure their employee health care costs. The stock had been a stock market darling as many investors had been taken with the company's aggressive management style and projections for rapid growth. In January 1992, the stock sold for over thirty times the May 1992 consensus estimate of about $1.80 and for only slightly less than thirty times the May 1993 consensus estimate of about $2.25. All of a sudden one day, however, the company mentioned that the recession was going to have some effect on earnings in the current quarter but just how much effect was uncertain. With such uncertainty, the stock dropped thirty points in one day to a price of $30. In my somewhat contrarian way, I thought that this may be an opportunity in that the company could not have changed that much from day-to-day although the stock market value had just plunged by 50%. What I found when analyzing the company, however, was that the company's financial behavior was quite difficult to characterize in a simple model. The difficulty was that the company has four different business lines—all of which had very different top-line growth rates and expense structures. The company itself gave very little direct information about how all these different sectors were performing, but in piecing together information from various sources I came up with a surprising financial model. In short, the operations with the most operating leverage and the highest margins were now growing very slowly and the operations with the least operating leverage and the lowest margins were growing at about three times the rate of the higher-margined segments. Adding insult to injury, the fastest growing segment, a reinsurance operation, required considerable capital to support its growth. Essentially, what was required for such an analysis was to build quarterly income statement models individually for all four sectors and then to aggregate the results together to have assumptions for my integrated financial statement projection program.

The results were startling which, as an aside, makes it appropriate to mention one of my simple principles of company analysis. This principle is that while company managements may lie and analysts may lie, reasonable numbers carefully thought through do not lie. The result of the careful numbers in EBP's case was that the faster the company grew its reinsurance business relative to the other businesses, the less money the whole company was going to make. Whereas revised analyst estimates after the January 1992 surprise were $1.55 and $1.90 for May 1992 and May 1993, respectively, my model produced estimates of $1.20 and $1.10, respectively. Another thing to note about this example was that management was impossible to reach by phone after the surprise. In one brief conversation I finally had with a member of management, very little was acknowledged about anything and there seemed to be little top-down recognition that the business behaved the way it had been characterized by my model. By the time I had concluded that my analysis was sufficient to cause me to avoid the stock the share price had declined further to $23. Avoiding the stock was the proper decision as well, given that the stock fell below $10 per share within the next six months.

CONCLUSION

This concludes my discussion of a "private market" orientation to small cap investing using a business management approach. In closing, I would like to summarize various aspects of the approach and the benefits from such aspects.

Early Discovery

The emphasis on being an early investor provides a number of benefits. Most simply, there is less competition for good investment ideas, as most investors would rather wait until stocks were more in the mainstream and the stocks had "started to work." Beyond that, however, an early investor has the opportunity to invest in the truly great small cap names very early and at valuations such stocks are unlikely to ever see again for some time. An investor with an early orientation is also forced to actively recognize emerging trends both with individual companies and their industries and with the economy as a whole. Such active recognition of trends provides synergistic benefits, both in exploiting opportunities and in managing risks that are not as acutely available to more reactive investors.

Original Research

Relying on one's own efforts in the research process provides many benefits and risk management techniques. To begin, original research will always bring one closer to the sunlight rather than the shadows in which most investment decisions are made. Beyond the additional understanding about each company in itself, however, there is a cascade of benefits available from such understanding.

Comprehensive screening allows one to focus one's time more efficiently. Systematic opportunity assessment forces more consistency and comparability across the companies researched, allowing firmer conclusions about company prospects. Risk assessment provides both systematic quality control and a considerable amount of intellectual stimulation about the true value of a company when subjected to a risk management perspective. Continuing review is ongoing quality control but is also more efficient than many monitoring approaches in that its structure has built-in controls and that the prior comprehensive original research provides a strong hypothesis that is easily checked for change or variance. All in all, such benefits work synergistically to manage risk aggressively and to provide the framework for a rational business management approach.

Strict Buy/Sell Discipline

The buy/sell discipline, along with portfolio optimization, results in minimal slippage between projected investment results and actual investment results. In addition to the rational framework it provides to act on investment opportunities, there are also considerable risk management techniques. The buy discipline not only suggests which stocks have the highest projected returns but it also forces an investor, in the environmental assessment, to proceed on a number of additional risk management steps. The sell discipline not only forces an investor to take profits but also manages risk by protecting an investor against a later negative surprise, which will eliminate all profits or even produce a loss. The sell discipline also enables more efficient use of investor time as sell decisions are both relatively automatic and are based on simple, rational criteria. More efficiency is seen in the case of being forced to sell a stock that later has a negative surprise. The investor is then spared the inevitable wrangling with management about what went wrong and the resulting intellectual gymnastics about what to do with the position at that point. Portfolio optimization provides one more control and rational management procedure to help achieve objectives. The investor can actively manage portfolios while being aware of portfolio return prospects instead of waking up and finding that the overall portfolio now has relatively poor returns prospects at a time that is disadvantageous for establishing more productive portfolio positions.

Systematic Approach

The process outlined in this chapter is uniquely designed for the risks and opportunities of small cap investing. Very thorough original research is possible with small companies, and so a step-by-step business management approach has been designed to do such research most effectively.

The inherent riskiness of small cap investing requires more rational and controlled portfolio management processes than are usually practiced in the investment business. Although all or portions of such an approach could probably be applied to all or a portion of an approach for larger-sized equities, I believe that the unique opportunities of small cap investing are exploited very effectively by a process specifically designed for small-cap investing, such as by the systematic process outlined in this chapter.

Chapter 10

The Evolution of a Small Cap Investor

William Martindale
Managing Principal
Martindale Andres & Co.

INTRODUCTION

During the late '50s I would come home at night after basketball or foot-
ball practice and my dad would be reading the stock pages. As you might
expect, I developed an interest in the companies he used to follow. I began
to read the stock pages in the newspaper just as he did, to learn from what
he was doing. That was really my initial exposure to investing. Of course,
at that time I didn't have any money to invest.

I went on to college and majored in business and minored in math.
After graduation, I was earning a little bit of money as an officer in the Air
Force. It wasn't much in those days, but I decided that investing in the
stock market might be a pretty good idea. I found a local broker and
bought a mutual fund here and there. I also started listening to his ideas
about what might be a good investment, and he came up with some small-
company names. I didn't have any real knowledge of the companies; they
just sounded like they could grow, so I got involved with them.

I remember Clopay Plastics and Stepan Chemical, but the one that
stands out the most is Radio Shack, which later became Tandy. I can remember having purchased $1,000 of the stock in 1966, holding it for a year
or so and deciding to sell it at a very minor profit. That $1,000, had I held

on to the stock, would have been worth $500,000 by 1982. There's a prime example of a growth stock, a company that compounded its earnings and cash flows to something significant in the future.

Throughout my period of time in the service, my interest in stock investing grew larger. After serving five years in the Air Force I decided to begin a new career. I was so interested in stocks and investing that I decided to become a stock broker. Eventually I took a job with Dean Witter in Philadelphia. I quickly found out that I knew little about investing and even less about selling. I tried emulating those around me with very little success. Four months into the business I started opening an account here and there because I was developing a style of my own and my sincerity began to show through. I learned that I had a keen interest in investing and the attendant thought process.

Seeking superior returns was and is very important to me. I was never really focused on sales commissions. I would study and try to find companies to invest in. Learning how to invest during that volatile period in the stock market was no honeymoon. Stocks had been down since 1968 and there was a big bottom in 1970, followed by a big move up in '71 and '72 that helped me emerge as somebody with a reasonable level of success in the business.

It was about that time that I stumbled across a little company through a fellow I knew. It was called Automated Environmental Systems and no one had ever heard of it. They were in the process of merging with a textile company called Universal Dye and Finishing. The merged company was named Unifi. I purchased 50 shares of that stock in 1970 at about $4.00 a share. At the time there were about 600,000 shares outstanding. Thinking, "Well, here's a fledgling little company that I can grow with over the years," I remember setting the goal that some day I would own 10,000 shares of that stock and it would be worth $100 a share. That would make me a millionaire!

GROWING WITH SMALL COMPANIES

In the early '70s I went about the business of trying to develop a client base and get them interested in putting a little bit of their money, not very much, in small companies that could grow. I did the normal things that a broker does, but I developed an interest in Unifi and set up a twenty-year goal of growing with it. Gradually I introduced it to my clients and they thought I was probably off my rocker, but acquired 100 shares here and 100 shares there anyhow.

The stock market turned rocky in '73 and '74, and the $10,000 or $12,000 that I had invested diminished to about $1,000 by the bottom of the market in December of '74. I concluded that this was tuition for my education. It is called the school of hard knocks, where I learned the vagaries of the marketplace. It was a relatively inexpensive education.

During the '73–'74 period, I broadened my investment scope to involve more than one company, recognizing that a portfolio approach made some sense. Unifi moved from $4.00 a share to $20.00 a share, before it started its precipitous decline to less than $1.00 a share. Not much was happening with the company, fundamentally, but expectations had certainly changed in the minds of investors.

I identified several smaller companies that had promise in various fields—Adams Russell in cable TV and Fab Industries in textiles. They all had one thing in common: they were smaller growth companies. I decided that if I was going to make my mark or make my fortune, it was going to have to be through investing in smaller companies with the basic premise that from little acorns, big oaks grow. The approach was compelling because if you were right on one of several, that one winner could make up for virtually all of your mistakes and provide a superior portfolio return.

I did some of the mathematical calculations to find out what it would take to build a million dollars in capital. Never stating it as a goal, I believed that 15% to 20% compounded rates would be enough to achieve the objective. I didn't think 15–20% was possible with bonds or blue chip stocks.

Over the next several years the stock market improved and my business grew. I remained in sales and was one of the better producers in the office, but certainly not the top one. Most important, I was beginning to recover financially from those very difficult years. My portfolio had recovered to where it was worth $15,000 or $16,000. All in all, not much money one way or the other.

I developed other interests, yet my avocation remained studying small companies and their stocks. During that ten-year period, I began to establish certain criteria to warrant making an investment in a company. I was searching for a company that was undervalued (low P/E) and was growing, giving me a leveraged position. I later called this the "double whammy," which meant investing in a company when earnings growth would take place and the price earnings ratio would increase as investors began to notice the company's accomplishments. I also wanted companies where management had a significant equity interest. I looked for companies that could, but did not, pay dividends because I felt they were taking the opportunity to reinvest in their own business, and that this choice was so compelling that they wouldn't waste the money on the double taxation of any of their earnings. I preferred companies that had strong financials, high internal rates of return, companies that were dominant in their marketplace, operating in niche markets, and perhaps most important, I required companies that told the truth in terms of how and what they reported to their shareholders.

In terms of evaluating a company over the long term, it is mandatory to read their quarterly and annual reports. One must see what they have to say to their shareholders and then see if they can honestly face up to the issues that they are dealing with and reflect them properly to their shareholders. It takes some practice to read between the lines and interpret what is said to pass judgment on their capability of managing the firm to see what direction they are taking and if they are truly focused on the long term.

TIME IS OF THE ESSENCE

My sense has always been that the largest component of earning a positive return is time. It takes time to compound capital. You need a multiple-year outlook, and three to five years seems to be a reasonable period of time. My sense is that if the management is committed to what it is doing, there's probably an indefinite period of time you can look to hold a stock, maybe never selling the stock. If you look back over history at the companies that have survived and thrived in this country and grown to become world dominant, there's rarely been a time to sell. Coca Cola, Hewlett-Packard, and WalMart are good examples of this buy-and-hold philosophy. On the other hand, there are companies that get too big, too mature and like humans may suffer from old age and actually die. Certainly if companies don't adjust to changing conditions that is what's destined to happen to them.

Having determined that I needed to hold my investments for a long period of time, I found that it was really insufficient to make just one investment decision in a particular company and never concern myself with that decision again. I had to make a continual series of decisions over that period of time. In fact, it has been proven many times, no matter what price or value I thought a stock might achieve, it would always be cheaper at some point in the future. It is often two or three years before the stock really begins to perform.

The fortune of having a stock go straight up from the moment you buy it, although alluring on the surface, is neither likely to occur nor a major factor in becoming a successful investor. I began a process of screening a wide range of companies based on my own list of fundamentals. It had to have the right market capitalization. It had to have the right management/ownership. It needed an earnings track record. Dividends were of no consequence; I was looking for high reinvestment rates. The type of business was not particularly significant because I felt that it wasn't necessarily the industry growth rate, rather it was the ability of the management to operate in the business that they were in. Sure, it would be nice if the industry was in a growth cycle. When that's the case, it draws a lot of capital and it also draws a lot of competition.

In my process of screening, I would whittle down a long list to a much narrower group of companies and try to determine which ones would be the most useful to sample.

I would acquire a relatively few shares of stock in order to begin to get reports and to get a sense of the management and what they had to say to their shareholders, how they viewed their business and how they assessed their own potential. Then I needed to do the comparative analysis of other companies and see if I could justify a position in that company. I wanted to think like the people inside that company even though I wasn't an insider.

An investor/owner focused on long-term compounding avoids the frictional costs of trading, paying taxes, and making too many decisions. After you make investments, things do change. Judgments must continue even in an investment one wants to stay with over the long term. One must eliminate investments that just don't work out for fundamental reasons and be willing to take losses, usually not less than 50% and in some cases 100%. You can only lose 100% of what you invest, but your return on the upside is theoretically infinite.

If you have a portfolio of stocks and one or two of those investments begin to do what you expect them to do, they become, over time, a disproportionate share of the overall assets. The question you have to ask then is: Do I try to maintain a diversified portfolio or do I allow my successful investments to dominate the portfolio? Having a broadly diversified stock portfolio diminishes both risk and return. The realization of superior return is best accomplished by staying with your successful investments, eliminating your mistakes, and accepting this imbalance that has to occur in the portfolio over time.

In the arcane world of small-company stocks, having a sound foundation of knowledge and confidence in the management is critically important. That knowledge is what's going to support you in your investment process when emotions have gone in the wrong direction or to extremes. Emotions portrayed in stock prices come out in the form of volatility. When you are dealing with smaller-company stocks, they are more volatile and price swings are more frequent and more extreme.

In order to take advantage of a buying "opportunity" one has to have cash and also the courage to buy the stocks when they are down. Knowledge is the basis that provides the courage to invest when others are selling. This form of dollar cost averaging is really what small cap investing and achieving superior return is all about. I found that stock prices can vary 30%, 40%, or 50% in a relatively short period of time, while larger companies' variance is not nearly as great.

THE SUCCESSFUL LONG-TERM INVESTOR

Finally, you have to adhere to certain fundamentals in making a new investment selection, although you probably will never find everything that you want in any particular stock. If you do, you're going to be paying too much for it. You are looking for a company that has an established position in its market, preferably a dominant position—a company that's in the process of creating its own monopoly, a low-cost producer, a dominant player in its field. Ideally, you are looking for a company with a pristine balance sheet, where the shareholders are the true owners of the company, and where the strength of the company can carry it through hard times.

Primarily, you are looking for a company that has the depth of capital to carry it during difficult periods. You want companies where the principals have significant ownership interest, and that's where their return, their own wealth-building, comes from. Any company that's growing is a consumer of capital, but if it has a high enough growth rate and a high enough rate of return, it should generate free cash flow, which gives it the ability to finance its growth.

For successful long-term investors in small companies, the challenge is to build the wealth of knowledge that's required to truly understand what these companies are doing just as if you were an insider. One of the ways to accomplish this is to read and understand the shareholder information (quarterly releases and annual reports), enable yourself to think as if you were management of that company, and assess whether management is doing the things that are correct for the long term. Measure them against other companies in the field. Pay far less attention to short-term phenomena and use your knowledge base to reduce acquisition costs and increase your return over time.

This system can work. Unifi, the company in which I purchased 50 shares in 1970, is today a world leader in polyester and nylon texturizing. In 1993 Unifi will have worldwide sales of over $1.2 billion. The 50 shares of Unifi purchased in 1970 at $4 per share are now, with splits, over 1,200 shares and were recently selling around $35 per share. That's a *210 to 1* return over twenty-three years. Somehow my goal appears modest now.

A QUESTION-AND-ANSWER SUMMARY OF THE MARTINDALE SMALL CAP INVESTMENT STYLE

Q.   *How would you describe your investment style?*

A.   My philosophy involves investing in smaller companies for a long period of time, which allows compounding to work to your advantage and to reduce frictional costs such as taxes and commissions. I buy companies with good balance sheets and earnings records in niche markets where they can grow to dominate their market.

Q.   *What do you mean when you say smaller companies or smaller capitalization?*

A.   The focus is on companies with $50 million to $100 million, as a minimum market capitalization, to companies on the upper range of $1 billion in market capitalization. The company has gone through the embryonic stage or the venture stage and is now viable with a track record of earnings, typically several years in age.

Q.   *What are the top three characteristics that you look for in choosing a stock?*

A.   I am interested in a company's historic earnings record, the company's balance sheet, and the company's position in its market. All of those things reflect the competence and capability of management. What I am really interested in is the management, and I decide over a period of time if they have what it takes to make the company a good long-term investment.

Q.   *How do you search for these companies? How do you find them? Where do you look?*

A.   Many different sources help me go through this process. Published information such as that furnished in *The Wall Street Journal, Barron's, Fortune, Forbes,* and *Business Week* is basic. I also use an extensive network of individuals throughout the country that ferret out regional companies that meet our criteria. Additionally, we create investment ideas through thematic conceptualizing. We look at where we are today and how the future might unfold. If there's a high probability of success for a company that is involved in an emerging industry (videoconferencing equipment, CDMA or HDTV), we will make an investment selection based on this broad long-term theme.

Q.   *You use a buy-and-hold strategy. Typically, how long will you hold a security?*

A.   I believe that in the long run a good investment should never be sold. That's not meant to copy some of our famous investors like Warren Buffet. But the basic investment philosophy is to buy and hold a security; add shares to that security as it validates our choice—as long as the company management and financials are strong and dependable. During the accumulation process events may change one's opinion as to the original basis for making the investment, so a culling process is employed. Generally, I hold investments through a market cycle of three to five years, culling stocks as necessary.

Q.   *When you decide that there's a company in which you are interested in accumulating positions, are there particular points in time when you make more or less of a commitment?*

A.   I like to use a modified dollar cost averaging approach to the securities that I buy. In smaller companies with less liquidity and significantly higher price volatility, I see price changes that do not necessarily reflect any fundamental change in the company or its outlook. Recognizing this and the vagaries of the market, I accumulate over a long period of time, willing to step up to the plate, so to speak, when prices are down.

Q.   *To follow up on your buy-and-hold strategy, do you also have a sell discipline?*

A.   There's not a point in time, based on price, that a stock should be sold. Having the long view, we are far less price sensitive than most investors. So, the sell discipline is basically fundamental. Sell when it is clear that management has altered its course or when it is clear that management has not been able to produce intended results within the projected time frame.

Q.   *Do you have any kinds of performance expectations for your stocks, either absolute or relative, and if so, over what time frames?*

A.   Our stated objective of course is to outperform the market. In order to be realistic about that objective we have to have an investment horizon that is longer than traditional investment horizons, usually three to five years, not three to five months. Time moderates risk. Our basic belief is that a company can have the ability to grow consistent with its internal rate of return, or return on equity. Over time, compounding of the internal rate of return will be reflected in market price.

Q.   What do you mean when you use the phrase "double whammy"?

A.   I use "double whammy" to emphasize the impact in the valuation of a security into the future that includes both earnings growth and multiple (price to earnings) revision. Earnings growth, as exemplified by the reported numbers, and multiple revision, as exemplified by the market's perception of those earnings, can lift prices geometrically as the market starts to perceive this growth.

Q.   What do you think about the issue of risk and liquidity in small cap stocks that you select?

A.   The risk that one takes in a small cap stock is largely a liquidity risk. We're not terribly concerned about the ability to resell the security in the short term. Recognizing that it's relatively difficult to accumulate the position in a short period of time, we have the confidence that liquidity will develop several years out.

Q.   How much do you rely on Wall Street and also on regional investment banking houses for research ideas?

A.   Over the years I've placed very little emphasis on research reports and the information provided by Wall Street. However, more recently that's been modified as some of the regional firms have been able to focus on companies in their own areas. Research staffs at national wire houses or the large investment banks tend to ignore smaller companies that cannot be bought in size by large institutions.

Q.   How do you stay on top of day to day and month to month developments?

A.   We have state of the art on-line information systems for providing news as it occurs. It's imperative to monitor that information, as it can give you clues as to how and when to act in the marketplace. Although you are continuously reading and evaluating information as it comes through, you also know there's an emotional side to the market that causes people to act in what I perceive to be an irrational fashion. This explains why security prices are constantly seeking their true value but never attaining it.

Q.   *Could you describe your best and your worst stock picks?*

A.   Well, the worst stock pick is easy—the one where you've lost all your money. And that's the downside of any investing: 100% loss. For some reason my memory fails me on that subject. The upside is infinite. I think over the years the best return in the long run has come out of Unifi. The best short-term return was from a company called ROLM, back in the late '70s and early '80s.

Q.   *If you had a wish list of the ideal fundamentals and/or other characteristics of a company as a prospect for your style of investing, what parameters would be on that wish list?*

A.   I would begin with being able to identify, critically review and decide that there's a management team in place dedicated to the long-term growth and well-being of the enterprise. Their goals must be appropriate for their business and they must have an enduring commitment to achieving those goals. I would love to see a pristine balance sheet and a representation of past achievement through a credible earnings record. I'd love to see a company that talks honestly and openly to their shareholders—a company that enables the shareholder to benefit either in the form of a steadily increasing stream of dividends or of corporate repurchase of stock at appropriate times to reduce the capitalization, a company employing its capital to optimize its internal rate of return.

Q.   *You have just described your wish list. Does that characterize what you call the "bottom-up" approach?*

A.   Yes. The "bottom-up" approach focuses on the company and what they are about as opposed to the industry within which they operate or any broader economic projections.

Q.   *Do you use diversification in your portfolio and if you do, typically how many stocks will you hold within a portfolio?*

A.   Diversification is integral to any investment strategy in portfolio management. It is not my objective to broadly diversify a portfolio because I think it undermines overall investment performance. My optimum portfolio at this juncture will have twenty-five to thirty different securities, with representation in all of the eight broad Dow Jones industrial groupings.

Q. *As a small cap manager in a market of small cap stocks, do you feel limited or is there some total size that can be effectively managed vis-à-vis what is out there?*

A. The overall equity market has to be in the several trillion dollar range. The securities that comprise the generally perceived small cap portion of that may approximate $100 billion dollars of market capitalization. Owning twenty-five to thirty securities with an average market capitalization of $200 million dollars would limit our universe to $500 million dollars. The exit strategy for this approach is to allow our companies to grow to such a size that they become larger than the small cap limit and thereby attractive to significant institutional pools of capital.

Q. *In constructing a portfolio of small cap securities as you define them, what happens when you have some big winners?*

A. I think the question is what type of rebalancing effort is employed over time in regard to the management of the investment portfolio. Given the strategy of buying and holding, allowing winners to run, culling from the bottom, and eliminating losers, there's a very clear potential for a certain few securities to become abnormally large in terms of the percentage of the portfolio. This is something that I passively allow to occur, recognizing that in the vast majority of investment portfolios the successes are what really enable the overall portfolio to outperform and not the elimination of those successes.

PART FOUR: STRATEGIES FOR TRADING AND PORTFOLIO MANAGEMENT

Chapter 11

Minimizing Transaction Costs in Small and Mid Cap Strategies

Sandip A. Bhagat, CFA
Senior Vice President
Travelers Investment Management Co.

INTRODUCTION

The historical outperformance of small-company stocks remains one of the most curious and debated anomalies within the U.S. equity market. The Ibbotson small company index[1] has gained 12.2% annually from 1926 to 1992, while the broad market as measured by the S&P 500 has advanced at an annual rate of 10.3% over the same period. This widely publicized annual return differential of 1.9% embodies the so-called size effect. In fact, the importance of the size effect as a key determinant of overall equity returns has been elevated further in recent studies (see Fama and French in References).

While the relative merits of views supporting or refuting the size effect are discussed in other chapters, we will focus our attention here on one of the arguments rejecting the size effect—the high cost of trading these small and mid cap stocks. Those who dismiss the size effect view small-company excess returns as the premium for bearing additional risks, including liquidity risk. They argue that these nominal excess returns disappear on a risk-adjusted basis.

It is widely acknowledged that the small and mid cap subset of the equity universe is characterized by thin trading volumes and high bid-asked spreads. Can these excess returns be realized after accounting for the real-world friction of trading costs in this less liquid market? For example, the annualized spread of 190 basis points mentioned above would be wiped out by transaction costs associated with annual one-way portfolio turnover of less than 100%. Such a level of portfolio turnover is not unusual and probably underestimates the experience of the median small-company active manager.

The impact of transaction costs on small and mid cap returns is an important consideration for both portfolio performance and asset allocation decisions. Since a penny saved is a penny gained, any savings in trading costs will flow through directly to improved performance. In this context, there may be as much potential to add value in small and mid cap strategies through controlling trading costs as in the stock selection process itself.

Strategic asset allocation models typically assign a modest weight to small and mid cap stocks based on historical returns and risk. If these gross returns are overstated because they ignore trading costs, then a constrained optimization using transaction costs will most likely reduce the optimal allocation to small and mid cap stocks.

What factors create frictional costs during the trading process and how can they be controlled to reduce total trading costs? Our discussion in this chapter attempts to answer these questions within an overall framework for understanding the trading process for small and mid cap stocks. We have organized our analysis into the following sections. Section I describes stock market microstructure and its implications for trading small and mid cap stocks. We identify the various sources of liquidity available to execute these trades and examine the factors contributing to the higher cost of trading. Section II provides a framework for identifying and measuring components of total trading costs. The relative importance of these components for small and mid cap trading is discussed, along with the effects on trading strategy created by sole emphasis on any one criterion. Section III integrates expected liquidity effects into the overall equity management process and discusses the use of pre-trade analytics to define the overall difficulty of a pro forma trade. Finally, the development of an optimal trading strategy and implementation are discussed in Section IV.

STOCK MARKET MICROSTRUCTURE AND IMPLICATIONS FOR SMALL AND MID CAP STOCKS

Liquidity and Efficiency

A good starting point to analyze stock market microstructure and its implications for trading decisions is to understand the features of an ideal market. An ideal market should be liquid and efficient; provide depth, breadth, and resiliency; and allow fair and orderly trading. While these are all desirable attributes of any market, their coexistence may be unattainable at all times because of some mutual incompatibility. We address this observation after providing some basic definitions of these market attributes.

A liquid market is characterized by depth, breadth, and resiliency. Depth and breadth imply that a large number of buyers and sellers can execute several transactions in a short period of time with only minor price impact. A resilient market will tend to revert back to more appropriate price levels after experiencing a severe price jolt created by demand imbalance. In a liquid market, therefore, orderly trading is easy to achieve. A number of transactions can be executed without creating big price swings. New equilibrium levels can be established with gradual price changes in a liquid market.

A standard measure of market liquidity is defined as the ratio of dollar trading volume to the change in price over a given time period. Bernstein (see References) provides a good overview of alternative measures of market liquidity.

However, the dampening effect of a liquid market on price changes can be seen to be inconsistent with market efficiency. In an efficient market, we want prices to adjust as rapidly as possible, *not gradually*, to reflect new information as soon as it becomes available. To the extent that a liquid market prevents rapid adjustment of price, it is incompatible with the notion of market efficiency. In practice, however, this natural conflict between liquidity and efficiency does resolve itself. Liquidity tends to disappear when unambiguous news or information appears in the market, paving the way for efficiency to assert itself through a discontinuous price change. This observation can be traced to the economics of the market maker function and will be examined shortly in light of the discussion on bid-asked spreads.

It is also important to understand the different motives for trading and the influence of different trading styles on both liquidity and efficiency. Harris (see References) provides a comprehensive description of various trading motives and identifies winning and losing styles. For the narrow scope of our discussion, we will classify each trader into one of two basic categories—noise traders and information traders. Noise traders are those traders who think they have information but really do not (See Black for a discussion on the influence of noise in financial markets). Noise traders move prices away from equilibrium. Information traders, on the other hand, use information to bring prices back to equilibrium. This information could be based on either fundamental value or changes in fundamental outlook.

Information traders contribute primarily to market efficiency, while noise traders increase both market liquidity and volatility. While noise traders implement a losing style of trading, their presence is important because it creates the profit motive for information traders to supply liquidity and restore efficiency.

Sources of Liquidity

This brief background on trading markets can be put into perspective within the microstructure of the U.S. stock market. The market for trading stocks in the U.S. has been organized in the following forms: the listed exchanges, the upstairs market, and the over-the-counter (OTC) market. Each of these markets is differentiated in terms of the role and competitiveness of market makers, their supply of capital, and the mechanisms provided to maximize liquidity.

A fourth market for trading stocks has evolved in recent years. This trading alternative is generally characterized by an absence of traditional *market-making* intermediaries and allows *natural* buyers and sellers to trade with each other within a crossing network. Most of these crossing networks tend to maximize liquidity by concentrating it into one point of time. In one platform, a single price auction even facilitates price discovery while others "borrow" prices from the continuously traded market. These crossing networks can range from a formal computer facility provided by different vendors, which electronically matches buyers and sellers, to an informal arrangement between institutions to cross stocks at predetermined prices.

The Instinet system has a unique position among all trading alternatives because it combines features of a crossing network and a continuous auction market. The Instinet system is an electronic market where institutional traders can enter bids and offers at any time for both listed and OTC stocks. These orders are then displayed along with dealer quotes for OTC stocks in an "open" book. This dissemination of aggregate liquidity allows narrower spreads to develop for OTC stocks and forms the basis for price discovery through a continuous auction.

During market hours, institutional traders may use the Instinet system to simply cross small trades with each other within the best current bid-asked spread. On the other hand, the price discovery feature of Instinet usually comes into play when fundamental information released during *off-market* hours gets translated into new price levels within its continuous electronic market. It is very common these days for Instinet to discover a different stock price before the market open for companies announcing unexpected corporate developments after the prior day's close of trading.

A discussion of the fourth market trading alternatives will be deferred at this point and pursued later in the chapter. The crossing networks can be considered more as an important trading tool and distinct from traditional forms of market organization, which offer *immediacy* through market makers. Since one of the primary objectives of this section is to understand the impact of the market maker on the bid-asked spread, an analysis of the fourth market within such a context is somewhat moot.

A continuously traded market such as the U.S. stock market requires a structure to provide immediacy, i.e., the ability to transact at any time. The order flow from buyers and sellers is random and separated over time in the absence of major fundamental news. Immediacy can be provided only through intermediaries who will assume the role of temporary counterparty. The market maker performs this role and retains interim positions in inventory until a natural offsetting trader can be found. Buyers and sellers transfer price risk to the market maker by demanding liquidity and immediacy.

The market maker's compensation for this transfer of risk results in the bid-asked spread. The market maker will buy from a seller at the bid price and then later sell to a buyer at the asked or offered price. The market maker, therefore, bridges the time gap between orders and makes continuous trading possible. The presence of the market maker smooths price changes and prevents discontinuous price jumps under normal market conditions.

On the listed exchanges, liquidity is provided by a monopolistic specialist. For the privilege of making an exclusive market in certain stocks and being able to charge the bid-asked spread on all trades, the specialist is assigned the task of facilitating orderly trading. This requires the specialist to make a market, i.e., quote a bid and an asked price for a certain minimum size at all times and to accommodate any orders that may come along at any time at those prices up to the quoted size.

In the event of a severe imbalance in supply and demand, the specialist may obtain permission from the exchange to temporarily halt trading in any given stock. The trading halt advertises the imbalance and helps the specialist attract additional interest on the counterside of the imbalance. In these instances, the specialist commonly turns to the "upstairs" market, the block trading desks of major investment banks and brokerage houses, for additional liquidity.

The role of the upstairs market in terms of providing liquidity has increased in recent years. Block traders have until recently served as agents to facilitate large transactions in single stocks. In a typical transaction, the buyer of a large block of stock places an order with a block trading desk. The block trader searches for enough sellers to take the other side of the trade at a sufficiently large clearing price.

This traditional role changed a few years ago in two important ways. The upstairs market is now willing to play a bigger role as principal by committing capital to provide liquidity. Also, with the evolution of the derivatives market, it is now possible for the upstairs market to facilitate large program or basket trades instead of single stock transactions on a principal basis. This process is easier because the net positions in the overall "book of business" created from both customer order flows and proprietary trading can be effectively hedged with various index options and futures. In fact, the cost of a principal program trade for a given trade portfolio will depend on what effect it has on this aggregate book. A trade portfolio that helps diversify the book will attract a lower charge.

And, finally, for companies whose stock does not trade in sufficient volume to warrant exchange membership, or those who choose not to be encumbered by exchange affiliation requirements, there is a network of broker-dealers who together make up an over-the-counter (OTC) market for these stocks. This network is not organized on a physical exchange but is instead linked electronically. The OTC market provides competitive market making among several broker-dealers for each stock. The Instinet system integrates institutional trading interests with the liquidity indicated by traditional market makers for OTC stocks.

We might reasonably expect the competitive structure of the OTC market to offer greater liquidity and lower trading costs than the monopolistic specialist system on the listed exchanges. Several researchers have investigated this issue using different measures of liquidity.

Cooper, Groth and Avery, and Marsh and Rock (see References) find, however, that liquidity on the listed exchanges is better than that encountered in the OTC market, though not by a big margin. We also observe that bid-asked spreads tend to be larger for OTC stocks than listed stocks. These observations assume greater significance for our discussion because a large proportion of the aggregate market value of the small and mid cap universe trades in the OTC markets. We show the concentration of small and mid cap market value in OTC stocks and their larger bid-asked spreads in Tables 11.1 and 11.2.

The examples used in this chapter to illustrate the differences between large cap and small/mid-cap trading issues make reference to the following benchmark indexes. The S&P 500 index serves as our proxy for the large cap universe. The Russell 2000 index best represents small size as defined by a capitalization limit of $500 million. The S&P 400 index is used to represent the mid-cap sector. However, the S&P 400 index has a liquidity bias built into it by the selection criteria used for membership. We have, therefore, also chosen a fourth benchmark, the Russell 2500, to represent the broad cap-weighted mid/small cap universe. The Russell 2500 provides a more realistic estimate of trading costs for mid/small cap stocks.

Market data used in these analyses was compiled during April 1993. Trading volume and bid-asked spread information may change over longer time periods.

Table 11.1—Percentage of Index Market Value Traded on Different Exchanges

Exchange	S&P 500 %	S&P 400 %	Russell 2500 %	Russell 2000 %
NYSE	96.1	69.5	58.7	40.2
AMEX	0.3	2.4	4.6	7.9
Regional	0.0	0.0	0.1	0.1
OTC	3.6	28.1	36.6	51.8
Total	100	100	100	100

Source: TIMCO

Table 11.1 shows the percentage of the market value of the various indexes traded on different exchanges. While less than 4% of the market value of the S&P 500 index trades in the OTC market, that proportion increases to over 50% for the Russell 2000 index.

Table 11.2—Bid-Asked Spreads for Index Stocks Traded on Different Exchanges

Exchange	S&P 500 %	S&P 400 %	Russell 2500 %	Russell 2000 %
NYSE	0.37	0.69	0.95	1.34
AMEX	1.12	0.68	1.51	1.65
OTC	0.77	1.40	2.55	3.13
Average	0.39	0.89	1.56	2.29

Source: TIMCO

The capitalization-weighted average bid-asked spread for different indexes is shown in Table 11.2. We can see that the average bid-asked spread increases from about 0.40% for the S&P 500 to almost 2.30% for the Russell 2000 index. The bid-asked spread for OTC stocks also tends to be higher than the spread for listed stocks within each index.

It can be seen from Tables 11.1 and 11.2 that the implementation of small and mid cap strategies requires costlier execution in the OTC market to a much greater extent than with other equity strategies. It is, therefore, important to understand the reasons for the higher expected cost of trading small stocks. In order to do so, we must gain some insights into the mechanisms that govern the pricing of the bid-asked spread.

Pricing of Bid-Asked Spreads

Several studies have investigated the pricing of the bid-asked spread. Stoll; Amihud and Mendelson; and others (see References) have focused on the inventory costs of the dealer function. These costs arise from the need to maintain an ongoing presence in a continuously traded market and can be largely considered fixed in nature.

Glosten and Milgrom, and Copeland and Galai (see References) attribute the size of the bid-asked spread to the adverse information bias that the market maker is exposed to. We observed earlier that the informed trader uses information to achieve a successful trading style. The risk of trading with such informed traders exposes the market maker to this adverse information bias. The market maker wins against the noise trader and loses to the informed trader. The market maker hedges adverse information risk through the bid-asked spread.

We now examine some other determinants of the magnitude of the bid-asked spread. The bid-asked spread tends to be larger for more volatile stocks. For a given pattern of trade flows, the market maker assumes greater inventory risk, i.e., exposure to unfavorable price moves before the position can be laid off, when underlying asset volatility is high. This inventory risk is also higher when the trading volume in a stock is low. Infrequent trading spaces alternate buyers and sellers further apart in time and increases the average holding period for the market maker. In this instance, the market maker either bears a greater price risk or a greater cost to hedge aggregate net long or short positions.

The adverse information risk discussed earlier assumes greater proportions with the degree of neglect in research and analysis in any stock. An informed trader is more likely to obtain an information edge in neglected stocks. This increases the likelihood of losses by market makers to such informed traders who may possess fundamental information not yet widely disseminated.

And last but not the least, the wider spread on OTC stocks can be attributed to the mechanism governing the disclosure of information on all available bids and offers. The transaction price and the bid-asked prices on the listed exchanges evolve as a result of a continuous auction among all traders during trading hours. The rules of the organized exchanges allow for a more favorable customer bid or offered price to supersede the specialist's bid or offered price. For example, the specialist's book may show the best bid to be 20 dollars per share for 5,000 shares from one of several buyers. The best offer may be from the specialist at 20 1/2 for 1,000 shares. Any other seller may now bypass the specialist and offer 5,000 shares (or any other size for that matter) at, say, 20 1/4. The buyer may now choose to complete execution at 20 1/4 for the appropriate number of shares. As you can see, this procedure allows for a narrower bid-asked spread to develop and for the spread component of execution costs to be lower.

Except for the Instinet system, there is no provision to supersede the market maker's bid or offered prices in the OTC market. We mentioned earlier that the ability to advertise institutional trades in competition with dealer quotes leads to narrower spreads for OTC stocks in Instinet. After identifying the best inside market from competing market makers, there is no *other* mechanism in the OTC market by which a prospective buyer, for example, can get information about the best offered price from traders other than the dealer.

In our previous example, the new seller's offered price of 20 1/4 may not get disclosed to the buyer. If the buyer wants immediacy to shed price risk, the transaction could get completed at a price of 20 1/2. On the other hand, if the seller is more anxious to trade, the transaction price could be 20. Even if both the buyer and seller complete their trade at the same time, there is no satisfactory mechanism by which the traders, and not the market-maker, can profit from the two-sided liquidity. We can, therefore, see how bid-asked spreads tend to be higher in OTC stocks, where all available liquidity is not deployed to establish a clearing or transaction price.

Implications for Trading Small and Mid Cap Stocks

What does all this mean for trading small and mid cap stocks? We are aware that this universe tends to be more volatile, is more neglected, includes more OTC stocks, and trades very thinly. It is now easier to understand why trading costs for small stocks are higher. Low trading volume and higher volatility increase the inventory costs of making a market in these stocks. Adverse information risk is higher due to the neglect factor.

And, finally, the wider spreads permitted by incomplete disclosure of best bids and offers for OTC stocks have a greater influence for small and mid cap stocks.

The presence of low trading volumes and high bid-asked spreads in the small and mid cap universe is illustrated below in Table 11.3 and Figure 11.1, respectively.

Table 11.3—Distribution of Market Value in $100 Million Index Trade Portfolios for Different Ranges of Relative Trade Size

Trade Size to Avg. Daily Volume	S&P 500 %	S&P 400 %	Russell 2500 %	Russell 2000 %
Less than 10%	100.0	60.8	78.2	47.6
10% to 25%	0	31.7	17.7	30.5
More than 25%	0	7.5	4.1	21.9
Total	100	100	100	100

Source: TIMCO

Figure 11.1—Distribution of Index Market Values for Different Ranges of % Bid-Asked Spread

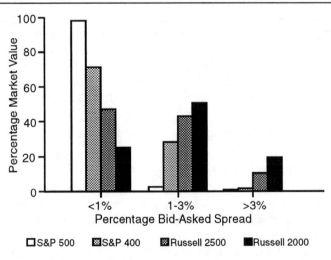

Source: TIMCO

In Table 11.3, we analyze the distribution of market value in $100 million trade portfolios for the various indexes in terms of the ratio of trade size to average daily trading volume. For example, 100% of the $100 million S&P 500 portfolio is traded in stocks where each individual stock trade represents less than 10% of that stock's recent average daily trading volume. The low proportion of daily trading volume required to transact in each stock implies a fairly liquid portfolio which should be easy to trade.

We can also see that low trading volume in the small and mid cap universe forces a greater dollar value into trade sizes for individual stocks that represent a larger portion of average daily trading volume. Almost 22% of the dollar value of a $100 million Russell 2000 portfolio is in stocks where the trade size exceeds 25% of daily trading volume.

Figure 11.1 depicts the distribution of index market value for different ranges of bid-asked spreads. While more than 95% of the market value of the S&P 500 is in stocks with a bid-asked spread of less than 1%, only 23% of the Russell 2000 index is in such liquid stocks. On the other hand, more than 50% of the Russell 2000 and 45% of the Russell 2500 is represented by stocks with a bid-asked spread between 1 and 2%. Almost 20% of the Russell 2000 is in stocks with a bid-asked spread of greater than 3%.

This completes a brief discussion of the influence of stock market microstructure on trading patterns for small and mid cap stocks. A working knowledge of these issues will be useful in understanding the more critical components of transaction costs discussed in the next section and then the key factors in developing a careful trading strategy.

MEASUREMENT AND COMPONENTS OF TRANSACTION COSTS

We discussed one component of transaction costs, the bid-asked spread, in the previous section. Before moving on to an analytical framework for developing an optimal trading strategy, we need to understand all sources of slippage that are encountered in the trading process. The interaction between the different components of trading costs will shed light on how to minimize the aggregate effect of all sources of friction. To do this, we must first develop a comprehensive measure of trading costs.

We begin with an overview of the different measures of trading costs that have found application in the equity management process so far. The earlier measures of transaction costs focused attention on executed trades only. These measures ignored the opportunity costs of unexecuted trades. The simplest such measure of execution costs compares the transaction price to the high, low, and the closing price on trade day. Here, stocks bought at or near the low price of the day and stocks sold at or near the high price of the day represent superior execution.

An improvement to this simple measure is the volume-weighted average price (VWAP) calculated for the trade day. The transaction price associated with each trade on the trade day is weighted by the proportion of daily volume represented by the respective trade size. The VWAP reflects an average price level for the traded stock during the course of the trade day. Here, the trader's objective is to execute at prices better than the VWAP, i.e., buy below the VWAP and sell above the VWAP.

In addition to ignoring opportunity costs, these measures suffer from other limitations. These methods ignore the costs associated with the bid-asked spread and any execution beyond the adverse side of the spread (a component of cost that we will soon define as market impact). In many cases, the trader can manipulate trades to look good against these measures. The effect of market movement during trade execution is also not adequately reflected in the analysis.

These limitations give rise to two ill-conceived notions. First, these approaches shift undue emphasis to commission costs. Commission costs are by far the smallest component of total transaction costs but that is not always reflected in these methods. If the difference between execution price and the VWAP happens to be low, commission costs may appear to be the dominant component of cost. Second, these methods create the illusion of negative trading costs. This happens when the execution price is sufficiently better than the VWAP to overcome commission costs. We will soon show that it is almost impossible for total trading costs to be zero or negative.

Implementation Shortfall

The most comprehensive measure for total trading costs has been proposed by Perold (see References). Within his framework, a paper portfolio is constructed at time t = 0, assuming costless execution at the benchmark price. This benchmark price is most commonly defined as the midpoint of the bid and asked prices when the decision to trade is made. The value of this paper portfolio (VPP) is then compared with the value of the actual portfolio (VAP) over time. The difference in the value of these two portfolios at any point of time t > 0 is known as the implementation shortfall (IS) **over time t. The implementation shortfall, at any time t, can be formulated** as:

$$IS(t) = VPP(t) - VAP(t)$$

The implementation shortfall over time is shown in Figure 11.2.

Figure 11.2—Implementation Shortfall Over Time

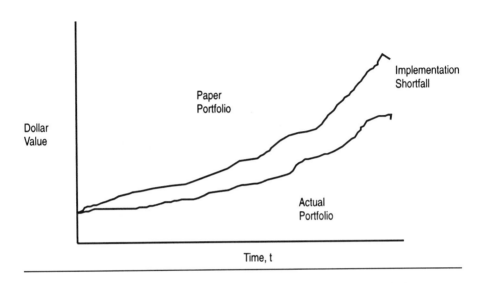

What frictional costs detract from the value of the actual portfolio and, therefore, contribute to the implementation shortfall? The answer to this question will identify all the components of total trading costs. The first component is easy to recognize and measure—commissions. Brokerage commissions represent explicit and direct costs. It is important to note that the impact of commissions on total asset value is a function of the stock price. Commissions are quoted on a per-share basis. Since the number of shares to be traded will be higher for lower-priced stocks, the percentage total commission cost will be higher.

The impact of commissions can be captured by normalizing the commission cost per share by the stock price per share (or the market value weighted price for a program trade of a basket of stocks). For example, a 3 cents/share commission charge will expend 25 basis points of total asset value for a $12 stock (0.03 divided by 12). Since the average price per share is lower for small and mid cap stocks, even this most basic cost assumes greater proportions for these stocks.

The next component should be intuitive and easy to identify after our earlier discussions on the role of market makers. We have seen that the cost of immediacy is the bid-asked spread. In the absence of intermediaries, it is reasonable to expect the *instantaneous* fair price to be the mid-point of the bid and asked prices. The size of the bid-asked spread, therefore, represents the loss in asset value incurred in a round-trip transaction in any security. Consider a stock bid at 24 1/2 and offered at 25. A round-trip transaction in one share of this stock will dissipate 1/2 from a starting asset value of 25. As a percentage of total wealth, this represents a significant loss of 5%.

Again the absolute magnitude of the bid-asked spread does not reveal enough information on expected loss of wealth. The appropriate measure expresses the bid-asked spread as a percentage of price per share. For a portfolio of stocks, the percentage portfolio bid-asked spread will be the ratio of the market value weighted bid-asked spread to the market value weighted price. One half of the percentage bid-asked spread reflects the intermediation cost for a one-sided (buy or sell) trade.

Buying at the offered price or selling at the bid price may sometimes be an optimistic expectation. We have noted that liquidity at the bid or offered price is finite and may, at times, be insufficient for the actual transaction volume. In such instances, additional liquidity may be available only at prices inferior to the current bid or offered prices (higher than the offered for purchases and lower than the bid for sales). Execution prices that penetrate the adverse side of the spread reflect market impact. Market impact is an important element of trading costs and can be considered to be the price dislocation caused by a demand for liquidity beyond the size prevailing at the current bid and offered prices.

In a liquid and resilient market, one would expect bid-asked spreads to be small, market impact to be insignificant, and any price deviations caused by such market impact to be short-lived. Unfortunately, the market for small and mid cap stocks is far removed from this ideal configuration.

The final component of trading costs takes into account the opportunity costs of unexecuted trades. Unexecuted trades in the actual portfolio will be represented by either unused cash or, alternatively, benchmark index exposure if futures are being used to achieve broad asset class exposure from the beginning of trading. In either instance, the *relative* performance of unexecuted trades will also cause the performance of the actual portfolio to differ from that of the paper portfolio.

These four components—commissions, bid-asked spread, market impact, and opportunity costs—capture all elements of trading costs and lead to a measurement of the implementation shortfall. A comparison of the relative magnitude of these costs for a one-way trade in stocks of different-sized companies is shown in Table 11.4.

Table 11.4—Measurement and Components of Transaction Costs

Component of Transaction Costs	S&P 500 bps	S&P 400 bps	Russell 2500 bps	Russell 2000 bps
1. Commissions +	10	15	20	25
2. 1/2 Bid-Asked Spread +/-	20	45	75	115
3. Market Impact +/-	Path-dependent	Path-dependent	Path-dependent	Path-dependent
4. Opportunity Costs	Path-dependent	Path-dependent	Path-dependent	Path-dependent

Source: TIMCO

Both market impact and opportunity costs will depend on the actual pattern of order flows, liquidity shifts, and security prices. It is, therefore, difficult to estimate them on an ex-ante basis. While it is possible that either of these components may turn out to be a negative cost (i.e., portfolio savings) in rare instances, it is virtually impossible for both to be negative at the same time. The latter observation holds because of the inverse relationship between market impact and opportunity costs.

Market Impact and Opportunity Costs

The trade-off between market impact and opportunity costs has significant implications for the development of a successful trading strategy. It is, therefore, important to examine the interaction of these two components in some detail. Market impact can be controlled through patient trading. If the trade size exceeds available liquidity at the margin, the trader's objective is to execute the additional shares as close to the adverse side of the spread as possible. Patient trading is most commonly implemented with the use of limit orders. An example of a limit order to buy either a single stock or a portfolio of stocks would be to specify a limit price equal to the current asked price + 1/4. In other words, the trader is trying to limit market impact to no more than 1/4. Another way to trade patiently is to spread the trade size over time. In this case, only partial positions get executed at any one time.

Any effort to mitigate market impact through such patient trading will most likely lower its cost. But, in such instances, opportunity costs are likely to be significantly adverse because unexecuted trades will probably occur in those stocks whose superior relative performance has moved them farther and farther away from price limits. Indeed, the easiest way to minimize opportunity costs is to complete all trades instantaneously with market orders. This will solve the problem of unexecuted trades. We can see, however, that market impact in this instance will be very large. The unfortunate truism is that any effort to control opportunity costs comes at the expense of market impact and vice versa.

In the context of the implementation shortfall and its components in Table 11.3, if all trades can be executed instantaneously at no worse than the adverse side of the spread, total trading costs will range between commission costs at best and the sum of commission and bid-asked spread costs at worst, i.e., $1 \le$ trading costs $\le (1 + 2)$.

The shape of the trading cost curve as a function of time is shown in Figure 11.3.

Figure 11.3—Total Trading Costs Over Time

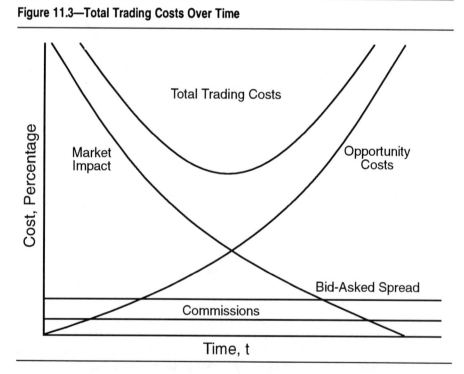

Commission costs can be considered invariant over short time periods. Bid-asked spread costs remain fairly constant over short trading horizons. We can see that opportunity costs increase as time goes by while market impact costs are highest at t = 0 and then decline over time. The total trading cost curve, therefore traces a parabolic path with a minimum at some discrete t > 0. In other words, total trading costs can be minimized by trading patiently enough to lower market impact to some extent but yet not so patiently so as to incur large opportunity costs.

We will see later that certain subsets of a trade list are better suited for patient trading, while other stocks in the trade list may warrant more aggressive execution. The accurate timing of individual trades within an overall program trade still remains an art form rather than a precise science. We will discuss guidelines in the last section on implementation issues to lend more structure to the trading process.

The inverse trade-off between market impact and opportunity costs is even more dramatic for small and mid cap stocks. Low trading volume in these stocks increases the magnitude of market impact from aggressive trading. The lack of depth can produce transaction prices far in excess of the originally prevailing bid or offered price with simple market orders.

An analysis of small stock returns also shows significant autocorrelation. This implies that streaks of consecutive positive or negative returns are more frequent and longer for these stocks. One reason for this pattern in returns may be the role of momentum investors in small and mid cap stocks. The growth style of investing is more popular in this universe and these investors tend to rely heavily on earnings and price momentum in their buy or sell decisions. This observation suggests that opportunity costs for small and mid cap stocks are likely to be higher, i.e., delaying the purchase of a favorably rated stock because of market impact concerns may eventually cost more. Low trading volume and serial price correlation create steeper curves for market impact and opportunity costs, respectively.

Patient trading is also vulnerable to the pitfalls of a subtle but consistent bias known as adverse stock selection. The effect works as follows. Stocks most likely to be executed with limit orders are those exhibiting unfavorable momentum. With patient trading, we are more likely to buy underperforming stocks on relative weakness and to miss execution in outperforming stocks whose price action takes them further away from original price limits. A similar trend develops on the sell side. This is completely counter to the outcome needed for superior portfolio performance; we want to buy the winners as soon as possible and sell the losers as soon as possible. Our discussion of price momentum and autocorrelation in small stock returns magnifies the dimensions of this problem for small cap **trading. While the benefits of patient trading can be large, so can the dangers!**

If the total trading costs curve were redrawn for small and mid cap stocks, we would observe higher levels of commission and bid-asked spread costs and sharper trends in both market impact and opportunity costs over time. These patterns point to the greater difficulty in trading small and mid cap stocks and the greater costs of poor execution.

With this background on the different sources and elements of trading costs, we now move on to the key question—how can we mitigate this potentially high cost? We address this question in the next two sections.

STOCK SELECTION AND PRE-TRADE ANALYSIS

Stock Selection

Our knowledge of transaction costs so far can be applied in two separate areas of the equity investment process. The obvious application is in the development of an appropriate trading strategy. Another application which, however, tends to be overlooked is in the front-end process of stock selection.

We begin with a discussion of the use of liquidity information in the portfolio construction process. We will discuss this application within the context of both passive and active equity management. The idea here is fairly simple. While total trading costs can be measured accurately only ex-post, they can be reasonably estimated on an ex-ante basis. If we accept this notion, it seems reasonable to evaluate the trade-off between these expected costs and the contribution to tracking accuracy in passive portfolios or expected return in active strategies.

Let us examine each case separately. In the passive implementation, each stock in the benchmark makes a contribution to tracking accuracy proportional to its market value weight in the index. The decision to include any index stock in the tracking portfolio should depend on the trade-off between its contribution to tracking accuracy and its expected trading cost. Here, the expected trading cost is evaluated in terms of both original acquisition and during ongoing rebalancing. It is interesting to note that in certain indexes that are created from a market value ranking scheme (i.e., the Russell 2000 and Russell 2500), the smaller, less-liquid stocks are also most vulnerable to index turnover during the periodic rebalancing.

It is quite likely that some of these less-liquid stocks get excluded by using such an approach. Their exclusion may increase tracking error to some extent but so will their inclusion because of higher trading costs. This is likely to be a favorable trade-off because *known* trading costs that reduce portfolio returns are being avoided at the expense of slightly higher tracking error, which theoretically should have *no long-term influence* on average portfolio returns.

An important assumption here is the use of sufficiently robust statistical sampling or optimization procedures that replace the less-liquid stocks with other index constituents that possess a similar profile of characteristics.

In active strategies, most stock selection methods create a rank of relative attractiveness for all stocks in the selection universe based on expected returns. These valuation methods range from conventional dividend discount models to broader multifactor models. Such methods may be supported either by traditional fundamental research or quantitative interpretation of consensus analyst forecasts. The expected return estimates from these approaches form the basis of buy/sell decisions.

With the knowledge that a certain portion of this expected return will be lost in the trading process, it seems reasonable to perform the cross-sectional evaluation of stocks on the basis of "transaction-cost-adjusted" expected returns. It might be appropriate to penalize a less-liquid stock for its expected high trading cost in the stock selection process itself. The more traditional risk-return trade-off can be expanded to become a risk-return-cost analysis.

In both cases described above, it is important to incorporate the effect of low liquidity on covariance and the influence of the liquidity risk premium on historical and expected returns into the modeling process with sufficient rigor.

Another way to affect portfolio composition with liquidity information is by limiting positions in any stock to a certain percentage of average daily volume. Such a consideration will limit both entry and exit costs. It also allows existing positions to be sold within a reasonable period of time in the event of a major change in the fundamental outlook. Given the low trading volumes for small cap stocks, these limits can still represent a large percentage of average daily volume. As an example, such a limit may range from 50% of average daily volume for broadly diversified portfolios to 200% for more-concentrated, aggressive portfolios.

Using such guidelines, it is possible to create liquid trade portfolios that still achieve the desired risk and expected return objectives. These trade lists will include stocks that trade in reasonable volume and do not have a large bid-asked spread.

Pre-Trade Analytics

Trading strategy will depend on the specific composition of the trade basket. Pre-trade analytics allow us to assess the overall level of difficulty of any trade. Several factors can make a trade potentially difficult to execute. These factors are listed below and can be used to create an overall difficulty index for any trade.

Table 11.5—Factors Affecting Difficulty of Trade

	Easy	*Moderate*	*Difficult*
Exchange Affiliation	Listed	Listed/OTC	OTC
Trade Size to Avg. Daily Volume	Low	Medium	High
Size of Bid-Asked Spread	Small	Medium	Large
Urgency to Trade	Low	Medium	High

Source: TIMCO

As we discussed earlier, OTC stocks tend to be less liquid and are more difficult to trade. A trade also becomes difficult to execute when the number of shares to be traded represents a big percentage of daily trading volume. A stock whose bid-asked spread is large is generally more difficult to trade. And finally, it is more difficult to complete urgent trades while controlling market impact. A program trade that contains the following features can be assigned the highest level of difficulty:

- a high proportion of OTC stocks,
- several positions representing a large percentage of average daily trading volume,
- several stocks with high bid-asked spreads, and
- an urgent need to complete execution.

An analysis of the pro forma trade list for a rating on these measures also helps in the development of a trading strategy. The key parameters in a trading strategy involve choosing the appropriate source of liquidity and deciding just how aggressive to be with different portions of the trade portfolio. As we will see in the next section, the pre-trade liquidity analysis provides insights into such issues.

OPTIMAL TRADING STRATEGY AND IMPLEMENTATION ISSUES

Before addressing the design of an optimal trading strategy, it is necessary to review different trading alternatives and alternative sources of liquidity. This discussion provides a window into the various options available to a trader.

The exposure to price risk during trading differentiates one form of trading arrangement from another. Trade formats can range from the simple market order trade on one end to a blind principal trade that guarantees predetermined execution prices. The different alternatives in between progressively transfer execution risk away from the trader to the broker.

In discussing these various trade structures, we will use an example of a stock bid at 30 and offered at 30 1/2. Last sale was at 30 3/8 and there are 5,000 shares bid for and 10,000 shares offered. We assume a buy order of 30,000 shares. Market orders guarantee immediate execution but offer no protection against market impact. In our example, a market order of 30,000 shares may get executed as follows: 10,000 shares at 30 1/2, another 5,000 at 30 5/8, and the next 15,000 at 30 7/8. There is no price certainty beyond the liquidity available at the offered price. For a less-liquid stock, the last slice of the order could get executed at a still higher price.

Market limit orders specify a limit price in an attempt to control market impact. We may specify a limit price of the current offered price in our example. Here, we get execution on 10,000 shares at 30 1/2. Our order replaces the old bid price and now becomes the best bid at 30 1/2. The size at the new bid price is our remaining 20,000 shares. If the next sell order on the specialist's book is 5,000 shares at 30 5/8, the new market in the stock now becomes 30 1/2 - 30 5/8, 20,000 × 5,000. While we have controlled market impact by specifying a limit price equal to the original asked price, we now begin to incur opportunity costs.

If new buyers appear who are willing to pay a price greater than 30 1/2, two things will happen. Our bid of 30 1/2 will slip farther back in the specialist's book in terms of price precedence and, more importantly, the stock price gets further and further away from us. If the price reaches 32 3/8 in a few days, our opportunity cost to save an additional 3/8, or 1.2%, will turn out to be a significant 5% of asset value. On the other hand, if new sellers dominate the trading after our partial execution on the first 10,000 shares, we may end up buying our remaining 20,000 shares below 30 1/2! In this instance, opportunity costs will be negative. However, there is little solace in this outcome because the ability to buy into weakness will most likely create negative realized returns in the portfolio.

Traditional Trade Formats

Trade formats where the broker commits capital to reduce execution risk for the investor can be structured in several ways. Single orders are typically sent to the block traders, whereas a portfolio of stocks is traded on the program trading desk. As we discussed in the first section, the block trading function has changed from the role of an agent providing a search service to that of principal committing capital.

In the purest form of price protection for a program trade, the broker guarantees prespecified execution prices without prior knowledge of trade portfolio constituents, but with specifications of overall characteristics. This arrangement provides the trader a price level that is unaffected not only by market impact from the trade itself, but even by any advance notification of such an impending trade. Such a trade will bear the highest commission cost to compensate the broker for use of capital and higher price and execution risk.

Other variations of the principal trade provide less price protection. As an example, the guaranteed execution price may be specified at a point of time after the broker has an opportunity to work the trades in the market over some time period. The broker may receive the trade portfolio before the opening of trading on trade day and guarantee that day's closing price. The price protection is lower because the guaranteed price here is influenced by market impact from our trading activity.

In all configurations of agency or principal trades, an incentive can be arranged that allows the broker to retain a certain percentage of profits realized relative to the strike price. The shared profit comes on top of a base level of commission charge.

EFP Trades

In addition to these traditional trade formats, we must mention a couple of alternatives that are becoming increasingly popular. One of them is known as the EFP (exchange-for-physical) trade, and the other is the basis trade.

As implied in the name of the former alternative, a futures position can be exchanged in this transaction for a desired portfolio of stocks or vice versa. An EFP trade refers to the exchange of a trade portfolio that *closely* resembles the underlying index of the futures contract or vice versa. EFP trades typically find application in passive or quantitative portfolios. A trade portfolio that deviates significantly in composition from the underlying futures index is more suited for the basis trade.

The EFP trade is generally quoted net of commissions and in terms of the futures basis. The futures basis is defined as the difference between the futures price and the underlying cash index price. As an example, let the price of the S&P 400 mid-cap index be 160.55. The fair value of the S&P 400 futures may be computed as 161.22. The fair value of the futures basis, therefore, is 0.67. A plain EFP trade in terms of the mid-cap futures basis may be bid at 0.25 and offered at 1.05. This allows us to sell a long futures position at a basis of 0.25 at the close of trading on trade day and receive in exchange an index-like basket of stocks. The difference of 0.42 index point between the fair value of the futures basis and its transaction value represents the cost of the trade. This cost of 0.25% of trade value is relatively small compared to the expected cost of the trade in the cash market.

The EFP trade may become attractively priced at any given time if an imbalance between stocks and futures develops in the broker's book of business. A broker may be more aggressive on one side of the EFP quote or the other in such an instance. If the aggressive quote representes the other side of our trade, it provides an opportunity to further lower trading costs. In our example above, another broker who would like to unload a long stock position in exchange for futures may bid the EFP at 0.65 and offer it at 1.55. Here, we could sell our futures at fair value and convert to a long position in stocks for no commission cost!

If the trade portfolio does not track the underlying futures index perfectly, the EFP trade will contain a risk premium to reflect the tracking error of the trade portfolio in addition to the normal spread around the fair value of the futures basis.

The EFP trade is one of the rare examples in which trading costs can truly be eliminated. Now this may sound too good to be true to several of our readers. But this startling observation can be understood in the context of our earlier discussions on the market making function. In these instances, we become a supplier of liquidity to a counterparty who needs to hedge certain systematic or specific exposures. Our trade affords a cheaper hedge to the counterparty than any other alternative, and so we are able to extract a premium for essentially providing a market making function. This premium can be in the form of zero trading costs!

Basis Trades

The basis trade strikes a balance in terms of the transfer of risk and subsequent cost between an agency trade on one hand and a principal trade on the other. The trade works as follows. For example, an investor may want to establish a long position in a basket of stocks from an initial cash position. He or she would instruct the broker to establish a long futures position on his or her behalf in the broker's account. The investor bears the market risk during this initial phase of execution. An average futures price is calculated to achieve the appropriate nominal equity exposure.

The trade portfolio is next evaluated for its basis risk or tracking error relative to the underlying futures index. The basket of stocks is then transferred to the investor at a price that reflects the average futures price and the basis risk. In this implementation, the investor self-insures the market risk borne until the futures position can be established and then transfers the tracking error risk of the trade portfolio to the broker.

We may observe similar opportunities to lower trading costs in the basis trade if the broad portfolio characteristics of our trade portfolio suggest a diversifying effect on the broker's aggregate book. For example, if our active trade portfolio has a greater concentration in health care stocks, it may represent a good hedge for a broker who recently took on a short position in health care stocks to execute a principal trade with some other customer.

Crossing Networks

We discussed the various sources of liquidity in the U.S. stock market in Section I of this chapter—the specialist on the listed exchanges, the upstairs market, and the competitive market makers in the OTC market. We discussed the benefits provided by the Instinet system in terms of the price discovery feature even during off-market hours and narrower spreads for OTC stocks created by augmenting institutional trading interests with dealer liquidity. We also mentioned the fourth market crossing networks as an additional source of liquidity. We discuss this trading alternative in greater detail in this section.

Crossing networks now play an increasingly important role in the institutional investor's drive to lower trading costs. These networks perform an electronic match-making function between natural buyers and sellers. Buyers and sellers enter orders into an electronic black box. These could be market orders or they may carry price limits. Traders have the option of advertising their trade to other participants in order to attract liquidity or keeping it anonymous and hidden. At a pre-specified point of time, or in some instances on a continuous basis, a computer match identifies buyers and sellers whose orders can be crossed. Matched market orders are typically traded at the mid-point of the then prevailing bid and asked prices.

Several crossing networks have come into existence over the last few years. These include BARRA-Jeffries' POSIT, Instinet's Crossing Network, and Morgan Stanley's MATCHPLUS. These crossing networks typically do not perform a price discovery function but instead "borrow" prices from the traded markets. Some of these are open for trading during regular stock market hours, while others are available even after the close. The NYSE also provides a crossing session after the close of trading for trades to occur at market closing prices.

The Arizona Stock Exchange (AZX) is another source of liquidity in the fourth market. This electronic exchange uses the structure of a single price auction to bring buyers and sellers together. Buyers and sellers create a quantity-price supply and demand schedule in each stock in the time leading up to the auction. At the time of auction, which takes place once a day outside regular trading hours, an equilibrium price is established for every stock from the intersection of the supply and demand curves. Buyers who bid more than the clearing price and sellers who offer less than the clearing price trade with each other at the clearing price.

The discovery of transaction prices within this single price auction would normally require the AZX to be registered as an exchange. It has, however, been exempted from this requirement because of a limited volume provision. However, it appears that the price discovery mechanism has not been fully exploited in this platform for lack of enough liquidity, as most transactions have occurred at or very close to the market closing price. In this context, the AZX so far has served primarily a crossing function to its users.

We complete this brief note on crossing networks by discussing the implications of this source of liquidity for small and mid cap trading. The elimination of the bid-asked spread due to the absence of an intermediary in this alternative offers big savings in trading costs. As we have seen earlier, the bid-asked spread component of cost is especially large for small and mid cap stocks. Therefore, the use of crossing networks in small and mid cap trading is likely to pay handsome dividends.

Optimal Trading Strategy

We now turn our attention to the development of an optimal trading strategy for small and mid cap stocks. The key consideration in this exercise is to exploit all sources of liquidity and match different subsets of the trade portfolio to each of these avenues. We have recognized by now that there are dangers in pursuing either a very aggressive strategy or trading very patiently with these stocks. We can, therefore, conclude that a middle ground is more desirable.

All trades within the overall trade list should be considered to exploit liquidity in the crossing networks. While the crossing networks offer the potential to reduce trading costs, their prolonged use will likely lead to patient trading and expose the portfolio to significant opportunity costs. Pre-trade analytics can next be used to identify trades that need to be worked carefully. OTC stocks and less-liquid stocks can be classified into this category. The best bid and asked prices can be sought for the OTC stocks from competitive market makers or within Instinet, while the less-liquid stocks may have to be traded in the upstairs market on a block basis.

We can balance the overall demand for liquidity in the remaining trade portfolio by identifying the level of urgency required by different types of stocks. It makes sense to pay up for market impact for only those stocks that are likely to be exposed to adverse opportunity costs. Information-based trades fall into this category. The purchase of a stock following a positive earnings surprise is one such example. A higher level of urgency is justified because the information content is likely to be short-lived and opportunity costs are likely to be high over that time period. On the other hand, a value-motivated trade buying out-of-favor cheap stocks on relative weakness can be executed patiently. Indeed, patient trading may provide superior execution if such a stock continues its downward momentum.

We summarize these guidelines for controlling trading costs in Table 11.6. The precise formulation of an optimal trading strategy will be specific to each trade list and its overall level of difficulty and also depend on market conditions prevailing at the time of implementation. If the overall investment style is value-oriented, a greater emphasis can be placed on patient trading. Growth investors, on the other hand, may have to adopt a more aggressive style. The relative emphasis on patient and aggressive trading may change during periods of high market volatility. When market volatility increases, both bid-asked spreads and opportunity costs are likely to be higher. It requires a skillful trader to gauge the relative magnitude of these effects in the midst of high uncertainty.

Table 11.6—Guidelines for Trading Small and Mid Cap Stocks

| | | Market Limit Orders | |
Crossing Networks	Worked Trades	Aggressive	Patient
All Trades	Poor Liquidity	Information-Based	Value-Oriented
	Most OTC	Good Liquidity	Moderate Liquidity
		Favorable	Adverse
		Price Momentum	Price Momentum

There are other nuances in the implementation of any trading strategy that assume added importance for small and mid cap stocks. Should the trader prefer a block trade and accept the resulting price concession or self-insure and attempt to seek liquidity independently for indeterminate cost? If the trader chooses the latter, should he or she advertise the entire position in order to attract liquidity and risk the danger of front-running or trade partial positions and risk the danger of driving prices farther away with each successive slice? These are difficult questions to answer with one standard formula. Traders can add significant value, especially for small and mid cap stocks, by making the right choice in such issues.

CONCLUSION

Our stated objective at the beginning of this chapter was to provide a better understanding of transaction costs for small and mid cap stocks and offer insights into means of mitigating the impact of these potentially high costs. We hope that the material discussed here provides a clear perspective of the issues surrounding small and mid cap trading.

Our goal here was to provide a unified framework within which to accommodate these issues. In order to accomplish this, our treatment of several background topics was very brief and, in some instances, offered just a partial discussion of the sub-topics. We chose to limit these discussions to be better able to view and understand the big picture.

Small and mid-cap trading can be very expensive. Total round-trip trading costs can range from 200 to 300 basis points under normal implementation conditions and could be even higher in the face of unfavorable market impact and/or opportunity costs. These costs detract from overall portfolio performance. With an annual turnover of 150%, the performance barrier to simply break even with the passive alternative would be as high as 300 to 450 basis points.

The incentive to control trading costs is particularly high for small and mid cap stocks. In order to minimize these costs, we have created a framework within which to understand the different forces that create friction during the trading process for small and mid cap stocks and developed guidelines to mitigate their influence.

ENDNOTE

[1] Ibbotson Associates, 1992 Yearbook, *Stocks, Bonds, Bills and Inflation.*

REFERENCES

Fama, E. F., and K. R. French, "The Cross-Section of Expected Stock Returns," *Journal of Finance*, Vol. 47:2 (June 1992), pp. 427–465.

Bernstein, P., "Liquidity, Stock Markets and Market Makers," *Financial Management* (Summer 1987), pp 54–62.

Harris, L., "The Winners and Losers of the Zero-Sum Game: The Origins of Trading Profits, Market Efficiency and Liquidity," Presentation at the Institute for Quantitative Research in Finance, Spring 1993 seminar.

Black, F., "Noise," *Journal of Finance* (July 1986), pp. 529–543.

Cooper, S. K., J. C. Groth, and W. E. Avera, "Liquidity, Exchange Listing and Common Stock Performance," *Journal of Economics and Business* (February 1985), pp. 21–33.

Marsh, T., and K. Rock, "Exchange Listing and Liquidity: A Comparison of the American Stock Exchange with the NASDAQ National Market System," American Stock Exchange Transactions Data Research Project Report #2, January 1986.

Stoll, H. R., "The Supply of Dealer Services in Security Markets," *Journal of Finance* Vol. 33 (1978), pp. 1133–51.

Amihud, Y., and H. Mendelson, "Dealership Markets: Market Making with Inventory," *Journal of Financial Economics* 8 (1980), pp. 31–53.

Glosten, L. R., and P. R. Milgrom, "Bid, Ask and Transaction Prices in a Specialist Market with Heterogeneously Informed Traders," *Journal of Financial Economics*, Vol. 14:1 (1985), pp. 71–100.

Copeland, T., and D. Galai, "Information Effects of the Bid-Asked Spread," *Journal of Finance*, Vol. 38:5 (December 1983), pp. 1457–69.

Perold, A., "The Implementation Shortfall: Paper Versus Reality," *Journal of Portfolio Management* (Spring 1988), pp. 4–9.

Chapter 12

Risk Modeling and Small-Company Stocks

Josh Rosenberg
Senior Consultant, Equity Model Research
BARRA

INTRODUCTION

Investing involves balancing predicted returns against predicted risk. Risk predictions depend on a model of the underlying factors that drive security returns. Thus, risk model estimation provides an understanding of market structure and security behavior. This chapter will discuss the theory and techniques used to develop the BARRA SMALLCAP risk model and insights gained in estimation and use of the model.

WHY BUILD A SMALL CAP MODEL?

BARRA offers two models to forecast the risk and explain the returns of United States equities. The U.S. SMALLCAP risk model provides precise risk forecasts for small stocks, while the U.S. Equity 2 (U.S. E2) model focuses on large stocks. BARRA built a separate model for small stocks because research on the United States equity market indicates that different factors are responsible for small and large stock behavior. A separate model for small stocks allows more-precise risk forecasting, return attribution, and optimization.

Small stocks behave differently than large stocks because of structural differences between small and large companies and their securities. Small companies tend to be more heavily dependent upon a single product line in a single industry, and are thus more sensitive to changes in product demand and input prices. As a result, small stocks tend to have greater total volatility, specific volatility, and higher betas than large stocks. Table 12.1 illustrates some of these contrasts in risk characteristics.

Table 12.1—Risk Characteristics of Small- and Large-Company Stocks
August 1992

	Small Stocks	Large Stocks
Average predicted annual risk	43.5%	34.6%
Average predicted annual specific risk	33.0%	23.0%
Average predicted beta with respect to HICAP market	1.1	1.0

Source: BARRA Database, SMALLCAP model.

The relative neglect of small stocks also distinguishes them from large stocks. Securities analysts follow large stocks more thoroughly than small stocks, and there is also less public information about small companies. Some small stocks are also thinly traded, which increases the chance they can be mispriced.

The contrasting risk and returns of well-diversified small company (SMALLCAP) and large company (HICAP) portfolios illustrate the risk-reward trade-off for these stocks. As Figure 12.1 illustrates, small stocks have historically experienced higher risk and higher return than large stocks. From January 1979, through August 1992, the SMALLCAP portfolio returned 172% above the cumulative return to three-month Treasury bills. Over the same period, the HICAP portfolio returned 138% above the T-bill return. However, over this period, the annual risk (standard deviation) of the SMALLCAP portfolio was 19.3% compared to 16.1% for the HICAP portfolio.

WHAT IS A SMALL CAP STOCK?

A commonly accepted definition of a small stock is one issued by a company with a market capitalization between $10 million and $500 million. However, for the purposes of model building and investability, it is impor-

Figure 12.1—Cumulative Excess Returns to SMALLCAP and HICAP Markets

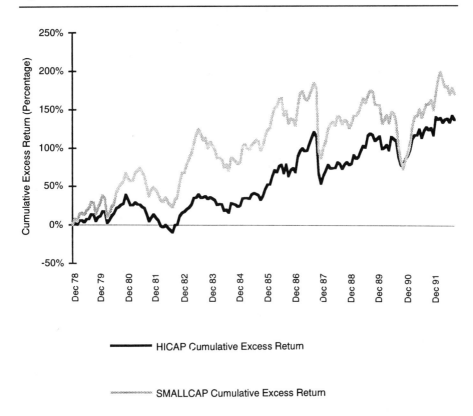

──────── HICAP Cumulative Excess Return

∞∞∞∞∞∞∞∞∞∞ SMALLCAP Cumulative Excess Return

Source: BARRA SMALLCAP and U.S. E2 Model

tant to delineate a fairly stable universe of stocks to be considered small stocks. One of the most significant problems in constructing a universe of small stocks is that monthly membership can change significantly. High turnover means high transaction costs, especially for small-company issues.

In the SMALLCAP model, several rules ensure that the SMALLCAP universe contains a large cross-section of small stocks and has reasonably low turnover. The general rule for inclusion in the universe is that an asset's capitalization is between annually determined upper and lower bounds, has a market price greater than five dollars, and is not a foreign issue.

To reduce turnover, universe membership is determined once per year. Assets in the universe during the year remain in the universe unless they have an extreme change in capitalization. A grandfathering rule further reduces turnover, so that stocks in the SMALLCAP universe as of the last year have looser requirements to remain in the universe.

In August, 1992, the SMALLCAP universe contained about 2,200 assets with a median capitalization of about $100 million. Ninety-five percent of SMALLCAP assets had capitalizations between $17 million and $550 million. The turnover of the universe from August 1991 to August 1992 was about 14% in terms of capitalization and 16% in terms of names.

THE STRUCTURE OF THE SMALLCAP MODEL

The BARRA U.S. SMALLCAP Equity Model is a multiple-factor risk model designed to provide risk forecasts, identify current and past sources of risk and return, and facilitate construction of portfolios with desired characteristics. Over 6,000 U.S. equities are included in the SMALLCAP database and risk forecasts are updated monthly. The basis of the SMALLCAP model is the separation of asset returns into returns due to industry groups, risk indices, and specific events. This relationship is described by the following equation:

$$r_n = X_1 f_1 + X_2 f_2 + \ldots X_{53} f_{53} + e_n$$

The left side of the equation lists monthly asset returns of SMALLCAP assets (r_n) for a given date. The right side of the equation lists SMALLCAP asset exposures ($X_1 \ldots X_{53}$) to factors and factor returns ($f_1 \ldots f_{53}$). Factor exposures are determined using the fundamental, market, and industry characteristics of each asset. Factor returns are estimated using a technique called *generalized least squares regression*. This estimation produces factor returns (f's) that best explain the relationship between factor exposures and asset returns.

Factors in the model are selected to identify and explain returns to groups of securities. In most equity markets, assets in the same industry tend to move together, as do assets with similar fundamental and market characteristics. The BARRA model uses these relationships in return attribution and risk forecasting.

SOURCES OF RISK AND RETURN FOR SMALLCAP STOCKS: PERFORMANCE ATTRIBUTION

Performance attribution is one example of the type of analysis that can be conducted using the SMALLCAP risk model. Factor exposures and factor

Figure 12.2—Separation of Asset Returns SMALLCAP Model

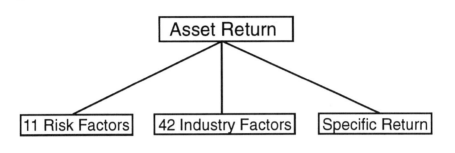

returns can be used to analyze the sources of portfolio risk and return over a given time period. Figure 12.2 indicates how returns are separated into different components.

What were some of the sources of return for the Mauna Loa Macadamia Nut Company (NUT) over August 1992? NUT's excess return (–1.4% over August 1992) can be separated into return due to risk indices, return due to industry factors, and specific return.

NUT has an exposure of 1 (or 100%) to the Agriculture and Food industry, and an exposure of –1.1 standard deviations below average to the Volatility risk index. The estimated Agriculture and Food industry factor return was –3% and the Volatility risk index factor return was –2%. Using this data, it is clear that a –3% return (an exposure of 1 times a return of –3%) was due to NUT's exposure to the Agriculture and Food industry. NUT also experienced a return of 2.2% (an exposure of –1.1 times a return of –2%) due to its exposure to the Volatility risk index.

With a history of portfolio exposures and factor returns, this type of analysis can be extended to answer questions such as, "Which factor bets were most successful?" "Which had the greatest contribution to risk?" or "What is the contribution to return of specific asset selection compared to factor exposures?"

ESTIMATING THE SMALLCAP MODEL: INSIGHTS AND RESULTS

The goal of the model estimation process is identification of the factors that explain co-movements of small stocks. Since these factors differ between large and small stocks, the BARRA SMALLCAP research process involved creating and testing an expanded list of potential explanatory variables. Estimation was conducted in two stages: estimation of industry factors and estimation of risk index factors.

Industry Factors

The first step in identifying important factors was to determine which industry groups best characterized asset behavior. This process involved testing the importance of the 55 industry factors used in the U.S. E2 model, and searching for additional industry factors. In the end, 42 industry factors were selected. Some SMALLCAP industry factors are combinations of several separate industry groups in the U.S. E2 model, while others are entirely new industry groups.

One important new industry group that was identified during the estimation process was Semiconductors. Research indicated that small semiconductor stocks performed differently than stocks of other small electronics companies. From January 1979 through August 1992, the Semiconductor factor had a cumulative return of 451% and annual risk of 29.3%, compared to a cumulative return of 185% and an annual risk of 22.9% for the Electronics industry. These differences in risk and return characteristics led to the decision to incorporate separate Electronics and Semiconductor industry factors in the SMALLCAP model.

Another result of the investigation of industry factors was the identification of significant differences in behavior of industries in the SMALL-CAP and U.S. E2 models. For example, one can ask the question, "Are small bank stocks and large bank stocks interchangeable?" By comparing the risk and return of the Bank industry factor in the two models, we can see that, net of other factors including SIZE, small banks still perform differently than large banks.

Figure 12.3 shows that over the past twelve years, net of other factors, a portfolio of large banks had a cumulative return of 54% compared to 132% for small banks. Annual risk was 19.3% for large banks and 18.2% for small banks. Thus, we can increase our explanatory power for small bank stocks by modeling them separately from large bank stocks.

The most volatile industry factors in the SMALLCAP model are Precious Metals and Semiconductors, while the least volatile are Electric Utilities and Gas Utilities. The two largest industries in the SMALLCAP model, based on percentage of capitalization, are Banks and Producer Goods.

Risk Index Factors

The second estimation stage involved identification of the fundamental and market attributes of small stocks that determine their return behavior. A database of about seventy potential explanatory variables (called de-

Figure 12.3—Cumulative Returns to SMALLCAP and HICAP Bank Industry Factors

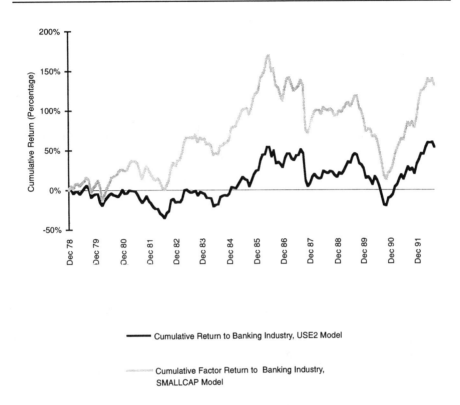

Cumulative Return to Banking Industry, USE2 Model

Cumulative Factor Return to Banking Industry,
SMALLCAP Model

Source: BARRA SMALLCAP and U.S. E2 Model

scriptors in BARRA parlance) was generated for each stock for each month over the estimation period. These variables include market descriptors such as historical beta and monthly share turnover as well as fundamental descriptors such as earnings-to-price ratio and historical earnings growth.

During the estimation of the SMALLCAP model, 40 descriptors were selected and combined into nine risk indices. Two additional risk indices, Large Capitalization and Low Price, account for different behavior of stocks outside the estimation universe. Table 12.2 lists the twelve SMALL-CAP risk indices.

Table 12.2—Risk Indices in the BARRA SMALLCAP Model

Volatility	Momentum	Interest Rate Sensitivity
Liquidity	Size	Growth
Operating Value	Fundamental Value	Financial Stability
Large Capitalization	Low Price	

For example, the SMALLCAP risk index Operating Value captures different risk and return for assets that are priced cheaply or expensively compared to their earnings and cash flow. The Operating Value risk index is calculated using a weighted combination of a twelve-month earnings-to-price ratio, a five-year earnings-to-price ratio, and a twelve-month cash-flow-to-price ratio.

FACTOR PERFORMANCE

Examining the performance of risk index factors provides additional insight into the behavior of SMALLCAP assets. Two risk indices are particularly interesting: Operating Value and Interest Rate Sensitivity.

The Operating Value factor measures the relative price of an asset compared to its operating value. Over the past twelve years, the Operating Value factor has had significantly positive average returns. This indicates that, net of other factors, SMALLCAP assets with larger exposures to Operating Value outperformed those with smaller exposures. Figure 12.4 shows that a SMALLCAP portfolio identical to the SMALLCAP market except for an active Operating Value exposure of 1 would have experienced a cumulative active return of 68% over the past twelve years.

This type of behavior is the basis for factor tilt portfolios. Factor tilt portfolios are designed to exploit historical factor behavior to generate positive active returns. Factor tilt portfolios may be constructed so that they have positive exposures to factors with significantly positive average returns, negative exposures to factors with significantly negative average returns, and neutral exposures to all other factors. Since portfolio construction requires balancing risk and return, factor tilt portfolios are constructed using a risk model and an optimizer such as BARRA's ACTIVOPS program.

Another risk index, Interest Rate Sensitivity, identifies assets whose returns are linked to the bond market. Descriptors that are used to calculate this risk index include bond beta, which relates asset returns to bond market returns, current yield, and payout ratio.

Figure 12.4—Cumulative Return to SMALLCAP Operating Value Factor

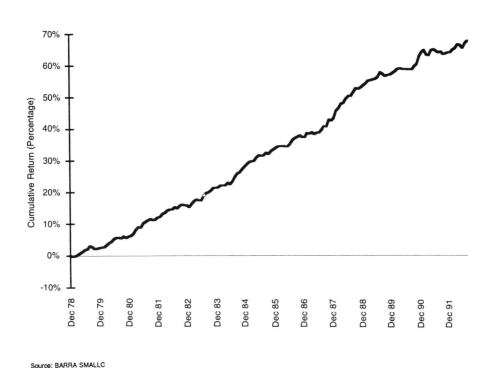

Source: BARRA SMALLC

The Interest Rate Sensitivity risk index provides insight into links between the macroeconomy and the SMALLCAP risk model. Over the past twelve years, the returns to this factor and the bond market have been correlated at about .36. This indicates that companies that the model characterized as interest rate sensitive tend to move together, and their performance is positively related to changes in bond prices.

FORECASTING RISK

The SMALLCAP model is designed to forecast several types of portfolio risk and to identify sources of risk. In BARRA models, risk is defined as the volatility, or standard deviation, of return. Intuitively, this means that a portfolio with an annual total risk of 20% will experience returns between –20% and 20% in two out of three years. As total risk increases, the probability increases that the portfolio will experience wider swings in returns.

As of August 1992, the total predicted risk of the SMALLCAP market is 24.7%, compared to 20.3% for the HICAP market.

Risk can be separated into components in the same way that returns are separated. This motivates definitions for several types of portfolio risk. As mentioned previously, total risk refers to the volatility of portfolio returns. Table 12.3 lists the total risk of some of the most stable and most volatile SMALLCAP assets in August, 1992.

Table 12.3—SMALLCAP Risk Forecasts August 1992

Risky stocks	Total Annual Risk Forecast
Chips and Technologies	76.8%
Videocart Inc.	73.0%
Zeos Intl. Ltd.	72.9%

Stable stocks	Total Annual Risk Forecast
Cascade Natural Gas Corp.	25.6%
Mobile Gas Services Corp.	25.5%
Maine Public Services Company	25.3%

Source: BARRA SMALLCAP Model.

Instead of the total risk of a portfolio, a manager may be interested in knowing how closely a portfolio tracks a benchmark. *Active risk* or *tracking error* provides this information by measuring the volatility of the difference between two portfolio returns. For instance, the tracking error of an actively managed SMALLCAP growth-oriented portfolio might be 5% relative to the SMALLCAP index. This implies that in two of three years, the active portfolio return will be between –5% and 5% of the portfolio return.

Another method of analyzing portfolio risk is based on the Capital Asset Pricing Model (CAPM) perspective of risk and return. Risk is separated into a component due to covariance with the market portfolio, or *systematic risk*, and risk uncorrelated with market portfolio, or *residual risk*. This leads to a risk measure known as *predicted beta*, which is a forecast of the relationship between the portfolio return and the market return. Often, a sixty-month realized beta is used as a proxy for predicted beta. The predicted beta, estimated using the SMALLCAP model, is significantly more accurate since it uses the current risk index and industry characteristics of the portfolio and of the market rather than their historical characteristics.

SPECIFIC-RISK MODEL

The SMALLCAP model incorporates separate models for common factor and specific risk. Common factor risk forecasts utilize factor exposures and factor variances. Specific risk forecasts utilize factors that predict an asset's sensitivity to idiosyncratic events. Specific risk predictions are based on a two-part model. The first part models assets' relative specific risk, and the second part models the average level of specific risk.

Three important factors that determine relative specific risk are industry exposure, market capitalization, and historical residual risk. For instance, gold companies tend to have larger-than-average specific risk, because their returns are significantly related to unpredictable events such as discovery of a new vein. Utility companies have below-average specific risk, because important events tend to affect the industry as a whole, rather than a specific company. Larger companies tend to be affected less by idiosyncratic factors than smaller companies, and companies with higher historical residual risk tend to have higher future specific risk.

Asset-specific risk is also related to the average level of specific risk. The average level of specific risk can be predicted using a time-series model of recent average levels. A January dummy variable accounts for the "January effect" in which average specific risk has a predictable increase in that month.

FORECASTING RISK: DETAILS

Total portfolio risk forecasts incorporate the two components of risk: common factor and specific. Common factor risk is due to portfolio exposures to industry and risk factors. Specific risk is due to a portfolio's sensitivity to idiosyncratic events. An average SMALLCAP asset has about 28% annual common factor risk and 33% annual specific risk. As portfolio size increases, diversification tends to reduce specific risk. For example, an average 500-asset SMALLCAP portfolio has about 1.5% annual specific risk.

A simple example of a risk calculation makes the risk forecasting process more clear. Consider a one-factor risk model and a portfolio with one asset. Common factor and specific risk forecasts for this example are a simplified version of those for a portfolio using a multiple-factor risk model.

Common factor variance forecasts depend on factor exposures and factor variances. (Variance is the square of risk.) Common factor exposures are determined using fundamental, market, and industry data. Common factor variances are based on the historical variance of factor returns. The predicted common factor variance is the product of the factor exposure and the factor variance.

In a multiple-factor model, common factor variance forecasts are more complicated. Instead of using the variance of a single factor, a matrix is used that forecasts the variance of each factor and the relationships between the factors. This matrix is called a *factor covariance matrix*.

The second component of total risk is specific risk. For a one-asset portfolio, the portfolio-specific risk is equal to the asset's specific risk. If more than one asset is in the portfolio, then the specific risk prediction is the square root of the weighted sum of the asset specific variances. The weights are the squared holdings of the assets in the portfolio.

WHAT CAN YOU DO WITH A RISK MODEL?

Case Study: Operating Value Tilt Strategy

To observe the SMALLCAP model in action, we can compare the risk and return to two portfolios that are based on the same strategy but are constructed using different techniques. The portfolio strategy is to exceed the return to the SMALLCAP market through active exposure to the Operating Value risk index, while minimizing active risk.

Portfolio 1 is constructed by selecting the 100 assets with the largest Operating Value exposures from the SMALLCAP universe, and assigning them weights proportional to their capitalizations. Portfolio 2 is constructed using the SMALLCAP risk model and the BARRA ACTIVOPS optimizer. The Operating Value factor is assigned an annual expected return of 3.8%, which equals its historical performance. The optimizer constructs Portfolio 2 so that it has minimum active risk and maximum active return for a given level of risk aversion.

Using portfolio characterization (PORCH) software, we can identify how well each portfolio implements the strategy. Portfolio 1 has an expected return of 6.8% due to its exposure of 1.8 to the Operating Value risk index, so it satisfies the first objective of the strategy. However, Portfolio 1 also has an active risk of 5.7%, which is higher than desired. This level of active risk is due to large incidental bets including substantially underweighting the portfolio in the Oil Service industry and overweighting the Thrifts industry. Portfolio 1 does not meet the second objective of the strategy.

Using PORCH, it is possible to identify the assets in Portfolio 1 that contribute most to active risk. These assets might be the first to be considered for down-weighting in the portfolio. In addition, assets from underrepresented industries might be added to the portfolio for risk control.

Portfolio 2, built using the ACTIVOPS optimizer, satisfies both objectives of the strategy. It has an expected return of 6.0% and an active risk of 3.9%. The reduced level of active risk with a high level of active return is due to the optimizer selecting a diversified portfolio that has a large exposure to Operating Value.

In addition to PORCH, which characterizes current portfolio risks, performance analysis software (PERFAN) can be used for historical analysis of portfolios and backtesting. Using PERFAN is beyond the scope of this chapter; however, it would facilitate comparison of risks and returns to the two portfolio building strategies if they were implemented historically.

CONCLUSION

Differences between small and large company assets arise from a number of factors. Precise analysis of risk and return for small-company assets requires a dedicated model estimated over this universe. The BARRA SMALLCAP model and risk analysis software help investment practitioners understand the sources of risk and return in their SMALLCAP portfolios and to implement their insights in portfolio construction.

APPENDIX: CALCULATING RISK FORECASTS

The equation to calculate total variance forecasts incorporates several elements: portfolio exposures to common factors(X_p), the factor covariance matrix (F), portfolio holdings (h_p), and the specific covariance matrix (O). The portfolio's total variance forecast is v.

$$v = X'_pFX_p + h'_pOh_p$$

Active risk is determined by calculating active portfolio exposures (X_{pa}), which are the differences between portfolio and market factor exposures, and active portfolio holdings (h_{pa}), which are the differences between portfolio and market holdings. An intuitive way of understanding the active risk calculation is that the active risk of a portfolio is its scaled distance from the market portfolio. The portfolio's active variance forecast is v_a.

$$v_a = X'_{pa}FX_{pa} + h'_{pa}Oh_{pa}$$

Predicted beta is determined by forecasting the covariance between the portfolio and the market due to common factors (X'_pFX_m), the covariance due to common asset holdings (h'_pOh_m), and the total variance of the market portfolio ($X'_mFX_m + h'_mOh_m$). The equation is similar in structure to the regression coefficient used in calculation of historical beta. The portfolio's predicted beta is b.

$$b = \frac{X'_pFX_m + h'_pOh_m}{X'_mFX_m + h'_mOh_m}$$

Risk forecasts and beta forecasts are examples of portfolio diagnostic information that the SMALLCAP risk model provides.

REFERENCES

Grinold, Richard, and Ronald Kahn, "The Factor Model Project: Multiple Factor Models for Portfolio Risk," April 1992. BARRA unpublished paper.

Kahn, Ron, "Smallcap Indices Without Tears," BARRA Newsletter, March/April 1991, No. 135. pp. 6–8.

Rosenberg, Barr, and Vinay Marathe, "The Prediction of Investment Risk: Systematic and Residual Risk," Proceedings of the Seminar on the Analysis of Security Prices, University of Chicago, November 1975, pp. 85–225.

Rosenberg, Josh, "The New SMALLCAP Model," BARRA Newsletter, January/February 1991, No. 134. pp. 21–25.

Rudd, Andrew, and Henry Clasing, Modern Portfolio Theory: The Principles of Investment Management (Orinda, CA: Andrew Rudd, 1988).

Chapter 13

Capturing Return and Controlling Risk in Managing a Small-Stock Portfolio

Varilyn K. Schock, CFA
Vice President and Director of Quantitative Strategies
Denver Investment Advisors, Inc.

John S. Brush, Ph.D.
President
Columbine Capital Services, Inc.

INTRODUCTION

The basic motive for investing is to build financial resources. Many of us shy away from investments that are likely to be the most rewarding, however, because of risk. Hence, the essence of the investor's dilemma is how to receive high returns without excessive risk.

Our interest in this dilemma resulted in designing an approach that captures small-stock returns, historically one of the most profitable segments of the stock market, while controlling risk throughout the process. Our research indicates that substantially higher returns with similar or lower volatility than small-stock indices is attainable with institutional-sized portfolios. This chapter discusses the thought process, model devel-

The authors wish to thank Michael Anselmi and David Ament, Columbine Capital Services, for research and suggestions; Ken Penland, Denver Investment Advisors, for helpful comments; and Brad Lafay, Denver Investment Advisors, for general assistance.

opment, testing, evaluation, and portfolio management strategy involved in our small-stock approach.

THE ATTRACTIVENESS OF SMALL STOCKS

Studies have shown that over long periods small-capitalization stocks outperform all other size segments of the equity market (as well as bonds and inflation).[1] A well-known study by Ibbotson reports that from 1926–1992, small stocks were the highest performing asset class at 12.2% annually compared to 10.3% for a larger common stock index, the S&P 500.[2] Despite periods of relative underperformance and periodic suggestions that the "small-stock effect" is dead, a compelling reason has not been advanced for why small stocks won't continue to outperform all other size segments and asset classes in the future.

At the same time, data that pertain to risk typically receive less attention. While risk in the financial world can have a number of definitions, "real risk" is so far known only after the fact. From a shareholder's point of view, if a stock rose during his or her ownership, it was not a risky stock; if it fell, the stock exhibited risk. However, as investors have been unsuccessful so far in perfectly predicting when real risk, or loss, will occur, risk is often viewed as the uncertainty of future returns and is estimated by measuring the variability of past returns. We and others use this definition of risk and measure variability, or volatility, by calculating the standard deviation of returns over time. We also examine the potential for experiencing capital loss.

According to Ibbotson, the volatility of returns of small stocks, measured by standard deviation, is 35.0% annually, compared to 20.6% for common stocks in general. Consequently, the annualized data indicate that an investor who owned a typical small-stock portfolio would have enjoyed an 18% increase in return over the S&P 500, while the level of risk increased by 75%. Since most investors own a portfolio of stocks for much less than 66 years—and short-run negative periods in a standard deviation calculation can be particularly uncomfortable—is the reward of small-stock investing worth the volatility? The answer depends on how well an investor can capture return and control risk.

THE ATTRACTIVENESS OF LOW VALUATION

Research over the decades continues to confirm that excess returns are achievable if an investor focuses on buying stocks with low valuations.[3] The return associated with two measures of value—low price/earnings ratio and low price/book value ratio—has been estimated by the consulting firm BARRA, Inc. If the influence of price/earnings ratio is isolated from all other influences on a stock's return, BARRA estimates that the contribution from low price/earnings ratio would have been 3.4% per year from 1973 to 1992. The influence of low price/book value is estimated to have been 3.0% per year. It is important to note that these returns are essentially *incremental* returns attributable to these value measures. Low price/earnings and price/book ratios have been more powerful indicators of future return than any other widely used characteristic—more powerful than a stock's earnings growth, price momentum, low leverage, popularity in the marketplace, or dividend yield.[4] Without a compelling case for why low-valuation stocks would change course and underperform in the future, it makes sense to focus on building high returns by starting with low valuation.

Our investment strategy was founded on the intellectual and common-sense appeal of combining the attractive performance characteristics of small stocks with the incremental returns associated with low valuation. From this starting point, our goal was to distinguish between stocks that had low valuations and those that were undervalued—the latter being stocks that would have the highest likelihood of outperformance. At the same time, our goal was to control risk, such that the return/risk trade-off of investing in small stocks was also attractive.

FORMULATING THE STRATEGY

We believe that the effort, expertise, and attention to detail applied in strategy formulation and design is critical to the integrity and reliability of an investment methodology. Our first priority is to meet the needs of clients from return and risk perspectives. To fulfill this objective, the key tenets of our investment philosophy are the following:

1. *We invest only in small-capitalization stocks.* The stocks must be small enough to achieve the returns suggested by the Ibbotson data but large enough to be utilized in institutional-sized portfolios.

2. *We use a methodology that focuses on valuation.* To capture the excess returns from undervaluation, we begin with proven value measures, including low price/earnings multiple and low price/book value ratio, to evaluate stocks. We enhance this value strategy by using measures that our research has shown increase returns. The measures used must make sense theoretically and from a practitioner's point of view. The methodology's emphasis on value is maintained by requiring that value measures always comprise at least 70% of the model developed to evaluate stocks. The value focus combined with enhancements is the model's contribution to our "Enhanced Value Discipline," the process for selecting stocks.

3. *We control risk throughout the process.* Risk is controlled from the evaluation stage, to buy-and-sell disciplines, to portfolio construction.

With these principles as a starting point, there were additional requirements to address "real-world" investment considerations:

1. When investing in small stocks, we believe it is important to develop a model for evaluating stocks that is custom-tailored to the small cap sector. Why? Small companies tend to operate in niche businesses and, if successful, can be less susceptible than large companies to macroeconomic or overall industry forces. On the other hand, smaller businesses typically have fewer products, which can result in more erratic sales and earnings patterns and more volatile share prices. Small firms are more likely to operate in regional rather than global markets; hence, foreign currency fluctuations can affect small and large stocks differently. Financial leverage and share liquidity can also produce differences in price behavior. These examples suggest that models for small and large stocks should be different, and that a model specifically designed for small stocks is likely to provide higher returns than a general model applied to the sector.

2. The technique used to construct a model should not be based on arbitrary or flawed assumptions about the equity market. Unfortunately, a widely used construction technique produces a linear relationship between a particular measure for stocks, such as price/earnings ratio, and their subsequent returns.[5] For example, as the multiple falls in a list of stocks ranked by P/E ratio, the future return is presumed to rise by the same relative magnitude all along the P/E spectrum. In the marketplace, this relationship is seldom perfectly linear—the distortions caused by simplistic model-building assumptions weaken the descriptive and predictive power of the financial model. In contrast, our approach uses an innovative technique that allows for linear and nonlinear relationships between stock characteristics and future returns.

3. The model should evolve and be responsive to change in the influences of stock returns over time.

4. Important company information that cannot be quantified in the model should be utilized in the buy-and-sell process.

5. The approach must add value over a reasonably long time period that spans a variety of financial and economic environments.

6. The approach must add value after subtracting the higher trade execution costs involved with small stocks.

7. The weight in a particular economic sector should not introduce uncompensated or excessive risk to the portfolio.

DESIGNING THE STRATEGY

Designing a process to bring the investment strategy to life involves defining a universe of stocks, dealing with data integrity issues, selecting an appropriate model construction technique for achieving the overall objective, determining a methodology for using data, and deciding portfolio construction rules and constraints.

Small Cap Universe

The Universe is designed to contain only small stocks. We begin by using a database of stock information that is created from Compustat data and checked for data integrity.[6] We rank these stocks by market capitalization at the end of each year, eliminate the 1,000 largest stocks from consideration, and examine the next 600. We remove limited partnerships, real estate investment trusts, and stocks with very low actual trading volume or float to produce the Small Cap Universe which typically consists of slightly less than 600 stocks. (At the beginning of 1993, the Small Cap Universe had a market capitalization range of $150–$750 million.)

Gradient Maximization

The model used to evaluate stocks is constructed using a mathematical technique called "gradient maximization." Gradient maximization identifies and takes advantage of relationships between stock characteristics, or inputs, and subsequent returns. First, the user defines an objective; then, the technique enables the user to determine which inputs are useful in achieving the objective and the relative importance of those inputs. (Appendix A to this chapter provides a more detailed description of the technique.)

For example, an investor wishing to maximize his or her investment return may face a common source of confusion: a stock with a high price/earnings ratio and a low price/book ratio. As the investor, would you avoid the stock because it appears expensive or buy it because it looks cheap? A model using gradient maximization would likely indicate that both measures are useful, and the technique would indicate the best weighting for each measure in order to achieve the objective.

The ways that gradient maximization differ from more common methods of modeling stock market information are significant: (1) gradient maximization takes advantage of both linear and nonlinear relationships between stock characteristics and returns in the equity market, (2) achieving a specific investment objective drives the technique's selection of stock characteristics and determines their relative importance in the model and, (3) the technique combines variable selection with portfolio construction in the model development process, incorporating constraints on turnover and trade execution costs. In essence, the advantage of using gradient maximization to develop a strategy is that it provides more realism in building a model, constructing a portfolio of stocks over time, and achieving an investment objective. To a large extent, the closer a model incorporates the realities of investing, the more reliable the results, and the greater the likelihood of higher excess returns.

Model Objective

The objective of many equity models is to maximize return. Risk controls often have secondary importance in the process. However, as the Ibbotson data show, the added return associated with investing in small stocks can be overwhelmed by their incremental risk. Our strategy attempts to address this imbalance, beginning with the model's objective. The model is designed to outperform the Small Cap Universe and control risk; to achieve this goal, the model objective is to maximize the ratio of return divided by risk (similar to the Sharpe ratio[7]). The equity characteristics used and their weights in the model are based on achieving the highest return/risk ratio over time using stocks from the Small Cap Universe.

Moving Data Window

The model is designed to evolve with changes in the equity market. As illustrated in Figure 13.1, the model was constructed using ten years of data from 1971 to 1980. The model was then tested on ten years of new data from the period 1981–1990. For each year of the test period starting with the beginning of 1981, the model is constructed using the previous ten years of data. At year-end, the oldest year's data is dropped off and the new data is added. The old model is then adjusted using new information, and the new model is used to rank stocks through the next year. Thus, the model always utilizes a ten-year "moving window" of stock market information.

The ten-year moving window technique was designed to provide sufficient and varied data for building a reliable model and, at the same time,

Figure 13.1—Ten-Year Moving Window

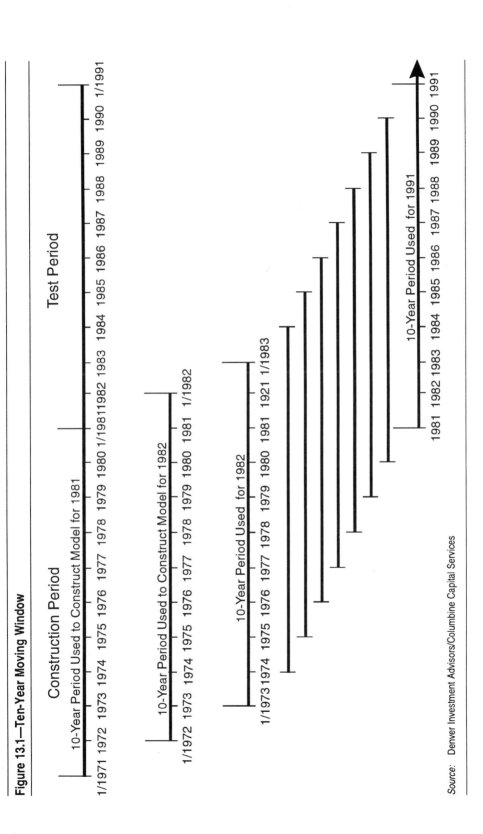

Source: Denver Investment Advisors/Columbine Capital Services

to make the model responsive to evolutionary changes in sources of return in the equity market. Ten years typically includes an array of financial and economic environments, including at least one full economic cycle; it typically also spans multiyear rotation within the stock market. At the same time, the data for the model is not fixed at an arbitrary point in history that is likely to become less relevant with each passing year. A much shorter time frame would likely produce a model heavily weighted toward an input that performed well in the recent past—just as the market stopped rewarding it.

Our methodology uses data from the most recent ten years in conjunction with gradient maximization to determine the combination and weighting of stock characteristics that outperform and produce the highest return/risk ratio over the ten-year period. This optimal combination of stock characteristics and weights comprises the model used to evaluate stocks in the subsequent year. At year-end, the ten-year data window moves forward one year, the model is reconstructed, and the new model is used to maximize return and control risk for the coming year.

Table 13.1 summarizes these and other strategy criteria, how they were addressed in the process, and the impact on return, risk, and reliability of the approach.

EVALUATING THE TEST RESULTS

Test results from the ten-year period 1981 to 1990 were evaluated on two levels: (1) efficacy of the model, based on return and risk analyses compared to the Small Cap Universe, and (2) viability of the approach as a money management strategy, based on return and risk comparisons with publicly available small cap indices. To adequately address this latter point, we first examine the issues involved in selecting appropriate well-known benchmarks.

Selecting a Publicly Available Benchmark

Investors tend to prefer benchmarks that are publicly available and widely disseminated. The advantages of these indices are that they are well-known, data are easily obtained, little additional effort is required from the client or manager to use the indices, and benchmark performance is independently calculated and reported. However, the disadvantages of using these indices for performance comparisons are considerable: (1) an index may not be an "investable" alternative to an active strategy; (2) benchmark returns may not be achievable; (3) the benchmark's economic sector or industry weighting may not reflect a neutral starting point for some clients; (4) the weighting difference alone between public benchmarks (typically capitalization-weighted) and many portfolios (typically equal-weighted) can produce return disparities; and (5) dividend income may not be included in return calculations.

Many small-stock indices are not "investable" and consequently are not realistic passive alternatives for institutional-sized portfolios. A significant portion of most small indices consists of stocks with very small market capitalizations or thinly traded shares.[8] Institutional investors and money managers are reluctant to own large positions in these companies due to: (1) increased regulatory burden if an investor owns more than 5% of a company's market capitalization; (2) acquiring a position may take several months, during which time the investment rationale for owning a stock could change and, importantly; (3) selling a large position in an illiquid stock is likely to drive the price down and significantly reduce the client's return.

Publicly available small-stock indices typically overstate the performance that investors can receive because trade execution costs are not deducted from benchmark performance. In simplest form, execution costs include brokerage commissions, the difference between the bid or offer price and the market-clearing price, and the adverse impact that filling an order has on a stock's price. Compared to large companies, most small companies have fewer shares outstanding and trading volume is typically lower. This illiquidity produces wider "bid/ask spreads" and increases both the likelihood of "market impact" and the potential magnitude of the impact. The typical result is substantially higher execution costs for investing in small stocks, and wider performance disparities with public indices. Investing institutional-sized portfolios is likely to generate greater market impact, raise costs further, and exacerbate these performance differences.

Execution costs would be incurred with either a passive approach that mimicked an index or with active management. Additionally, public benchmark performance does not reflect the investment management fees that would be incurred with passive, small-stock approaches.

Many indices have larger weightings in industries or economic sectors than a client may want in the managed portfolio. For example, it is common today for financial stocks to comprise approximately 20% of a small cap index.[9] Clients with actively managed portfolios should be comfortable with *at least* 20% of the portfolio in financials to allow for periodic over-weighting of the group. Otherwise, the index would not be a truly representative benchmark.

Lastly, some well-known small cap indices include dividend income in performance calculations while others do not. The impact of even low dividend income compounded over time can affect cumulative return enough to make the difference between whether or not an investment strategy outperformed a benchmark.

Table 13.1—Summary of Strategy Criteria and Design

Strategy Criteria	Design Response	Impact on Return, Risk, and Reliability
Small stocks.	Annually construct Small Cap Universe by ranking Compustat database on market capitalization, eliminate the largest 1,000 stocks and use the next 600 minus limited partnerships, investment trusts and stocks with very low float.	Small stocks have exhibited higher return, higher risk than the overall market over time.
Value focus.	Model that ranks stocks on attractiveness includes value and other proven measures; value measures are required to comprise at least 70% of the model.	Value measures increase return. Proprietary measures increase return or reduce risk or both. Value has lower risk than growth.
Control risk throughout the process.	Model objective: Maximize return divided by risk. Indicator(s) used in the model reduce risk. Sell discipline: A stock is sold if it ranks below the top 30% in any economic sector. Sector neutrality: Economic sector weights in the portfolio approximate those in the Small Cap Universe. Diversification: 50-60 stocks.	Maximizes return per unit of risk. Reduces risk. Reduces risk. Reduces risk. Reduces risk.
Model designed to outperform with small stocks.	Model is designed using the Small Cap Universe.	Increases reliability.
Model construction technique should allow for "real-world" equity dynamics.	Gradient maximization allows for linear and non-linear relationships between stock indicators, and indicators and returns, which enables the model to have superior predictive power.	Increases return. Increases reliability.

Table 13.1 Continued

Strategy Criteria	Design Response	Impact on Return, Risk, and Reliability
Model should evolve.	Stock characteristics used in the model change over time. Importance of a particular stock characteristic changes over time. Model is reconstructed annually. 10-year moving window balances the need for data that spans cycles in the market with the importance of using data that is continually relevant to the present.	Increases return per unit of risk. Increases reliability.
Approach must add value over a reasonably long time frame.	Construct the model using a 10-year period; test the approach in a subsequent 10-year period. Rank stocks monthly using the model, buy the highest ranked 10% in each sector, sell those that rank below the top 30% in each sector.	Increases reliability.
Approach must add value given higher execution costs.	Execution costs of 3% round trip included in results. Annual turnover constrained to 100% or less.	Reduces return. Increases reliability of outperformance with institutional-sized portfolios.
Test should have integrity and reliability.	Database is screened for errors. Financial data is lagged to only utilize data available at the time. All stocks that existed in any year were candidates to be included in the Universe. 10-year period used to construct the model, subsequent 10 years of fresh data used to test the approach.	Increases reliability.

Source: Denver Investment Advisors/Columbine Capital Services

Given these considerations, we examined the characteristics of widely disseminated small-stock benchmarks as well as several consultants' style portfolios. The CRSP 6-8[10], an index consisting of stocks in the 6th to 8th deciles ranked by market capitalization, and the Russell 2000 appeared to be the most appropriate small-stock benchmarks for our strategy. In general, characteristics of the CRSP 6-8 are closer to our Universe than the Russell 2000, while the latter benchmark is more widely known. (Appendix B to this chapter lists summary characteristics.)

The trade-offs involved in selecting these benchmarks were the following: (1) the majority of the capitalization of both benchmarks is currently in the $100–750 million range, which is similar to the Small Cap Universe; (2) the performance of the Russell 2000 could, however, be substantially swayed by its 20% weighting in stocks with market capitalizations of less than $100 million, which are likely to be extremely illiquid; (3) benchmark performance data does not allow for trade execution costs or fees; (4) overall, economic sector weights of the benchmarks are similar to our Universe with the CRSP 6-8 the most similar—yet, weight differences in Consumer Discretionary with the Russell 2000 and Financial Services with both indices could cause performance dissimilarities; (5) our strategy is equal weighted and the indices are capitalization weighted—however, the performance impact may be small, given the relatively narrow capitalization ranges involved; and (6) the performance of both benchmarks includes dividend income, removing a potential concern that our strategy might be perceived as having an artificial advantage.

Efficacy and Viability Tests

The strategy's results over the ten-year test period were evaluated using a rigorous battery of tests[11] based on six fundamental criteria:

1. Did the strategy meet the objective of outperformance and higher return relative to risk?
2. Are the characteristics of the portfolios consistent with the strategy design?
3. How consistent are the returns? What is the downside experience?
4. Does the model provide excess returns within economic sectors?
5. Could particular stocks in the underlying portfolios have produced skewed or misleading results?
6. Would the strategy add value, given the low trading volume that characterizes many small stocks?

Figures 13.2 to 13.8 provide information from the test results that address these considerations. Figure 13.2 is a reward/risk diagram with the

Figure 13.2—More Reward, Less Risk

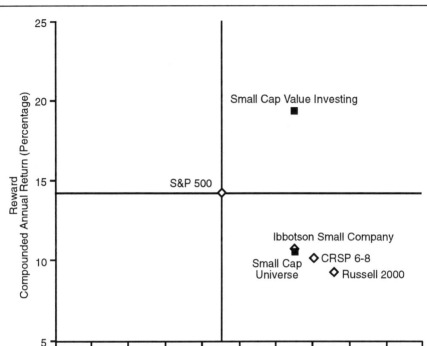

Source: Denver Investment Advisors/Columbine Capital Services

S&P 500 at the "cross-hairs" that shows the results of our strategy and small-stock indices. From 1981 to 1990, the S&P 500 returned 13.9% on an annualized basis, while volatility of returns was 17.2%. Data on the Ibbotson small-stock index is included for comparisons with the long-term Ibbotson study cited earlier.

The Small Cap Value strategy's return of 19.0% compounded annually is significantly higher than the Universe at 10.0%, the CRSP 6-8 at 9.8%, and the Russell 2000 at 8.5%. At the same time, the strategy's annualized volatility of returns is slightly less than volatility in the other indices. (Appendix C to this chapter provides annual data.) It is also important to note that our strategy includes execution costs, while the other indices do not.

To quantify this trade-off between reward and risk, we calculated the ratio of average monthly returns over the annualized monthly standard deviation of returns to produce "modified Sharpe ratios" over the period.

The model was designed to maximize return per unit of risk in each ten-year window, and the ratios below indicate that the strategy produced an attractive return/risk trade-off in the years following the model construction windows.

Modified Sharpe Ratios for the Period 1981–1990

Small Cap Value Investing	Small Cap Universe	CRSP 6-8	Russell 2000	Ibbotson Small-Stock	S&P 500
1.02	.60	.63	.51	.58	.88

Small Cap Value Investing's returns slightly more than offset the risk involved, and the relationship is substantially more attractive than the return/risk trade-off of the Universe, CRSP 6-8, or the Russell 2000. It is also intriguing that, during this period when large stocks generally outper-

Figure 13.3—Price/Earnings Ratio

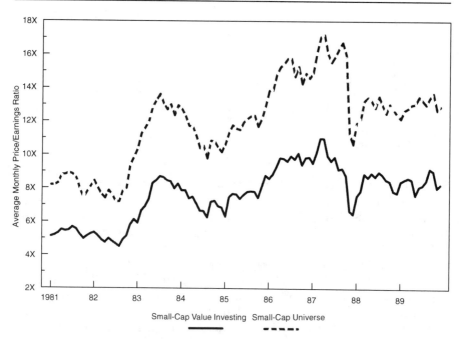

Notes: Small-Cap Value Investing: equal weighted, negative earnings removed.
         Small-Cap Universe: equal weighted, negative earnings removed.

Source: Denver Investment Advisors/Columbine Capital Services

formed small stocks, the Small Cap Value strategy outperformed the broad market and offered a superior return/risk relationship.

Figures 13.3 and 13.4 indicate that the characteristics of portfolios over time are consistent with the strategy's value-based philosophy. Figure 13.5 shows that the strategy produced excess returns over the Universe and benchmarks in three-fourths or more of the quarters—rather than having a few "home runs." Additionally, Small Cap Value Investing had twelve negative quarters, substantially fewer than the benchmarks, and outperformed the benchmarks over 80% of the time in quarters when small stocks declined. On an annual basis, the strategy would have produced two negative return years in ten. The worst downside experience occurred in 1990, when the strategy would have lost –13.6%. However, the loss is smaller than the CRSP 6-8 at –18.1% and the Russell 2000 at –19.5%. The strategy's quarterly and annual performance in down periods, and its simi-

Figure 13.4—Price/Book Value Ratio

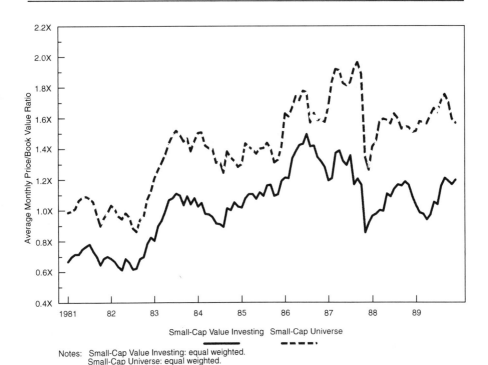

Small-Cap Value Investing   Small-Cap Universe

Notes: Small-Cap Value Investing: equal weighted.
        Small-Cap Universe: equal weighted.

Source: Denver Investment Advisors/Columbine Capital Services

Figure 13.5—Analysis of Quarterly and Annual Returns 1981–1990

	Small Cap Universe	CRSP 6–8	Russell 2000	Small Cap Value Investing
Down quarters	16	16	17	Outperformed 13 of Universe's down quarters Outperformed 13 of CRSP's down quarters Outperformed 14 of Russell's down quarters
Total quarters	40	40	40	Outperformed Universe 31 quarters Outperformed CRSP 30 quaraters Outperformed or equalled Russell 32 quarters
Calendar years	10	10	10	Outperformed Universe 9 years Outperformed CRSP 9 years Outperformed Russell all 10 years
Annualized standard deviation of quarterly returns	21.4%	22.7%	23.4%	21.0%
Average quarterly return	3.0%	3.0%	2.8%	5.0%

Source: Denver Investment Advisors/Columbine Capital Services

lar-to-better overall volatility than the benchmarks suggests that the strategy's risk control techniques are working.

The model's ability to identify attractive stocks within economic sectors is depicted in Figure 13.6. The chart shows the average excess return of stocks that ranked in the top 10% of each sector using the model. Portfolios were constructed on a monthly basis. The model added value in each of the ten economic sectors, with an average excess return over sectors of the Small Cap Universe of 7.1%.

At the individual stock level, equal weighting the portfolios and diversifying with fifty stocks prevented a few stocks from having an overwhelming impact on the returns. As the portfolios' economic sector weights mirrored those in the universe, returns were not driven by what could be unrealistically large sector differences.

Figure 13.6—Top-Ranked Stocks Outperform in Every Sector

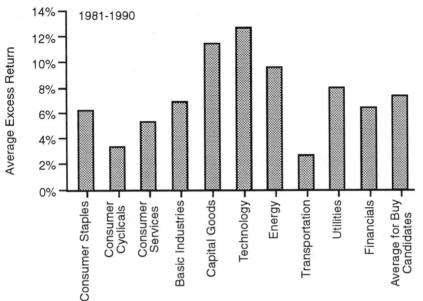

Performance of Equal-Weighted Buy Candidates by Sector vs.
Equal-Weighted Sectors of Small-Cap Universe

Source: Denver Investment Advisors/Columbine Capital Services

Lastly, the effect of low trading volume in small stocks can be critical to whether institutional-sized portfolios can achieve excess returns. Low trading volume can drive up trading costs, make a large position essentially impossible to buy, or require extra time to establish or sell a holding. Testing the impact of less liquid stocks in a strategy is not a simple task, however. Historic trading volume data for small stocks is often incomplete or unavailable, and data on stocks that trade over-the-counter are likely to be overstated.

With these difficulties in mind, we created two scenarios to investigate the model's excess returns in the face of stocks with low liquidity. In the first case, we wanted to know whether and by how much the strategy would outperform the Universe if the least liquid stocks were not purchased. However, as historic liquidity data was unavailable, we used a stock's market capitalization as a proxy. On a monthly basis, we ranked stocks using the model, alternately excluded the smallest 25%, 50%, and

66% of the Universe, constructed 50-stock portfolios of the remaining stocks, and calculated the portfolio's excess return (including 3% transaction costs) over the test period. Figure 13.7 shows the results.

We expected the excess return to decline as more stocks were removed from consideration, causing the portfolios to contain a mix of stocks from lower in the model's ranking. It was somewhat surprising that the excess return did not decelerate at a quicker rate, however. The data suggest that the strategy would have outperformed the Small Cap Universe by 7.3% with as much as two-thirds of the Universe removed from consideration.

One caveat is that by using capitalization instead of actual liquidity data, the resulting portfolios become progressively more biased toward larger stocks that performed well during the 1980s. On the other hand, the Universe was designed to exclude large stocks—and its capitalization range is relatively narrow, suggesting that any benefit in this period from simply moving to larger stocks was likely to be small. In addition, market capitalization is likely to be an increasingly accurate proxy for liquidity the smaller the stock. Consequently, we believe it is reasonable to conclude that at least when the smallest 25% of the stocks (based on either market

Figure 13.7—Small Cap Value Outperforms without the Smallest/Least Liquid Stocks

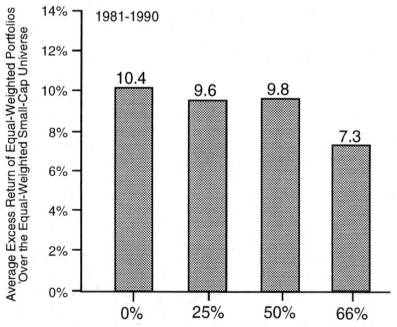

Source: Denver Investment Advisors/Columbine Capital Services

capitalization or liquidity) are not purchased, there is only a modest decline in excess return over the period.

In the second scenario, we addressed the impact on excess returns of trading institutional-sized positions in small stocks. We included execution costs of 3% in our research, which is higher than would be expected in similar circumstances for trading large-stock portfolios. The extra cost was included to defray the likely effect on stock prices of trading larger positions. To allow for extra time involved for establishing or selling a large position, we tested the effect of delaying the execution of trades by one and two months. Figure 13.8 indicates that while the combined effect of higher transaction costs and longer trading periods reduces returns, the strategy still adds substantial value.

In sum, the test results indicate that:

- The model is a powerful tool for identifying undervalued stocks.

- The approach produces value-focused portfolios that over time provide higher return relative to risk than similar indices.

Figure 13.8—Small Cap Value Outperforms When Trade Execution Is Delayed

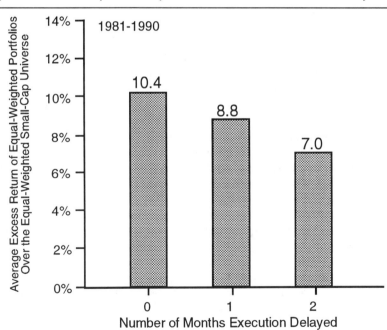

Source: Denver Investment Advisors/Columbine Capital Services

- In addition to slightly less overall volatility, the approach produces fewer and lower negative returns when small stocks in general decline.

- The model adds value within each economic sector.

- The results are not skewed by a few exceptional short-term periods or a few heavily-weighted stocks.

- The results appear to be achievable with institutional-sized portfolios.

With the foundation of a solid evaluation and portfolio construction strategy, we move from research to investing.

MANAGING A SMALL-STOCK PORTFOLIO

Investing in a portfolio of stocks is something like taking an airplane flight. We know that the laws of physics and aerodynamics are fundamental to air travel. We expect that proven principles of propulsion and navigation are used as the basis for rising above the ground and reaching our destination. We rely on thorough testing of the aircraft before flight and the sophisticated instruments, navigation systems, and radio signals that make many flights a routine operation. We have good reason to feel confident when a high level of sophistication and technology is amassed in the systems of commercial aircraft. In fact, we would not choose to fly without it.

At the same time, if we knew that an airplane would be operated entirely by "autopilot," most of us would refuse to board the plane.

In the investment world, there are no hard and fast laws that determine success or failure. This is one reason why outperforming a benchmark can be at least as complex as flying an airplane. Similarly, we believe that it is important in the financial world to utilize all resources available, combining the advantages of a sophisticated investment model with the advantages of experienced portfolio management when investing a client's assets.

The advantages of good quantitative models are organization, discipline, documentation, and an empirically demonstrated *raison d'être*. Good qualitative decision-making provides integration of varied types of information, interpretation, intuition, and an ability to factor in the dimension of human behavior. We combine quantitative research from our model with qualitative information assessed by the portfolio manager for a more complete picture of the potential rewards and risks of an individual stock. In so doing, we add the final element of the approach to further enhance the portfolio's risk-adjusted return.

In broad terms, the portfolio manager's function is to 1) meet the client's needs, and 2) provide invaluable information from the investment "front lines" regarding maintaining and improving the quality of our approach.

Meeting the Client's Needs

Meeting the client's needs involves capturing the returns of small value stocks and controlling risk—better than a relevant benchmark, minimizing execution costs, and communicating regularly about the portfolio and the approach.

Capturing return and controlling risk. The first function of portfolio management is implementation. The portfolio manager does not evaluate all stocks in the Universe; the model ranks stocks from most attractive to least attractive within each economic sector. At the same time, the model does not invest in stocks; we invest in stocks through disciplined use of the model. The portfolio manager uses the strategy determined in the process of building the model. The portfolio manager evaluates highly ranked stocks, typically the top 10% in each sector, as candidates for purchase. This is portfolio management's role in the Enhanced Value Discipline. Using the list of purchase candidates, the portfolio manager weighs quantitative and qualitative information, as well as liquidity and portfolio considerations, and selects stocks. The resulting portfolio typically consists of 50–60 stocks. Once a stock ranks below the top 30% in each sector, it is automatically sold. The portfolio manager may choose to eliminate a purchase candidate from consideration or sell a stock early based on information not contained in the model.

Effective portfolio management requires a thorough understanding of the model, the strengths and weaknesses of quantitative models, the dynamics of small companies and small stocks, and the current investment environment. Importantly, the portfolio manager must know when quantitative information is more likely to determine the future direction of a stock price, and when qualitative information may supersede it. In essence, the portfolio manager must know when to "stay out of the way" of the model and when to intercede in the interest of the client.

Portfolio manager involvement is designed to complement the model. One way this is achieved is by identifying cases where company data used by the model is an unreliable indication of the firm's future performance. Recent earnings announcements, the company's business progress, and customer/competitor information move stock prices and may not have entered the database that drives the model.

The operations of small businesses can be heavily influenced by the business fortunes of customers or unusual situations within the company. A work stoppage at a major manufacturer, for example, can be a crippling blow to a small supplier, or senior management defections can leave a small firm adrift. A portfolio manager can assess and react to these situations at the time, rather than wait for subsequent financial results to flow through the database to the model.

The portfolio manager can also reduce the client's potential risk by avoiding the occasional stock that appears to have unknowable or incalculable risk. As an example, smaller companies can be more susceptible than larger firms to legal actions where the outcome could severely impair the company's business or drive it into bankruptcy. If the stock price zigs and zags with every new development, it may be advantageous to own another stock ranked highly by the model.

If two stocks are both ranked highly, information learned by the portfolio manager may suggest that one stock is more attractive than the other. These cases can be the essence of undervaluation: when a stock is among the most undervalued in the universe as ranked by the model, and the portfolio manager observes a business on the cusp of potentially dynamic change.

Finally, a portfolio manager, like a pilot, anticipates and reacts on a real-time basis to what is not known today. It is the extra element of control and safety that we require in air travel and that makes sense in the management of assets.

Minimizing execution costs. Once individual stock decisions are made, a second function of portfolio management is to minimize cost in trade execution. Since public small cap benchmarks do not include costs, an invested strategy's performance will lag behind these benchmarks at the moment the first trade takes place. In addition, the larger the asset base, the more trading costs can reduce returns at the beginning and going forward. Consequently, a small-stock strategy requires serious attention to trading.

At the model level, our approach was designed to outperform with annual turnover of 100% or less and after subtracting round-trip trading costs of 3%. The constraint on turnover was included to lessen the extent that trading costs could reduce performance. Portfolio management takes this research a step further to execute actual trades in a cost-effective manner.

In addition to the three components of execution costs previously mentioned—commissions, bid/ask spread, and market impact—a fourth element can be the opportunity cost of a trade. This is the lost opportunity or "cost" of a trade not executed because the stock's price has moved substantially and against the investor's interest. Except for brokerage commissions, the size of these costs depend on characteristics of the stocks being traded, share liquidity, portfolio turnover, the methodology, and the medium used to trade. The portfolio manager may determine liquidity thresholds for purchase candidates, develop trading strategies to minimize costs, and is involved in monitoring the results. Finally, a subtle but important benefit of portfolio manager involvement in trading strategies is the integration of small-stock trading realities into the investment decision-making process. Table 13.2 summarizes portfolio management involvement in the day-to-day investment process.

Table 13.2—Summary of Portfolio Management Involvement in the Strategy

Strategy Criteria	Portfolio Management Role	Objective for Return, Risk, and Reliability
Meet clients' needs from return and risk perspectives.	Disciplined implementation of the approach. Evaluate stocks in the top 10% in each sector; automatically sell stocks that rank below the top 30% in each sector.	Maximize return per unit of risk.
Important nonmodel information included in the strategy.	Assess qualitative information to complement model's quantitative ranking. Select stocks to buy.	Increase return, reduce risk.
Control risk throughout the process.	May sell a stock ahead of model indication based on nonmodel information. Liquidity analysis.	Reduce risk, increase reliability. Reduce risk.
Approach must add value given higher execution costs.	Minimize cost in trade execution.	Increase return.

Source: Denver Investment Advisors/Columbine Capital Services

Communicating with clients. Meeting clients' needs involves communicating frequently and providing responsive service. Clearly, long-term client relationships result from actions rather than from paper statements. Yet, as communication and service are as important as meeting a client's performance needs, we briefly offer a few areas where portfolio management keeps clients informed.

A portfolio manager is a conduit between research, the equity market, and the client. Portfolio management can provide insight into the small cap sector of the market, as well as regularly provide the portfolio's style characteristics that confirm its small-stock, value focus. The portfolio manager can discuss why the approach is leading or lagging its benchmark; he or she listens to clients' observations and can describe current research into improving the process.

Improving the Investment Approach

The approach was designed to be dynamic and, in some ways, to automatically improve over time. The formulation of the model allows for new measures to be included and existing ones to gain or lose importance, while the portfolio maintains its consistent value theme. The model is updated annually based on the most recent ten years of stock market information. Portfolio manager involvement in implementation allows qualitative information to continually flow through the process, and provides a check-and-balance method for enhancing risk-adjusted return. The importance of trading costs to the bottom line drives the investigation of new strategies to reduce costs.

We capitalize on one of the strengths of a quantitatively based approach by tracking results at various stages in the process. This research allows us to monitor aspects of the approach and is one source of ideas for improving the approach. The result is a feedback process for improving the strategy which is depicted in Figure 13.9.

SUMMARY OF THE PROCESS

Figure 13.10 is a diagram of the Small Cap Value Investing approach that we have described.

Our research suggests that investing for high returns without incurring unrestrained risk may not be an intractable dilemma. The incremental return and risk of small stocks can be balanced in an investment approach so that investing in small stocks makes sense, given both dimensions. Moreover, our effort indicates that capturing excess returns and controlling risk in small-stock investing is not only possible but a profitable approach to building financial resources.

Figure 13.9—Strategy Improvement Process

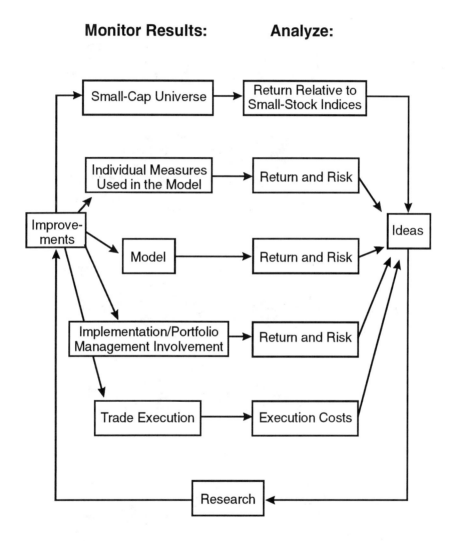

Source: Denver Investment Advisors/Columbine Capital Services

Figure 13.10—Small Cap Value Investing Process

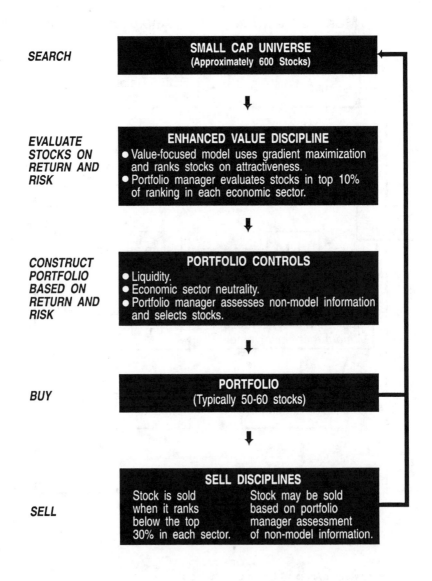

ENDNOTES

[1] A recent study is, Mott, Claudia E., Daniel P. Coker, and Michele C. Eschert, *Small Cap Monthly*, Prudential Securities (March 18, 1993), p. 4.

[2] Ibbotson Associates, *Stocks, Bonds, Bills, and Inflation: 1993 Yarbook*, Ibbotson Associates, Chicago, Illionis, p.33.

[3] Two recent articles are Eugene F. Fama and Kenneth R. French, "The Cross-Section of Expected Stock Returns," *The Journal of Finance*, Vol. 47 #2 (June 1992), pp. 427–465; B. Jacobs and K. Levy, "Disentangling Equity Return Regularities: New Insights and Investment Opportunities," *Financial Analysts Journal* (May 1988), pp. 18–43.

[4] BARRA, Inc., Berkeley, California

[5] A statistics technique called "linear regression."

[6] Standard and Poor's Compustat database, Englewood, Colorado.

[7] William F. Sharpe developed the Sharpe measure, which is defined as (the average rate of return for a portfolio – the risk-free rate)/the standard deviation of returns. William F. Sharpe, "Mutual Fund Performance," *Journal of Business*, Vol. 39 #1, Part 2 (January 1966), pp. 119–138.

[8] For example, on a capitalization-weighted basis, 59% of the Russell 2000 and 17% of the Wilshire Small Cap consist of stocks that have less than $250 million in market capitalization. At the same time, 24% of the capitalization of the Russell 2000 and 62% of the Wilshire Small Cap's weight comprises more than 25% of the included stock's average daily trading volume. (The Russell 2000 is constructed by Frank Russell Company and represents the bottom two-thirds of the largest 3,000 common stocks domiciled in the U.S. The Index consists of 2,000 companies and has an average market capitalization of $139 million. The Wilshire Small cap is constructed by Wilshire Associates to track the performance of small stocks. Small stocks are selected from the Wilshire Next 1750, which is derived from taking the largest 2,500 stocks ranked by market capitalization and eliminating the largest 750 stocks. The Wilshire Small cap contains 250 stocks and has an average market capitalization of $492 million.) Claudia E. Mott, "Benchmark Study III—The Small Cap and Mid Cap Pictures," *Prudential Securities* (September 29, 1992); and Claudia E. Mott, Daniel P. Coker, and Michele C. Eschert, "Benchmark Study III.V—Year-End 1992 Small Cap and Mid Cap Updates," *Prudential Securities*, (February 25, 1993).

[9] In the study cited, five out of eleven small-stock indices have a weighting of 20% or more in *Financial Services*. The *Financial Services* weighting in five of the remaining six is greater than 17%. Claudia E. Mott, Daniel P. Coker, and Michele C. Eschert, "Benchmark Study III.V—Year-End 1992 Small Cap and Mid Cap Update," *Prudential Securities*, (February 25, 1993).

[10] The CRSP 6-8 was developed by the University of Chicago Center for Research in Security Prices. It is constructed by ranking all stocks on the New York Stock Exchange by market capitalization, forming deciles, and including stocks from the American Stock Exchange and the NASDAQ National Market System (NMS) that are within the capitalization cut-offs of the 6th-8th declines. The benchmark consists of 1,215 stocks currently and has an average market capitalization of $254 million. Claudia E. Mott, Daniel P. Coker, and Michele C. Eschert, "Benchmark Study III.V—Year-End 1992 Small Cap and Mid Cap Updates," *Prudential Securities*, (February 25, 1993).

[11] An excellent article on evaluating strategy test results is: John D. Freeman, "Behind the Smoke and Mirrors: Gauging the Integrity of Investment Simulations," *Financial Analysts Journal*, (November–December 1992), pp. 26–31.

REFERENCES

Fama, Eugene F. and French, Kenneth R., "The Cross-Section of Expected Stock Returns," *The Journal of Finance*, 47, No. 2 (1992), pp. 427–465.

Freeman, John D., "Behind the Smoke and Mirrors: Gauging the Integrity of Investment Simulations," *Financial Analysts Journal* (November–December 1992), pp. 26–31.

Ibbotson Associates, *Stocks, Bonds, Bills and Inflation: 1993 Yearbook*, p 33.

Jacobs, Bruce and Levy, Kenneth, "Disentangling Equity Return Regularities: New Insights and Investment Opportunities," *Financial Analysts Journal* (May 1988), pp. 18–43.

Mott, Claudia E., "Benchmark Study III—The Small Cap and Mid Cap Pictures," *Prudential Securities*, September 29, 1992.

_____, Coker, Daniel P., and Eschert, Michele C., "Benchmark Study III.V—Year-End 1992 Small Cap and Mid Cap Updates," *Prudential Securities* (February 25, 1992).

_____, "Small Cap Monthly," *Prudential Securities* (March 18, 1993), p. 4.

Sharpe, William F., "Mutual Fund Performance," *Journal of Business*, 39, No. 1 (1966), pp. 119–138.

APPENDIX A—BUILDING EQUITY MODELS USING

GRADIENT MAXIMIZATION

Suppose you must select a "best" portfolio from a large group of stocks. For each stock you have a number of factor rankings such as book/price, earnings/price, etc. To identify a most attractive portfolio out of the large number of potentially buyable stocks, you will have to face the problem of combining all these rankings into a single composite number. Since the various factor rankings may have different predictive power when used alone, and since different factor rankings have varying degrees of correlation with one other, there is no simple way to know what the best combining recipe might be.

Gradient maximization is an approach to addressing this problem. Gradient means "slope along a specific direction"—uphill in a mountain climbing sense. Maximization is proceeding uphill to reach a maximum. A step-by-step description of the process for a hypothetical problem is the best way to present the critical ideas:

1. Start by choosing some initial weighting. To combine two simple factors it might be: 40% book/price and 60% earnings/price.

2. In a multiyear database, rank order all of the stocks every month using the initial weighting combination of factors as a ranking model.

3. Measure the multiyear performance of a portfolio holding the highest-ranked 10% of all stocks each month. Associate this overall return with the weighting that produced it. This is the return that we are going to try to increase to the maximum amount possible.

4. Explore the region around the current weighting combination by sequentially changing each factor weight up and then down a bit from the original weighting chosen and recompute the monthly returns and final multiyear returns. Associate the final return with each unique weighting combination that produced it.

5. Consider which weight changes lead to the largest increase and decrease of overall return. If every change up and down from the current weighting results in a decrease in return, you are at the maximum return point since the weights you have cannot be improved upon. In general, the experiments of step 4 will suggest that some weights should be increased, some decreased. The magnitude of the change planned for each weight is proportional to the beneficial change in overall, multiyear return. In our two-vari-

able problem this could be as simple as: increase the weight on book/price, decrease the weight of earnings/price.

6. Now, change the weights at the same time as suggested from 4 and 5 by increasing amounts. The overall returns should rise, peak, and then decline. Take the peak in return and the weightings that achieved it as a possible maximum point. This peak is the apparent maximum in the best or steepest uphill-improving direction defined from the last locally explored point tested. Either this is the final maximum or there is a new direction leading further uphill in return sense.

7. Return to step 1 and explore the region around the new weighting. If you are very lucky, no improvement will be possible and you have reached the desired maximum return point. Usually, due to the irregular shape of the variable/return surface, a new direction of possible improvement will be found and you will move off in that uphill direction.

8. Eventually, after multiple reiterations of this process, you will find a set of weights that cannot be improved upon. This means you have achieved a candidate maximum. You got there by a sequence of local explorations and upward moves along the local maximum gradient.

Restarting the whole process from different arbitrary weights will verify that the same "best" model is found. Local maxima can exist, so multiple restarts or equivalent procedures are necessary. Depending on the process, a coarse search of initial starting points can be made to avoid a bad initial guess of weights.

Gradient maximization is very flexible at simulating realistic portfolio returns. Transaction costs, economic sector constraints, and more elaborate turnover reducing strategies can be applied if desired. Instead of excess return one could use a ratio of return/volatility as a measure to be maximized.

Gradient maximization is expensive in computer time and requires considerable human intervention along the way. Modern computers and efficient sorting algorithms make it practical. For a typical real-world problem of 1500 stocks, 20 years of monthly data, and six variables, selecting a best 150-stock portfolio can take 1 minute per simulation. This speed is attainable only with specialized software and experienced programmers. Literally hundreds of runs must be made to reach the best weighting combination.

APPENDIX B

SIZE DISTRIBUTION OF SMALL CAP UNIVERSE AND BENCHMARKS

	PERCENTAGE OF COMPANIES			MARKET CAPITALIZATION WEIGHTED		
Market Capitaliza-tion Range (12/92)	Small Cap Universe %	CRSP 6-8 %	Russell 2000 %	Small Cap Universe %	CRSP 6-8 %	Russell 2000 %
$750M–$1.5B	–	–	0.3	–	–	0.1
$250M–$750M	99.5	42.1	15.0	99.8	63.1	40.0
$100M–$250M	0.5	53.2	33.4	0.2	35.5	38.5
Less than $100M	–	4.8	51.3	–	1.4	20.0

Sources: Denver Investment Advisors/Columbine Capital Services and Prudential Securities.

ECONOMIC SECTOR DISTRIBUTION OF SMALL CAP UNIVERSE AND BENCHMARKS

	PERCENTAGE OF COMPANIES			MARKET CAPITALIZATION WEIGHTED		
Russell Economic Sectors (12/92)	Small Cap Universe %	CRSP 6-8 %	Russell 2000 %	Small Cap Universe %	CRSP 6-8 %	Russell 2000 %
Autos & trans.	5.5	4.0	3.7	5.4	4.1	4.5
Cons. discret./svcs.	23.3	21.4	16.6	24.0	23.6	16.4
Consumer staples	2.2	3.5	3.0	2.1	2.9	2.4
Financial services	11.4	18.4	17.6	11.6	18.5	19.5
Healthcare	12.6	12.3	14.0	11.9	11.8	12.9
Integrated oils	2.2	0.4	0.2	2.4	0.6	0.3
Materials & proc.	9.8	7.1	11.3	10.0	7.3	11.0
Other energy	3.1	4.9	4.5	3.0	4.2	4.2
Producer durable	8.4	7.2	7.2	8.1	6.8	5.7
Technology	12.8	13.3	14.3	12.6	13.1	15.1
Utilities	6.4	4.5	3.8	6.2	4.6	5.8
Other	2.2	3.0	2.4	2.6	2.5	2.1

Sources: Denver Investment Advisors/Columbine Capital Services, Center for Research in Security Prices, and Frank Russell Company.

APPENDIX C

SMALL CAP VALUE INVESTING TEST PERIOD PERFORMANCE AND INDEX RETURNS

	Small Cap Value Investing*	Small Cap Universe**	CRSP 6-8**	Russell 2000**	Ibbotson Small Company**	S&P 500**
	(equal-wtd 50-stock portfolios)	(equal-wtd)	(cap-wtd)	(cap-wtd)	(cap-wtd)	(cap-wtd)
1981	17.4%	5.5%	5.0%	2.0%	13.9%	–5.0%
1982	26.2	20.3	25.6	24.9	28.0	21.5
1983	41.1	31.6	28.7	29.1	39.7	22.4
1984	10.1	–2.2	–0.9	–7.3	–6.7	6.2
1985	49.3	30.2	32.2	31.0	24.7	31.6
1986	20.6	8.7	8.4	5.7	6.9	18.6
1987	–5.5	–3.1	–6.4	–8.8	–9.3	5.3
1988	33.9	22.3	23.4	24.9	22.9	16.6
1989	25.7	17.6	19.1	16.2	10.2	31.6
1990	–13.6	–19.2	–18.1	–19.5	–21.6	–3.1
Compound annual return	19.0%	10.0%	9.8%	8.5%	10.7%	13.9%
Annualized standard deviation of quarterly returns	21.0	21.4	22.7	23.4	21.3	17.2

*   Includes 3% execution costs.

** Does not include execution costs.

Sources: Denver Investment Advisors/Columbine Capital Services, Center for Research in Security Prices, Frank Russell Co., Ibbotson Assoc., and Standard & Poor's.

Chapter 14

Tactical Style Allocation Using Small Cap Strategies

Rosemary Macedo
Vice President Quantitative Research
Bailard, Biehl & Kaiser

INTRODUCTION

Other chapters in this book expound on the nature, returns, and diversification benefits of small cap stocks domestically and internationally, effectively covering the why, what, where, and how of small cap investing. This chapter focuses on the when of small cap investing, namely tactical style allocation.

Most large funds hire multiple managers, each specializing in a particular style, such as large cap or small, value or growth. More often than not, management of the overall style mix is guided by a rearview mirror: recent underperformers are abandoned, often just before their style comes back into favor. Instead of basing decisions on recent past performance of a style, however, it makes more sense to consider which style is likely to perform best in the coming months. Such a discipline already has been applied successfully at the stock-picking level, using a bottom-up approach. (See Arnott, Kelso, Kiscadden, and Macedo [1990], and Arnott, Dorian, and Macedo [1992].) This chapter explores the benefits of applying a style management discipline at the portfolio level, using a top-down approach to style allocation.

The chapter begins by highlighting the need for a disciplined approach to managing the allocation between small cap value and small cap growth strategies. After an appraisal of the potential rewards, I will show how quantitative models can help investors anticipate which small cap style is likely to shine, and I will discuss the indicators that drive the models. Since there are, of course, times when both small value and small growth are out of favor, tactical style allocation between large cap and small is also addressed. The chapter concludes with a discussion of how such a discipline could be used by fund managers.

THE CASE FOR STYLE MANAGEMENT

Returns at the fund level are dramatically affected by the allocation among specialty managers of different styles. The role of size and value as principal determinants of expected return at the portfolio level—surpassing even beta—has been well documented in the literature. Probably the most widely known example is the recent paper by Fama and French [1992].

Investment styles are often compared historically to make a point about which is least volatile or produces the highest returns. Such analysis is highly sensitive to which period of time is chosen, and, in any case, past results offer no guarantee of future performance. One historical observation that is dependable, however, is that no style does well all the time. A discipline that forecasts when styles will go in and out of favor could exploit these changes. Indeed, looking ahead at Figure 14.1, one might surmise that the need for such a discipline has been growing.

Style management typically occurs only at the sponsor level, where it tends to be more reactive than active, and is usually limited to shifting money out of recently unsuccessful styles into those that performed well recently (a sell low, buy high strategy). Investors who took money away from large-cap managers in the mid 1980s, from growth managers in 1988 and 1989, and from small-stock and value managers in 1990, did so only to see superior results in the very style they had just abandoned.

With a tactical style allocation discipline, an investor could seek to anticipate which styles are likely to do well. A disciplined process, which is responsive to changing market and economic conditions, could alert investors to upcoming opportunities. It could be a valuable guide for an investment committee deliberating whether to terminate styles that have underperformed recently.

SMALL VALUE VERSUS SMALL GROWTH

Table 14.1 tabulates the differences in annual performance of small value and small growth. Small growth dominated from 1978 to 1981, small value

Table 14.1—Annual Return Comparison

	Small Growth[1]	Small Value[1]	S&P 500
1978	27.33%	11.23%	6.57%
1979	51.78	22.84	18.60
1980	52.75	18.56	32.13
1981	(1.25)	25.00	(4.91)
1982	19.16	35.90	21.11
1983	22.56	42.29	22.37
1984	(9.05)	22.10	6.11
1985	26.45	42.11	32.03
1986	10.13	23.48	18.55
1987	(8.64)	(3.08)	5.22
1988	19.30	22.39	16.82
1989	18.72	18.12	31.53
1990	(19.02)	(19.39)	(3.18)
1991	56.80	49.00	30.57
1992	13.20	29.23	7.60

1   Wilshire Style Indexes

from 1981 through 1988, and neither for very long thereafter. Figure 14.1 illustrates just how dramatic and volatile the differences in performance are from quarter to quarter. Even when one style was dominant for a long period, there were opportunities to add value through style timing. A switch from small value into small growth for the nine months beginning in October 1982, for example, would have added about 20% relative to staying in small value. Recently, the opportunity for style timing has been even greater, with more frequent swings. Each of the last three years has seen a swing of 10% or more.

The potential to add value with such a discipline is presented in Table 14.2, which compares a perfect foresight portfolio (100% in best style) to a fixed allocation of 50% small value/50% small growth, from January 1981 through December 1992. The 12.27% annualized added value is *net* 5.6% transaction costs (280% turnover/year × 2%/round-trip). Actually, one would have done almost as well by simply holding small value for the whole period. The problem is, how could one have known that at the beginning of 1981?

Figure 14.1—Difference in Quarterly Returns, Small Value-Small Growth

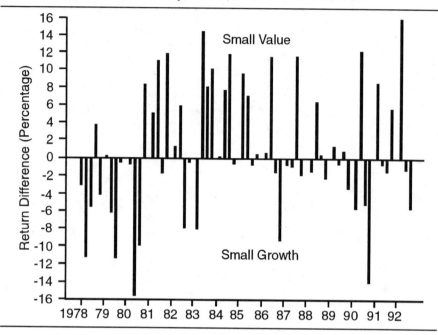

Table 14.2—*Potential* for Style Timing, Small Value & Small Growth, 8101-9212 (Perfect Foresight)

	Perfect Foresight	50/50 Normal[1]	Potential Added Value
Annualized return[2]	28.90%	16.63%	12.27%
Standard deviation	15.97%	17.12%	4.52%
Information ratio	1.81	0.97	2.71
Turnover	280%		

1 Systematically rebalanced, 50% small value, 50% small growth.

2 Net of transaction costs: 2% round-trip for small cap, 0.5% for large.

The rest of this chapter focuses on models that seek to capture this potential, using only the information that would have been available at the time. The actual amount of value added by models in such a simulation is relatively unimportant; the performance differences between styles, i.e., the potential rewards to successful timing, may be greater or smaller in the future. What is important about the models is that they be able to predict *ex ante which* style will outperform, and that the reasons they make those calls are sound.

The returns presented throughout this chapter are based on Wilshire Associates' passive style indexes[1]. One could argue that there are more representative or better-performing indexes or funds with these same styles, but that would not alter the basic conclusions as to whether this kind of timing works. The timing either does or does not add value for any given set of specialty managers. Clearly, the more skillful the active managers in each style, the greater the rewards that can be reaped with effective timing. In the case of passive managers, the more concentrated the style bets, the greater the potential rewards for timing.[2]

STYLE INDICATORS, SMALL VALUE VERSUS SMALL GROWTH

The investigation into return forecasting for style portfolios concentrated on three primary areas: valuation, economic, and market indicators, such as the equity risk premium, producer price inflation, the leading indicator, and volatility. This research confirmed several powerful relationships (see Table 14.3).

Table 14.3—Style Return Indicators for Small Capitalization Stocks, Value versus Growth, 7801-9212

Indicator	Style Favored	Correlation[1]	t-Statistic
Equity risk premium	Small growth over small value	−0.355	−5.1
Market volatility	Small growth over small value	−0.201	−2.7
Interest rate volatility	Small growth over small value	−0.174	−2.4
Leading indicator trend	Small value over small growth	0.242	3.3
Bond yield	Small value over small growth	0.188	2.6

1   Correlation with *subsequent* difference in returns, small value − small growth. All t-statistics are significant at the 95% level.

Equity risk premium is the strongest discriminator for future style performance. A high-equity risk premium favors riskier portfolios. Growth stocks are longer-duration investments than value stocks, hence they are perceived to be more risky and so tend to do well when the equity risk premium is high.

In turbulent markets, there is frequently a "flight to quality" during which risky stocks tend to be sold cheaply, and less risky stocks tend to be bid up due to high demand. *After* a period of high volatility, the cheap small-growth stocks outperform the expensive small value.

Similarly, small-growth stocks will be oversold during periods of high interest rate volatility. *After* such periods, they rebound.

Evidence of a healthier economy, such as a strong year-over-year rise in the leading indicator, signals that value is likely to outperform growth.

High bond yields are associated with times when value-oriented portfolios outperform growth-oriented portfolios.

Valuation, economic, and market conditions do affect the future performance of various investment styles in ways that we can predict. Multivariate models were constructed for each style using these intuitively appealing indicators, emphasizing consistent performance and reasonable turnover as well as value added.

PERFORMANCE TESTS, SMALL VALUE VERSUS SMALL GROWTH

To test the efficacy of style forecasting models as decision-making tools, the small value versus small growth forecasting model was applied to the corresponding style indexes.

The model forecasts were generated under a rigorous *ex ante* framework, where the only information used for each forecast was that which would have been available prior to the period being forecast. Data available from January 1978 to December 1980 were used to predict January 1981 returns. Data available from January 1978 to January 1981 were then used to predict February 1981 returns. This recursive process was repeated through December 1992, resulting in twelve years of monthly forecasts.

These *ex ante* forecasts were used to rebalance the portfolio each month, with 100% of the portfolio being put into the most attractive style. Changes were made whenever the expected difference in returns exceeded transaction costs. A benchmark portfolio with 50% small value and 50% small growth was used as a normal, and was systematically rebalanced whenever market movements caused a drift of 1% or more from this fixed weighting.

Table 14.4 summarizes the results of an *ex ante* performance test of this strategy. The tactical portfolio was able to add 6% annually to the fixed mix, after transaction costs, and with only 19% annual turnover. Figure 14.2 shows the trailing three-month added value from tactical style allocation over the twelve-year *ex ante* test period. During this period, the tactical portfolio tended to bet on value, not because value did well, but rather because market and economic conditions were generally more favorable for value-oriented strategies during this period. The following discussion traces the performance record and the indicators that drove the model.

Table 14.4—*Ex ante* Performance Test, 8101-9212
Tactical Style Allocation Between Small Value and Small Growth

	Tactical Style	50/50 Normal[1]	Added Value
Annualized return[2]	22.65%	16.63%	6.02%
Standard deviation	14.23%	17.12%	6.38%
Information ratio	1.59	0.97	0.94
Turnover	19.00%		

1 Systematically rebalanced, 50% small value, 50% small growth.

2 Net of transaction costs: 2% round trip for small cap, 0.5% for large.

Only two out of the twelve quarters between January 1978 and December 1980 favored value, yet the model correctly called value at the beginning of 1981 *without* look-ahead bias. How? At the end of 1980, the equity risk premium plunged, correctly signaling the move out of small growth. The subsequent calls and outcomes are recapitulated below.

Volatility decreased in mid-1981, strengthening the signal for small value. The model tripped at the end of 1981, incorrectly calling small growth because of brief increases in equity risk premium and volatility. Results were mixed for 1982, with the model tending to favor small value. From January 1983 through December 1985, the model signaled small value for all thirty-six months, missing the dominance of small growth in early 1983 but capturing the dominance of small value over the following two and a half years. In early 1983, the model signaled small value due to the below-average equity risk premium and volatility, and above-average trend in the leading indicator. Thereafter, as the equity risk premium and volatility decreased further, and the leading indicator trended upward more steeply, the signal for small value became even stronger, and the model added value with good consistency throughout the next thirty months. In 1986, the model missed only one month, correctly calling three out of four small-growth months and eight out of eight small-value months.

In 1987, the model stuck with small value through the October crash, missing several small-growth months but more than making up for it by

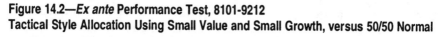

Figure 14.2—*Ex ante* Performance Test, 8101-9212
Tactical Style Allocation Using Small Value and Small Growth, versus 50/50 Normal

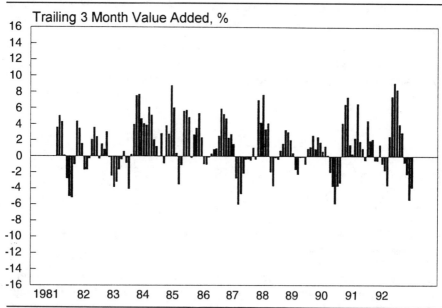

capturing the 13% excess return to small value over small growth in Octo-ber 1987. Due to the crash, the volatility numbers shot up and the model correctly switched into small growth after October. From January 1988 through the end of 1992, the model heavily favored small value. There were only seven small-growth signals during this period, but all of them were correct. Low volatility and close to average equity risk premium kept the model out of small growth in early 1990 and late 1992, causing under-performance in those periods.

Over these twelve years, this disciplined approach to style manage-ment successfully added value, using only the information that would have been available at the time. Forecasts for a given month were based on market data through the previous month only, and economic data through, at most, two months previous (according to reporting lags). For-ward-looking management of the style mix between small value and small growth appears both possible and promising.

LARGE CAP VERSUS SMALL CAP

It has been shown above how a disciplined approach might be used to enhance returns from the small cap portion of a portfolio by actively man-

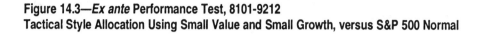

Figure 14.3—*Ex ante* Performance Test, 8101-9212
Tactical Style Allocation Using Small Value and Small Growth, versus S&P 500 Normal

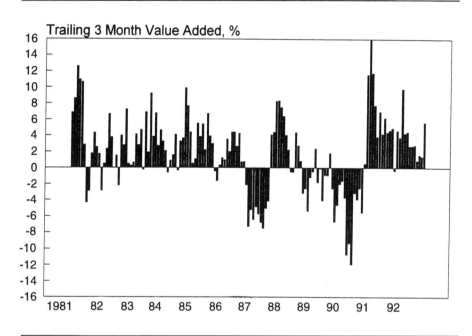

aging the style mix between value and growth. Similarly, value can be added by actively managing the style mix between large cap and small cap.

Although small cap outperforms large over long periods, there are times when large outperforms small. Figure 14.3 revisits the trailing three-month returns to the tactical small value, small growth portfolio, showing the added value relative to the S&P 500 rather than the 50/50 normal. Small cap performs well overall, but 1987 and 1990 were dreadful. The logical question is, could one have predicted large cap's dominance in those years beforehand?

INDICATORS, LARGE CAP VERSUS SMALL CAP

Several powerful indicators of large cap versus small cap performance were identified. Table 14.5 presents the correlations and t-statistics for selected valuation, economic, and market indicators. Many of the same indicators that drove the small value versus small growth model are effective for large cap versus small cap forecasting as well.

Table 14.5—Style Return Indicators, Large Capitalization versus Small 7801-9212

Indicator	Style Favored	Value Correlation[1]	t-Stat	Growth Correlation[1]	t-Stat
Equity risk premium[2]	Small over large	–0.187	–2.5	–0.314	–4.4
Market volatility	Small over large	–0.144	–1.9	–0.270	–3.7
Cash yield trend	Large over small	0.218	3.0	0.166	2.2
Leading indicator trend	Large over small			0.176	2.4
Exchange rate volatility	Small over large	–0.213	–2.9		

1 Correlation with subsequent difference in returns, large-small. Blanks indicate t-statistics that were insignificant at the 95% level.

2 Two different measures were used.

Equity risk premium again is the strongest discriminator for future style performance. A high equity risk premium favors portfolios perceived as more risky, so small cap is indicated over large when the equity risk premium is high.

After a period of high volatility, small cap stocks can be expected to outperform large, since small cap tends to be oversold during the "flight to quality" that occurs in turbulent markets.

Rising Treasury bill yields favor large cap over small cap.

Small companies outperform large at the beginning of a recovery. After there is evidence of a healthier economy, such as a strong year-over-year rise in the leading indicator, large tends to outperform small.

Large stocks are more leveraged to overseas earnings growth than small stocks. Consequently, large stocks are penalized when the exchange rate is highly volatile.

A multivariate model was developed for large cap versus small cap, using these indicators, emphasizing consistent performance and reasonable turnover as well as value added.

PERFORMANCE TESTS, S&P 500 PLUS SMALL VALUE AND SMALL GROWTH

A second simulation was run, this time adding the S&P 500 as an investment option using the large versus small and small value versus small growth models. As before, all forecasts were *ex ante*, using only information that would have been available at the time. The portfolio was always invested 100% in the most attractive style.

Table 14.6 summarizes the results of an *ex ante* performance test of this strategy. Another 3.5% was added annually, relative to the test using only small value and small growth.

Table 14.6—*Ex ante* Performance Test, 8101-9212
Tactical Style Allocation Using S&P 500, Small Value, and Small Growth

	Tactical Style	50/50 Normal[1]	Added Value
Annualized return[2]	26.10%	16.63%	9.47%
Standard deviation	14.94%	17.12%	6.85%
Information ratio	1.74	0.97	1.38
Turnover	35%		

1 Systematically rebalanced, 50% small value, 50% small growth.
2 Net of transaction costs: 2% round-trip for small cap, 0.5% for large.

Comparing Figures 14.3 and 14.4(A), the charts of trailing three-month added value before and after the large versus small model was added, one can see that this added value came from "sitting out" small cap at the end of 1987, and most of 1989 and 1990. Figure 14.4(B) is comparable to Figure 14.3, showing added value relative to the S&P 500.

Until 1987, small cap outperformed large cap handsomely. How did the model know to get out of small cap in 1987? The most consistent indicator throughout the period was volatility, which was below average most of the time, indicating large over small. The equity risk premium also tended to be average or lower, strengthening the signal for large.

Forward-looking management of the style mix among large cap, small cap value, and small cap growth also appears both possible and promising. What about using large value and large growth as well? Figure 14.5 illustrates all the timing possibilities. All the graphs are set to the same scale so that one can easily compare the relative potential. Between January 1978

Figure 14.4—*Ex ante* Performance Test, 8101-9212
Tactical Style Allocation Using S&P 500, Small Value, and Small Growth

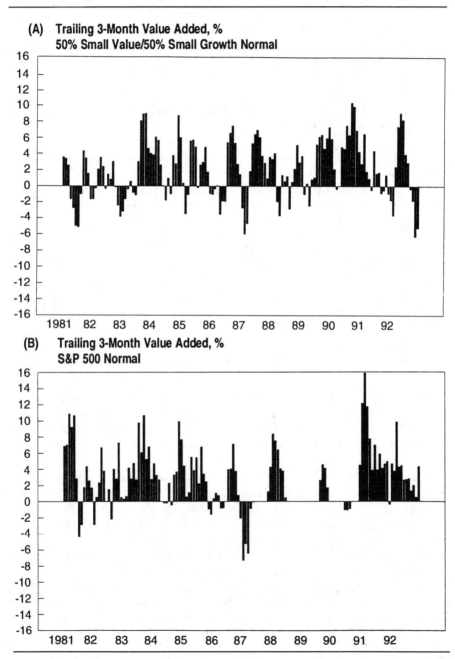

(A)   Trailing 3-Month Value Added, %
       50% Small Value/50% Small Growth Normal

(B)   Trailing 3-Month Value Added, %
       S&P 500 Normal

Figure 14.5—Difference in Quarterly Returns, Style Matrix

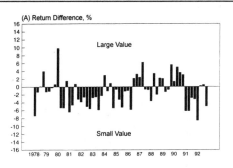

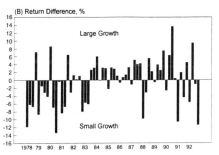

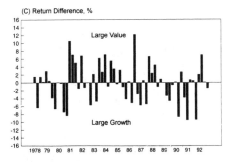

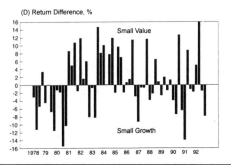

and December 1992, small value versus small growth presented the greatest opportunities for active management.

One final simulation uses all four style portfolios, large value, large growth, small value, and small growth. Results are presented in Table 14.7: 10.12% was added relative to the 50/50 small cap value/small cap growth normal portfolio, with turnover of just over 41% and an information ratio of 1.4 (reward/risk) (see Figure 14.6).

Table 14.7—*Ex ante* Performance Test, 8101-9212
Tactical Style Allocation Using Large Value, Large Growth, Small Value, and Small Growth

	Tactical Style	50/50 Normal[1]	Added Value	S&P 500 Normal	Added Value
Annualized return[2]	26.75%	16.63%	10.12%	14.64%	12.11%
Standard deviation	15.57%	17.12%	7.16%	15.78%	7.06%
Information ratio	1.72	0.97	1.41	0.93	1.72
Turnover	41%				

1 Systematically rebalanced, 50% small value, 50% small growth.

2 Net of transaction costs: 2% round-trip for small cap, 0.5% for large.

IMPLEMENTATION, OR "MILEAGE MAY VARY"

A tactical style allocation discipline could be implemented several ways: through futures, through shifting assets between specialty managers, or through a dedicated swing portfolio.

Some benefit may be gained through use of a futures overlay, particularly in large cap versus small cap. A full implementation of style management would have to wait for a wider range of futures contracts to become available.

By anticipating which styles are likely to be rewarded, a plan sponsor could take better advantage of the relative merits of managers with diverse styles. Any added value from style management using active specialty managers will be leveraged according to the managers' skill. In this case, the logistics involved must be weighed against the benefits.

The most practical way to implement the strategy is through a dedicated swing portfolio. Rather than moving some portion of assets between two managers, one manager could move the same portion of assets be-

Figure 14.6—*Ex ante* Performance Test, 8101-9212
Tactical Style Allocation Using Large Value, Large Growth, Small Value, and Small Growth

(A)   **Trailing 3 Month Value Added, %**
       50% Small Value/50% Small Growth Normal

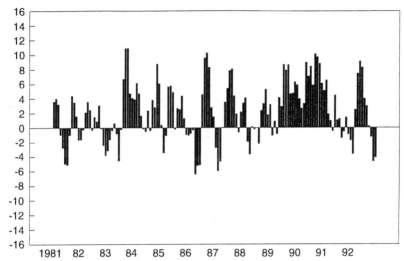

(B)   **Trailing 3 Month Value Added, %**
       S&P500 Normal

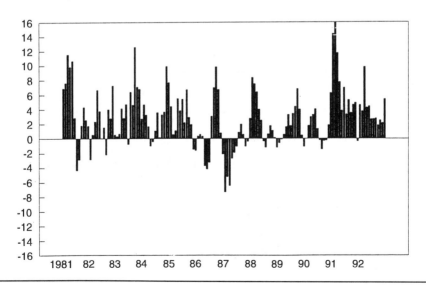

tween two or more styles. The returns to a swing portfolio would depend on the style-timing skill plus the manager skill within each style. Historically, the interquartile range (25th percentile-75th percentile) of annualized returns within each style has averaged 8%. The implication of this is that stock selection skill could easily add another 4% to the swing portfolio returns, or easily subtract 4%. Alternatively, passive style portfolios could be used in a swing portfolio to eliminate specialty manager selection risk.

CONCLUSION

Sometimes it is more important to know when to invest in small cap stocks than to know which small cap stocks to invest in. Even when small cap stocks on the whole are doing well, there can be startling differences in the returns to different styles of small cap stocks.

There are powerful *ex ante* indicators of style performance that can form the basis of a forward-looking approach to style allocation within small cap, and style allocation between small cap and large cap. Most importantly, these leading indicators of style performance make sense. Besides avoiding the pitfalls of "rearview mirror" management, such an approach offers the possibility of significant and consistent added value.

ENDNOTES

[1] Wilshire Passive Style returns are *index* returns, and as such are not net of any management fees or transaction costs. They are constructed as follows:

Individual portfolios are capitalization weighted and are rebalanced quarterly. Approximately 40% of the Wilshire 2500 ends up in portfolios.

WSV: To construct the passive small value portfolio, Wilshire screens companies with capitalization ranks from 751 to 2500. Only those with high ranks in earnings-to-price, book value-to-price, and yield are included. Any with less than two years of history are dropped.

WSG: To construct the passive small-growth portfolio, Wilshire screens companies with capitalization ranks from 751 to 2500. Stocks with high yield, little or no earnings growth, and low beta are eliminated from the portfolio, and those with less than two years of history are dropped.

WLV: To construct the passive large-value portfolio, Wilshire screens companies with capitalization ranks from 1 to 750. Only those with high ranks in earnings-to-price, book value-to-price, and yield are included. Any with less than five years of history are dropped.

WLG: To construct the passive large growth portfolio, Wilshire screens companies with capitalization ranks from 1 to 750. Stocks with high yield, high book value-to-price, little or no earnings growth, and low ROE are eliminated from the portfolio, as are those with less than five years of history.

[2] Bailard, Biehl & Kaiser implements the tactical style allocation strategy using more concentrated passive style portfolios. In addition to more concentrated style bets, the portfolios are better diversified across industries than Wilshire Associates'. The Wilshire returns are presented here because they are widely known.

REFERENCES

Arnott, Robert, John Dorian, and Rosemary Macedo, "Style Management: The Missing Element," *Journal of Investing* (June 1992).

Arnott, Robert, Charles Kelso, Stephen Kiscadden, and Rosemary Macedo. "Forecasting Factor Returns," *Journal of Portfolio Management* (Summer 1990).

Fama, Eugene, and Kenneth French, "The Cross-Section of Expected Stock Returns," *The Journal of Finance*, Vol. XLVII, No. 2 (June 1992).

Chapter 15

Value and Growth Cycles in Small Cap Investing

Kenneth L. Fisher
President and Chief Investment Officer

Joseph L. Toms
Senior Vice President and Director of Research

Fisher Investments, Inc.

INTRODUCTION

Many people associate small capitalization stocks with the notion of "growth." A common misperception is that the reason for small cap exposure is to get those "little fast growing companies." The reality, however, is that just as there are value and growth stocks in the large cap world, there are also value and growth stocks in small cap. Small cap value stocks have distinct characteristics differentiating them from small cap growth stocks. This leads to different performance characteristics, so that just as there are value and growth *cycles* in large cap stocks, similar cycles exist in small cap.

It is important to note that the magnitude of these cycles is much larger in small cap than in big cap. Achieving median or better big cap returns with minimal out-of-phase volatility requires both growth and value allocations. This is even more true with respect to small cap. Without small cap value as a significant portion of a small cap allocation, underperformance is guaranteed.

To illustrate this point, refer to Figures 15.1 and 15.2, which show the performance of big cap and small cap stocks over three-year rolling periods.

Figure 15.1 measures the returns of big cap growth and big cap value stocks. The group's returns are then compounded on a three-year moving average basis to minimize single-year aberrations and smooth out the cycle. The "growth" return is subtracted from the "value" return to derive a relative performance spread. Thus, as the trendline rises, value is outperforming growth; as it falls, growth is outperforming value.

As mentioned, value and growth cycles also exist in small cap. As Figure 15.2 shows, an identical "cycle" effect is produced, whereby as the trendline rises, small cap value outperforms small cap growth, and as it falls, small cap growth does better than small cap value.

To properly quantify this "cycle" phenomenon within the small cap world requires a redefinition of how the market consensus presently views the equity markets. Current market indexes are insufficient to measure broad market and small cap performance for reasons that will be outlined below.

Instead, we analyze the market by dividing it into four quadrants based on capitalization and valuation. This "Four-Quad" analysis (along with derivative exercises) is the optimal methodology for looking at stock market style cycles, particularly in small cap stocks. Further, as we will show through this new and simple methodology, small cap value is the best-performing style over the long term. Contrary to common opinion, it is essential to own small cap value stocks to achieve the long-term returns associated with small cap.

EXISTING MARKET INDEXES ARE INADEQUATE

Academic research into stock returns has shown that the two most critical determinants of a stock's performance are capitalization and valuation.[1] The market's return over the past twenty years can be explained by these two variables. Given this fact, how does one best measure the market? Historically, investors used the Dow Jones Industrials or the S&P 500. In the past decade, indexes like the NASDAQ Composite or the Russell 2000 were introduced as more appropriate small cap benchmarks. Yet these indexes share one common weakness—they are all market cap-weighted (or price-weighted in the case of the Dow), thus making their portrayal of the market suspect. Why? There are several reasons.

Figure 15.1—Big Cap Value versus Growth
3-Year Value Return Minus Growth Return, 3-Year Rolling Periods

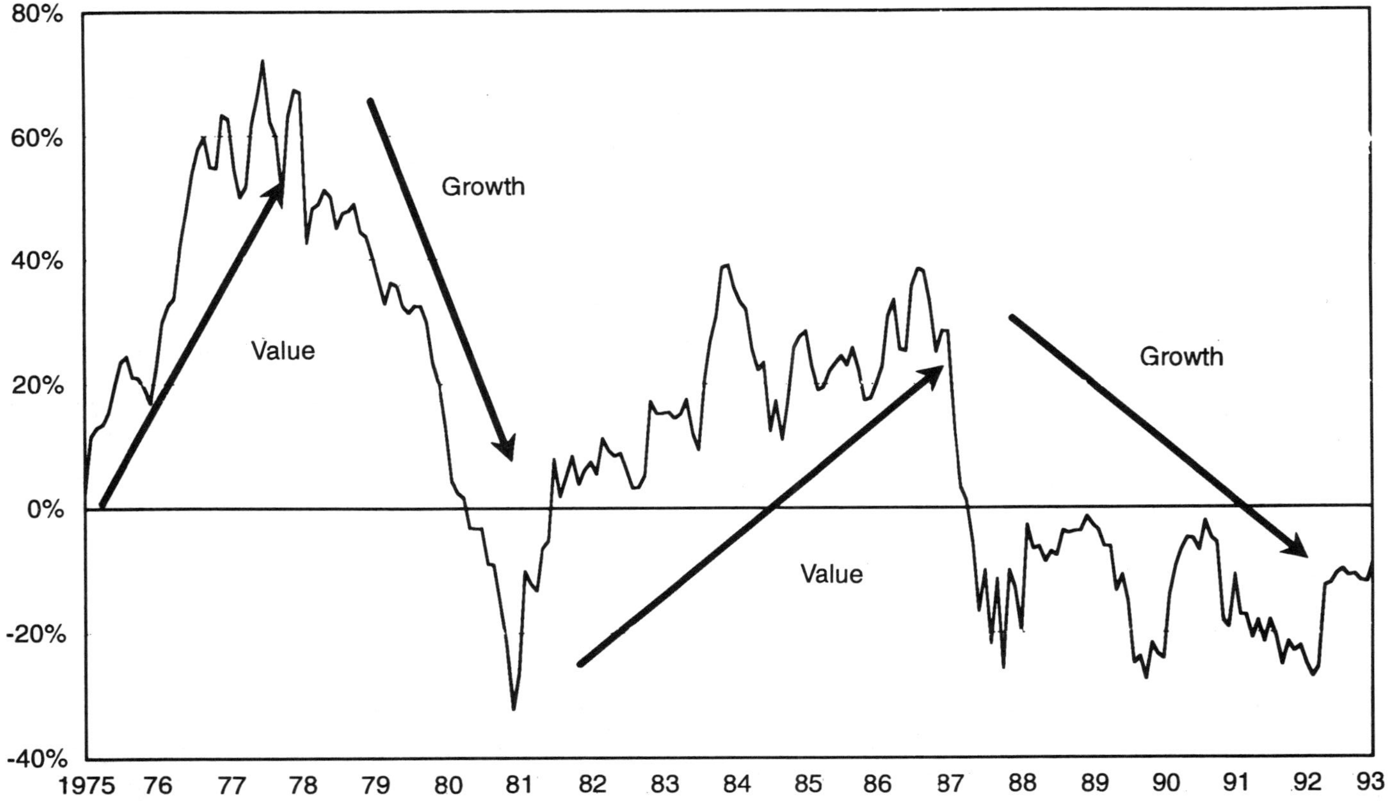

Figure 15.2—Small Cap Value versus Growth
3-Year Value Return Minus Growth Return, 3-Year Rolling Periods

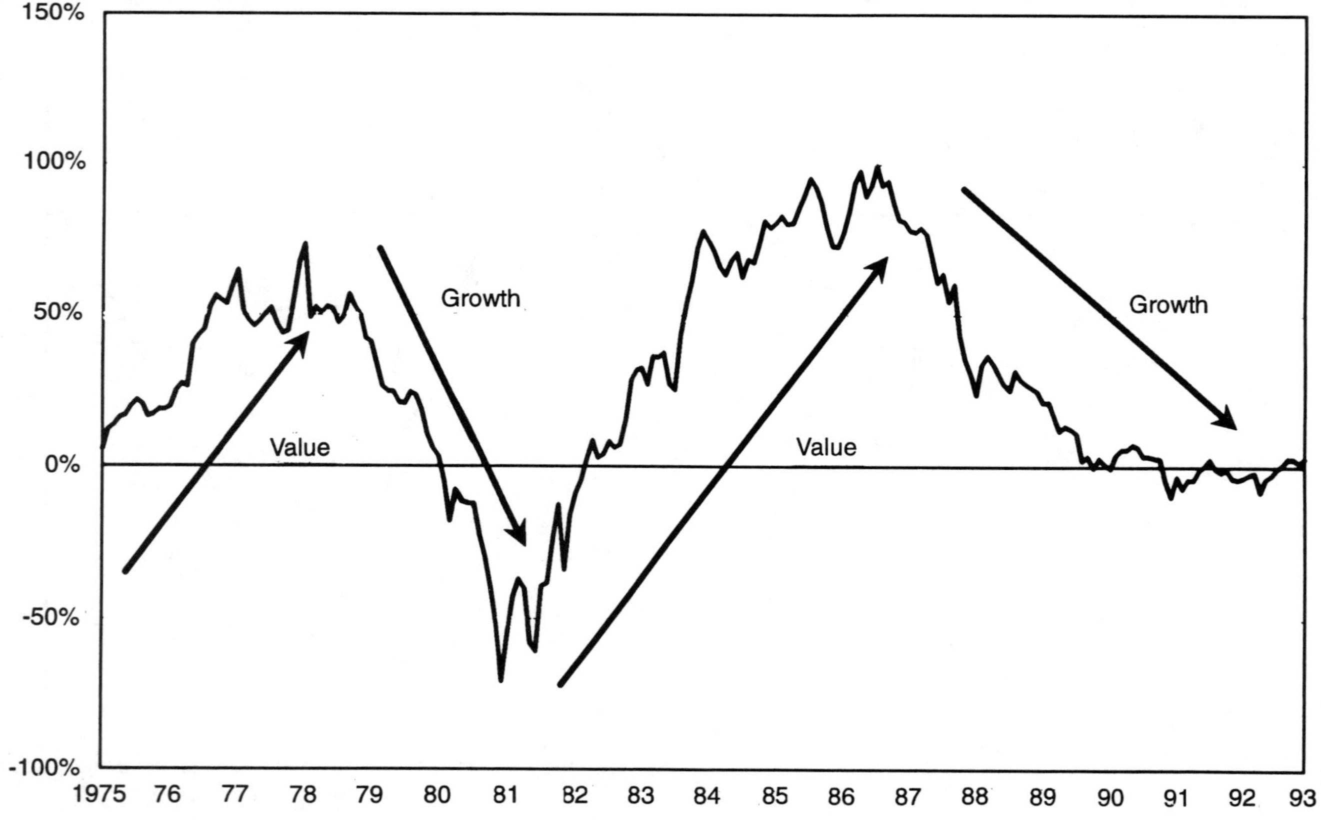

First, any cap-weighted index gets its impact from the biggest stocks in the index and thus by definition does not have adequate small cap representation. In the S&P 500, for example, as of March 31, 1992, the ten largest stocks carried the same weight in the index as the 335 smallest stocks among the 500—so that 2% of the stocks had the same power on the index as 67% of the stocks in the index. The performance of smaller cap stocks is masked by the performance of the biggest stocks, which can be seen by calculating the same index on an equal-weighted basis. Consider the first quarter of 1992. The S&P 500 was down 2.5%, but the *equal-weighted* S&P 500 was *up* 3.0%. Why the discrepancy? Logically, the smaller stocks in the index must have outperformed the larger stocks. And they did—the largest ten stocks were down 5.67% versus the 335 smallest S&P 500 stocks (having the same aggregate weight in the index), which were up 5.52%. Thus, the performance of the vast majority of the stocks was not reflected in the index's return.

In addition to having a big cap bias, market cap-weighted indexes have another flaw—they mimic the performance of, and thus derive their impact from, the "hottest" investment management style of recent years. Because market caps are determined by price and shares outstanding, it follows that if an index is market cap-weighted, a stock's price determines its weight in the index. Thus, when a stock's price appreciates relative to the index, its impact within the index grows. So the index will reflect the stocks that have done best in the recent past—and in the most recent past. So when a style is "hot" over an extended period, the stocks of that style increase their weighting in cap-weighted indexes, which can become quite overweighted in that style.

Thus, commonly used indexes don't do justice to the various styles. And since capitalization and valuation are the crucial elements in determining performance, one must look beyond traditional indexes to isolate equity style returns.

FOUR-QUAD ANALYSIS

For analytical purposes, we break down the market into four distinct quadrants. First, via Standard & Poor's Compustat Database, we take the 2,000 largest stocks based on market cap.[2] This group comprises 98.5% of the aggregate value of the equity market and is the only truly "liquid" portion from an institutional perspective. Interestingly, the remaining percentage of the market consists of about 3,300 publicly traded companies whose total value is less than the market cap of the two largest stocks. The 2,000 largest stocks are then divided into two groups on the basis of market cap: (1) the 500 largest cap stocks, which is actually the traditional big cap stock universe; and (2) the next 1,500 stocks by market cap, which is the small cap universe. Currently, the 1,500 stocks run from about $80 million to $1.1 billion in market cap, with the median cap being $325 million. This is the liquid or "tradable" portion of the small cap universe.

The next step is to use the price-to-book (P/B) ratio to split each group into equal halves. Those stocks with a P/B above the median are defined as growth stocks; those with below-median P/Bs are classified as value stocks. The result is four distinct quadrants: 250 big cap value stocks, 250 big cap growth stocks, 750 small cap growth stocks, and 750 small cap value stocks.

Our quadrant analysis is a simple, easy-to-understand methodology in which all institutionally buyable stocks are easily categorized and tracked. The beauty of this separation into quadrants is that it not only "purifies" each specific style, thus allowing one to isolate performance, but it also allows for the equal weighting of each stock to see how each area is truly performing. Consequently, it avoids the intrinsic problem of market cap weighting, wherein a few big stocks may totally mask the performance of the majority of stocks.

Figure 15.3 shows the median market capitalization and the median P/B for each quadrant.

Note that the attributes of each quadrant are quite different. The median cap is at least eight times larger in the big cap than the small cap quadrants. Likewise, the difference in P/B between the value and growth quadrants is also large at 2.5 times.

Since our focus is on the small cap area, it is instructive to look at the differences between the companies in the small cap growth quadrant and the small cap value quadrant. As Figure 15.3 demonstrates, the average P/B of the small cap growth quadrant is 3.65, 2.1 times greater than the small cap value quadrant. But the differences extend beyond valuations to areas including industry distribution and company size. While the market caps of the two quadrants are similar, small cap value companies are larger than their growth counterparts, a function of selling at valuation discounts. The average small cap value company has $900 million in sales, much more than the small cap growth average of $432 million.

The differences in industry weightings between the two quadrants are even more dramatic. For instance, consider the exposure to financials and utilities of each quadrant:

	Small Cap Value	Small Cap Growth
Financials	10.98%	2.14%
Utilities	6.69%	0.27%
Total	17.67%	2.41%

Figure 15.3—Top 2,000 Market Cap Stocks Median Market Cap and Price to Book

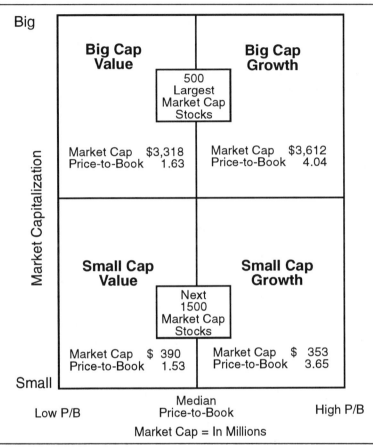

Financials and utilities comprise a large portion of the small cap value quadrant, but only a small piece of small cap growth. Because of their sensitivity to interest rates, the small cap value quadrant will receive a much greater impact from interest rate changes than the small cap growth quadrant. On the other hand, small cap growth will be affected much more by changes relating to the health care/drug sector:

	Small Cap Value	Small Cap Growth
Drugs/biotechnology	1.47%	7.24%
Health care svcs. & mgmt.	2.01%	6.17%
Medical prods. and supplies	.94%	4.83%
Total	4.42%	18.24%

While health care/drug stocks are the largest components of the small cap growth quadrant, their representation in the small cap value quadrant is minimal. There are many other less extreme examples of differences in industry weightings between the two small cap quadrants. Since different industries are influenced in a different manner by economic events, the result will be different performance in the two quadrants. This in turn leads to distinct performance cycles for small cap growth and small cap value. The point here is that small cap is not a monolithic grouping—there are significant differences between small cap value and small cap growth companies, which has important implications for asset allocation and returns, as detailed below.

A LONG-TERM LOOK AT PERFORMANCE

The next logical step for us is to consider performance of the four quadrants over three-, ten-, and twenty-year periods. The performance for the longest time frame of our study, the twenty-year period from December 1972 to December 1992 is included in the four-quad chart in Figure 15.4.

The performance for each quadrant in the intermediate term is shown in Figure 15.5.

The performance over the past three years is shown in Figure 15.6.

Not surprisingly, there is a rotation in performance over time, whereby different quadrants dominate at different times. Over the longest period, the past twenty years, the top-performing quadrant has been small cap value. The value style in aggregate has beaten growth by over 6% per year. Clearly small cap value has boosted the good long-term performance of small cap overall. Owning only small cap growth over the past twenty years would have resulted in sub-par returns—only 8.54%, the worst performance of all four quads.

In the past ten years, big cap stocks have clearly outperformed small cap stocks. However, value stocks also beat their growth counterparts. The story changes when one looks at the past three years. Here, big cap growth has been the dominant style—with big cap beating small cap overall. The bottom line is simply this: by dividing the stock world according to cap size and valuation, we can vividly observe that different quadrants lead the performance parade at varying times.

Figure 15.4—20-Year Annualized Performance from December 1972 to December 1992

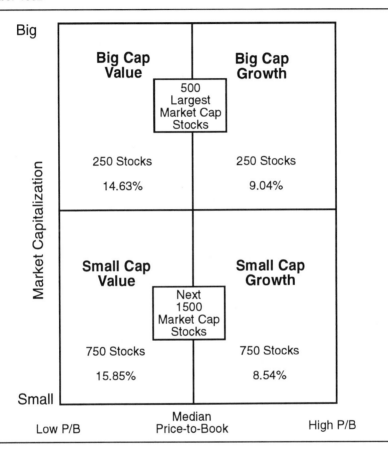

Big

Market Capitalization

Small

Big Cap Value

500 Largest Market Cap Stocks

250 Stocks

14.63%

Big Cap Growth

250 Stocks

9.04%

Small Cap Value

Next 1500 Market Cap Stocks

750 Stocks

15.85%

Small Cap Growth

750 Stocks

8.54%

Low P/B   Median Price-to-Book   High P/B

TRACKING STYLE DOMINANCE WITHIN MARKET CYCLES

Capitalization

Which style will dominate the next cycle? To answer this question we must first look at the issue of small cap versus big cap. It is generally accepted that big cap and small cap stocks perform in alternating multiyear cycles.

Figure 15.5—10-Year Annualized Performance December 1982 to December 1992

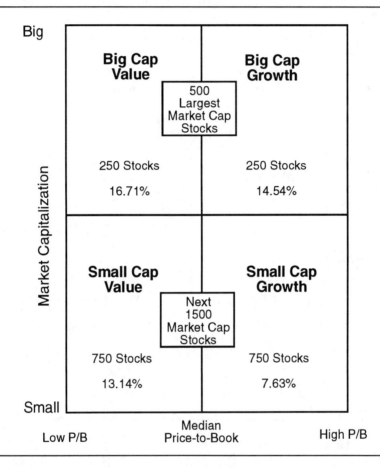

Figure 15.7 gives a historical as well as a visual perspective. It takes the performance of the smallest 50% of the New York Stock Exchange (NYSE) and subtracts from it the performance of the big cap S&P 500. The resulting number represents the "spread" between small cap stocks and big cap stocks. When the spread is positive, small cap is outperforming; likewise, when it is negative, big cap is outperforming. To minimize single-year aberrations, the performance is measured over three-year periods.

By graphing the performance spread between small cap stocks and big cap stocks over three-year rolling periods, a clear cyclical picture emerges. There have been four distinct periods of small cap outperformance and four periods of big cap outperformance. One time frame, the 1950s, produced mixed results.

Figure 15.6—3-Year Annualized Performance December 1989 to December 1992

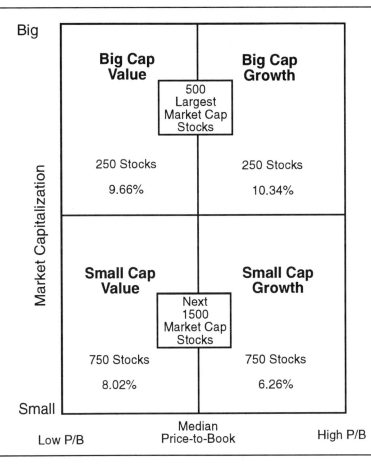

The four-quad approach lends itself to a new form of analysis, which we call "market share" analysis. It allows an in-depth look at which style has and will likely continue to dominate within a market cycle. Basically, it consists of determining the percentage of the overall market's value—or "market share"—represented by a quadrant or combination of quadrants at any time. The market share can then be compared to the market shares in previous cycles, or at peaks and troughs, with an eye to gauging possible future price movements based on past market share.

For example, by determining today's small cap "market share" and what it was in the past, it is possible to view its possible future. In this case, market share is the percent of the aggregate value of the total stock market represented by small cap. The four-quad approach facilitates this

**Figure 15.7—Small Cap versus Big Cap
3-Year Relative Performance Spread
3-Year Rolling Periods**

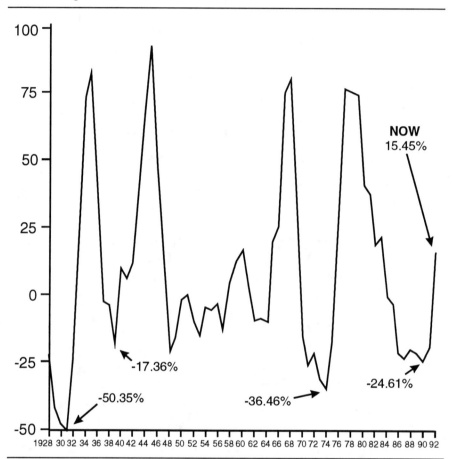

process by allowing us to simply sum the market values of the stocks in the small cap growth and small cap value quadrants and compare that to the total value of all four quadrants. This examines small cap's market share over time, as shown in Figure 15.8.

Note: when small cap has done well, it started with a low historical market share relative to big cap. For instance, in 1974, small cap's market share was only 14%. By the time it peaked in 1983, it had grown to 22% of the market. In hindsight, 1974 was the best opportunity to own small cap stocks since the end of the Great Depression. Small cap's market share hit

Figure 15.8—Small Cap's Capitalization as a Percent of the Markets

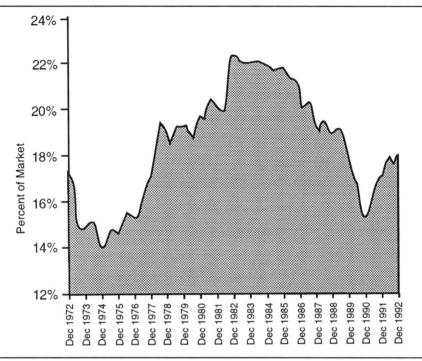

a low again in late 1990, with market share at 15%. Not surprisingly, small cap has done better than big cap since October 1990.

Low market share for a style within the context of past market share history is one indication of minimal downside and good upside potential. Why? It indicates how faddish a style is. When a style has a large share of the market compared to history, it means the style has become more popular. When a style has a low share of the market compared to history, it means the style has been losing popularity. Generally, styles that are too popular have already been bid up in price—all the buying has been done.

Valuation

The next issue that begs analysis is what the other determinant of performance—valuation—will favor. As we said earlier, just as big cap and small cap stocks perform in alternating cycles, so also do value and growth stocks. One can see these cycles within big cap by taking the returns of the low 30% of P/Es and subtracting from it the returns of the high 30% of

P/Es—to derive a spread. Again, we use three-year rolling periods to smooth out individual quarters' gyrations. Actually, we refer here to the "big cap value versus growth" chart mentioned earlier and reproduced in Figure 15.9.

To reiterate, when the spread is declining and becomes negative, growth stocks are leading. Likewise, when it is rising and positive, value stocks are dominating. The graph in Figure 15.9 shows distinct periods of value and growth dominance. Big cap value dominated from late 1974 to

Figure 15.9—Big Cap Value versus Growth
3-Year Value Return Minus Growth Return
3-Year Rolling Periods

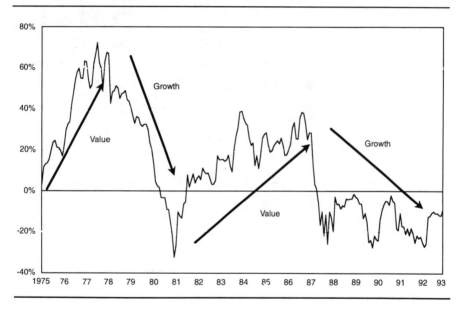

1978. Then big cap growth took over, leading value from 1979 to 1980. Value again led from 1981 to 1986, after which growth dominated once again, from 1987 to 1991.

We also maintained that the same cyclicality between value and growth holds true in small cap stocks (see Figure 15.10).

Not surprisingly, the same time periods apply.

Value dominates from 1974 to 1978, growth from 1979 to 1980, value from 1981 to 1986, and growth again from 1987 to 1991. Further, if you

Figure 15.10—Small Cap Value versus Growth
3-Year Value Return Minus Growth Return
3-Year Rolling Periods

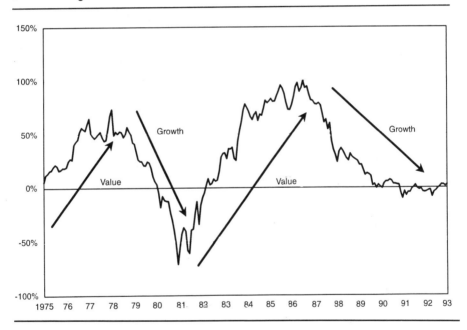

overlay the two previous graphs (see Figure 15.11), you can really appreciate that the magnitude of the swings between value and growth is larger
in small cap than in big cap, a misunderstood and greatly underappreciated point.

The market share analysis outlined above is also very useful when
looking at growth and value cycles. Value's share of the total market has

**Figure 15.11—Value-Growth Cycles for Big Cap and Small Cap Stocks
3-Year Rolling Periods**

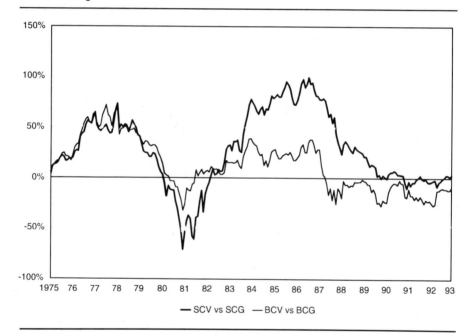

Figure 15.12—Value's Capitalization as a Percent of the Market's

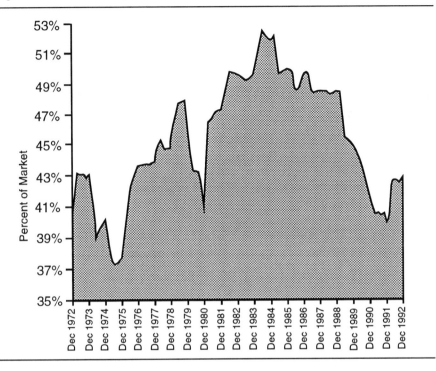

ranged from a low of about 37% in 1975 to a high of around 53%, as shown in Figure 15.12.

At the end of 1991, value's market share stood at 38%, lower than it was in 1981 and only slightly above its 1975 bottom. Thus, market share analysis suggested minimal downside risk and superior upside potential for the value style. Upside potential can be determined by calculating returns achieved after previous bottoms. In this case, the actual annualized returns for value and growth in the periods following the value bottoms were:

	May 1975-July 1979	Dec. 1980-Nov. 1984
Value	+26.5%	+19.6%
Growth	+20.3%	+ 1.9%

This illustrates the utility of market share analysis—it allows you to assess a given style's position relative to other styles and other time periods.

VALUE AND GROWTH PEAKS

Perhaps an even more visually powerful way to see how the four quadrants change in relation to each other is to examine them as four sector pie charts at both value and growth peaks. For instance, Figure 15.13 shows two examples of growth peaks (May 1975 and November 1980). Both represent periods where growth's market share peaked, followed by significant underperformance relative to value stocks. Note that in both cases the big cap growth quadrant clearly dominates the other three in terms of overall size. In this case, big cap growth is 55.19% of the total aggregate market value. Combined with small cap growth's share at the peak in May 1975, growth constituted about 63.56% of the total value of the market. Also note that at the November 1980 growth peak, the total growth share was 60.93%, this time with a heavier small cap growth representation.

We can apply the same analysis to value peaks, as shown in Figure 15.14. Value peaked in July 1979 at a 48.48% market share and in September 1986 at 50.54%. Note that the pie becomes much more "even" when a value peak occurs as compared to when growth peaks occur. Value controls just about half of the total market at its tops, while growth accounts for close to 65% of the market's aggregate value when it peaks.

AN ANALYSIS OF THE PRESENT SITUATION

Next, consider how the market is currently configured. Our analysis indicates that growth peaked in December 1991. Look at the four quadrants as of December 1991. Big cap growth was at 53.02%, which is very close to the high it reached in May 1975. Growth's total market share was at 61.80%, thus surpassing its 1980 peak and coming very close to its 1975 peak (see Figure 15.15).

Four-quad analysis has shown that when any one quadrant dominates returns, the opposite style quadrant tends to perform the worst. Thus, if big cap growth is the "hot" style, then the opposite style—small cap value—should be the worst performer, the logic being that big cap is the opposite of small cap, and growth is the opposite of value. The elements that make big cap growth attractive to investors at any given time will be lacking in small cap value, which will perform poorly as a result. The same holds true in the case of big cap value and small cap growth. Diagonal styles then are counter-cyclical to each other stylistically within the stock universe.

A look back to the mid-1980s shows how the diagonal style impact works. For instance, from June 1983 through September 1986, big cap value was the dominant style. In fact, a quick perusal of *Pensions and In-*

Figure 15.13—Total Market Value Broken Down by Quadrants

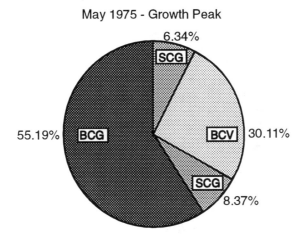

May 1975 - Growth Peak

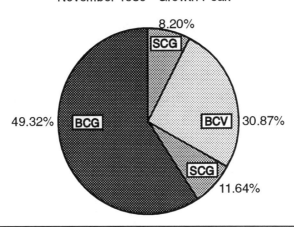

November 1980 - Growth Peak

vestments "Money Movers" section in late 1986 finds the pension world clamoring for the services of big cap value managers. But, as we have seen, styles rotate—much like a clock. Imagine a clock with only one hand overlaid onto our four quadrants. A graphic representation of big cap value as the dominant style in this scenario would show the clock's hand sweep from 9:00 (June 1983) to 12:00 (September 1986), through the big cap value quadrant. Figure 15.16 displays this along with specific returns for each quadrant.

Figure 15.14—Total Market Value Broken Down by Quadrants

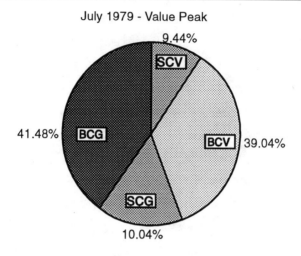

July 1979 - Value Peak

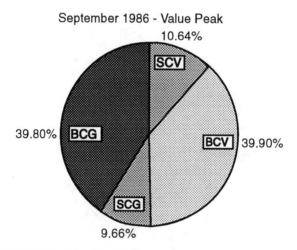

September 1986 - Value Peak

The number-one style was big cap value, with a total return of 74.0%. The worst performer was big cap value's diagonally opposed style—small cap growth—with a return of 9.3%.

Using the same analogy, as the clock's hand sweeps through the big cap growth quadrant from 12:00 (September 1986) to 3:00 (October 1990), it is not surprising to find that the best performance came from this quadrant (see Figure 15.17). The worst performer—small cap value—is again big cap growth's diagonally opposed style.

Figure 15.15—Total Market Value Broken Down by Quadrants

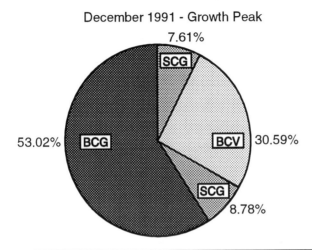

December 1991 - Growth Peak

The clock continues. From 3:00 (October 1990) to 6:00 (December 1991) the clock sweeps through the small cap growth quadrant (see Figure 15.18). The best performer was small cap growth. The worst, naturally, was big cap value—again the diagonal opposition.

MARKET CYCLE CATALYST

Value Versus Growth

What provides the impetus for cycles to change? And more specifically, what caused the current value cycle to start? We hold that the answer lies in the direction of interest rates. We found that when interest rates drop significantly, with a time lag, a value cycle ensues. Likewise, when rates rise significantly, again with a time lag, the result is a growth cycle. Thus, over the long term, there is a direct correlation between the behavior of interest rates and whether value or growth will be the dominant style.

The relationship between interest rates and style cycles becomes apparent by examining the periods when the Federal Reserve has made aggressive attempts to lower interest rates. We define these periods as any time the Fed has cut the discount rate at least three times over the course of a twelve-month period. Figures 15.19 to 15.24 show the returns for the value and growth portions of the quadrants after three discount rate cuts

Figure 15.16—Top 2,000 Market Cap Stocks
Performance of Each Quadrant June 1983–Sept 1986

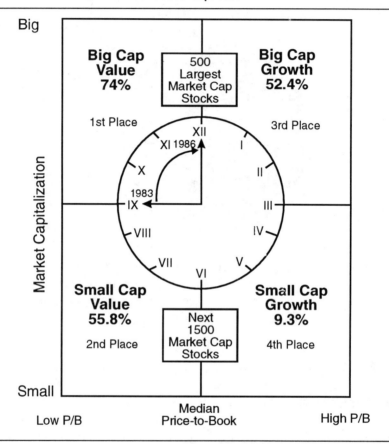

within a twelve-month period. Returns are provided based on three different valuation measures: P/Es; P/Bs; and PSRs.

The graphs in Figures 15.19 to 15.24 detail performance for the years
1971, 1975, 1980, 1981, 1985, and 1991, at intervals from three months to
two years after the third interest rate cut. (Note that in every case, the
market was higher two years after the cuts.) In four out of the five occur-
rences, value stocks beat their growth counterparts. Only in 1971 did this
not hold true—a classic case of "the exception that proves the rule." 1971
was exceptional due to two notable elements unique to the period. First,
the price of oil tripled, thus hurting value companies, which are by and
large more energy-dependent than growth stock firms. Second, wage and
price controls were implemented, the only time this has occurred in a

Figure 15.17—Top 2,000 Market Cap Stocks
Performance of Each Quadrant Sept 1986–Oct 1990

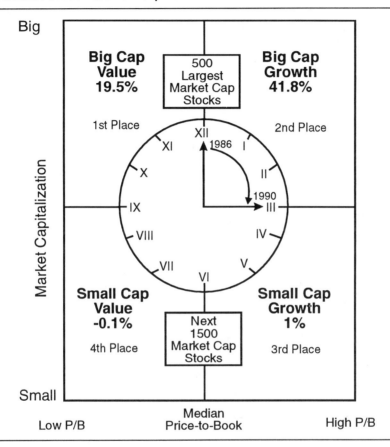

peacetime environment since World War II. Both of these factors had a dramatic impact on the economy and created a substantially different economic climate from the other four periods as well as from today.

Why do falling interest rates benefit value stocks? Many investors would think this counterintuitive. Many argue, particularly those weaned on the dividend discount model, that growth stocks should profit from falling rates, not value stocks. Were all else equal that would be true. But the real world is not *ceteris paribus*. The data prove otherwise. While about 50% of the time growth stocks performed better *initially* (over the first year or so), this was primarily due to investors scurrying to own "quality" in a time of typical economic concern. But this impact is temporary, and by the end of the cycle, value clearly wins. The reason is quite simple. It relates to

**Figure 15.18—Top 2,000 Market Cap Stocks
Performance of Each Quadrant Oct 1990–Dec 1991**

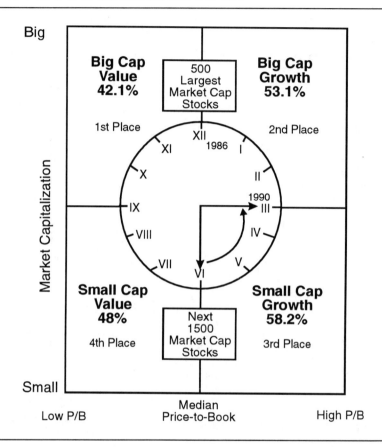

the overall level of debt (both short- and long-term) that value companies carry relative to growth companies. Look at Figure 15.25, which portrays the amount of short- and long-term debt each quadrant has. (We removed finance and utility companies from this comparison to prevent their highly leveraged balance sheets from obscuring reality.)

The value quadrants have much more debt than the growth quadrants—by a factor of 140% to 160%. This "extra" leverage results from it making more sense for growth stock firms to raise capital by offering equity than by issuing debt. The trade-off is simple. If a growth stock sells at 30 times earnings, that translates into an earnings yield of 1/30, or 3.3%. Selling stock at this level is, in essence, "borrowing" money at a 3.3% interest rate as compared to mid-1992 levels of long-term rates of about 7.5%,

Figure 15.19—Small Cap Growth versus Value Returns Starting with the Third Discount Rate Cut in 1971

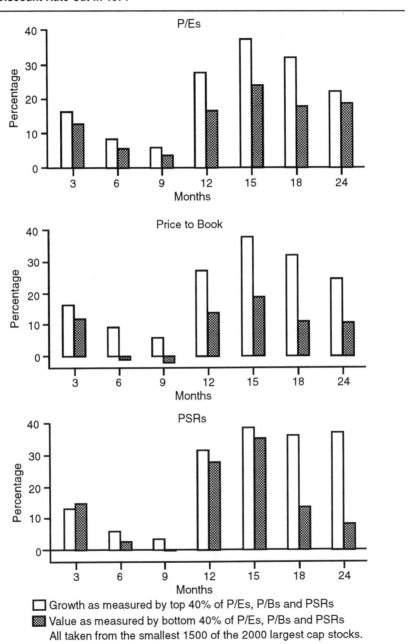

☐ Growth as measured by top 40% of P/Es, P/Bs and PSRs

▨ Value as measured by bottom 40% of P/Es, P/Bs and PSRs

All taken from the smallest 1500 of the 2000 largest cap stocks.

Figure 15.20—Small Cap Growth versus Value Returns Starting with the Third Discount Rate Cut in 1975

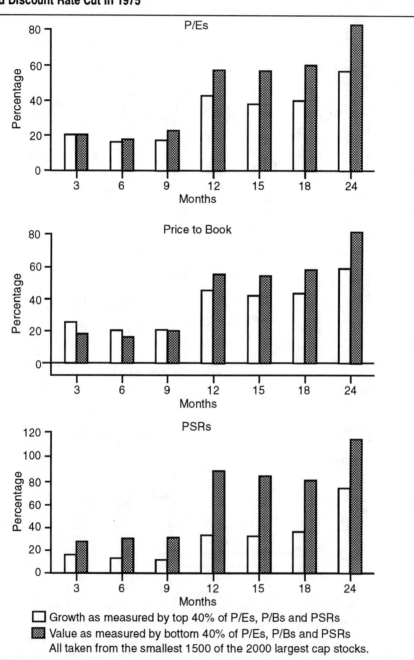

Growth as measured by top 40% of P/Es, P/Bs and PSRs
Value as measured by bottom 40% of P/Es, P/Bs and PSRs
All taken from the smallest 1500 of the 2000 largest cap stocks.

Figure 15.21—Small Cap Growth versus Value Returns Starting with the Third Discount Rate Cut in 1980

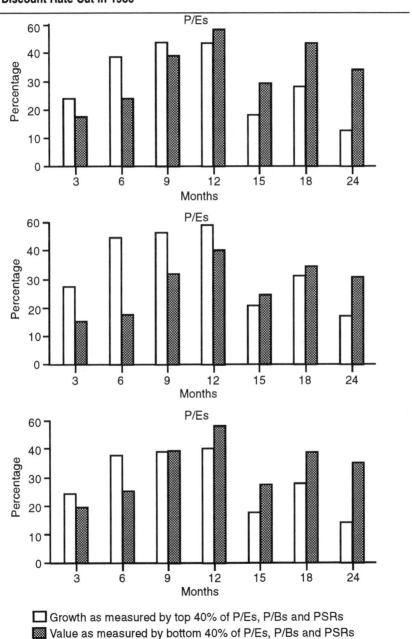

Growth as measured by top 40% of P/Es, P/Bs and PSRs
Value as measured by bottom 40% of P/Es, P/Bs and PSRs
All taken from the smallest 1500 of the 2000 largest cap stocks.

Figure 15.22—Small Cap Growth versus Value Returns Starting with the Third Discount Rate Cut in 1981

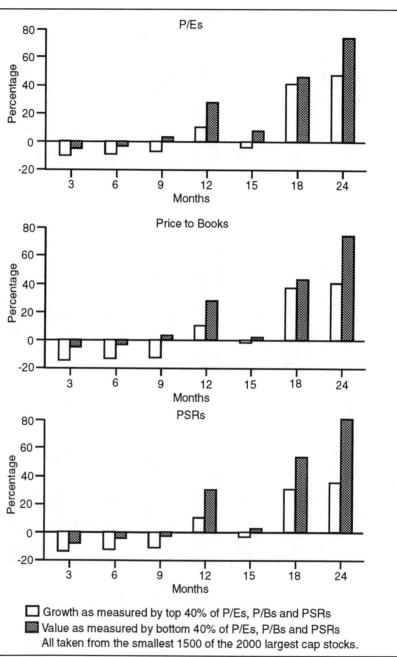

Growth as measured by top 40% of P/Es, P/Bs and PSRs
Value as measured by bottom 40% of P/Es, P/Bs and PSRs
All taken from the smallest 1500 of the 2000 largest cap stocks.

Figure 15.23—Small Cap Growth versus Value Returns Starting with the Third Discount Rate Cut in 1985

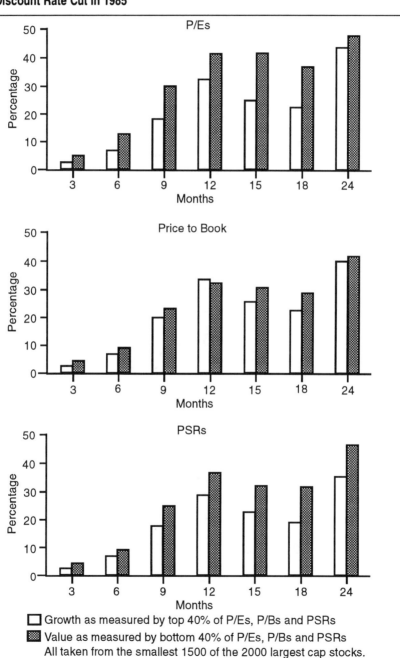

Growth as measured by top 40% of P/Es, P/Bs and PSRs
Value as measured by bottom 40% of P/Es, P/Bs and PSRs
All taken from the smallest 1500 of the 2000 largest cap stocks.

**Figure 15.24—Small Cap Growth versus Value Returns Starting with the
Third Discount Rate Cut in 1991**

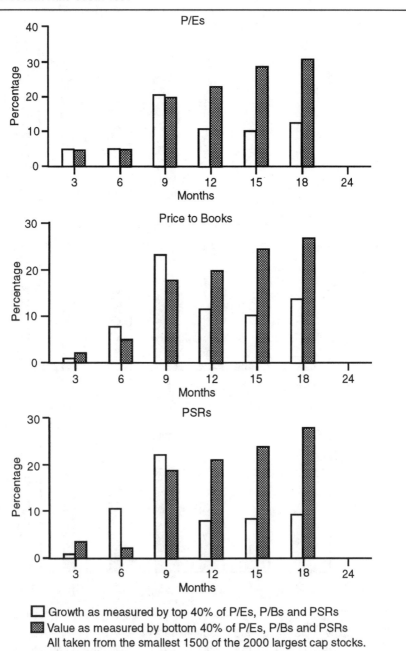

Growth as measured by top 40% of P/Es, P/Bs and PSRs
Value as measured by bottom 40% of P/Es, P/Bs and PSRs
All taken from the smallest 1500 of the 2000 largest cap stocks.

Figure 15.25—Top 2,000 Market Cap Stocks
Total Company Debt/Total Capital for Each Quadrant

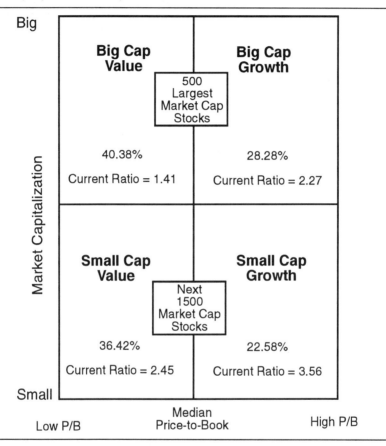

saving the company over 4.2%. This trade-off doesn't work as well for value companies, which sell at much lower valuations and thus have higher earnings yields—a P/E of 10, for instance, implies a 10% earnings yield, making 7.5% debt seem cheap. The result is that value companies tend to look to debt for additional capital, while growth stocks look to equity.

The impact of this difference in leverage is that when rates rise—after a time lag to work through maturity schedules—the interest costs of value companies rise faster than growth companies, thus negatively affecting the earnings of value companies relative to those of growth companies. The obvious effect is that value stocks' suppressed earnings produce poorer performance than their growth counterparts.

The opposite effect occurs after rates fall. Value stocks' earnings improve—because of reduced interest costs—on an absolute level and also relative to growth stocks. With ANY economic recovery—regardless of intensity or velocity—the relative potential in earnings increases on the value side become dramatic.

Not surprisingly, when 90-day Treasury bill rates are overlaid with growth and value cycles, the cycles tend to follow with a reasonable degree of closeness, after a time lag, the longer-term direction of interest rates (see Figure 15.26).

Figure 15.26—90-Day Treasury Bills and Growth and Value Cycles

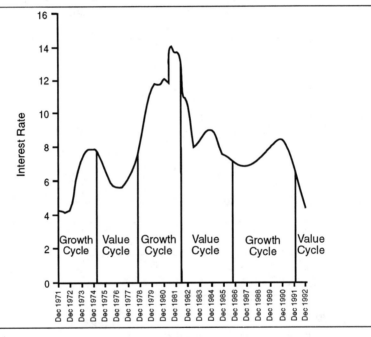

There is often a time lag, as it takes time for the interest rate change to translate into investor expectations. But as this happens, the cycle changes.

Big Cap versus Small Cap

The same analysis can be applied to the big/small side of the equation. Just as value outperforms in a falling interest rate environment, so also does small cap. As Table 15.1 shows, small cap outperformed big cap by an average of 9% over the same five periods outlined previously.

Table 15.1—Returns after Three Successive Discount Rate Cuts within a Year

			The 500 Largest Market Caps				
Date of Last Cut	3 Months	6 Months	9 Months	12 Months	15 Months	18 Months	24 Months
Jan '71	0.67	5.01	5.41	18.90	26.24	23.41	26.60
Feb '75	15.71	12.39	17.48	32.83	31.92	37.07	39.05
Jun '80	13.18	22.76	27.94	26.35	12.64	21.06	11.27
Nov '81	−9.54	−9.93	−3.57	15.19	22.53	35.52	40.02
May '85	1.00	8.38	23.83	34.69	38.54	36.38	53.17
Apr '91	4.05	7.65	14.36	15.47	18.96	20.52	
Average	4.18	7.71	14.22	23.91	25.14	28.99	34.02
			The Fisher 1500—the next 1,500 in size				
Date of Last Cut	3 Months	6 Months	9 Months	12 Months	15 Months	18 Months	24 Months
Jan '71	14.76	4.16	3.47	24.20	36.60	26.20	17.20
Feb '75	19.73	17.30	19.24	48.23	46.18	48.88	67.71
Jun '80	20.73	30.09	39.10	44.07	22.79	33.54	24.02
Nov '81	−9.64	−8.01	−4.17	21.00	34.72	58.09	59.38
May '85	2.95	8.01	21.36	33.46	28.96	25.92	42.15
Apr '91	2.28	8.78	12.35	15.46	15.90	18.34	
Average	8.47	10.06	15.80	31.07	30.86	35.16	42.09

CONCLUSION

Four-quadrant analysis is a simple and effective way of isolating equity styles within the stock market. More important, four-quad analysis indicates the importance over the long term of maintaining an exposure to the small cap value asset class. Owning only small cap growth is a guaranteed way of underperforming the small cap return for extended time periods. In light of this, small cap value should be seen as a long-term investable universe for institutional investors.

This is particularly true because most plans have a heavier weighting, in aggregate, in big cap growth stocks than big cap value stocks (and virtually NO weighting in small cap value stocks). The "market share" chart in Figure 15.27 looks at small cap value as a percentage of big cap growth.

Figure 15.27—Small Value as a Percent of Big Cap Growth Capitalization

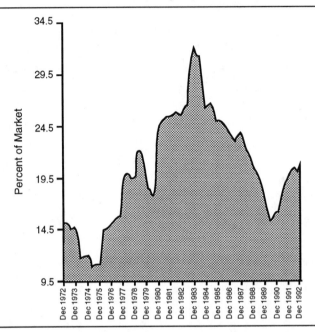

Recall the principle of diagonal opposition—that when small cap value does well (1975–1979, 1981–1985), big cap growth does poorly. When big cap growth does well (1979–1981, 1986–1991), small cap value does poorly. Given the tendency for diagonal quadrants to have opposite performance, the obvious "hedge" for plans weighted toward big cap growth is to increase their small cap value weighting relative to the total. This would lead to increased performance and reduced risk through diversification.

ENDNOTES

[1] See specifically "The Cross-Section Of Expected Stock Returns," by Eugene F. Fama and Kenneth R. French, Graduate School of Business, University of Chicago.

[2] Primary source for all research data and graphs is *Standard & Poor's Compustat Database* unless otherwise indicated. All total return data were calculated on an equal-weighted basis.

Chapter 16

The Value Approach to Small Cap Investing

Peter Carman
Senior Vice President and Chief Investment Officer

Richard S. Pzena
Director of Investment Management Research

Matthew S. Baker
Senior Research Analyst

Sanford C. Bernstein & Co.

INTRODUCTION

For most investors the concept of small capitalization equity investing has been synonymous with emerging growth. We would argue that there are two assumptions that underlie this assertion.

- Assumption one: The small cap performance effect that has been documented by a number of academic studies[1] is produced by the impact of many small, rapidly growing companies within the small cap universe that provide the earnings growth that generates the excess returns for the small cap universe.

- Assumption two: Concentrating portfolio investments in companies characterized by rapid earnings growth, within the small cap universe, is the most reliable method both for capturing the small cap effect and for outperforming the small cap averages. That is, if you can find the next Wal-Mart, Sun Microsystems, or Microsoft, a larger performance premium is assured.

We will argue that both of the assumptions outlined above are wrong. In fact, we believe that substantial evidence exists that the premium performance generated from small cap investments is the consequence of investors mispricing out-of-favor companies characterized by modest growth rates, unspectacular futures, and unimpressive financial characteristics. This is the domain of value.

We believe that the process by which small cap stocks outperform large is merely an extension of the process by which small cap value outperforms the small cap universe. As we move from large cap to small cap to small cap value, the characteristics of the universe move from more growth-like to more value-like. It is precisely these value-like characteristics that generate long-term outperformance (see Table 16.1).

Table 16.1—Total Annualized Return 1978–1992*

Large cap	17.5%
Small cap	18.8%
Small cap value	24.5%

*   Large cap is S&P 500; small cap is Wilshire Associates Next 1750; small cap value is Wilshire Associates Small Cap Value.

In that regard, we will explore four major issues:

- What is the composition of the small capitalization universe[2] in terms of various financial and industry characteristics?

- Specifically how should we define value within the context of small cap?

- How well do simple value strategies such as low P/E or low price-to-book work in the small capitalization universe?

- What is the stock-pricing process that leads to creation of the value performance premium?

THE SMALL CAP UNIVERSE IS RICH IN VALUE

To understand the "value" attributes of the small cap universe, a first step would be to look at the industry makeup of the small cap universe itself. Table 16.2 compares the small cap universe to the large cap universe. The two groups are somewhat similar in terms of industry makeup, but the small cap universe is slightly more "value" in nature. The small cap universe is dominated by financial, consumer, and industrial companies, which are all highly cyclical; hardly the domain of the traditional growth stock manager. In fact, cyclical companies make up 58% of the small cap universe compared with only 39% of the large cap universe. The traditional growth industries—technology and consumer growth (which includes both medical suppliers and traditional consumer products manufacturers and retailers) are actually underrepresented in the small cap universe as compared to large cap. The single largest industry difference between the two universes is the size of the financial services sector, which in small cap consists primarily of hundreds of publicly traded local, state, and regional banks. Again, these traditionally are not growth stocks.

Table 16.2—Sector Breakdown, Small Cap versus Large Cap

	Large Cap	Small Cap
CYCLICAL:		
Housing	1%	3%
Finance	11%	20%
Consumer cyclical	9%	10%
Commodity	7%	10%
Capital equipment	8%	13%
Transportation	3%	2%
	39%	58%
GROWTH:		
Consumer Noncyclical	30%	18%
Technology	5%	10%
	35%	28%
OTHER:		
Energy	10%	4%
Utility	16%	10%
	26%	14%

As of October 1992
Source: Compustat and Bernstein estimates.

The second observation that can be made about the small cap universe is that the lion's share of companies in the universe have been in business for a very long time (see Table 16.3).

Table 16.3—Longevity—Small Cap versus Large Cap

% of Companies in Business for at Least:	Small Cap	Large Cap
5 Years	87%	93%
10 Years	62%	84%

Source: Compustat.

While the small cap universe is composed of companies with slightly shorter histories than the large cap universe, it does not appear to be dominated by emerging growth companies in the early stages of development. In fact, the average small cap company has sales of nearly $1 billion (see Table 16.10).

Finally, the small cap universe does not have financial characteristics normally associated with rapid growth. The companies tend to be depressed, with sub-par earnings and revenue growth rates and low levels of profitability, as shown clearly in Table 16.4. These, too, are the characteristics normally associated with a value style of investing.

Table 16.4—Financial Characteristics—Small versus Large Cap

	Large Cap	Small Cap
5-Year sales growth	8.1%	5.6%
5-Year earnings growth	7.0%	3.8%
Return on equity	14.2%	10.6%

Note: Average 5-year growth rates over the period 1973–1992. Average ROE over same period.
Source: Compustat.

It is interesting that the levels of profitability displayed in Table 16.4 for the small cap universe have been consistently low over the years. In every year since 1973 small cap companies have had an average return on equity significantly less than large cap companies. (See Figure 16.1).

Figure 16.1—Return on Equity Comparison Small Cap versus Large Cap

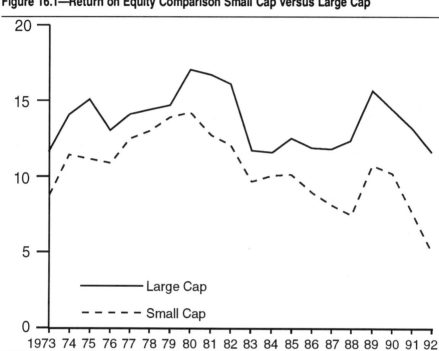

So the small cap universe is different from the preconceived notion of what small cap really is. Small cap does not mean new. Small cap does not mean emerging growth. Small cap does not mean exciting financial characteristics. And small cap does not mean small size. Small cap means small market value.

Small market value is caused by investor reaction to these unattractive characteristics, which produces underpriced stocks. The small cap universe is, therefore, particularly appropriate for traditional value investors.

As Table 16.5 illustrates quite clearly, the market prices small cap stocks at a discount to their large cap brethren—precisely due to their relatively unattractive characteristics.

**Table 16.5—Valuation—Small Cap versus Large Cap
Average—1973–1992**

	Small Cap	Large Cap	Small Cap Discount
Price/book	1.3	1.6	15%
Price/sales*	0.5	0.7	28%
Price/earnings	12.0	11.6	(4)%
Leverage*	45.7%	41.3%	n.m.

* Excludes Financial Companies
Source: Compustat.

Over the past 20 years, the small cap universe has sold at an average of 15% less than the large cap universe on the basis of price-to-book, although that discount has been as large as 40% in 1974 (see Figure 16.2). Using price-to-sales (Figure 16.3), the small cap discount has averaged 28% and has been as high as 60%. Interestingly, on the basis of price to earn-

Figure 16.2—Small Cap Discount to Large Cap Price-to-Book Value

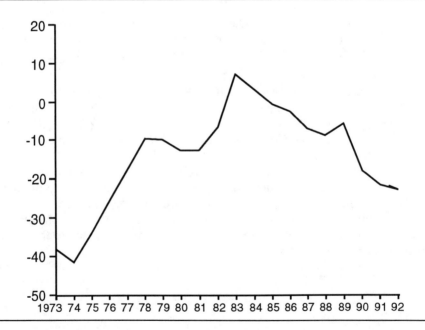

Figure 16.3—Small Cap Discount to Large Cap Price-to-Sales

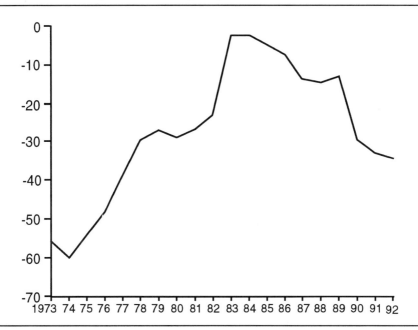

ings (Figure 16.4), the two universes sell for roughly the same price on average with a range of a 30% discount to a 40% premium.

The implication of this discrepancy is that on the basis of size—measured by sales or book value—the small cap universe is cheap. But, on the basis of current earnings, the small cap universe is not cheap. In aggregate, its return on sales (i.e., profit margin) and its return on equity are depressed. We observe these characteristics of the small cap universe when we measure them directly—sub-par profitability, poor recent growth rates, and hence depressed stock prices. Thus, on the basis of current earnings power, the small cap universe does not appear cheap on average.

But as we shall see later, depressed profitability tends to recover in subsequent years—this is what gives rise to the small cap effect. But first, let us define the concept of value in small cap stocks in a little more detail.

VALUE INVESTING—APPLICATION TO SMALL CAP

A value approach to investing is an attempt to purchase securities that sell in the marketplace at a discount to their long-term intrinsic worth. Generally, current conditions do not favor this particular class of companies.

Figure 16.4—Small Cap Discount to Large Cap Price-to-Earnings

Typically, some companies are facing problems that depress their earnings power below its normal level. Those problems can be temporary—such as an economic cycle—or permanent—such as a loss of competitiveness or an obsolete product.

The objective of a value investor is to find those companies whose share prices are depressed because of an overreaction to what later turns out to be a temporary problem. The keys to success in finding those opportunities are: first, to find basic measures to screen the large number of companies in the small cap universe to find a more manageable group of statistically attractive "value" opportunities; and second, to review the specifics of those companies to distinguish between temporary and permanent problems.

Several financial characteristics are often associated with a value portfolio. They include low price to book value, low price to sales and low price to earnings.

If we divide the universe of small cap companies into quintiles based on the price of the company relative to these measures of intrinsic worth, we find a substantial spread between the most and least conservatively valued quintiles.

Table 16.6—Small Cap Valuation by Quintile[1]

	Price/Book	Price/Earnings	Price/Sales
Cheapest quintile	0.6x	9.4x	0.2x
Second quintile	1.0	9.4	0.4
Third quintile	1.3	10.7	0.4
Fourth quintile	1.9	12.9	0.7
Most expensive quintile	4.1	23.1	1.1

1   Quintiles formed on the basis of price-to-book ratio.
Source: Compustat.

The stocks in the cheapest quintile sell for six-tenths of book value, while the stocks in the most expensive quintile sell for around four times book value. The stocks in the cheapest quintile sell for nine times earnings, compared to twenty-three times in the most expensive quintile. Similarly, cheap stocks sell for 0.2 times sales, compared to 1.1 times for expensive stocks.

Investors obviously have optimistic expectations for the future performance of the most expensive stocks and are more reserved with regard to the future prospects of the cheapest quintile.

Clearly, the stocks of companies characterized by above-average profitability and the potential for rapid earnings growth deserve to sell at meaningful price-to-book or P/E premiums. Similarly, the stocks of more ordinary, less profitable companies deserve no such premium and, in fact, to the extent that their earnings growth and profit structure is permanently sub par, they should sell at a discount to the market.

Value managers believe that these assertions are correct; however, they also believe that investors systematically overestimate and overvalue the persistence of the growth and profit characteristics of well-positioned companies and equally systematically overstate the persistence of sub-par economic performance for companies with low P/Es and low price-to-book.

In the ensuing discussion, we will define value as those companies with the lowest price-to-book value ratio, since price-to-book has, in our studies, shown the highest correlation with investment performance. Recognize, however, that all stocks with low price-to-book value ratios are not "values." Some deserve the low ratio. Nevertheless, despite its shortcomings, price-to-book is a good proxy for value.

The validity of the value managers' case can be supported by investigating a phenomenon called regression to the mean, as it applies to company economic performance. With regard to company profitability, this concept suggests that companies with superior return on equity should exhibit a strong tendency to regress toward the average level of profitability for the universe, while companies with sub-par return on equity should show improving results as their financial performance moves toward that of the average company. This case of regression to the mean for company financial performance can be supported by the following analysis.

In Figure 16.5 we track the profitability of our small capitalization universe over multiple five-year periods. First we classify the companies into quintiles ranked by return on equity. Then we look at the average ROE of each of those quintiles over the next five years. The impact of the process of regression to the mean is obvious. For the worst companies, profits recover over that five-year interval, while the profitability of the best companies deteriorates significantly. This process shouldn't be surprising since in the real world low levels of profits result in management actions, including cost cutting, facility rationalization, and product improvement. This frequently occurs just as depressed markets recover on a cyclical basis. Similarly, highly profitable companies often attract competition, which tends to result in pressure on their profit structure while growth prospects

Figure 16.5—Small Cap ROE Regression 1/73–11/92

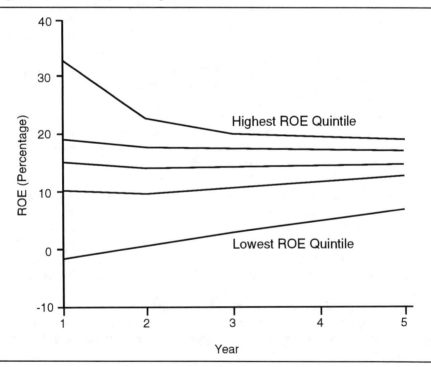

diminish over time as markets become saturated or as competition emerges.

Since depressed companies tend to recover and superior companies tend to return to more normal levels of profitability, the discrepancy in valuation between the quintiles is probably exaggerated. Accordingly, cheap companies, as defined by price/earnings and price/book value relationships, should outperform the market over time. Similarly, expensive companies should underperform. This is exactly the case, as shown in Table 16.7.

Table 16.7—Annual Total Return to Investors by Price-to-Book Quintile 1973–1992 Annual Rebalancing

Cheapest quintile	18.0%
Second quintile	17.4%
Third quintile	14.4%
Fourth quintile	12.1%
Most expensive quintile	10.6%
All stocks	14.4%

Source: Compustat.

During the last twenty years, a simple strategy of buying the companies with the lowest price to book value ratios in our universe and rebalancing the portfolio annually would have returned 18% per year, 3.6% better than the universe average. On an annual basis (using price-to-book as the measure of value), the strategy would have outperformed in fourteen of the last twenty years (see Figure 16.6).

If we used price-to-earnings as the measure, the results over the same twenty-year period would be similar, as shown in Table 16.8.

The reason why such simple strategies work is that investors tend to overreact to their concerns about near-term industrial performance creating valuations that are depressed relative to the underlying value of the firm. It continues to work because it is fundamental human nature to avoid anxiety. Each year a different set of investments cause concern and are mispriced.

Investors who are willing to tolerate the discomfort can reap superior returns.

Figure 16.6—Small Cap Value versus Small Cap Annual Total Return

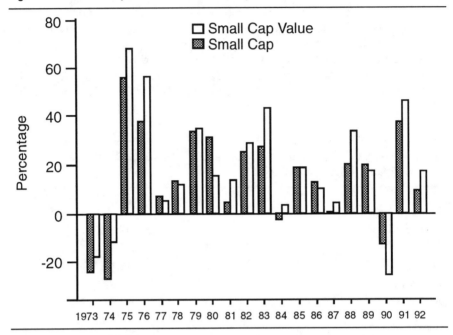

Table 16.8—Annual Total Return to Investors by Price-to-Earnings Quintile 1973–1992 Annual Rebalancing

Cheapest quintile	17.4%
Second quintile	17.4%
Third quintile	14.4%
Fourth quintile	12.1%
Most expensive quintile	10.6%
All stocks	14.4%

Source: Compustat.

IS THE SMALL CAP EFFECT ITSELF A VALUE PHENOMENON?

Thus far, we have argued that a value approach to small cap investing can provide superior returns to a small cap index. We will now go even further and make the case that the entire small cap effect itself is a value phenomenon.

There are a number of academic studies that address the issue of small capitalization equity returns that strongly suggest that the related concepts of value investing, low price-to-book and regression to the mean play a powerful role in the excess returns that accrue to the small capitalization stock universe.

Fama and French (1992) found that "two easily measured variables, size and book value to market equity provide a simple and powerful characterization of the cross-section of average stock returns for the 1963–1990 period."[3]

In a related study, Fama and French (1990) also found that the behavior of small-stock fundamentals was determined not by actual company size as defined by assets, but by the way that size was defined (market capitalization).[4] Small market capitalization companies in fact tend to be characterized by substandard earnings, higher leverage, and low price-to-book ratios. When companies are sorted by physical size (i.e., total assets) those financial differences disappear.

The most important insight that we can draw from the Fama and French studies is that *small cap companies are not necessarily small companies.* In fact, when we divided our small cap universe into size on the basis of physical measures such as sales or assets, performance results differed dramatically from the results when size is measured by market cap. This information is analyzed in Tables 16.9 and 16.10.

Table 16.9—Small-Company Characteristics When Size Is Based on Total Sales, 1973–1992

	Small Companies	Large Companies
Return on equity (%)	12.6%	13.4%
5-Year sales growth (% per year)	8.7%	8.3%
5-Year earnings growth (% per year)	7.6%	6.7%
Total return to investors (% per year)	12.6%	11.3%
Memo: Average 1992 sales ($ m)	$723	$8,640
Average 1992 market cap ($ m)	$762	$6,882

Source: Compustat.

Using sales as an indication of size (Table 16.9), we have broken up our universe into the 25% largest companies and the 75% smallest. The largest have average sales of $8.6 billion compared to the smaller group's average of $723 million.

What is truly interesting about this data is that the profitability and growth measures are virtually identical for both small companies and large companies. The traditional belief that small companies grow much faster and are much more profitable than large companies simply because they are small is a myth. During the last twenty years, large companies grew their sales at an average of 8.3% per year, virtually the same as small companies' 8.7% annual pace. Small-company earnings growth was within 1 percentage point of the large-company average. And small-company profitability as measured by return on equity was actually less than large-company profitability.

What is even more striking is that the total return to investors is somewhat independent of company size. Although small companies earned their owners 12.6% per year compared to 11.3% for large companies, the entire "small cap effect" cannot be captured by simply investing in those companies that are just physically smaller.

When size is measured in terms of market capitalization, the data is very much in line with what we would expect from the Fama and French analysis.

Table 16.10—Small-Company Characteristics When Size Is Based on Market Value 1973–1992

	Small Companies	Large Companies
Return on Equity (%)	10.6%	14.2%
5-Year sales growth (% per year)	5.6%	8.1%
5-Year earnings growth (% per year)	3.8%	7.0%
Total return to investors (% per year)	14.4%	10.8%
Memo: Average 1992 sales ($ m)	$933	$7,848
Average 1992 market cap ($ m)	$615	$7,402

Source: Compustat.

Companies with small market values have very unappealing financial characteristics. They are much less profitable than their large cap counterparts. The average return on equity for the small cap universe over the last twenty years has been 10.6% compared with 14.2% for large cap companies. The small cap companies have seen their sales grow at only a 5.6% rate compared with 8.1% for larger companies. Furthermore, earnings have grown at a rate of only 3.8% for the small cap universe versus 7% for the large cap universe.

While these companies are clearly physically smaller than those companies with large market caps, it is not the physical size that gives them their unattractive characteristics. In fact, there are many substantial-sized companies in the small cap universe.

Yet despite these unattractive characteristics, these companies earn a return to their shareholders that substantially exceeds the return to the more attractive large cap companies. Here the "small cap effect" is clearly evident, averaging 3.6% per year over the past twenty years.

What phenomenon is at work here? How can small companies have financial characteristics similar to large companies when companies with small market caps look so different? And, why do those weak financial characteristics produce such a large performance premium?

There is only one reasonable explanation: small cap is a proxy for depressed stock price. Small physical size is a characteristic that changes only slowly. Companies do grow and shrink; however, the turnover of both the large cap and the small cap universe based on physical size is quite modest (see Table 16.11).

Table 16.11—Average Turnover of Universe 1988–1992

	Size Determined by:	
	Sales	*Market Cap*
500 largest companies	6%	10%
Small cap	11%	19%

Source: Factset, Compustat.

Over the last five years, the largest 500 companies, as measured by sales, turned over on average 6% per year. The next 1,500 companies turned over on average 11% per year. When size is measured using market cap, the turnover is much higher—10% for the large cap universe and 19% for the small cap universe.

Size based on market capitalization is relatively volatile, since it is influenced by investors' psychology and their perceptions of valuation, while, as we have seen, physical size is much more stable. These perceptions are, of course, closely related to the economic performance of each company. When a firm's earnings deteriorate, the market value of the company will often fall by much more than the decline in the physical size of the company. If it later turns out that the earnings slide was temporary (as is very likely given the phenomenon of regression to the mean discussed earlier), the market value will recover disproportionately as well.

The small cap effect that we witness is clearly related to this kind of recovery. It must be—otherwise, we would be able to witness significant differences between small companies and large based on physical size. Such differences do not exist. The small cap effect comes from the volatility of the small cap universe. Every year, a different group of companies becomes depressed. Because the universe is a fluid, volatile universe, there will always be investment opportunities due to the overreaction of investors to temporary phenomena.

To put it somewhat differently, small capitalization companies are depressed *because of their sub-par profitability* not because they are small companies. When a company does poorly, its stock price drops. Since stock price is the primary determinant of market cap, these companies fall into the small cap universe. As profitability recovers, these stocks outperform.

While we have been discussing the "value" concepts of sub-par profitability and regression to the mean, these concepts apply equally well to the entire small cap universe when compared to large cap companies. Hence, our conclusion that the small cap effect itself is a value effect.

ADDITIONAL SUPPORT FOR A VALUE APPROACH TO SMALL CAP

Several other studies have been done that we believe indirectly support our contention that the small cap effect is a value effect. One such study is an analysis of securities returns based on trading location. Christopherson and Trittin (1990)[5] determined that there were significant differences in returns from small capitalization stocks based on trading location. Their data suggest that the small cap effect is really an exchange effect. The small cap companies that trade on the New York Stock Exchange outperform the small cap companies that trade over-the-counter (see Table 16.12). Their analysis of stock characteristics and returns by trading location is very interesting and has important implications for our value thesis.

Table 16.12—Selected Small Cap Equity Characteristics—December 31, 1989

	NYSE	OTC
Price/book	1.4x	1.9x
Price/sales	0.4x	0.7x
Sales/growth	7.3%	13.5%
Debt/capital	38.0%	27.5%
Average returns	19.4%	16.1%

Source: Christopherson and Trittin, *The Effects of Trading Location on Small Capitalization Stock Returns* (1990), p. 3.

The NYSE segment has lower price-to-book, lower price-to-sales, slower sales growth, and more leverage than stocks traded over-the-counter. According to the study, the OTC universe is particularly notable for a set of characteristics that are normally associated with growth companies and has a high exposure to growth sectors such as technology and health care. The NYSE universe, on the other hand, had greater exposure to cyclical and interest sensitive stocks.

Despite its statistically unattractive characteristics relative to the other trading locations, the NYSE small cap sample outperformed the OTC small cap stock subset by 3.4% during the period of the study, from 1973 through August 1989.

We have updated this performance history and taken it further to emphasize the point. Table 16.13 takes a similar approach and compares total return for New York Stock Exchange small cap stocks to OTC small cap stocks.

Table 16.13—Total Return for Small Cap Stocks by Trading Location 1976–1992

	NYSE	OTC
All small cap stocks	18.1%	16.9%
Stocks with more than 3 years' trading history	18.2%	17.6%

Source: Compustat

During the period from 1976 to 1992, NYSE small cap stocks did in fact outperform OTC small cap stocks by about 1.2% per year. But, when we take the initial public offerings out of the picture (i.e., those companies with less than three years' trading history), the difference narrows to only 60 basis points per year. The implication is that the OTC market has a much higher proportion of emerging growth stocks than does the NYSE. It is these emerging growth stocks that help hold down returns. Adjusting for the higher proportion of emerging growth stocks in the OTC market emphasizes the point that the small cap effect is influenced more by "value" phenomena than it is by anything else, including trading location.

Another study that we completed also supports the case that the small cap effect is a value effect. We studied the migration of companies into and out of the small cap universe to see whether there was a steady stream of companies moving upward from tiny to small to large, or if changes in the universe came from "fallen angels." Not surprisingly, the "fallen angel" effect dominates the emerging growth effect, as shown in Table 16.14.

Table 16.14—Migration of Stocks into the Small Cap Universe 1988–1992

Market value of universe	$538 Billion
Emerging growth companies migrating upward	$10 Billion
Fallen angels migrating downward	$49 Billion

Source: Compustat.

During the last five years, the small cap universe had an average market value of $538 billion. Each year, approximately $10 billion of companies moved up from the micro cap sector into the small cap universe. Similarly, approximately $50 billion of companies fell from the large cap universe into the small cap universe. While not conclusive, the evidence supports the thesis that changes in the small cap universe itself are dominated by value phenomena rather than growth phenomena.

CHARACTERISTICS OF VALUE INVESTING

Besides offering superior returns over the long term, there are several other attractive characteristics of small cap value investing that are worth mentioning. These include:

- Value tends to be defensive.
- Value tends to be less volatile.
- Value tends to have lower turnover.

The value style of investing as we define it here—in terms of price-to-book—tends to be defensive. Most of the performance premium is earned in down markets, as shown in Table 16.15.

Table 16.15—Small Cap Value Performance in Various Markets 1973–1992*

	Up Markets	Down Markets	All Markets
Number of months	139	99	238
Average monthly performance:			
Small cap	4.9%	–3.9%	1.2%
Small cap value	5.0%	–3.2%	1.6%

* Through October 1992.
Source: Factset, Compustat.

Over the last 20 years (through October 1992), the small cap market was up in 139 months and down in 99 months. During the up months, a value style tends to perform in line with the market, earning 5% per month when the market is up (the market itself earns 4.9%). During the down months, however, the value style is substantially better at preserving capital and loses 3.2% per month compared with a 3.9% monthly loss for the universe.

Another advantage of a value approach to investing is that value portfolios tend to be somewhat less volatile than the small cap universe (see Table 16.16).

Table 16.16—Volatility Comparison—Small Cap versus Small Cap Value 1978–1992

Wilshire Associates Next 1750	19.1%
Wilshire Associates Small Cap Value	13.8%

Source: Wilshire Associates.

One of the other advantages that accrue to a value style of investing is relatively low turnover. Because transaction costs can be so high, controlling turnover will contribute to the performance premium of any small cap investment strategy. In our historical simulations of a value approach to small cap management, average turnover was 35% per year. Using a strategy of annual rebalancing for the low price-to-book value portfolio results in portfolio turnover of 45%. The small cap indices themselves turn over about 20% per year.[6] Accordingly, a value strategy is only modestly more exposed to transaction costs than an indexed strategy. As a consequence, the transaction cost savings produced by a value strategy provides a significant competitive advantage as well as providing a confidence that the theoretical results of this value portfolio can be translated into actual results.

ENHANCING A NAIVE SMALL CAP VALUE STRATEGY

Of course, there are "values" that do not in fact turn out to be good investments. Accordingly, research is an important tool for a value investor. The ability to understand which depressed companies won't regress to the mean can add significantly to returns. The risks, of course, are that the psychological fears that make a company cheap affect even the most experienced analysts, causing them to understate the recovery potential for underpriced stocks.

Nevertheless, by starting with a universe of cheap stocks (e.g., those with low price-to-book ratios) the odds of outperforming the market are high. It is a universe extremely rich in attractive investment opportunities. It is also defensive and thus somewhat less risky than emerging growth investments.

CONCLUSION

The small cap universe is extremely fluid. Each year there are those companies that migrate from small cap to large cap (as their earnings grow). In addition, some companies migrate from large cap to small cap (as their earnings decline). By continually adjusting a portfolio to purchase only the small cap companies (and hence the ones that are characterized by depressed earnings, low prices, and low price-to-book ratios), investors can capture the premium performance from the small cap effect and achieve an additional premium by focusing on a portfolio that emphasizes the most attractive segment of that universe.

The explanation of the small cap effect that we have outlined here is dramatically opposed to the emerging growth investment process that dominates the investment community. Clearly, emerging growth stocks do exist. However, we believe that the overall long-term impact of such companies is modest compared to the impact of the value phenomenon. There is no other way of explaining stock market return patterns where companies with low price-to-book ratios and low historical earnings and sales growth rates tend to outperform those with higher prices and better prospects.

What we have discussed so far is so obvious that it shouldn't persist. If our observations are correct, why wouldn't investors shift strategies and invest in low price-to-book stocks, thus eliminating the return advantage? The answer is both psychological and analytical. There is always a good reason for a company's stock price to be depressed. Investing in a company with sub-par profitability is uncomfortable. Investing in a company with an outstanding history and bright expectations for the future is comfortable and exciting. As long as investors react in this manner, value investing will continue to work.

To be fair, there is clearly a premium that can accrue to superior growth-stock managers. Their task is to select those companies whose superior growth and profitability characteristics regress to the mean much more slowly that the average growth company. Our real argument is that growth managers have a particularly difficult task because the competition to find long-term winners is so intense that prices are high, and thus the growth universe as a whole is not particularly rich in companies that are likely to provide a long-term performance premium.

The reverse is true for depressed, out of favor companies. Whereas the constant search of growth managers for the best of the best companies causes high prices, the overall lack of competition in the relatively unexciting world of value stocks leaves prices low and the chance for investment success high.

ENDNOTES

[1] Mark R. Reinganum, "Abnormal Returns in Small Firm Portfolios," *Financial Analysts Journal* (March–April 1981); Rolf W. Banz, "The Relationship between Return and Market Value of Common Stocks," *Journal of Financial Economics* (1981).

[2] We define "small cap" as the bottom 1,500 of the largest 2,000 companies. On 7/1/92 the universe had a market cap range of $100 million to $1.3 billion. Large cap is defined as the 500 largest publicly traded companies.

[3] Eugene F. Fama and Kenneth R. French. *Journal of Finance*, Vol. XLVII, No. 7 (June 1992), p. 429.

[4] Eugene F. Fama and Kenneth R. French, "April 1990, Small Firm Fundamentals." Unpublished paper presented at Center for Research in Securities Prices Conference, May 1991.

[5] Jon Christopherson and Denis J. Trittin, *The Effects of Trading Location on Small Capitalization Stock Returns* (Dec. 1990), pp. 5 & 7.

[6] Source: Wilshire Asset Management.

Chapter 17

Using Multifactor Models to Invest in Small Stocks

William W. Jahnke
Founder
Vestek Systems, Inc.

INTRODUCTION

In recent years the idea that portfolios can be managed using computers has emerged as a recognized investment style. Quantitative investing is based on evaluating what factors ("factor models") are associated with investment success, quantifying the factors, and using computer programs ("portfolio optimizers") to maintain portfolio exposures to desirable factors. Examples of factor models include low market-to-book ratios, low price-to-earnings ratios, and stock price trend reversal. More elaborate factor models include positive earnings trend revision and high expected returns from dividend discount models. Traditional managers often base their investment decisions on such factors; the difference lies in the degree to which stocks are systematically evaluated, the frequency of evaluation, the number of stocks evaluated, the number of factors evaluated, the formalization of the weightings used to produce a composite ranking of each stock's relative attractiveness, and the precision with which the stocks entering and exiting the portfolio is consistent with the objective of maximizing or meeting desirable factor exposures.

One essential difference between quantitative investing and traditional investing is that quantitative multifactor investing starts with a large pre-defined universe of securities and systematically determines purchases and sales using a defined but limited set of factors, while traditional investing evaluates smaller universes of stocks in a less defined and more subjective manner. Quantitative investing seeks to broadly diversify where possible; traditional investing places emphasis on individual stock selection.

In this chapter we explore some of the issues involved in employing multifactor models to invest in small stocks. We also present some empirical evidence to support the employment of multifactor models in managed small-stock portfolios. Lastly, we make some comparisons between large- and small-stock investing, using multifactor models.

SINGLE- AND MULTIFACTOR MODELS

Single-factor models employ one factor in determining relative investment attractiveness. The factor model can be as simple as ranking stocks by their trailing twelve-month price-to-earnings ratio or as complex as ranking stocks by mispricing derived from a three-stage dividend discount model. The idea is that a universe of stocks can be evaluated by ranking stocks according to their exposure to a factor. The factor has merit in stock selection if the stocks with high rankings on average over time outperform the universe of stocks from which they are drawn. Highly desirable factor models produce a large periodic return relative to the universe with a small period-to-period variation in excess return. An example would be for the top decile to produce a monthly excess return over the universe of fifty basis points, with a monthly standard deviation of fifty basis points. This implies an investor could be approximately 67% confident that in any given month the top-decile-rated stocks would outperform the universe, while the prospect of underperforming the universe over time would diminish toward zero as the number of months increased.

The degree to which factor models produce superior performance is an empirical question. Some evidence is reported later on in this chapter. The reasons that some factor models have produced superior returns historically have "theoretical" explanations. It is up to the manager of a factor model to present a theory that explains why the factor model worked in the past and, more importantly, why it should be expected to work in the future. Purchasers of portfolio management services employing factor models are advised to get a plausible explanation of why the factor is expected to work in the future before investing. Interestingly, some purveyors of factor model investing do not profess to understand why their model produces superior performance, and more interestingly, their clients don't require it.

In a rational, informed, and mature market, prices should be expected to be set fairly. This means the returns to factor models should produce random outcomes after adjusting for nondiversifiable risk. The fact that over a given investment horizon a number of factor models produce statistically significant performance relative to their universe is to be expected, due solely to random variation in the return generating process. Test 100 factors and 5 should be expected to produce statistically significant performance in a time period of any given length.

If the market is rational but misinformed, a factor model that captures a pricing anomaly will produce superior returns until such time as a large enough group of investors wakes up to the fact and reprices stocks to eliminate the expectation of future above-average returns. In the process, investors already exposed in their portfolios to the factor will experience a windfall gain. Henceforth the periodic return to the factor will fluctuate randomly about the return of the universe, as new information is impounded in stock prices. The reason the return to a fairly priced factor is expected to fluctuate randomly is that new information is a random variable. Sometimes new information is good and sometimes not. Sometimes new information is very significant and sometimes not.

Unfortunately, investors who evaluate factor models based on past performance alone are often drawn to a factor model whose performance is a product of randomness in the return generating process. To bet on a factor model is to bet the market has not yet figured out that it is acting foolishly by permitting some informed investors to earn superior risk-adjusted returns at the expense of the uninformed investors.

The idea behind multifactor models is that the market is mispricing more than one factor at a point in time, and by exposing a portfolio to multiple factors, the periodic risk of underperformance relative to the benchmark can be reduced by factor model diversification. The weighting of the factors in a multifactor model is determined by the expected excess return to the factor, the expected stability or consistency of the return to the factor, and the expected correlation of returns across the factors. By identifying factor models where the returns are expected on average to be positive and where the periodic returns have low or negative correlation, the risk of the multifactor model underperforming in any given period is reduced.

SMALL STOCK INVESTING USING MULTIFACTOR MODELS

The objective of a small-stock multifactor model is to produce realized return in excess of the performance of the universe of small stocks from which the portfolio is drawn. The performance benchmark should be a capitalization-weighted small-stock universe. The main reason for capitalization weighting is that the results of an equally weighted index are impossible to replicate due to the demands of rebalancing back to equal weights. Capitalization-weighted benchmarks are usually replicatable by index funds with small tracking errors in performance, and the average active return to an investment style is governed by the capitalization-weighted universe and the costs associated with active management. The problems with the small capitalization benchmark are only partially reduced by capitalization weighting. The migration of stocks into and out of the universe and the associated implicit transaction costs are a problem for both active and passive small-stock investors.

The choice of what constitutes a small-stock universe is a matter of judgment. Stocks not in the S&P 500, excluding stocks with market capitalization under $50 million, is one choice. The second-largest 1,000 stocks by market capitalization redefined quarterly is one of a number of others. Some investors view small-stock investing as mid-cap investing. There is no industry standard. Once a universe and updating frequency is determined, the next question to be answered is what factors to use.

The factors commonly used in multifactor models usually fall into several categories: low valuation, relative valuation, earnings revision, past success, and risk factors. Low valuation factor models include low price-to-earnings, low market-to-book, low price-to-sales, low price, high dividend yield. No attempt is made to relate price to future earnings or cash-flow projections. The idea is that low-valuation stocks are on average out of favor and prices are on average too low but no attempt is made to validate price paid relative to expected cash flow. Relative valuation factor models include dividend discount models, low price-to-forecasted earnings, and high forecasted growth-to-price earnings. These factor models require forecasts of future earnings or cash flows. Consensus earnings forecasts are often employed in relative-value factor models. Earnings-revision factor models monitor changes in consensus forecasts. Companies experiencing increases in earnings forecasts from Wall Street analysts have an impressive track record in predicting future relative performance. Past-success factor models look at historical growth rates in earnings, return on equity, and past stock market performance. Some factor models like strong past performance; some favor weak past performance. There are a large number of risk factors employed in multifactor models. These include CAPM risk measures beta and sigma, market volatility measures, and financial statement leverage and capital adequacy measures. There are in addition a number of other factors to choose from not mentioned here.

The choice of factors going into a small-stock multifactor model should be theoretically based and empirically supported. It is better to start with a theory and test it than it is to find out what worked in the past and then come up with a theory. Worse yet is to find something that worked in the past and not bother with a theory. If your firm does not have the computer resources to backtest multifactor models, there are a number of organizations who are in business to assist your firm for a fee. The best tests, and the only tests of a multifactor model that really count, test multifactor models with real money. This is especially true with small-stock multifactor models because of the difficulty in measuring cost of trading.

Testing multifactor models comes in two forms: model backtesting and portfolio simulation. Model backtesting tests to see whether or not the rankings from the multifactor model outperform the universe of stocks being evaluated. By evaluating the degree of outperformance of the top-rated stocks (top decile or quintile) in relation to the model's rate of turnover and implied transaction costs, the question of doing a portfolio simulation is answered. Portfolio simulations employ a portfolio optimization program to simulate the management of a portfolio, using historical data, a multifactor model, and portfolio diversification and turnover constraints. The simulation should incorporate explicit estimates of trading costs in the evaluation of rankings coming from the multifactor model and the imputation of trading cost in the portfolios performance based on the liquidity of the stock, the percentage of average trading volume represented by the trade, and the opportunity cost of not getting the trade done at the time the optimization was run. Generally several interactions are run that evaluate different levels of portfolio diversification and turnover. It is hard to avoid the look-back trap at this point in choosing the degree of diversification and portfolio turnover.

The optimizer used to construct the portfolios in the portfolio simulation is likely to be the same program used to implement the multifactor portfolio management strategy. The optimizer will seek maximum exposure to the multifactor models, subject to portfolio diversification constraints. Such models were employed by a number of investment management organizations in the 1980s. Most of the applications were limited to medium to large stock universes. The reasons for this include availability of data and ease of implementation. The higher transaction costs associated with small-stock investing, and their implications in adjusting stock ratings and dealing with the more difficult trading issues, favored implementation with larger stocks. From an optimization perspective, managing small-stock portfolios involves some additional work. The optimizer should be set up to recognize the cost of buying or selling. This can be done by converting multifactor ratings into estimates of excess returns net of transaction costs.

Experience, preferably real-time experience instead of backtesting, can be used to determine the translation of stock ratings to excess return expectations, called "alpha" by the quants. Given the problematic trading of small stocks, the process of optimization is likely to become more iterative as the portfolio is adjusted based on the ability to trade the stocks on the trade list produced by the optimizer. The separation between portfolio management and trading is likely to blur to a greater extent with small stock multifactor applications because of the trade list implementation problems. The importance of understanding the full cost of trading and developing trading strategies that do a good job of trading off price impact and opportunity cost is crucial. The desirability of implementing a trading cost execution performance evaluation system is high. The system needs to capture the full order flow coming out of the portfolio optimization process, capturing the called for trades that both did and did not get executed.

EVIDENCE THAT MULTIFACTOR SMALL-STOCK INVESTING WORKS

The evidence that small-stock multifactor models provide an opportunity to outperform small-stock universes is limited. Not much has been published on the subject. In some cases the underlying data required to build factor models has not been available or has been more limited for smaller capitalization stocks. Vestek Systems maintains a factor database for all publicly traded stocks going back to June 30, 1984. Databases of prices, fundamental data, expectational data, and corporate actions were updated monthly and avoid the survivorship problem and data availability problem evident in most reconstructed databases. In 1989 a 48-multifactor system was built to replace the 5-factor system Vestek initiated in 1984. The 48-factor returns database was back-built in 1989 to June 30, 1984, and updated monthly to the present. Monthly factor returns are calculated by regressing the cross-sectional monthly returns against standardized cross-sectional factor exposures as of the beginning of the month. Factor returns are also maintained by decile for each of the factors on a monthly basis.

In Table 17.1, the monthly linked and annualized factor returns for a small-stock universe—represented by the second thousand largest market capitalization stocks—is reported for the period December 31, 1984, to December 31, 1992. All the stocks in the universe for which there was data on the factor were ranked by the factor and sorted in descending order into deciles at the end of each month. Stocks with the highest calculated factor exposure were placed in decile 1 and those with the lowest were placed in decile 10. The equal-weighted total return was calculated for the following month. The returns were linked and annualized. Several of the factors had data going back to 1989, as indicated. The universe performance for the factors varied due to the number of stocks for which data was available.

The reader can get a good idea of what factors worked by looking at decile 1 and 10 columns and comparing the returns with the universe. Now look across all ten deciles for each factor. The factors associated with big payoffs during the period are positive earnings revision, low valuation, and low risk.

The column labeled SPREAD/1-UNIV reports the difference between the top decile and the universe adjusted for missing data. The spread runs from a high of 18.5% to –19.2% per annum. Those are big numbers! Of interest but not reported are the standard deviations of excess returns and the cross-correlation of excess returns. Vestek uses this information to determine the optimal weightings of factor models.

SMALL-STOCK VERSUS BIG-STOCK FACTOR MODELS

Do factors models that work for big stocks work for small stocks? Some analysts would be surprised if the answer was yes. Looking again at the eight-year period ending December 31, 1992, Table 17.2 reports the performance of the 48 factors; this time for the S&P 500 universe of stocks, excluding foreign stocks. Several things are striking in comparing Tables 17.1 and 17.2. The ranking of factor performance is very similar. Just run your eyes down the listings. Surprise is at the top of the tables, followed by low valuation. High risk measures are at the bottom of the tables.

Another striking detail, the return spreads for the "big" stock universe (decile 1 minus the universe) are 11.6 to –9.7, approximately one-half as big as for the small-stock universe. Is the market more efficient in pricing large stocks? Will actively run small-stock portfolios employing multifactor models prove to be more successful in beating their benchmarks than big stock multifactor applications?

CONCLUSIONS

Small-stock multifactor models will be employed by a growing number of investment management organizations in the next five years. The backtest performance data suggest that the market is less efficient in pricing small stocks and that quantitatively managed portfolios employing multifactor models can provide positive excess return. Purveyors or patrons of small multifactor portfolio management are advised to operate based on theory as well as empiricism and to develop measures that monitor the various costs of implementation.

Table 17.1—Decile Return Report
Linked Return % Annualized—Equal Weighted 12/31/84–12/31/92

UNIVERSE: SECOND 1000 STOCKS

VALUE FACTOR	1	2	3	4	DECILE 5	6	7	8	9	10	UNIV	SPREAD 1-UNIV	BEGIN DATE
EARNINGS YIELD REVISION	27.8	23.1	15.2	11.2	11.3	8.2	5.8	3.0	1.6	-11.0	9.3	18.5	8/31/89
MONTHLY EARNINGS REVISION	28.9	23.2	16.1	9.5	11.9	11.2	14.0	6.7	-2.3	-8.7	10.7	18.2	5/31/89
WEEKLY EARNINGS REVISION	27.2	11.6	9.7	13.4	10.1	10.6	9.5	11.5	9.0	-5.4	10.6	16.6	5/31/89
EARNINGS REVISION-SURPRISE	29.3	29.6	23.2	18.7	14.3	12.7	12.9	7.3	4.0	-4.5	14.5	14.8	12/31/84
NON-CONSENSUS REVISION	21.4	21.8	19.1	19.6	11.7	9.1	3.4	1.1	6.8	-8.3	10.4	11.0	9/30/89
FORECAST EP	22.8	24.5	18.8	18.3	12.6	15.2	11.9	12.0	8.7	2.4	14.8	8.0	12/31/84
TRAILING EP	20.2	22.8	17.9	16.0	13.6	10.2	12.5	11.7	6.0	2.4	13.4	6.8	12/31/84
RECENT EARNINGS REVISION	17.0	18.4	14.5	18.1	14.4	11.4	7.0	2.0	7.1	-4.9	10.4	6.6	9/30/89
TRADE MOMENTUM PAST MONTH	18.3	15.1	15.3	16.9	15.9	14.3	12.5	10.5	9.4	10.9	14.0	4.3	12/31/84
STOCK REPURCHASE	15.8	13.1	13.9	11.5	14.2	14.4	15.7	12.4	9.4	9.1	13.4	2.4	12/31/84
MARKET PRICE	16.7	16.0	15.2	16.7	16.1	16.8	15.7	8.7	11.3	14.2	14.8	1.9	12/31/84
18 MONTH RELATIVE RETURN	14.3	16.3	13.5	14.7	14.3	15.5	11.9	11.9	7.5	2.7	12.4	1.9	12/31/84
PV RATIO 2	15.7	20.9	17.6	18.0	16.4	15.1	16.1	14.2	8.1	4.7	14.8	1.0	12/31/84
SALES TO PRICE	13.9	14.0	13.7	15.9	14.5	9.7	13.3	13.1	12.2	7.9	13.0	1.0	12/31/84
EXPECTED RETURN 2	15.7	21.6	17.9	15.9	18.0	16.6	13.8	13.7	8.6	5.3	14.8	0.9	12/31/84
1 QUARTER RELATIVE RETURN	12.8	13.3	13.5	13.0	12.9	15.7	16.0	12.7	13.5	2.9	12.9	0.0	12/31/84
LONG TERM EPS GROWTH	14.0	10.8	12.8	14.0	14.1	14.6	14.8	16.9	14.6	10.7	14.0	-0.1	12/31/84
1 MONTH RELATIVE RETURN	14.0	9.8	14.0	14.2	15.9	17.3	15.6	13.0	15.9	7.2	14.2	-0.1	12/31/82
LTG DISPERSION	13.3	13.0	13.4	12.2	19.6	15.5	15.0	12.9	12.2	11.7	14.0	-0.7	12/31/84
RETURN ON EQUITY	12.4	15.0	16.5	15.4	15.1	15.4	14.2	8.8	10.9	7.0	13.2	-0.8	12/31/84
CASH FLOW TO PRICE	12.2	17.0	16.6	17.4	15.5	12.6	10.8	12.1	9.8	6.6	13.2	-1.0	12/31/84
CURRENT INDICATED YIELD	13.3	19.8	15.6	13.8	13.5	10.6	9.7	10.5	21.0	14.4	14.8	-1.5	12/31/84
HIST EPS GROWTH	12.1	11.9	16.3	15.1	15.5	10.8	15.4	16.5	13.3	10.4	13.9	-1.8	12/31/84
HIST EPS INSTABILITY	12.1	14.2	12.3	12.5	11.9	14.7	16.6	13.5	14.7	15.1	13.9	-1.8	12/31/84
LONG TERM TAX EFFECT	11.6	2.2	10.0	12.3	13.2	15.0	17.2	20.2	18.2	14.3	13.9	-2.3	12/31/84
YEAR 1 EPS YIELD GROWTH	11.5	14.7	16.0	18.3	19.4	17.8	13.1	13.0	12.5	2.6	14.0	-2.5	12/31/84
ANALYST COVERAGE	11.3	13.5	18.5	13.6	16.6	16.3	15.5	12.4	10.1	11.1	14.0	-2.7	12/31/84
INTEREST RATE SENSITIVITY	11.8	14.7	16.0	16.5	15.0	16.7	21.8	12.0	11.6	8.9	14.9	-2.7	12/31/84
LOG OF MKT CAPITALIZATION	11.6	15.0	14.1	13.1	17.3	14.0	12.0	13.3	22.4	11.5	14.8	-3.2	12/31/84
ADJUSTED ANALYST COVERAGE	10.7	14.5	16.7	15.0	16.1	13.4	15.5	12.8	14.2	9.8	14.0	-3.3	12/31/84
SHORT TERM TAX EFFECT	9.7	6.6	14.4	13.8	16.9	16.0	15.9	15.6	15.5	8.8	13.9	-4.1	12/31/84

Table 17.1 Continued

UNIVERSE: SECOND 1000 STOCKS

VALUE FACTOR	1	2	3	4	DECILE 5	6	7	8	9	10	UNIV	SPREAD 1-UNIV	BEGIN DATE
5-YEAR RELATIVE STRENGTH	10.4	16.1	15.7	19.7	18.7	13.8	14.0	10.8	21.5	3.9	14.9	-4.5	12/31/84
BOOK TO PRICE	8.0	16.9	17.0	15.3	12.9	11.1	12.1	13.0	11.8	9.3	12.9	-4.9	12/31/84
HISTORICAL BETA	10.0	12.4	14.2	11.1	12.0	12.2	14.2	17.4	15.5	24.9	14.9	-5.0	12/31/84
DEBT CAPITAL	8.1	12.5	12.0	12.3	13.1	14.6	14.3	16.1	16.1	11.5	13.2	-5.1	12/31/84
TRAILING PE	10.3	12.1	12.7	9.4	15.0	15.8	16.9	17.2	24.5	19.4	15.4	-5.1	12/31/84
TRADING VOLUME PAST MONTH	9.8	16.1	17.5	13.9	12.4	14.0	12.4	13.0	12.8	22.2	14.9	-5.1	12/31/84
FUNDAMENTAL BETA	6.2	13.4	12.6	12.8	13.4	22.7	13.6	14.0	15.7	18.0	14.8	-8.6	12/31/84
MTHLY VOLATILITY PAST 5 YR	6.0	8.1	13.8	11.1	15.8	13.1	13.1	15.5	19.4	28.8	14.9	-8.9	12/31/84
12:MONTH EPS YIELD GROWTH	4.1	8.2	18.0	16.7	15.0	17.6	16.0	11.4	16.2	12.2	13.6	-9.5	3/31/89
TRADING VOLUME PAST QTR	4.9	12.5	15.2	14.9	16.4	12.5	15.3	14.1	14.3	23.4	14.9	-9.9	12/31/84
TREND REVERSAL	2.4	10.5	10.9	12.0	10.9	10.5	14.1	17.4	16.7	18.3	12.4	-10.0	12/31/84
FORECAST PE	4.7	10.1	12.1	10.7	15.8	13.7	15.0	20.3	24.0	22.9	15.2	-10.5	12/31/84
SPECIFIC RISK	3.9	10.9	13.4	13.2	13.6	11.7	15.7	15.7	18.2	29.2	14.9	-11.1	12/31/84
EPS DISPERSION	1.8	11.1	11.8	11.9	16.0	17.1	15.7	24.1	17.4	13.1	14.0	-12.2	12/31/84
WEEKLY VOLATILITY PAST YR	-0.7	8.3	9.1	11.8	15.1	16.3	16.5	13.2	17.3	17.6	12.7	-13.3	12/31/84
DAILY VOLATILITY PAST MTH	-5.7	7.4	12.6	16.1	17.7	18.4	17.3	18.4	18.9	14.3	13.5	-19.2	12/31/84

Table 17.2—Decile Return Report
Linked Return % Annualized—Equal Weighted 12/31/84–12/31/92

UNIVERSE: S&P 500

VALUE FACTOR	1	2	3	4	5	6	7	8	9	10	UNIV	SPREAD 1-UNIV	BEGIN DATE
WEEKLY EARNINGS REVISION	22.9	15.0	9.8	11.9	10.6	12.0	13.5	7.1	7.5	2.2	11.3	11.6	5/31/89
MONTHLY EARNINGS REVISION	18.7	16.3	19.9	10.2	14.6	12.3	6.8	3.2	7.6	2.5	11.3	7.4	5/31/89
EARNINGS REVISION-SURPRISE	23.8	21.1	21.3	20.2	18.3	16.1	13.4	16.0	13.6	2.4	16.7	7.1	12/31/84
EARNINGS YIELD REVISION	15.5	11.9	13.2	12.4	12.9	7.6	8.3	5.0	1.8	-1.2	8.9	6.6	8/31/89
STOCK REPURCHASE	22.6	17.8	16.7	15.7	14.4	15.9	14.5	20.1	12.6	11.6	16.3	6.2	12/31/84
FORECAST EP	22.6	20.3	21.7	17.6	16.1	16.1	15.6	14.7	12.7	8.4	16.8	5.8	12/31/84
RECENT EARNINGS REVISION	15.5	14.3	12.4	14.2	11.9	12.1	7.0	1.3	8.4	0.8	9.9	5.6	9/30/89
TRAILING EP	21.4	19.5	19.1	19.8	16.7	17.0	14.9	13.4	11.8	7.6	16.3	5.1	12/31/84
NON-CONSENSUS REVISION	14.4	17.9	15.0	11.4	10.8	9.3	7.7	4.3	5.4	-0.4	9.7	4.7	9/30/89
TRADE MOMENTUM PAST MONTH	19.4	17.1	17.5	17.7	17.2	16.7	18.7	15.1	13.2	10.4	16.4	3.0	12/31/84
5-YEAR RELATIVE STRENGTH	17.7	18.3	18.2	18.9	17.7	16.1	14.6	14.8	13.5	8.5	16.0	1.7	12/31/84
LOG OF MKT CAPITALIZATION	17.7	15.8	16.2	17.8	16.2	18.2	16.3	17.1	14.1	11.1	16.3	1.5	12/31/84
PV RATIO 2	17.8	20.2	19.1	20.0	20.5	19.4	15.9	14.0	10.0	9.9	16.8	1.1	12/31/84
ANALYST COVERAGE	17.3	14.1	16.1	17.3	15.7	17.5	17.5	17.1	15.7	13.8	16.4	1.0	12/31/84
RETURN ON EQUITY	17.0	18.7	16.9	16.3	18.2	15.7	18.4	14.6	14.1	11.4	16.3	0.7	12/31/84
EXPECTED RETURN 2	17.1	21.3	19.6	19.7	19.2	15.6	16.9	15.8	11.6	9.4	16.8	0.3	12/31/84
CURRENT INDICATED YIELD	16.6	16.6	21.6	20.4	16.0	16.8	16.1	14.6	14.2	8.1	16.3	0.3	12/31/84
18 MONTH RELATIVE RETURN	15.7	15.9	16.1	18.1	16.5	15.0	16.8	18.0	13.8	9.5	15.8	0.3	12/31/84
MARKET PRICE	16.1	16.8	18.8	17.7	18.6	17.9	14.2	17.9	13.5	9.4	16.3	-0.2	12/31/84
CASH FLOW TO PRICE	15.7	15.7	20.0	18.1	14.9	14.7	15.6	13.9	16.8	13.4	16.0	-0.3	12/31/84
HIST EPS GROWTH	16.1	18.6	18.2	20.2	17.9	15.9	15.9	15.2	16.2	12.4	16.8	-0.7	12/31/84
TRADING VOLUME PAST QTR	15.4	13.2	18.3	18.4	18.0	14.4	18.6	14.8	17.3	13.6	16.3	-0.9	12/31/84
TRADING VOLUME PAST MONTH	15.0	15.5	16.6	18.6	18.0	19.9	15.4	14.7	16.1	11.6	16.3	-1.3	12/31/84
INTEREST RATE SENSITIVITY	14.7	17.6	17.9	18.5	17.3	19.8	14.6	15.4	14.8	8.5	16.0	-1.4	12/31/84
1 QUARTER RELATIVE RETURN	13.8	14.2	16.2	14.8	18.1	14.9	18.0	16.9	19.1	10.3	15.8	-2.0	12/31/84
YEAR 1 EPS YIELD GROWTH	13.7	18.5	18.0	19.1	20.2	18.5	17.2	16.3	11.9	8.3	16.3	-2.6	12/31/84
LONG TERM EPS GROWTH	13.7	17.8	17.7	16.6	15.7	16.5	16.2	16.4	15.8	16.2	16.4	-2.7	12/31/84
1 MONTH RELATIVE RETURN	12.9	12.7	16.3	16.9	14.8	20.7	16.3	15.6	16.1	11.6	15.8	-3.0	12/31/84
ADJUSTED ANALYST COVERAGE	13.1	15.2	16.2	18.3	14.8	19.6	17.5	14.4	17.1	16.1	16.4	-3.3	12/31/84
SALES TO PRICE	12.4	14.0	16.9	17.4	16.7	16.3	15.4	16.3	17.8	15.9	16.1	-3.7	12/31/84
BOOK TO PRICE	12.3	20.7	17.6	19.0	14.5	13.4	15.8	15.4	16.8	13.4	16.0	-3.7	12/31/84

Table 17.2 Continued

UNIVERSE: S&P 500

VALUE FACTOR	1	2	3	4	DECILE 5	6	7	8	9	10	UNIV	SPREAD 1-UNIV	BEGIN DATE
TRAILING PE	12.8	11.7	14.8	17.8	16.0	18.8	20.4	17.8	21.3	21.2	17.4	-4.6	12/31/84
LTG DISPERSION	11.4	15.4	15.9	16.3	15.3	17.8	18.3	19.2	17.6	15.8	16.4	-5.0	12/31/84
TREND REVERSAL	10.7	15.2	19.7	16.2	13.9	13.0	16.7	16.5	18.0	16.8	15.8	-5.1	12/31/84
12 MONTH EPS YIELD GROWTH	8.6	13.5	9.0	17.9	17.8	16.8	14.8	14.8	13.8	10.6	13.9	-5.3	3/31/89
HIST EPS INSTABILITY	10.5	17.9	17.0	17.8	15.8	19.3	17.0	19.2	18.0	14.2	16.8	-6.3	12/31/84
FUNDAMENTAL BETA	9.8	12.5	14.5	15.0	13.8	17.2	18.3	19.1	20.2	19.8	16.3	-6.5	12/31/84
HISTORICAL BETA	9.2	14.1	16.5	16.2	16.4	17.3	16.7	16.7	18.4	16.6	16.0	-6.9	12/31/84
SPECIFIC RISK	8.8	12.9	14.3	16.8	16.7	16.9	17.1	20.2	17.4	17.4	16.0	-7.2	12/31/84
LONG TERM TAX EFFECT	8.0	15.1	17.5	16.3	19.6	17.3	16.1	17.7	15.8	10.7	15.6	-7.6	12/31/84
FORECAST PE	9.4	14.1	15.2	16.0	16.3	17.5	17.7	20.7	21.4	22.7	17.2	-7.8	12/31/84
MTHLY VOLATILITY PAST 5 YR	8.2	12.8	15.8	15.4	18.4	15.4	16.2	19.9	19.0	17.0	16.0	-7.8	12/31/84
SHORT TERM TAX EFFECT	7.7	19.9	17.1	18.8	19.6	16.3	15.0	17.5	13.8	8.8	15.6	-7.9	12/31/84
DEBT CAPITAL	7.9	15.6	17.3	17.2	18.1	18.7	14.7	17.4	17.1	16.6	16.2	-8.2	12/31/84
WEEKLY VOLATILITY PAST YR	7.5	12.6	13.7	16.7	18.3	17.0	18.5	18.2	15.8	17.1	15.8	-8.3	12/31/84
DAILY VOLATILITY PAST MTH	7.9	12.5	13.5	21.1	19.3	19.0	17.3	17.1	16.4	17.0	16.3	-8.4	12/31/84
EPS DISPERSION	6.6	12.4	13.5	15.9	17.3	16.9	19.2	17.9	19.9	22.5	16.4	-9.7	12/31/84

Chapter 18

Investing in Small Cap Stocks Using Financial Futures

Richard A. Crowell
President and Managing Director

Anthony W. Ryan
Manager, Global Investments

PanAgora Asset Management, Inc.

INTRODUCTION

Change brings opportunities. In June 1991, Standard and Poor's Corporation introduced the S&P MidCap 400 Index as a companion to the S&P 500 Stock Index. For years, the S&P 500 has served as a performance benchmark for major institutional investors. The S&P MidCap 400 Index extended the accurate measurement of stock performance to the next level of stocks in terms of size.

The introduction of the S&P MidCap 400 Index was a milestone event. It reflected increasing interest on the part of institutional investors in small capitalization (small cap) stocks. Traditionally, securities in this segment of the market have not received the amount of investor's attention that their larger capitalized competitors enjoyed. While it can be argued that MidCap is not "small cap," it is smaller than the S&P 500 and has opened the gates to a stream of small cap indices.

The development of the S&P MidCap 400 Index was followed by the introduction of trading in futures and options on the MidCap Index. This made the benefits of futures trading available to investors interested in mid cap and small cap stocks. Table 18.1 is a list of currently available futures and options on small cap and mid cap market indices. Futures trading has grown rapidly so that a large and liquid market is now available in S&P MidCap futures. Figure 18.1 shows the close relationship between the S&P MidCap 400 Index and the price of its futures. Figure 18.2 shows the level of trading in these futures. The February 1993, volume of trading of 677 futures contracts per day is equivalent to trading about $54,000,000 of MidCap stocks. The open interest of 9,412 futures contracts is equivalent to about $753,000,000 of MidCap stocks.

Table 18.1—Small Capitalization and Mid Cap Derivatives

Index	Derivatives	Exchange
S&P 400 MidCap	Futures	Chicago Mercantile Exchange
	Options on futures	Chicago Mercantile Exchange
	Index options	American Stock Exchange
Russell 2000	Futures	Chicago Mercantile Exchange
	Options on futures	Chicago Mercantile Exchange
	Index options	Chicago Board Options Exchange
Wilshire Small Cap	Futures	Chicago Board of Trade
	Option on futures	Chicago Board of Trade
	Index options	Pacific Stock Exchange
Value Line	Futures	Kansas City Board of Trade
	Index options	Philadelphia Stock Exchange

INVESTING IN SMALL CAP STOCKS

Typically, investors consider small cap stocks from one of two perspectives: (1) stock selection, and (2) the "small cap performance effect." Some investors look at small capitalization stocks as the ultimate stock selection opportunity. They diligently research the background and prospects for

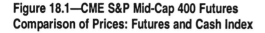

**Figure 18.1—CME S&P Mid-Cap 400 Futures
Comparison of Prices: Futures and Cash Index**

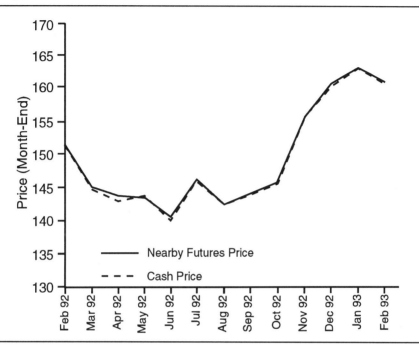

companies of potential interest. They search technical journals looking for breakthrough technological innovations. They watch trade shows for exciting new product offerings. They listen to advice from Wall Street experts and from their friends. The objective is to find the next Microsoft, Apple Computer, or even the next infant IBM. Investors who are lucky enough or smart enough to hit the big winner earn huge rewards. Of course, for every stock winner, there are losers that no one wants to remember. But that is the risk and reward of stock selection.

Other investors are interested in the "small cap performance effect." This is the well-documented tendency of small cap stocks to provide higher returns to investors over time. Consider the following data. Over the period from 1900 to 1992, small cap stocks outperformed big cap stocks by 10.1% to 8.1%. This small cap premium of 2.0% per year compounds to huge extra value over the years. Of course, small cap stocks do not outperform every single day, month, or year. There are long periods of underperformance when bigger stocks provide higher returns. Nevertheless, over many years, the small cap performance effect has been powerful and should be of interest to investors.

**Figure 18.2—CME S&P Mid-Cap 400 Futures
Monthly Trading Volume and Open Interest**

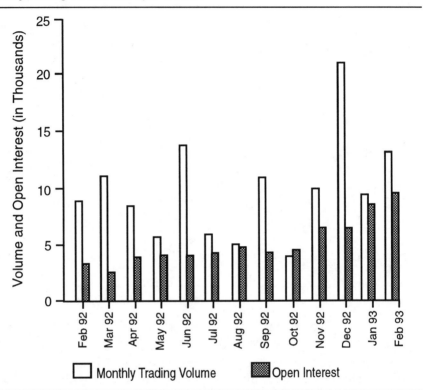

To capture the superior performance of the small cap performance effect, investors must hold a diversified portfolio of small cap stocks, perhaps a hundred or more stocks. Owning only a few small cap stocks does
not provide adequate diversification. A portfolio of a few small cap stocks
may do very well, much better than the small cap performance effect, *or* its
performance may be terrible. Most individual investors do not have the
financial resources to hold the number of securities required to capture the
small cap performance effect in a systematic way. Fortunately, there are
multiple ways to capture this effect. Mutual funds are one alternative. Mid
cap and small cap stock index futures and derivatives are another.

Both small cap stock pickers and investors capturing the small cap performance effect can successfully use futures to enhance return and reduce
investment risk. Since the composition of the financial marketplace is anything but homogeneous, there are numerous potential users of mid cap

and small cap futures contracts, including passive index funds (in the form of institutional commingled funds and mutual funds), active small cap investment managers, locals, and Wall Street brokerage houses.

WHAT IS A STOCK INDEX FUTURE?

Briefly, a future is a contractual obligation to buy or sell a market index at a specific date in the future. A stock index future must be traded on a futures exchange through an auction process. Initial margin is required as a good-faith deposit by the investor. This deposit is required by the futures exchange and deposited with your broker. The initial margin may be in cash or in securities. Exchanges typically set the initial margin requirements at 5% to 10% of the underlying value of the stock index. A change in the price of the future causes a daily mark-to-market. This is a daily cash flow in or out of your margin account depending on whether your futures position made or lost money each day. The cash flow occurs each morning based on yesterday's price change of the futures contract. This cash flow is called the variation margin.

Futures prices are set by auction trading. The fair value of an index future can be calculated from the price of the index which, in turn, depends on the prices of the stocks in the index. The theory of futures pricing is simple. Over the life of the future, there is an arbitrage between (1) the strategy of holding all the stocks in the index and (2) the strategy of holding Treasury bills and buying the future. The return from strategy (1) and strategy (2) should be identical. By definition, on expiration date, the future is priced at the same price as the underlying stock index. Since Treasury bill interest rates are often higher than dividend yields on stocks, this means the current value of the future must be *slightly higher* than the current price of the index. That is, between now and expiration date, the future must drop down to the price of the index by an amount sufficient to offset the extra yield on Treasury bills. Otherwise, holding Treasury bills and the future would exceed the return of holding the stocks.

For example, on March 16, 1993, the S&P MidCap 400 Index closed at $163.87. There were 95 days to the expiration of the June futures contract. Assuming Treasury bill interest rates of 3.17%, Treasury bills would earn $1.37 between March 16 and June. The dividend yield on the index was 1.92%, and dividends expected over the next 95 days were worth $0.83. The difference in income, $1.37 - $0.83, is $0.54 so the fair value of the futures contract is the closing price of the index plus $0.54 = $163.87 + $0.54 = $164.41.

The equation for the price of a stock index future is:

$$F = S * (1 + r - d)^t$$

where F = price of the future
       S = price of the stock index
       r = risk-free interest rate
       d = dividend yield on the stock index
       t = fraction of year until the expiration of the future

While this chapter is primarily about futures, many of the applications can be implemented with index options and/or options on futures. The primary differences are that (1) the payoff pattern of options is different, and (2) options may be more convenient for individual investors since options do not require the daily mark-to-market process.

USING FUTURES FOR SMALL CAP INVESTING

The many uses for the small cap and mid cap index futures contracts reflect the diverse universe of investors and their strategies. This chapter identifies five potential strategies for trading the small cap and mid cap futures. These strategies include cash management, arbitrage, transition management, asset allocation, and speculation.

Equitizing Cash

Many investors in small cap stocks almost always leave a substantial portion of their assets in cash while they search for the next small cap stock investment. This makes no sense for investors who believe that stocks, especially small cap stocks, will provide superior returns to cash. Investors who believe stocks will outperform cash should remain fully invested in stocks lest their portfolios lag the positive performance of stocks. Suppose a very optimistic small cap investor expects small cap stocks to return 20% per year. At the same time, suppose money market funds are earning 4% per year. If the investor has 25% of assets in cash in the money market fund and 75% in small stocks, the total expected portfolio return is 75% of 20% plus 25% of 4%, for a total expected return of 16% (0.75 * 20% + 0.25 * 4% = 15% + 1% = 16%). By not investing the cash in small cap stocks, the investor is suffering an opportunity loss of 4% per year (20% for stocks − 16% for the portfolio = 4% in opportunity loss).

Of course, there are other reasons for holding cash, such as that mutual fund managers must cover redemptions and expenses. However, this cash component of the portfolio can easily be hedged so that it does not lag the return of the index during a rising market. Cash may also be held for defensive reasons. An investor worried about a market correction will want to raise cash. Defensive cash is covered below under the topic of asset allocation.

The following example demonstrates the specifics of using futures to equitize cash (see Table 18.2). The basic calculations are straightforward. This example is based on a portfolio designed to track the S&P MidCap 400 Index, i.e., an index fund portfolio. The same principles apply to small cap portfolios. Suppose the $100 Million S&P MidCap 400 Index portfolio has 90% of the portfolio in stocks and 10% in cash.

Example:

August 31, 1992   SPM Closing Price: $142.71
December 31, 1992   SPM Closing Price: $160.55

The capital appreciation (price change) of the S&P MidCap 400 Index from August 31 to December 31 was 12.50%. Since the portfolio's equity exposure was only 90%, the portfolio's price change would be $11,250,000. This is calculated as follows:

(160.55/142.72) * $90,000,000 = $101,250,000

$101,250,000 – $90,000,000 = $11,250,000

Neglecting dividends and interest, the final portfolio value on December 31, 1992, would equal $111,250,000. This would represent an 11.25% gain for the overall portfolio. The return of the portfolio would lag the Index return by 125 basis points (1.25%) or $1,250,000 on the original $100 million portfolio.

The cause of this underperformance can be removed by simply hedging the cash exposure by purchasing stock index futures contracts. In this case, purchasing 140 MidCap futures contracts hedges the 10% cash component and the portfolio would have 100 % equity exposure. The number of contracts required to hedge the cash component is calculated in a straightforward manner. Keep in mind that an S&P MidCap futures contract is 500 times the S&P MidCap 400 Index. This is equivalent to saying that one contract is equivalent to 500 "shares" of the S&P MidCap 400 Stock Index.

Number of futures contracts = $ Amount to be Hedged/(500 * Index Level)
                            = $10,000,000 / (500 * 142.71)
                            = 140 S&P MidCap futures contracts

Since the futures contract will provide virtually the same return as the index, with 140 S&P MidCap contracts, the price change of the portfolio would then equal (or very close to equal) the price change of the S&P MidCap 400 Stock Index.

Table 18.2—CME S&P MidCap 400 Futures

	Monthly Volume	Average Daily Volume	Month-end Open Interest	Month-end Futures Price (nearby)	Month-end Cash Price
Feb 92	8,753	796	3,205	151.00	151.02
Mar 92	10,872	494	2,416	144.95	145.11
Apr 92	7,991	381	3,737	143.80	143.15
May 92	5,611	281	3,912	143.90	144.20
Jun 92	13,225	601	3,851	140.70	139.86
Jul 92	5,754	262	4,163	146.70	146.54
Aug 92	4,915	234	4,789	142.80	142.71
Sep 92	10,953	522	4,163	144.70	144.48
Oct 92	3,777	172	4,335	147.40	147.70
Nov 92	9,964	498	6,529	155.60	155.62
Dec 92	20,893	950	6,618	161.05	160.56
Jan 93	9,308	465	8,398	162.40	162.35
Feb 93	12,868	677	9,412	160.00	159.77

Source: Chicago Mercantile Exchange.

Well-managed index funds that must track the indices closely use this same process to hedge dividends that are declared but not yet paid. The total return or performance of the index includes not only the capital appreciation or loss caused by price changes, but also the income received in the form of dividend payments. To closely track the index, these dividend accruals must be hedged when the dividend is declared on ex-dividend date.

By equitizing cash, portfolio managers minimize the difference between the total return of the portfolio and the index. This difference is known as tracking variance. The total amount of dividends and cash must be hedged in order to minimize tracking variance. Since most investors expect stocks to outperform cash, buying futures to equitize their cash reserves results in substantial annual profits.

Arbitrage

While brokerage firms will continue to execute trades in individual stocks on behalf of their institutional and retail clients, they will also trade the mid cap and small cap futures contracts in order to control inventory risk, and to profit from the opportunities that arise as a result of arbitrage situations, both for their proprietary desks and their clients.

In the futures and cash markets, the potential for arbitrage exists when the current prices of the futures contracts are not in line with the expected fair value relative to the underlying cash market. The fair value of any futures contract is based on the underlying index level, as well as current short-term interest rates and the yield of the index.

The primary reason for participating in an arbitrage trade is to make a profit without market risk, and the greatest potential for profit exists when the markets are inefficient. Inefficiency means different things to different people. To an arbitrageur, inefficiency means the ability to execute the trade and still lock in the profit after market impact and commissions are taken into account.

For example, a significant opportunity existed to profit from this situation when the S&P 500 futures contacts were first introduced in 1982. Many firms made a great deal of money based upon their ability to detect mispricings between the futures contract and the underlying securities, and their ability to execute the necessary trades in both the futures and cash markets.

Over time, the markets have become much more efficient at fairly valuing futures contracts. Consequently, opportunities for arbitrage profit are now very limited, forcing some firms to cease participation. The primary reason for the increased efficiency is the continued introduction of faster, more powerful technology and communications. The inefficiencies are discovered more quickly, trades are filled faster, and the opportunities are exploited.

An arbitrage trade is relatively easy when trading a S&P 500 basket on a Super DOT Machine at the NYSE. However, executing a S&P MidCap basket is not as easy. This is primarily due to the differences in the two indices. Over 90% of the capitalization on the S&P 500 Index is traded at the NYSE. However, only 60% of the MidCap is traded at the NYSE. Over 30% of the securities in the MidCap Index are traded over-the-counter and are not available to electronic trading.

Trading in the OTC market is quite different than trading at the NYSE. It is not conducive to electronic trading capabilities and is, therefore, less efficient and potentially more profitable from an arbitrageur's point of view.

Transition Management

The small cap and mid cap futures contracts also provide an excellent vehicle for the implementation of transition management. These futures can be traded to facilitate the liquidation or construction of a long stock portfolio of small or mid cap stocks. This situation exists when an investor desires to purchase a small cap or mid cap stock portfolio, and is presently long some other basket of stocks. Futures enable the portfolio manager to liquidate the undesirable securities in such a fashion as to minimize the cost associated with the liquidation, while maintaining small cap or mid cap market exposure at the same time. As the securities are liquidated, futures would be purchased to hedge the sale proceeds.

The futures contracts can also be used to permit the investor to move from cash to a long stock portfolio or vice versa. Many brokerage firms will quote a spread—effectively a transaction price or fee—to trade a futures position for the underlying securities in the index, either by going long futures/short stock, or short futures/long stock. This type of trade, known as a basis trade or Exchange for Physical (EFP), is often a very economical way to gain or reduce exposure to the equity market.

Asset Allocation

Asset allocations can also be implemented in an efficient fashion through the utilization of futures trading. Futures contracts can be used to establish a strategic equity allocation, as well as increase or decrease that exposure based on a tactical asset allocation model. The existence of small cap and mid cap futures contracts creates at least two distinct opportunities.

First, the investor can gain equity exposure to nearly the entire equity market, large as well as smaller stocks, by purchasing a combination of the S&P 500, S&P MidCap and small cap futures in the appropriate quantities. The quantities would be determined by the relative capitalizations of each of the benchmarks. Collectively, the two S&P indexes represent greater than 90% of the capitalization of the U.S. equity market (S&P 500 75%, MidCap 15%) and small cap represents the remaining 10%.

Second, the futures also serve as vehicles to increase or decrease equity exposure in a cost-effective and efficient manner. The futures contracts will be utilized by portfolio managers desiring to make certain sector bets, not in the traditional sense with respect to industries, but with respect to capitalization sectors.

Traditional active managers of small cap portfolios will trade small cap and mid cap futures contracts to hedge cash, maintain exposure until trading opportunities exist, and to control the risk of poor relative performance if the manager's performance is judged relative to a market index of small cap stocks. By being long the futures contracts, the active manager effectively locks in the return of the index.

Speculation (as in Investing)

For most investors, the basic position is owning an asset. Here, the bet is that the price will go up. In the parlance of futures, this is a standard "long" position. The two other important positions are "short," selling an asset that you don't own in the expectation of falling prices, and "hedged." A "hedged" position is almost equivalent to holding cash because the portfolio value doesn't change if stock prices advance or decline. In the language of futures, a hedger typically owns an asset and sells a future against this owned position. A "speculator," on the other hand, believes that the price will move, up or down, and invests accordingly. A long speculator believes prices will rise and goes long in the futures market. Thus, a long speculator is simply an investor who invests in the expectation of rising prices.

All this is a long-winded way of saying that futures on small cap and mid cap stock index futures are an alternative way of investing in (going long) small cap and mid cap stocks. The procedure is simple: keep assets in cash equivalents and buy stock index futures on the index of interest to you. Your realized performance will then be very close to the performance of the index over the period the future is held. Of course, each future has an expiration date (comparable to a maturity date). So it is necessary to "roll" into the next date future on or before this date.

CONCLUSION

Trading in stock index futures is booming all around the world. In the U.S. and Japan, the underlying value of trading in futures *exceeds* trading in securities. As a result, well-developed, liquid futures markets are available for a variety of investment purposes. Investors in small cap stocks can take advantage of stock index futures to enhance their investment returns and to reduce investment risk in at least five different ways, including equitizing cash, arbitrage, transition into or out of long stock positions, asset allocation, and simply investing in expectation of higher prices. These tools are already several years old and have proven their value under a variety of market circumstances.

PART FIVE: INTERNATIONAL OPPORTUNITIES IN SMALL CAP INVESTING

Chapter 19

Indexing International Small Cap Stocks

Brian R. Bruce
Vice President and Unit Head

Peter G. Leahy
Vice President

State Street Bank and Trust Company

INTRODUCTION

As international investing continues to grow, small capitalization equities have emerged as an attractive market segment that can increase overall portfolio diversification. Small cap international stocks offer the potential for excess returns over full market cycles. In addition, their low correlation with other asset classes can reduce overall portfolio volatility.

A small cap international index fund provides international equity exposure beyond the capitalization ranges generally covered by the major international indices. With trading costs approximately double those of the larger cap issues, a low turnover strategy such as indexing has an enormous advantage over an active approach.

SMALL CAP INDEX CHARACTERISTICS

Several small cap international indices exist. We will concentrate on the Salomon-Russell Extended Market Index (EMI) as the benchmark index. This index is well-supported and disciplined in its construction methodology. Salomon Brothers and the Frank Russell Company have both committed significant resources to this project in order to ensure its success. The construction methodology is rigorous and publicly available. It is also user-friendly, which should make it easier to track. The EMI offers the greatest distinction in terms of capitalization coverage, industry representation, and the lowest correlation with EAFE of the various alternatives.

The EMI index has several other desirable characteristics. There is a corridor that has been established to reduce turnover from a pure capitalization screen. This means that a stock will not arbitrarily leave the EMI index because it has reached a specific capitalization level unless certain buffer levels are exceeded. Secondly, extensive efforts have been made to adjust for cross-holdings, thereby achieving a proxy for the investable universe. This adjustment is updated on an ongoing basis.

The EAFE Index, by comparison, is designed to capture approximately the largest 60% of the market capitalization in each of the 18 countries in the index. Combining the EAFE and the EMI-EPAC indices significantly increases overall market exposure. Small cap international index funds offer effective, low-cost exposure to the bottom 20% of the available international small capitalization equity universe.

The EMI-EPAC Index has an average market cap that is U.S.$2.6 billion less than the EAFE Index and holds nearly twice as many securities (see Table 19.1). Four hundred twenty-seven stocks, which comprise 24% of the EMI Index, are also included in the EAFE Index. To avoid duplication with existing EAFE exposures, small cap funds can be created without EAFE stocks. Table 19.1 shows a detailed capitalization comparison between the EMI and EAFE indices. A breakdown by market is shown in Table 19.2.

Table 19.1—Capitalization Comparison

	MSCI EAFE	SR EMI EPAC	SR EMI EPAC (EX EAFE)	Overlap (EAFE+EPAC)
# Stocks	1,050	2,210	1,770	440
Total Cap	3,075 B	591* B	430* B	161* b (27%)
Avg. Cap	2.9 B	267 MM	243 MM	367 MM
Wtd. Avg. Cap	13.5 B	556 MM	471 MM	785 MM

* Available

**Table 19.2—EMI-EPAC Index Composition by Country
March 31, 1991**

Market	# of Securities	Average Capitalization U.S.$ Millions	% of EMI EPAC	% of MSCI EAFE
Austria	13	118	0.2	0.6
Belgium	30	170	0.9	1.3
Denmark	31	141	0.7	0.8
Finland	2	100	0.0	0.3
France	123	265	5.5	6.7
Germany	126	327	7.0	7.4
Ireland	8	150	0.2	0.0
Italy	99	133	2.2	2.4
Netherlands	52	446	3.9	3.2
Norway	18	72	0.2	0.4
Spain	46	208	1.6	2.5
Sweden	37	140	0.9	1.7
Switzerland	114	157	3.0	3.7
United Kingdom	346	423	24.8	19.1
Europe	**1,045**	**289**	**51.1**	**50.0**
Australia	52	309	2.7	3.0
Hong Kong	44	290	2.2	2.5
Japan	1,018	247	42.7	42.7
Malaysia	27	125	0.6	0.0
New Zealand	5	120	0.1	0.3
Singapore	19	184	0.6	1.4
Pacific	1,165	247	48.9	50.5
TOTAL	**2,210**	**267**	**100.0**	**100.0**

RISKS AND RETURNS

Small cap international stocks offer many of the same portfolio benefits as found with U.S. small stocks. Historical results (Figure 19.1) would suggest that they offer the potential for excess returns over a market cycle. Figure 19.2 shows a significant outperformance in all the major markets, including Japan, the UK, France and Germany, over the period 1974 to 1989.

The low correlation with other asset classes should reduce overall portfolio volatility. Table 19.3 shows that the FT Small has the lowest correlation to the S&P 500 of any other index listed.

The relative liquidity of small cap stocks makes them ideal for indexing. With trading costs approximately double those of larger cap issues (Table 19.4) low turnover strategies such as indexing have an enormous advantage over any active approach.

Figure 19.2 and Table 19.5 show the superior returns of small versus large caps.

Figure 19.1—EMI EPAC versus MSCI EAFE Performance* March 31, 1991

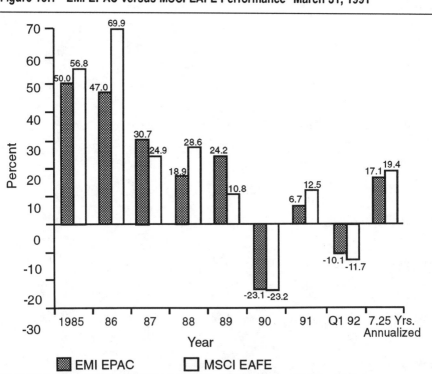

Figure 19.2—International Small Cap Effect (Jan. 1978–Dec. 1991)

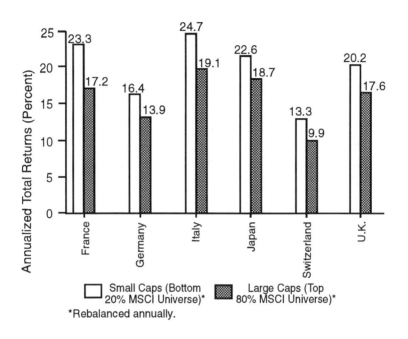

Small Caps (Bottom 20% MSCI Universe)*   Large Caps (Top 80% MSCI Universe)*

*Rebalanced annually.

Table 19.3—Correlation Matrix

	MSCI WORLD	EMI WORLD	MSCI EAFE	EMI EPAC	S&P 500	RUSSELL 2000	FT SMALL EUR+PACB
MSCI WORLD	1.00						
EMI WORLD	0.96	1.00					
MSCI EAFE	0.97	0.92	1.00				
EMI EPAC	0.90	0.93	0.95	1.00			
S&P 500	0.75	0.75	0.56	0.47	1.00		
RUSSELL 2000	0.57	0.64	0.38	0.32	0.89	1.00	
FT SMALL EUR+PACB	0.91	0.92	0.97	0.99	0.47	0.32	1.00
STD DEV	19.07	19.56	24.14	26.87	16.20	20.30	29.01

Based on monthly returns from June 89 through December 91

Table 19.4—EMI Cost Analysis—9/91

	Estimated Bid/Ask Spread
Australia	100.0
Austria	180.0
Belgium	125.0
Denmark	120.0
Finland	300.0
France	75.0
Germany	60.0
Hong Kong	75.0
Ireland	85.0
Italy	80.0
Japan	70.0
Malaysia	75.0
The Netherlands	65.0
New Zealand	65.0
Norway	105.0
Singapore	100.0
Spain	80.0
Sweden	150.0
Switzerland	70.0
United Kingdom	120.0

ACTIVE OR PASSIVE?

There are many reasons to index small capitalization stocks. Among the most important is the greater market coverage from indexing. An indexer will hold all of the issues in a particular index, while an active manager will typically hold a very small subset. Another reason is lower turnover. Indexes typically turn over 5% to 10% per year. An active manager will have turnover that can be ten times greater. With bid-ask spreads ranging from 60 to 300 basis points, an equity must have a very superior return relative to the index to justify the cost of trading. An index fund can also be invested more easily due to the reduced liquidity requirements involved in buying many names. Take, as an example, a $50 million investment. Spread across the EMI index, the trade will be only 42% of average daily volumes; 95% of the trade can be done in less than one day's volume. This is in marked contrast to an active portfolio. Also, by holding many names, the consistency of the small cap bias can be ensured. Finally, pas-

Table 19.5—Bottom 20% versus Top 80% Rebalanced Annually

	AUD	ATS	BEF	DKK	FIM	FRF	DEM	HKD	ITL	JPY	NLG	NZD	NOK	SGD	ESP	SEK	CHF	UKS	PORT	USD
Small vs. Large [Annlzd Diff] Basis Points	(250)	(100)	680	(349)	760	611	242	149	557	393	(494)	2200	NA	198	215	516	342	253	389	58
# Yrs Small Outperformed Large	3	6	7	5	3	8	9	8	10	8	6	3	–	7	6	5	10	8	7	8
# Yrs Small Under-performed Large	11	8	7	9	1	6	5	6	4	6	8	1	–	7	8	9	4	6	7	6
# Small Companies In Beginning Prd	13	1	5	1	5	15	18	3	11	43	6	4	1	6	4	4	6	25	162	2000
# Small Companies In End Period	18	4	7	5	7	26	25	11	28	97	9	3	6	13	13	13	21	45	351	2000
—Bottom 20%—																				
High Cap	153	139	374	176	96	434	332	174	161	1104	294	45	108	149	159	282	125	553	1104	–
Low Cap	16	28	143	40	31	50	20	45	39	244	89	29	94	25	22	113	24	46	22	–
Ave Cap	82	109	277	111	66	264	174	88	96	719	195	36	103	94	108	161	82	345	388	–
(Millions)																				

sive managers charge lower management fees. These fees are a direct hurdle for managers trying to outperform the index.

CONCLUSION

Small cap international index funds offer the opportunity to further diversify existing international exposure beyond the capitalization ranges generally covered by the major international indexes. Their ability to provide exposure to a new asset class with attractive transaction costs and management fees make them an investment all plan sponsors should consider.

Chapter 20

The Small Country Effect

Michael Keppler
President
Keppler Asset Management, Inc.

Heydon Traub
Senior Vice President
State Street Global Advisors

INTRODUCTION: A SIMPLE BUT REWARDING TECHNIQUE: EQUAL WEIGHTING*

A simple technique that has been used by many successful investors who are aware of the difficulty of realistic return estimates—especially for individual securities—is the equal weighting of each security in a portfolio.[1] A comparison of the annual price change of all companies included in the S&P 500 Index demonstrates the superiority of equal weighting over market-capitalization weighting: Over the 34 years through the end of 1991, an investor who bought the same dollar amount in each stock included in the S&P 500 Index[2] achieved almost three times the capital gains of an index investor who acted on the assumption of modern portfolio theory that a

---

*The authors thank Nicholas A. Lopardo, who made this joint study possible.

Table 20.1—S&P 425/500 Index Risk and Return Analysis (1958–1991)

Year	Annual Price Return S&P 425/500 Index Capitalization Weighted (CW) %	Annual Price Return S&P 425/500 Index Equally Weighted (EW) %	Return Difference (EW−CW) %	S&P 425/500 Index CW Cumulative Price Return (12/57=100)	S&P 425/500 Index EW Cumulative Price Return (12/57=100)
				100	100
1958	37.6	44.8	7.2	138	145
1959	9.4	16.2	6.8	151	168
1960	−4.7	1.0	5.7	143	170
1961	23.1	26.9	3.8	177	216
1962	−12.8	−14.5	−1.7	154	184
1963	9.5	20.5	11.0	169	222
1964	24.0	15.5	−8.5	209	257
1965	9.9	25.5	15.6	230	322
1966	−13.5	−10.7	2.8	199	288
1967	23.3	41.9	18.6	245	408
1968	7.5	21.7	14.2	263	497
1969	−10.2	−16.7	−6.5	237	414
1970	−0.6	−2.5	−1.9	235	403
1971	11.7	14.6	2.9	263	462
1972	15.6	12.4	−3.2	304	520
1973	−17.4	−18.2	−0.8	251	425
1974	−29.7	−25.0	4.7	176	319
1975	31.6	47.9	16.3	232	471
1976	19.2	28.1	8.9	277	604
1977	−11.5	−6.0	5.5	245	568
1978	1.1	2.5	1.4	247	582
1979	12.3	22.1	9.8	278	710
1980	25.8	25.2	−0.6	350	890
1981	−9.7	−0.9	8.8	316	882
1982	14.8	23.8	9.0	362	1091
1983	17.3	23.7	6.4	425	1350
1984	1.4	−1.2	−2.6	431	1334
1985	26.3	26.1	−0.2	544	1682
1986	14.6	12.2	−2.4	624	1887
1987	2.0	0.8	−1.2	636	1902
1988	12.4	13.9	1.5	715	2167
1989	27.3	21.6	−5.7	911	2635
1990	−6.6	−14.1	−7.5	851	2263
1991	26.3	32.4	6.1	1074	2996

Note: 1958–1971 S&P 425 Index, 1972–1992 S&P 500 Index
Source: Tweedy, Browne (1992)

market capitalization-weighted portfolio offers the best risk-adjusted return. The annual results of both the equally and market capitalization-weighted S&P Index are shown in Table 20.1.

SOME THOUGHTS ON RISK AND RETURN OF THE S&P 500 INDEX

A superficial review of the thirty-four-year test results may suggest that even though an equally weighted portfolio of S&P stocks returned 3.65% more in capital gains on average per year than a capitalization-weighted index, this was possible only at the cost of an increase in volatility[3] and therefore may not be all that desirable, even though the return/volatility trade-off was positive. However, a more thorough analysis of risk and return shows that it is only the volatility north of the zero-return line that increases with the equally weighted portfolio (see Table 20.2). The higher

Table 20.2—S&P 425/500 Index Risk and Return Analysis (1958–1991)

Risk & Return Measures	S&P 425/500 Index CW	S&P 425/500 Index EW	Value Added
Compound Annual Price Return (%)	7.23	10.52	3.28
Average Annual Price Return (%)	8.45	12.10	3.65
Standard Deviation (%)	15.80	18.47	2.68
Probability of Gain (%)	70.6	70.6	0
Average Gain in Winning Years (%)	16.83	21.72	4.89
Expectation of Gain (%)	11.88	15.33	3.45
Probability of Loss (%)	29.4	29.4	0
Average Loss in Losing Years (%)	−11.67	−10.98	0.69
Expectation of Loss (%)	−3.43	−3.23	0.20
Highest Annual Return (%)	37.60	47.90	10.30
Lowest Annual Return (%)	−29.70	−25.00	4.70
Probability of Highest Annual Performance (%)	38.2	61.8	23.53
Number of Years	34	34	NA
Number of Winning Years	24	24	0
Number of Losing Years	10	10	0
Number of Years with Highest Return	13	21	8
Risk−Adjusted Return (Keppler−Ratio)			
− Return per Unit of Expectation of Loss	2.46	3.75	1.29
Volatility−Adjusted Return (Sharpe−Ratio)			
− Return per Unit of Standard Deviation	0.53	0.66	0.12

Note: 1958–1971 S&P 425 Index, 1972–1992 S&P 500 Index

average gain in winning years, the higher expectation of gain, the smaller average loss in losing years, the larger highest annual return, and the higher lowest annual return indicate

1. A significant enough shift in the return distribution to the right to render the standard deviation unusable as a risk measure,[4] and
2. Positive skewness of the return distribution of the equally weighted S&P Index. In a non-symmetrical distribution, volatility measures, such as the standard deviation or the variance of return, are not suitable.

    Therefore, the Sharpe ratio is not accurate and should not be applied. Since many investors do apply volatility measures, regardless of the shape of the return distribution, they should be aware that the standard deviation of returns is misleading as a risk measure in direct proportion to the skewness of the return distribution. This means that, in the case of negative skewness, the Sharpe ratio shows a lower than actual risk, whereas in cases where the return distribution is positively skewed, the Sharpe ratio indicates more risk than there actually is.[5]

The results in Table 20.2 suggest that the equally weighted portfolio of S&P stocks dominates the market capitalization-weighted S&P portfolio. Why did we choose equal weighting? Equal weighting, which gives the same weight to small cap and large cap issues, can serve as a proxy for small capitalization investing. This technique allows investors to reap a large part of the performance advantages of small capitalization investing without having to have any knowledge of specifics, such as the size or the expected rates of return of the investments. Nevertheless, the investor has to make sure that there is sufficient liquidity to buy the individual securities without moving the price and that the bid-ask spread is not prohibitive. Details on the application of equal weighting to country selection for global equity portfolios are given at the end of this chapter.

EQUAL WEIGHTING OF NATIONAL EQUITY MARKETS

When we analyzed national equity market returns, we found that the same principles that were found with individual U.S. stocks can be applied to national equity markets: An equally weighted world index has a higher expected rate of return than a market capitalization-weighted world index. Our analysis was based on the returns of the 18 markets included in the Morgan Stanley Capital International (MSCI) World Index:[6]

Australia	Germany	Singapore/Malaysia
Austria	Hong Kong	Spain
Belgium	Italy	Sweden
Canada	Japan	Switzerland
Denmark	Netherlands	United Kingdom
France	Norway	U.S.A.

During the 20-year period ending in December 1989, the total return in local currencies (including reinvested gross dividends) was 15.51% for the equally weighted world index and 12.14% for the market capitalization-weighted MSCI World Index. The same relationship holds for a U.S. dollar investor: Over the same twenty-year test period, the total annual compound return of the equally weighted world index was 16.69%, beating by 3.43% the market capitalization-weighted MSCI World Index, which returned 13.26% per year in U.S. dollar terms.

When we first realized this relationship, we believed that it could be due only to the fact that smaller markets tend to have higher returns than larger markets. A more detailed analysis of the major markets was required to prove our ideas. At that time we also believed that, if we were right, the benefits of what we dubbed *The Small Country Effect* should even exceed those of equal weighting, since it was obvious that equal weighting can only partially exploit the small-(market) size effect.

A WELCOME COINCIDENCE

It was a welcome coincidence that we received a call in mid-1992 from the editors of this book, asking us for a contribution. That to us provided the impetus to the more detailed study on market size and returns in the global equities arena that is described below.

On the assumption that the odds of beating global stock market indices can be turned to the investor's favor by concentrating global equity investments in markets with below-average capitalization, we tested a number of buy-and-sell strategies over the 16 1/2 year period ending in June 1992,[7] constructing hypothetical portfolios made up of MSCI country indices.

SMALL COUNTRY INVESTING: DATA AND METHODOLOGY

Three portfolios were constructed, each consisting of six national markets according to the size of their market capitalization:

1. Large Size Markets Portfolio (*Portfolio 1*),
2. Medium Size Markets Portfolio (*Portfolio 2*),
3. Small Size Markets Portfolio (*Portfolio 3*),

The hypothetical portfolios were constructed with equal initial investments in each market, regrouped according to their market capitalization, and rebalanced to equal investments in each national market at the end of each quarter. The quarterly total returns for the various portfolios were calculated as the arithmetic average of the quarterly total returns of the national MSCI indices included in each portfolio. Total returns were calculated with gross dividends reinvested, as published by Morgan Stanley Capital International Perspective.

RESULTS: GENERIC, RATHER THAN TIME-SPECIFIC

Following are the most important findings of the analyses in local currencies detailed in Table 20.3:

1. In terms of their total annual compounded returns, *Portfolios 1, 2,* and *3* finished in the expected order: *Portfolio 3*—investing in the smallest markets in terms of their market capitalization—resulted in the highest total return (19.19%), 3.4 percentage points above the total return for the equally weighted benchmark index and 6.52% above the conventional benchmark, the market capitalization-weighted MSCI World Index, while *Portfolio 1*—investing in the largest national markets—resulted in the lowest total return (11.9%). The results are shown graphically in Figure 20.1.

    In terms of their total cumulative returns, during the 16 1/2 years ending in June 1992, an investment of 100 local currency units in *Portfolios 1, 2,* and *3* grew to 640, 1,118, and 1,811, respectively, while the same investments in the equally and market capitalization-weighted world indices grew to 1,123 and 716 local currency units (see Figure 20.2).

2. The average quarterly returns achieved with *Portfolios 1, 2,* and *3* were also negatively correlated with their size rankings: Returning 4.82%, *Portfolio 3* again beat the two other size portfolios and the two benchmark indices. The equally weighted benchmark index again occupied a middle position between the returns of *Size Portfolios 1* and *3* with a return of 4.02%, while *Portfolio 1* resulted in the lowest return: 3.11%. The latter also underperformed the market capitalization-weighted benchmark, which returned 3.31% per quarter.

Table 20.3—The Small Country Effect in Local Currencies
Dec 31, 1975–June 30, 1992

Risk & Return Characteristics *	MSCI World Index CW	MSCI World Index EW	Large Size Markets	Medium Size Markets	Small Size Markets
Compound Annual Return (%)	12.67	15.79	11.90	15.76	19.19
Average Quarterly Return (%)	3.31	4.02	3.11	4.13	4.82
Highest Quarterly Return (%)	17.16	18.42	16.76	22.47	22.90
Lowest Quarterly Return (%)	−23.80	−28.35	−25.41	−32.66	−26.96
Probability of Gain (%)	72.73	78.79	74.24	72.73	74.24
Average Gain in Winning Quarters (%)	6.62	6.65	6.05	7.98	8.30
Expectation of Quarterly Gain (%)	4.81	5.24	4.49	5.80	6.16
Standard Deviation of Quarterly Returns (%)	7.41	7.35	6.94	8.74	8.07
Probability of Quarterly Loss (%)	27.27	21.21	25.76	27.27	25.76
Average Loss in Losing Quarters (%)	−5.50	−5.76	−5.37	−6.13	−5.20
Expectation of Quarterly Loss (%)	−1.50	−1.22	−1.38	−1.67	−1.34
Longest Losing Streak (# Quarters)	4	4	4	6	6
Largest Drawdown from Previous High (%)	−27.19	−28.35	−25.41	−32.66	−26.96
Risk–Adjusted Return (Keppler Ratio):					
– Return per Unit of Expectation of Loss	2.21	3.29	2.24	2.47	3.60
Volatility Adjusted Return (Sharpe Ratio):					
– Return per Unit of Standard Deviation	0.45	0.55	0.45	0.47	0.60
Number of Periods (Quarters)	66	66	66	66	66
Number of Losing Quarters	18	14	17	18	17
Number of Winning Quarters	48	52	49	48	49
% of Quarters Outperforming MSCI CW	0	61	42	64	62
% of Quarters Outperforming MSCI EW	39	0	33	58	61

*) Total Returns with Gross Dividends Reinvested, Rebalanced Quarterly
CW: Market Capitalization–Weighted
EW: Equally–Weighted

3. The risk-adjusted return, i.e., the return per unit of expectation of loss, was highest for *Portfolio 3* (3.6) and lowest for *Portfolio 1* (2.24) among the three size portfolios, which means that *Portfolio 3* beat *Portfolio 1* by a factor of 1.6 on a risk-adjusted basis. The equally

**Figure 20.1—Compound Annual Return (%) in Local Currencies
Dec 31, 1975–June 30, 1992**

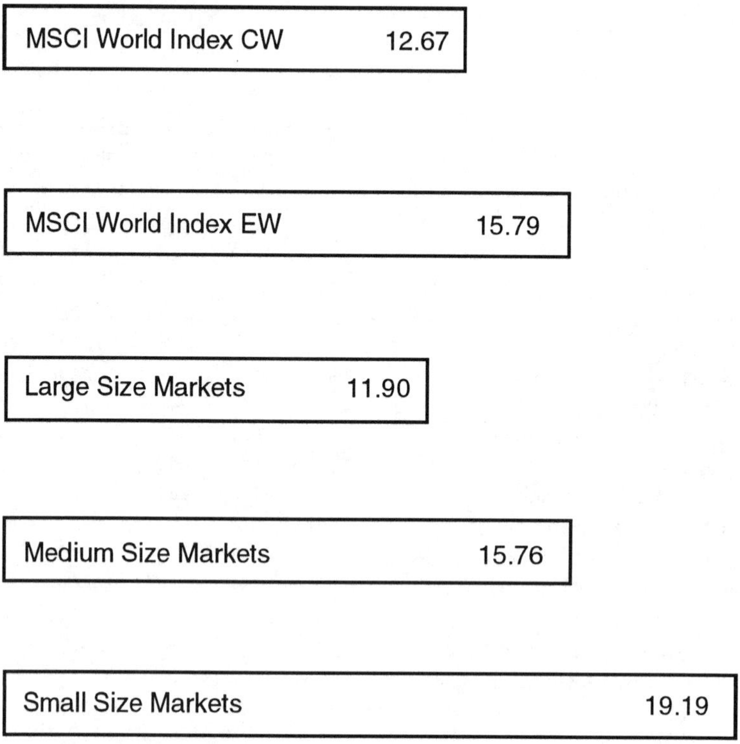

| MSCI World Index CW | 12.67 |

| MSCI World Index EW | 15.79 |

| Large Size Markets | 11.90 |

| Medium Size Markets | 15.76 |

| Small Size Markets | 19.19 |

weighted world index came in second (3.29), while the presumably most efficient global equity portfolio, the market capitalization-weighted MSCI World Index, turned in the lowest risk-adjusted return (2.21) and was even beaten by *Portfolio 1* (2.24), the portfolio consisting of the six largest markets. Figure 20.3 shows the risk-return relationship of the three size portfolios, the market-capitalization and the equally weighted world indices.

Our results suggest that investors are not getting paid for accepting higher risk. To the contrary, the most risk-averse investors, i.e., those who invest in the smallest-size markets or in equally weighted portfolios, reap the highest returns, which means that there is no trade-off between risk and return: Based on an analysis of *Portfolios 1* and *3*, the risk-return relationship is negative.[8]

**Figure 20.2—Cumulative Performance in Local Currencies with
Gross Dividends Reinvested**

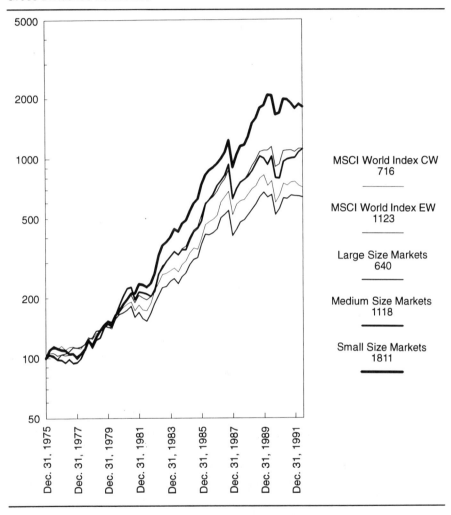

MSCI World Index CW
716

MSCI World Index EW
1123

Large Size Markets
640

Medium Size Markets
1118

Small Size Markets
1811

A frequency distribution of the return differences between the
quarterly returns of the *Small Size Markets Portfolio* and the quarterly returns of the market capitalization-weighted MSCI World Index shows the extent of the positive skewness of the excess returns
of the *Small Size Markets Portfolio* in relation to the market capitalization-weighted MSCI World Index: Not only are there sixteen additional observations on the positive side of the return distribution,
but the average returns of each interval (the numbers shown on

Figure 20.3—Risk-Adjusted Return in Local Currencies Dec 31, 1975–June 30, 1992

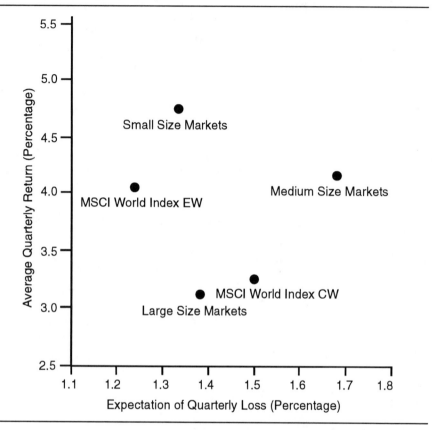

top of each distribution pillar), which indicate the magnitude of the return differences, are all in favor of the *Small Size Markets Portfolio* (see Figure 20.4).

4. The volatility-adjusted return, i.e., the return per unit of standard deviation of quarterly returns, was highest for *Portfolio 3* (0.6), and lowest for *Portfolio 1* (0.45). Thus, *Portfolio 3* beat *Portfolio 1* by a factor of 1.3. The volatility-return relationship for the three size portfolios, the market capitalization and the equally weighted world indices, is shown in Figure 20.5 (see also endnote 5).

5. While the other performance measures shown in Table 20.3 do not always point to the *Small Size Portfolio* as being the most attractive one, most demonstrate the dominating position of *Portfolio 3* over *Portfolio 1*. The alternative risk measures demonstrate the irrele-

Figure 20.4—The Small Country Effect
Frequency Distribution of Return Differences in Percent between Small Size Markets
Portfolio and the Cap Weighted MSCI World Index in Local Currencies

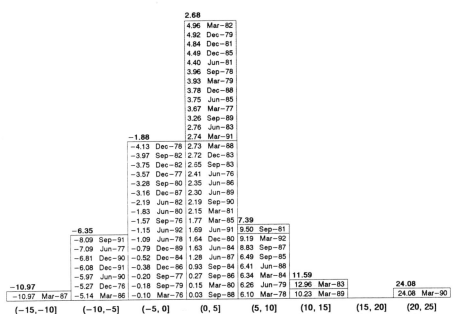

Note: The numbers indicate the amount of the deviation from the MSCI World Index return during each quarter in percent; negative numbers indicate underperformance, postitive numbers indicate superior performance. The averages of each interval, which are shown on top of each pillar, indicate the magnitude of the skewness of the return differences, while the shading indicates the frequency.

Note: The numbers indicate the amount of the deviation from the MSCI World Index return during each quarter in percent; negative numbers indicate underperformance, and positive numbers indicate superior performance. The averages of each interval, which are shown on top of each pillar, indicate the magnitude of the skewness of the return differences, while the shading indicates the frequency.

vance of the standard deviation as a risk measure for nonsymmetrical return distributions: While the standard deviation of quarterly returns for the *Small Size Markets Portfolio* is 8.07%, 8.9% higher than the corresponding 7.41% standard deviation of the quarterly market capitalization-weighted world index returns, the expectation of quarterly loss for the *Small Size Markets Portfolio* is more than 13% lower (–1.3%) than the expectation of quarterly loss for the market capitalization-weighted world index (–1.5%). Again,

Figure 20.5—Volatility-Adjusted Return in Local Currencies
Dec 31, 1975–June 30, 1992

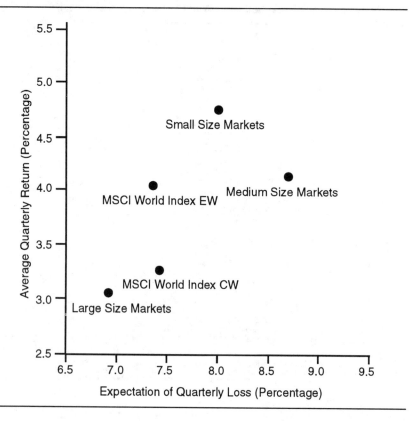

this demonstrates how questionable volatility measures may become if the return distributions are positively skewed.

6. The *Small Capitalization Portfolio* beat the equally weighted world index in forty-one out of the sixty-six quarters of the test period, i.e., 61% of the time, while the *Large Cap Portfolio* underperformed the equally weighted world benchmark in forty-four quarters, i.e., 67% of the time.

7. T-tests of mean return differences show that small cap *Portfolio 3* outperformed the equally weighted world index and the market capitalization-weighted MSCI World Index at significance levels 0.015 and 0.013, respectively. We also tested whether *Portfolio 3* outperformed the market capitalization-weighted MSCI World Index by at least 0.5% per quarter and found that a 0.5% or higher

performance advantage per quarter is significant at level 0.067. The t-tests show that the differences between *Portfolio 3* returns and both the market capitalization-weighted MSCI World Index and the equally weighted world index returns are statistically significant.

8. The stability of our basic findings is further demonstrated by the fact that subperiod results of the three 4-year periods, and one 4 1/2-year period are all in sequence and consistent with the results of the full 16 1/2-year test: Among the three size portfolios, the *Small Size Markets Portfolio* had the highest returns for each subperiod, followed by the *Medium Size Markets Portfolio,* while the *Large Size Markets Portfolio* returns came in lowest for each subperiod. Also, the equally weighted world index outperformed the market capitalization-weighted world index during each subperiod. See Table 20.4 for subperiod results.

Table 20.4—The Small Country Effect
Subperiod Results in Local Currencies—Compound Annual Returns in Percent

Subperiods	MSCI World Index CW	MSCI World Index EW	Large Size Markets	Medium Size Markets	Small Size Markets
12/31/75–12/31/79	9.43	10.55	9.42	10.49	11.26
12/31/79–12/31/83	17.58	21.09	14.15	21.30	27.47
12/31/83–12/31/87	17.45	18.21	13.87	18.13	22.27
12/31/87–06/30/92	7.30	13.82	10.44	13.67	16.68

9. The average holding periods were nineteen, twelve, and twenty-two quarters for *Portfolios 1, 2,* and *3,* respectively. The annual average turnover rate of the *Small Size Markets Portfolio* is therefore estimated at 18% without the quarterly rebalancing. Including quarterly rebalancing, we estimate the annual turnover rate at 31% of the portfolio.

While the value of the U.S. dollar against most foreign currencies fluctuated widely during the test period, the risk and return characteristics of the strategies tested follow similar patterns when measured in U.S. dollar terms. The U.S. dollar results, detailed in Table 20.5, suggest that, over the long term, currency considerations may be less important than many international investors are inclined to believe.

Table 20.5—The Small Country Effect in U.S. Dollars Dec 31, 1975–June 30, 1992

Risk & Return Characteristics *	MSCI World Index CW	MSCI World Index EW	Large Size Markets	Medium Size Markets	Small Size Markets
Compound Annual Return (%)	14.19	16.58	13.98	15.44	19.73
Average Quarterly Return (%)	3.68	4.22	3.62	4.07	4.95
Highest Quarterly Return (%)	22.65	22.64	24.98	31.19	27.57
Lowest Quarterly Return (%)	−18.13	−20.24	−17.45	−25.56	−17.70
Probability of Gain (%)	74.24	77.27	72.73	71.21	72.73
Average Gain in Winning Quarters (%)	7.10	7.27	7.16	8.46	8.74
Expectation of Quarterly Gain (%)	5.27	5.62	5.21	6.02	6.35
Standard Deviation of Quarterly Returns (%)	7.86	7.87	7.75	9.16	8.44
Probability of Quarterly Loss (%)	25.76	22.73	27.27	28.79	27.27
Average Loss in Losing Quarters (%)	−6.17	−6.18	−5.81	−6.77	−5.15
Expectation of Quarterly Loss (%)	−1.59	−1.40	−1.59	−1.95	−1.40
Longest Losing Streak (# Quarters)	5	5	5	6	3
Largest Drawdown from Previous High (%)	−24.00	−20.24	−23.18	−25.56	−17.70
Risk–Adjusted Return (Keppler Ratio):					
– Return per Unit of Expectation of Loss	2.31	3.00	2.28	2.09	3.52
Volatility Adjusted Return (Sharpe Ratio):					
– Return per Unit of Standard Deviation	0.47	0.54	0.47	0.44	0.59
Number of Periods (Quarters)	66	66	66	66	66
Number of Losing Quarters	17	15	18	19	18
Number of Winning Quarters	49	51	48	47	48
% of Quarters Outperforming MSCI CW	0	52	47	55	56
% of Quarters Outperforming MSCI EW	48	0	38	50	53

*) Total Returns with Gross Dividends Reinvested, Rebalanced Quarterly
CW: Market Capitalization–Weighted
EW: Equally–Weighted

Keppler Asset Management Inc., New York

Following are the most important findings of the analyses in U.S. dollars:

1. Compound annual and average quarterly returns are in the expected order for the three size portfolios and the equally and mar-

ket capitalization-weighted world indices: Small is beautiful, and if you know nothing, weigh your portfolios equally!

2. Both, the longest losing streak and the largest drawdown were least damaging for the *Small Size Portfolio.*

3. While the standard deviation of quarterly returns was high for the *Small Size Portfolio,* the lowest 1.4% expectation of a quarterly loss was shared with the equally weighted world index. The latter risk measure was higher for all other portfolios shown.

4. Both, risk- and volatility-adjusted returns—as defined in the local currency analysis—were most favorable for the *Small Size Markets Portfolio.*

5. T-tests of mean return differences show that the small cap *Portfolio 3* outperformed the equally weighted world index and the market capitalization-weighted MSCI World Index at significance levels 0.031 and 0.044 respectively. The t-tests show that the differences between *Portfolio 3* returns and both the market capitalization-weighted MSCI World Index and the equally weighted benchmark index returns are statistically significant.

5. Subperiod results again strongly support the overall results of the study: The *Small Size Markets Portfolio* had the highest returns of the three size portfolios for each subperiod, while the *Medium Size Markets Portfolio* occupied the middle positions, and the *Large Size Markets Portfolio* returns came in lowest during each subperiod. Subperiod results in U.S. dollars are shown in Table 20.6.

Table 20.6—The Small Country Effect Subperiod Results in U.S. Dollars
Compound Annual Returns in Percent

Subperiods	MSCI World Index CW	MSCI World Index EW	Large Size Markets	Medium Size Markets	Small Size Markets
12/31/75–12/31/79	11.73	14.56	13.77	13.55	15.79
12/31/79–12/31/83	14.09	9.46	8.63	9.06	10.07
12/31/83–12/31/87	25.75	28.52	23.30	26.43	35.46
12/31/87–06/30/92	6.94	14.82	11.11	13.67	19.12

CONSIDERATIONS FOR THE PRACTICAL APPLICATION OF THESE STRATEGIES

All of the results shown here implicitly assume a frictionless market, i.e., no transaction costs for the initial investment nor for rebalancing. Of somewhat lesser importance, we assume no taxes on capital gains, nor on dividends—we use gross dividends, when in fact most countries have a 15% net tax on dividends for U.S.-based investors.[9] Reasonable estimates of transaction costs have to include not only the fees and commissions, but also the market impact due to the size of the portfolio. For example, we may not have a problem giving Norway an equal weight in a six-country portfolio when we invest $1 million. However, for a $1 billion portfolio, we would face huge transaction costs.

In Table 20.7, we show an approximation of transaction costs (the average of buys and sells) in each market. These are based on moderate-size

Table 20.7—Estimated Transaction Costs in Percent		Table 20.8—Minimum Size Trade* for Market Impact in Million $	
Australia	1.00	Australia	$16.9
Austria	1.25	Austria	2.8
Belgium	1.75	Belgium	3.7
Canada	0.50	Canada	16.5
Denmark	1.10	Denmark	13.6
France	0.60	France	45.2
Germany	0.40	Germany	86.4
Hong Kong	0.75	Hong Kong	24.5
Italy	0.80	Italy	21.0
Japan	0.75	Japan	139.8
Netherlands	0.55	Netherlands	38.5
Norway	1.30	Norway	2.2
Singapore	1.00	Singapore	4.8
Spain	1.50	Spain	14.9
Sweden	1.25	Sweden	7.1
Switzerland	0.70	Switzerland	64.8
U.K.	0.70	U.K.	263.6
U.S.A.	0.40	U.S.A.	900.0

Source: State Street Global Advisors.

* Assuming an index strategy

Source: Morgan Stanley.

trades relative to the available liquidity in each market. As noted, costs increase progressively both above and below certain efficient threshold levels, which vary from market to market depending on size and liquidity. Assuming market capitalization weighting of countries, the implementation of a global index strategy with a $200 to 400 million portfolio would result in minimal transaction costs.

If one were to equally weight countries, the ideal size becomes less clear. A $40 million equally weighted global index fund would be reasonable for Belgium, but would not leave a sufficient amount for purchases in the U.S. or Japan to be efficient. A manager could not get a good sample of names and simultaneously keep transaction costs reasonable in the larger markets.

Most of the problems from a practical point of view arise with the smaller markets. In Table 20.8, we have shown thresholds for each market where significant market impact is currently likely to be felt if a manager attempted to complete an index trade in one day. As one would expect, the impact starts earliest with the smaller markets. Norway presents the tightest bottleneck: market impact would begin to pose a problem if one tried to invest only $2.2 million on a given day.

The extent of market impact on the performance of portfolios investing in small markets largely depends on portfolio turnover. In the *Small Size Markets Portfolio*, Austria, Denmark, and Norway were held throughout the entire test period. Belgium was held through most of the period, while Singapore, Sweden, Spain, Hong Kong, and Italy were also held at various times. Investments in all markets with the exception of Hong Kong and Italy were likely to involve transaction costs of 1% or more. Most of the illiquid markets, e.g., Austria, Belgium, Denmark, and Norway, were bought only once—they were never sold. The only country that went out of the portfolio more than once was Hong Kong, the most liquid of all the markets held. Thus, even for large portfolios the additional transaction costs that would have been incurred as a result of market impact and/or implementation shortfall should not have materially changed the results shown. The fact that the strategy does not depend on instant portfolio rebalancing when the market capitalization of national markets changes further contributes to its stability. Even if it took a whole quarter to move into a market, the incremental value added by the strategy would be about the same as with instant portfolio rebalancing.

There are ways to further reduce trading costs. Holding futures provides market exposure while increasing liquidity significantly. In addition, there are often tax benefits relating to the implied dividends one could capture via futures. Currently, futures on major market indices are available for fifteen of the eighteen markets included in our study. Only Italy, Norway, and Singapore/Malaysia do not yet offer futures. Unfortunately, most of the futures on the indices of the small markets were only recently introduced and therefore liquidity may still be a problem. However, this should improve over time.

In addition to futures, other investment vehicles that do not trade on exchanges can ease implementation. With the market for swaps now developed, brokers often provide reasonable quotes even for some of the smaller markets.[10] This provides exposure, and depending on the terms, it may also provide liquidity. Finally, several index fund providers, such as State Street Global Advisors, offer country index funds which, frequently provide opportunities to move in or out of a market without any transaction costs due to participants moving in opposite directions.

IMPLICATIONS FOR ACTIVE MANAGERS

If traditional (nonquantitative) portfolio managers were going to bias their portfolios toward the smaller markets, this might present a more difficult problem, especially for larger portfolios. Of all the markets involved, the only market where managers were materially concerned about liquidity was Austria.[11] However, this would probably change if they were to take sizable positions in several of the smaller markets. As presented in Table 20.9, the median manager's maximum position, shows the current *Small Size Portfolio* ranges from 5 to 10%. This number would probably be even lower for a global portfolio, as this survey was geared toward portfolios that did not include the United States. Since the U.S. represents about 40% of the MSCI World Index, the range may actually drop by 40% to 3% to 6%. Equal weighting would call for about a 17% weighting per country. Obviously, this goes far beyond what most managers would normally do.

Traditional managers' decision to limit the smaller markets is reasonable, however, given the normal turnover of most managers. The discussion above regarding transaction costs assumes index-weighted holdings within countries. This mitigates much of the potential transaction costs, as it is essentially a buy-and-hold strategy within markets. In addition, each security's weight in a given country results from the company's market value, which usually is a good proxy for liquidity. To a large extent the typical active manager holds equal weights of about one hundred securities. Thus, if a manager were to give large weights to the smaller markets, the market impact and/or implementation shortfall could become huge when trading in some of the smaller companies.

This liquidity burden would shrink if countries were equally weighted without concentrating investments in all of the smallest markets (since it is unlikely that an active manager would find only small markets attractive).

Table 20.9—Median Manager Maximum Weight in Percent

Australia	10.0
Austria	5.0
Belgium	7.0
Canada	10.0
Denmark	5.0
France	20.0
Germany	25.0
Hong Kong	10.0
Italy	12.4
Japan	60.0
Netherlands	13.2
Norway	5.0
Singapore	10.0
Spain	10.0
Sweden	8.0
Switzerland	13.7
U.K.	35.0
U.S.A.	N.A.

Source: Ennis, Knupp & Associates.

We have recently implemented the results of our research in our *Global Advantage Fund*, where we equally weight the most attractive markets and select the best securities in those markets. This will show in real time the practicality and advantage of equally weighting markets.

EMERGING MARKETS

Interestingly, the one area where equal weighting of countries (or some variation of it) has caught on is within the emerging markets. Particularly with some of the more quantitative managers, equal weighting of emerging markets has great appeal. Although we do not include the statistics here, it is true that, also with emerging markets, equal weighting of countries has provided superior returns to capitalization weights. Finally, were we to extend our universe to include both developed and emerging markets, equal weighting of markets would yield even higher excess returns.

Over most periods, the smallest markets have tended to do better than larger ones.

CONCLUSION

This study suggests that market size has significant predictive power with respect to the relative performance of broadly diversified global equity investments. Global investors with a three- to five-year investment horizon can achieve excess risk-adjusted returns by concentrating investments in a combination of smaller national equity markets. The size of national equity markets is thus a useful selection criterion for enhancing the returns and reducing the risk—if not necessarily the volatility—of global equity portfolios.

ENDNOTES

[1] State Street Global Advisors has employed primarily equal weighting of securities in each country in its international *High Value* portfolios since March 1984. Their performance ranks at or near the top of comparable measurement universes for most countries on a return basis, and equally important, ranks among the lowest risk portfolios in these universes. The slight small capitalization exposure which is generated through the concept of equal weighting has undoubtedly contributed positively to the performance.

[2] Tweedy, Browne Inc.: Interview in *Outstanding Investor Digest*, New York, 1992, Vol. VII, No. 9 & 10, p. 17. Prior to 1972 the S&P 425 Index was used.

[3] The standard deviation of the annual returns was 15.8% for the capitalization-weighted portfolio and 18.47% for the equally weighted portfolio.

[4] R. S. Clarkson, "The Measurement of Investment Risk," presented to the Faculty of Actuaries in the United Kingdom, February 20, 1989. Clarkson shows in a theoretical example of two investments A and B with symmetric return distributions, where every "reasonable" investor would prefer A to B regardless of the fact that investment A has four times the variance of investment B: "Suppose, for example, that we have two shares A and B, where the returns to a particular future date depend on certain scenarios, $X_1, X_2, \ldots X_n$. For each scenario X_i, the return on share A (which is always positive) is twice the return on share B. Since the return on share A is always greater than the return on share B, any reasonable investor will

regard share A as 'less risky' than share B regardless of the respective variances of return."

5 Even though the volatility concept on risk may be inaccurate and misleading due to the positive skewness of the returns of the equally weighted S&P Index, we show the results to allow interested readers to analyze the returns according to modern portfolio theory. Yet we do not represent that the application of the volatility concept to risk measurement is justified under the given circumstances.

6 Finland and New Zealand were not included since they did not enter the MSCI World Index until 1988.

7 The size of the national markets included in the MSCI World Index as a percentage of the MSCI World Index is published in the monthly editions of Morgan Stanley Capital International (MSCI) Perspective, New York. Our research starts at the end of 1975, since data on market size prior to that date was not available to us.

8 For other negative risk-return relationships see Robert A. Haugen, "The Link Between Growth/Value and Risk/Return," presented at the 6th Annual Asset Allocation Congress, sponsored by the Institute for International Research on February 25, 1992, in Palm Beach, Florida, and Michael A. Keppler, "Further Evidence on the Predictability of International Equity Returns." *Journal of Portfolio Management*, Fall 1991.

9 Since dividend yields and withholding taxes for the various size portfolios are similar, the return differences of the various strategies are not significantly affected by withholding rates.

10 Swaps are agreements typically offered by brokers to pay an equity market return to an investor in return for the LIBOR rate or some other debt market rate. Thus, the investor "swaps" a return he or she is earning on a fixed-income investment for an equity return without having to invest directly in a large number of equities.

11 Ennis, Knupp & Associates: 1992 Survey of Non-U.S. Stock Market Suitability, Chicago 1992.

Chapter 21

Small Capitalization Stocks in Switzerland

Hans Kaufmann
Head of Swiss Research Department
Bank Julius Baer

INTRODUCTION

Around 75%, or some SFr 200b of total Swiss stock market capitalization of SFr 270b at end-1992 stemmed from the fifteen largest capitalization stocks. The five largest companies alone (Nestlé, UBS, Roche, Sandoz, and Ciba-Geigy) accounted for some 50% of the market value of all listed Swiss stocks. The remaining SFr 70b, or 25%, was divided among 263 companies, which represents an average stock market capitalization of just under SFr 266m per company.

An analysis of daily turnover in securities during 1991 and 1992 produces a similar picture. Around 80% of all transactions were in the thirty most frequently traded stocks. The twenty-six permanently traded stocks generate more than 80% of the total turnover in shares on the Swiss stock markets. Thus secondary stocks accounted for less than 20% of turnover, although they represent over 90% of all stocks. The small market capitalization—possibly split into three categories of security—and the resulting inadequate marketability, is the chief problem with secondary stocks (see Table 21.1).

Table 21.1—Three Categories of Marketability

First-class (> SFr 10m*)	Good (SFr 5–10m*)	Adequate (SFr 1–5m*)	
Roche DRC	SBC PC	Holderbank B	Interdiscount B
UBS B	Winterthur R	Adia B	Swiss Re B
Nestlé R	Alusuisse B	Winterthur B	Sulzer R
Ciba-Geigy R	Swiss Re PC	Ciba-Geigy PC	Swissair B
BBC B	BBC PC	Sandoz B	Forbo B
Nestlé B	Zürich B	UBS R	Merck B
CS Holding B	Surveillance DRC	Winterthur PC	Merkur R
Sandoz PC	SMH R	Sulzer PC	Bâloise R
SBC B	Zürich PC	Elektrowatt B	Bobst B
Sandoz R	SBC R	Bâloise PC	Bührle B
Ciba-Geigy B	Roche B	Schindler PC	Baer Holding B
Zürich R	Swiss Re R	Ems-Chemie B	SMH PC
	Nestlé PC	Georg Fischer B	Alusuisse R
	Holderbank B	Swiss Volksbank R	Ares-Serono B
		CS Holding R	Sika PC
		Ascom B	Berner R
		BBC R	Kuoni B
		Pirelli PC	

*   Daily transaction volume.

UNSATISFACTORY MARKETABILITY

The remaining securities have daily turnover volume of less than SFr 1m, and their marketability must therefore be rated as unsatisfactory. Besides the quoted small capitalization stocks, another 200 small caps are traded OTC. Leading market makers in these stocks (regional banks, mountain railways and cable cars, hotels, etc.) are Willisauer Volksbank (Lucerne), Zürcher Kantonalbank (Zurich), and Bank Hoffmann (Zurich).

An interesting indicator of the market breadth is the volume of the Soffex shares (shares underlying traded futures and options) as a percentage of total volume. Volume figures for Swiss shares are available since April 1990 (see Figure 21.1).

Figure 21.1—Soffex Stocks

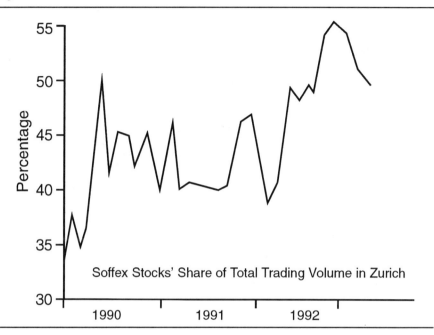

Soffex Stocks' Share of Total Trading Volume in Zurich

DRASTIC UNDERPERFORMANCE OF SECONDARY STOCKS

For about five years, i.e., since the worldwide stock market crash of October 19, 1987, secondary stocks have differed greatly from blue chips, particularly in terms of performance. Whereas the latter have largely recovered from their correction at that time, with price advances in excess of 60%, secondary stocks are still on the whole about 15-20% below their level of five years ago, despite good business results from many of the companies. Since its low in 1987 the SBC Index shows an increase in value of roughly 50%. We have made these calculations on the basis of a representative number of blue chips (30 stocks) and secondary stocks (60) without taking into account the differing market weighting (unweighted method of analysis). (See Figure 21.2.)

An important reason for the good showing made by the blue chips could well be international diversification by large foreign institutional investors who, by buying shares of large companies in each country have, over the last few years, built up index-like portfolios, which have high market liquidity. As a rule, blue chip and index portfolios can be hedged to a great extent over the short term with derivative instruments, and this is mostly impossible with secondary stocks. If one has secondary stocks

Figure 21.2—Blue Chips and Secondary Stocks

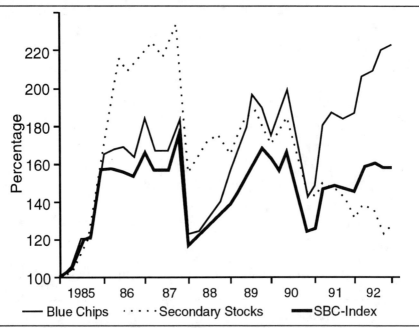

Blue Chips ····Secondary Stocks ■■■SBC-Index

and wants to counter a market weakness, one has no alternative but to sell, which in periods of weakness often means selling at a much lower price, owing to the lack of marketability. Hedging secondary stocks with derivatives, whose underlying stocks are blue chips, can even prove to be counterproductive. For example, in 1991 and 1992 most blue chips performed well, whereas most secondary stocks not only clearly underperformed the market but in many cases sustained price losses. The causes of the underperformance by the secondary stocks are numerous and are attributable in most cases to a cumulation of widely differing factors.

Only a few years ago, the little-regulated Swiss capital market still offered a means of raising risk capital to a broad spectrum of issuers. During the 1980s in particular, Swiss investors positively fell upon any new issues of equity. However, since the 1987 stock market crash the climate for new issues on the Swiss capital market has deteriorated appreciably. Today, even capital increases by established companies do not meet with a very warm response. On the contrary, they are regarded as a drug on the market.

In our opinion, there are four causes for this drastic alteration in conditions, particularly for small and medium-sized companies and most especially for companies controlled by individual families or other majority shareholders:

- In recent years, there has been a large increase in the number of **shareholders who are critical,** and so far the companies have done little or nothing to reduce their vulnerability to attack.

- The **internationalization and professionalization of the investment business** make greater demands on these companies, which so far they have only partially met.

- The **widespread use of modern portfolio theory** has an increasingly negative effect on companies with small market capitalization.

- Switzerland's steps in the direction of Europe could result in a permanently **higher level of interest rates,** which not only means a higher interest burden for the companies, but also opens up attractive alternatives for investors in the fixed-income sector.

INCREASING NUMBER OF CRITICAL SHAREHOLDERS

The rising number of critical shareholders is a reaction to the sometimes unfair practices of Swiss companies in the past. Many companies, particularly in the 1980s, took advantage of the favorable climate to open their companies to the public either by realizing part of their own shareholdings or by letting the public participate in a capital increase. Whereas in the former case the company was sold off, the proceeds going to the founding shareholders, a capital increase placed new resources at the disposal of the companies. The favorable situation on the Swiss capital market even made it possible to find providers of risk capital who were prepared to take the same financial risk as the founders, without, however, being granted a right of say commensurate with the risks they were taking. The **concept of different share categories with the same voting rights** is still widely used. It is based on the principle that each share has one vote, regardless of its par value. Nevertheless, as far as capital is concerned—i.e., dividends, subscription rights for capital increases, and any liquidation dividends—the relative par value is determinative. In this way, by putting in, for example, SFr 100, family shareholders were able to bring in SFr 500 of additional risk capital from the market, without ceding their voting majority.

Despite the creation of **different categories of stock,** many founder shareholders were able to demand a large capital input from the public which, in not a few cases, was used to accelerate corporate growth by means of acquisitions. Many of these takeovers were not part of a long-term strategy but rather the result of funds being too easily available (period of low interest rates). The number of fiascos was correspondingly high, often even jeopardizing the original business. Nonetheless, **having different categories of voting shares** does not guarantee perpetual control of a company. Apart from problems of succession, which can lead to the share packages being split up, it is possible that, a few years after going public and despite having to put in a disproportionately lower amount, the majority shareholder no longer has the necessary means to guarantee a voting majority by participation in a capital increase.

As a rule, income from dividends is not enough for majority shareholders to finance regular capital increases. This is true particularly for those shareholders who have financed their majority partly with borrowed funds and who need the earnings from dividends to pay the interest. Young companies are often very hungry for capital, since their growth is exceptionally rapid and often means large outlays in the form of start-up costs. They therefore have a tendency to retain as much of the profits as possible, i.e., the **pay-out ratio is low**. Moreover, from a tax standpoint, it does not make much sense for the majority shareholder to collect large dividends in order to reinvest them in the company at a later date. The public shareholder therefore usually has to accept a dividend policy dictated by the majority shareholder. However, established Swiss companies, with the exception of banks, also have low pay-out ratios in international comparison, which is something many investors do not much appreciate.

When a company goes public, the public shareholder voluntarily decides whether or not to accept a capital structure with voting shares, but this is not the case when such shares are introduced at a later stage. Nevertheless, in the past some large shareholders, who were no longer able to meet the financial needs of their companies out of their own pockets, have resorted to voting shares. They have succeeded, partly thanks to the proxy votes held by banks, to ensure the necessary qualified majority at a general meeting of shareholders. A further step would then often entail practically forcing the public shareholders to cede the voting shares due to them in a capital increase to the majority shareholder, either by **not listing certain categories of voting shares or even by de-listing them** on the stock market. Anyone not ceding his stocks to the majority shareholder would be left sitting on nontradable shares, which could only be sold again at a discount to the listed shares. The practice, whereby family firms quote only certain types of shares on the stock market, is still widespread. However, many institutional investors demand a minimum stock market capitalization. If this is not met, the company is neglected, i.e., the circle of possible demand for its shares is significantly restricted.

Another practice felt to be unfair by public shareholders is the provision in the statutes of some companies that gives the company **the right to**

convert its nonlisted registered shares into bearer shares. In this way family shareholders are free to change their registered shares into bearers and sell them on the stock market. On the other hand, unlike public shareholders, they benefit from more favorable tax rates for so long as the securities have not been converted.

The most unpleasant development during the last few years has been the bad habit some companies have developed of placing shares and PCs en bloc or gradually via the stock market and excluding existing shareholders. The justification often given for this, that issuing securities at the market price does not represent a dilution of existing shareholders' positions, is only superficially true. In fact, net asset value is given away to third parties, since the majority of Swiss companies are traded at prices that are below their true net asset value. Such **private placements** often also more than satisfy demand and thus the public shareholder is cheated out of the benefit of any upside in the price that might have arisen, had the supply not been altered.

The old Company Law permitted companies the use of yet another instrument to keep unwelcome shareholders at bay: *Vinkulierung,* **or restrictions on shareholders**. The willful limitation of share ownership by refusal to enter shareholders in the stock ledger was a common practice until the end of June 1992. Even today, refusal of stock ledger entry is permissible, although, after the expiry of the transitional period, the revised Company Law will limit the permissible grounds to three, of which two seem acceptable: the exclusion of a shareholder when the registered share has been acquired under a false name, or when the company has to prove its essentially Swiss character, for example as a national airline, or because it is subject to the real estate law Lex Friedrich. The third ground for refusal of stock ledger entry, when a shareholder's purchases exceed the company's statutory maximum percentage of voting stock, is still a kind of clause for the "protection of the homelands," which in the longer term will appear obsolete in a liberalized European market. The planned new Federal Stock Exchange Law will probably contain regulations on company takeovers, which will mean that many companies are likely to give up their quota regulations.

As if all these means were not sufficient to keep hold of power, a further instrument was created in 1965, by which risk capital could be obtained from the public without giving away the right of say: the **participation certificate** (PC). However, the PC was not primarily created to reinforce majority control by family shareholders. By means of the PC, which was not regulated by law, it was possible to raise authorized capital, which would not have been possible under the old Company Law through shares. Such authorized PCs meant that the necessary securities could be kept in readiness to cover conversion and option rights in a simple way, without the necessity of an issue. Additionally, unlike shares, there was no minimum nominal value laid down for PCs, which made possible the issue of the so-called "lighter" securities.

Participation certificates, which have no voting rights, have become less and less popular during the last few years. Although many, especially foreign, investors were prepared to invest in PCs of companies, in which otherwise only restricted registered shares were available to the public, as time went by the PCs were increasingly traded at a discount to stocks with voting rights. The greater the number of PCs that were issued in relation to the number of shares, the larger the price differential. When its capital is increased, however, a company has to fix the same issue price for all categories of shares, i.e., the issue price is geared toward the instrument on the market with the lowest valuation, which as a rule is the PC. The creation of risk capital therefore became increasingly expensive. Companies, which only have PCs outstanding with the public are hardly capable of going to the stock market because of the PCs' low valuation. It will be hard for them to procure further risk capital without issuing stocks with voting rights.

The justification often given for the issue of participation certificates is that they provide protection against takeovers because they have no voting rights. This is only true to a certain extent. In a takeover, the attacker does indeed try to obtain the voting majority and not necessarily the majority of the capital. The most recent experiences have shown, however, that **PCs are ignored in takeover bids**, i.e., they do not keep up with the price advances of the shares, which naturally enough annoys the holders of PCs. Nevertheless, PCs can even have a boomerang effect in a takeover bid, since the attacker has to find less capital to buy the company than if the company only had shares outstanding. The flood of conversion and option rights issued after the 1987 crash can be seen as the last attempt to place PCs with the public.

Company takeovers have become a particularly controversial issue in Switzerland during the last few years. On several occasions the public shareholders have had to stand by and watch the majority shareholder sell his share package at a premium, while they were not even bid the market price for their shares. It is therefore no wonder that rumors of takeovers are nowadays more likely to be greeted by the market marking the price down rather than by awarding it a premium. The Swiss finance minister Otto Stich seems to be justified in his demand that the planned new federal Stock Exchange Law should as a matter of urgency contain provisions to ensure fairer rules and regulations with regard to takeovers.

The purpose of this description of unpopular instruments and practices has not been to lay blame anywhere, but simply to demonstrate why the number of shareholders who are critical has grown so enormously during the last few years. Most of these vulnerable areas still exist and will make the procurement of new equity difficult for many companies. While the companies themselves can do much to meet the demands of the capital market, the three remaining factors, which have contributed to the drastically altered conditions do not, however, lie within their direct sphere of influence.

INTERNATIONAL DIVERSIFICATION HAS SET NEW STANDARDS

Since the 1980s, the Swiss stock market has benefited from the **trend toward international diversification**. The equity-oriented Anglo-Saxon institutions, in particular, have pursued this policy, because modern portfolio theory has demonstrated that an internationally diversified portfolio achieves a greater return combined with less risk.

As the fourth largest European stock market with a market capitalization of around 10% of the European total, Switzerland rates as a much-sought-after investment market. However, foreign institutional investors have never appreciated the lack of transparency in the presentation of accounts by Swiss companies, which makes international comparison difficult. Although in the early 1980s some adjustments were made to make the hyperconservative Swiss accounts comparable, during the last two to three years investors have gone over to regarding the published figures as the "true" ones.

The fact that it was principally the large capitalization companies that complied with the foreign institutions' demands for greater transparency, altering their accounts to conform to EC or IAS standards has accelerated this trend. Nevertheless, some foreign institutions have confused greater transparency with a moving away on the part of Swiss companies from their conservative accounting methods. Since, under the new methods, published profits were not greatly different from those previously declared, and in some cases lower, it was widely thought that the true profits of Swiss companies were never higher than those published, which in our view is a false conclusion. As we have already mentioned, a more open presentation of accounts in no way means a moving away from the good old Swiss principle of caution. In most cases, the earnings quality of Swiss companies is still to be rated higher than that of foreign competitors.

Nonetheless, the still patchy transparency in accounting methods and conservative principles have in some cases led to Swiss companies appearing overvalued in international terms. Every year, for more than twenty years, the Swiss Association of Financial Analysts and Portfolio Managers has examined the quality of reporting by Swiss companies. Although massive progress has been made over the years, one cannot help but notice that the bottom third of the list is made up almost exclusively of family firms. To be fair, though, it must be said that some family-controlled companies have recognized the signs of the times and come into the top section of the association's list because of their exemplary accounts. Overall, however, one can state that the secretiveness of family firms is still a great handicap.

Swiss institutions have also begun to diversify more internationally, although the ceilings laid down by law for pension funds and life insurance companies limit the trend to a certain extent. For Swiss companies this means greater difficulty in raising equity, as they are now in competition with foreign firms. They can no longer automatically count on there being Swiss pension funds wishing to invest. This is all the more true as some of the funds have already reached the limit of their permissible quota of voting stock in some companies.

Increased participation by professional investors in the last few years has led to a different way of looking at **capital increases**. The Swiss myth that subscription rights are a kind of extra dividend is beginning to wear thin. Institutional investors are perfectly aware that the rights are simply compensation for the dilution of net asset value and earnings that result from a capital increase. They are no longer prepared to exercise such rights, if management has no clear objective for the use of these new resources. It is therefore not surprising that nowadays capital increases are more often a drug on the market than the stimulus they were in the past. Today investors demand a higher return on the risk capital they have made available. In future, institutional investors will no longer be satisfied with a return on equity that is lower even than the rate of interest paid on Swiss government bonds.

Institutional investors are playing an increasingly active role at **annual general meetings**. The political pressure that is sometimes put on the managers of pension funds in Switzerland in order to silence their opposition, may conceal the problem temporarily but it will not solve it. As in the U.S., collective saving in Switzerland—the compulsory accrual of large assets—will encourage a tendency by institutional investors to exert influence on managements and boards of directors. If a large pension fund does not wish to spread its assets too widely, but to concentrate on no more companies than it can easily monitor, this can lead to a situation where positions are taken up in some securities that are several times higher than their daily trading volume. A large investor is then unable to liquidate a large position within a reasonable timescale without making a considerable loss. For this reason, institutional investors will increasingly have to strengthen their **contacts with managements**. Small investors may feel this to be unfair special treatment, but in the last resort it is also to their advantage that the stock price does not fall through the floor as the result of large-scale selling. In this connection, the question also arises as to what purpose is served by **listed cooperatives**, whose shares only have   indirect voting rights through delegated proxies. Moreover, the choice of these proxies is to a large extent decided by the management concerned. It might be more advantageous in the long run to preserve the ability of such firms to raise money on the capital market by converting them into limited companies, despite the one-off costs this would entail.

SERIOUS ECONOMIC CONSEQUENCES OF PASSIVE PORTFOLIO MANAGEMENT

Modern portfolio theory has not only encouraged international diversification but also led to a situation where an increasing number of investment advisers have gone over to managing assets passively, i.e., by linking them to an index. This change has also made a substantial contribution to the decline in the prices of secondary stocks. Institutional investors attempt to minimize the risk of individual stocks and try to reproduce at least the average performance of the various markets through diversification into the few securities that dominate them. A portfolio manager no longer concentrates on a company's valuation, but on the risk of the stock price deviating from the market average. The higher the valuation of the share, the greater its relative weighting in the index. Index-oriented investors will thus invest comparatively more money in the most expensive stocks. On the other hand, small companies with low valuations have virtually no significance for the overall index and are accordingly neglected by investors.

Family firms are not included in the mostly narrowly based indices, either because trading volume is too thin or because only some of their shares are listed. They also do not come into the running as underlying stock for **derivatives** such as futures and options. Institutional investors, however, prefer stocks whose prices can be temporarily hedged cheaply by means of derivatives.

Passive portfolio management has led to a **concentration of stock market trading volume** on a few blue chips. Although in terms of numbers, secondary stocks and family firms account for the lion's share, i.e., 80% of all listed stocks, measured by stock market turnover and capitalization, they only represent some 25-30%. The concentration of stock market trading on a few stocks also affects research by banks and brokers, who in turn limit themselves to a small number of stocks. Today each Swiss blue chip is seriously studied by around 25 analysts, by means of company interviews, studies, and earnings estimates. Between five and ten analysts regularly submit earnings estimates on medium-sized companies to I/B/E/S, which is an information service that collects and assesses worldwide earnings estimates covering over 10,000 companies. As a rule, there are less than five analysts studying the smaller companies. If, on grounds of cost-effectiveness, banks cease in future to analyze companies with little marketability, they will also stop doing active marketing for these stocks. Analysts will concentrate on those companies whose managements have an open information policy and are therefore helping to make their companies known to existing and potential investors. We too shall follow this policy more consistently in the future.

The miserable performance by secondary stocks over the last five years and the restricted tradability of the shares of majority-owned companies have led to a changed attitude on the part of the stock market banks. For example, at the beginning of September a large British brokerage firm announced that in future it would no longer act as market maker for around 300 companies in the U.K. The Swiss banks and brokers have announced no such measures, as there is no official market making for individual stocks. However, with the present **low rates of commission**, banks and brokers are no longer prepared to take up risky positions in secondary stocks and family firms, even to effect a block transaction. Family firms have taken this service for granted for too long and only in a few cases have they bothered a great deal about encouraging a regulated market in their shares.

COMPANIES FACE NEW CHALLENGES FROM THE MOVE TOWARD EUROPE

Finally, **the altered monetary environment** has contributed to the difficult situation for family firms. In saying this we are referring to the central bank's restrictive monetary policy over the last three years, which has caused a recession, plunged many domestically oriented companies into earnings difficulties and further undermined investors' willingness to take risks with small and medium-sized companies. Moreover, Switzerland's steps in the direction of Europe could bring about a permanently higher level of interest rates. Even if real interest rates, which in the case of Swiss government bonds have a historical long-term average of 0.9%, were to double in the context of a further approach to the EC, Switzerland would still remain an island of low interest rates within Europe. Although its EEA membership was rejected by the majority of the electorate on December 6, 1992—with 49.7% in favor and 50.3% against—another attempt to join the EC in one way or the other will probably be made in the years ahead. EC membership would be likely to bring SFr interest rates up to the

European level, which in the longer term would certainly mean yet higher rates.

One consequence of this would be a **growing interest burden** for companies. Another consequence would be that higher interest rates would open up attractive **alternative investment opportunities** for investors. It would then make sense for investors to take on the extra risk of equities only if by doing so there were the possibility of achieving a higher return than that of low-risk government bonds. In order to fulfill this condition, listed companies will have to achieve **substantially higher returns on equity** than in the past. If they do not, their stock prices will remain at a low level or even fall further. Lower stock prices lead to higher capital costs, which in turn have an adverse effect on earnings, which leads to lower stock prices, etc. This vicious circle, in which some family firms are already trapped, then continues and is particularly disastrous for a company, whose **competitors** have found considerably greater acceptance on the market and whose cheaper refinancing gives them significant competitive advantages. The trend toward Europe will favor the large concerns with good marketability at the expense of medium-sized and smaller companies.

ACCESS TO THE CAPITAL MARKET IS VITAL FOR THE SURVIVAL OF COMPANIES

The demands on public companies have recently increased enormously. Although the **ability to raise capital on the market** cannot be measured in balance sheet terms, it is, however, a **prerequisite for long-term survival**. In order to achieve or regain this, it is not enough merely to get rid of the restrictions on shareholders. This is only to take into account the revised Company Law. Even share splits and the abolition of PCs are taken for granted when it comes to improving marketability. Real progress would imply the abolition of **special shares with voting rights** coupled with share repurchases, although the latter makes no sense at present on tax grounds. All the same, some companies have drawn the appropriate conclusions in this direction and bought back the shares of subsidiaries that no longer had ready access to the capital market (e.g., Nestlé: Frisco-Findus; Georg Fischer: Buss; Ciba-Geigy: Zyma). Other companies are likely to follow suit. Companies that do not fulfill the following six conditions in the medium term are likely to disappear from the capital market sooner or later which, we could well envisage, might mean going private:

- good business performance
- improved transparency in the presentation of accounts

- open information policy in the course of, as well as at the end of, the year
- active solicitation of current and future investors by means of road shows, receptions for large investors and analysts
- progressive dividend policy (pay-out ratio of at least 30-40% of net profit)
- fair treatment of public shareholders when majority shareholders sell share packages, etc.

Several Swiss companies aware of their difficult situation founded a federation called "Pro Swiss Invest" in late 1992 to cope with these problems. Sixteen companies have joined the club to date (e.g., Holvis, Phoenix Mecano, Elco Looser), having as prime target the improvement of accounting methods (transparency) and shareholder rights.

HOW TO INVEST IN SWISS SMALL CAPITALIZATION STOCKS

An easy way to invest in small capitalized Swiss stocks are investment funds or similar instruments (see Table 21.2).

Table 21.2

Fund or Company Name	For Further Information Contact	Size End-1992	
Special Swiss Stock Fund	Bank Julius Baer, Zurich	SFr	20m
Swiss Small Caps	Zürcher Kantonalbank, Zurich	SFr	50m
Vontobel Small Cap. Fund	Bank Vontobel, Zurich	SFr	120m
IST-Schweizer-Aktien-Ergänzungswerte (tax-exempt, for Swiss pension funds only)	Bank Julius Baer, Zurich Pictet & Cie., Geneva	SFr	60m
Asselsa Ltd.	Maerki, Baumann, Zurich	SFr	25m
Total		SFr	275m

HOW TO MEASURE THE PERFORMANCE OF SMALL CAPITALIZED STOCKS

At the end of 1992, there were four indices available to measure the performance of small capitalized Swiss companies.

- **VSC-Index** (small companies)   (Bank Vontobel, Zurich)
- **SILO** (small caps.),   (Lombard, Odier, Geneva)
- **MILO** (medium-sized companies),   (Lombard, Odier, Geneva)
- **"Ausserbörsliche"-Index** (OTC stocks) (Willisauer Volksbank, Lucerne)

VSC-Index—This index includes companies with a market capitalization of less than 0.2% (i.e., SFr 500m) of total market capitalization. Although some 60% of all quoted companies are covered, they represent only 8% (31.12.1991: SFr 18.2b) of total market capitalization.

The **Lombard-Odier indices** are calculated on a not-reinvested basis, starting at 1000 on January 1, 1980:

MILO (medium capitalization index)—94 shares (bearer, registered, participation certificates) of the 50 largest Swiss companies not included in the SMI. The market value totalled SFr 51.5b, i.e., 19.9% of total market capitalization, or 18% of all listed companies, as of June 30, 1992.

SILO (small capitalization index)—295 shares (bearer, registered, participation certificates), which represent 75.5% of all listed companies. The market capitalization of this index amounted to SFr 21.2b, i.e., 8% of total market capitalization, as of June 30, 1992.

"Ausserbörsliche"-Index (31.12.1981: 100)—This index excludes OTC companies with a market capitalization of less than SFr 15m (banks), SFr 10m (industry), and SFr 5m (railways). The remaining 51 OTC stocks represented a market capitalization of some SFr 1.8b by the end of 1992.

HOW TO STRUCTURE A PORTFOLIO OF SMALL CAPITALIZED SWISS COMPANIES

A comparison of the sector weightings of blue chips and secondary stocks shows a complete difference between the two (see Table 21.3).

ATTRACTIVE SWISS SMALL CAPITALIZATION STOCKS

Investors looking for individual, unique investment opportunities in small capitalization stocks may use the following names as a starting point for further analysis (see Table 21.4).

Table 21.3

End-1992 (as a %)	SPI	Blue chips	Secondary stocks
Banks	20.2	21.1	17.5
Insurance	9.7	10.0	8.8
Transport	0.5	0.0	2.1
Retail	1.0	0.0	4.0
Other services	6.2	1.4	20.1
Services	**37.7**	**32.5**	**52.5**
Machinery	2.3	0.0	8.9
Utilities	1.6	0.9	3.6
Chemicals/pharmaceuticals	31.2	39.6	7.4
Food	17.1	21.5	4.7
Electrical engineering	5.2	5.6	4.0
Construction	2.1	0.0	7.9
Other industries	2.9	0.0	11.0
Industry	**62.3**	**67.5**	**47.5**
Market capitalization (SFr b)	**272.0**	**201.2**	**70.8**

Table 21.4

Company	Sector
APG	outdoor advertising
Atel/EG Laufenburg	international electricity wholesalers
Baer Holding	portfolio management, broker
Bobst	paperboard processing machinery
Danzas	forwarding (No. 1 in Europe)
Feldschlösschen	brewery
Forbo	linoleum (No. 1 worldwide)
Fuchs Petrolub	lubricants
Georg Fischer	casting, spark erosion machinery
Globus	department stores
Gurit	elastic connectors, special coatings
Hilti	fixing and demolition techniques
Holvis	non-wovens

Table 21.4 Continued

Company	Sector
Intershop	commercial real estate management
Keramik Laufen	tiles, coarse ceramics
Kuoni	tourist operator
Lindt & Sprüngli	chocolate (top quality)
Merkur	news stands, mattresses
Mikron	machine tools
Motor-Columbus	power plants, technology
Mövenpick	catering, hotels
Oerlikon-Bührle	shoes (Bally), military products
Rieter	spinning machinery, noise insulation
RIG	paperboard and plastic packaging
Saurer	textile machinery
Siegfried	OTC products for health, dried medical herbs
SIG	packaging machinery
Sika	building chemicals
Sprecher & Schuh	low-voltage electrical equipment, industrial automats
Von Moos	steel
Von Roll	steel, environmental technology
Walter Rentsch	office equipment distributor
Zellweger	textile machinery, house installation, gas warning devices
Zürcher Ziegeleien	construction materials

The following Appendix provides information on price/earnings ratio (Figure 21.3), price/cash flow ratio (Figure 21.4), and price/book value ratio (Figure 21.5).

APPENDIX

Figure 21.3—Price/Earnings Ratio 1970–1994

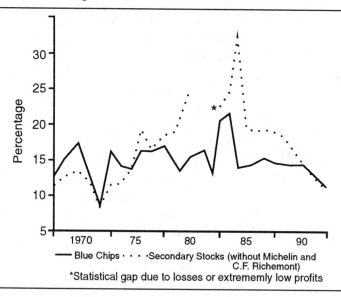

Blue Chips · · · Secondary Stocks (without Michelin and C.F. Richemont)
*Statistical gap due to losses or extrememly low profits

Figure 21.4–Price/Cash Flow Ratio 1970–1993

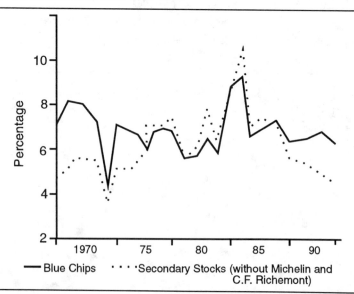

Blue Chips · · · Secondary Stocks (without Michelin and C.F. Richemont)

Figure 21.5—Price/Book Value Ratio 1970–1993

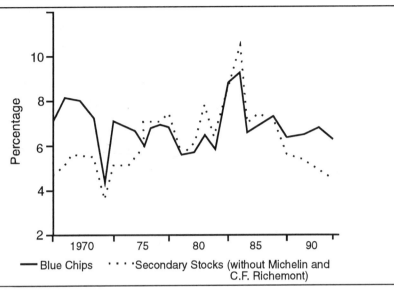

Index